Resisting War

In civil conflicts around the world, unarmed civilians take enormous risks to protect themselves and stand up to heavily armed combatants. This is not just counterintuitive – it is extraordinary. In this book, Oliver Kaplan explores cases from Colombia, with extensions to Afghanistan, Pakistan, Syria, and the Philippines, to show how and why civilians are able to influence armed actors and limit violence. Based on original fieldwork as well as statistical analysis, the book explains how local social organization and cohesion enables both covert and overt *nonviolent* strategies, including avoidance, cultures of peace, dispute resolution, deception, protest, and negotiation. These "autonomy" strategies help communities to both retain civilian status and avoid retaliation by limiting the inroads of armed groups. Contrary to conventional views that civilians are helpless victims, this book highlights their creative initiative to maintain decision-making power over outcomes for their communities.

OLIVER KAPLAN is an assistant professor at the Josef Korbel School of International Studies at the University of Denver. He was previously a postdoctoral Research Associate at Princeton University in the Woodrow Wilson School and at Stanford University as an affiliate of the Empirical Studies of Conflict project. His research for *Resisting War* received the Diskin Dissertation award honorable mention from the Latin American Studies Association.

Resisting War

How Communities Protect Themselves

OLIVER KAPLAN

University of Denver

CAMBRIDGE
UNIVERSITY PRESS

University Printing House, Cambridge CB2 8BS, United Kingdom

One Liberty Plaza, 20th Floor, New York, NY 10006, USA

477 Williamstown Road, Port Melbourne, VIC 3207, Australia

4843/24, 2nd Floor, Ansari Road, Daryaganj, Delhi – 110002, India

79 Anson Road, #06–04/06, Singapore 079906

Cambridge University Press is part of the University of Cambridge.

It furthers the University's mission by disseminating knowledge in the pursuit of education, learning, and research at the highest international levels of excellence.

www.cambridge.org
Information on this title: www.cambridge.org/9781107159808
10.1017/9781316671887

First published 2017

A catalogue record for this publication is available from the British Library.

Library of Congress Cataloging-in-Publication Data
NAMES: Kaplan, Oliver Ross, author.
TITLE: Resisting war : how communities protect themselves / Oliver Ross Kaplan.
DESCRIPTION: Cambridge, United Kingdom ; New York, NY : Cambridge University Press, 2017.
IDENTIFIERS: LCCN 2016044944 | ISBN 9781107159808 (Hardback)
SUBJECTS: LCSH: Community organization–Colombia. | Civilians in war–Colombia. |
    Civil war–Protection of civilians–Colombia. | Nonviolence–Colombia. | Colombia–History–
    1946–1974. | Colombia–History–1974–
CLASSIFICATION: LCC HN303.5 .K37 2017 | DDC 303.6/109861–DC23
    LC record available at https://lccn.loc.gov/2016044944

ISBN 978-1-107-15980-8 Hardback

To the campesinos *of Colombia: the true experts*
on making peace.
To Ben.

Contents

Table of Contents

Figures

Tables

Preface and Acknowledgments

This project began with a question and a curiosity. How can we tell if civilians in conflict settings can protect themselves through social movements? The reigning theories all said this was unlikely, and yet there were cases that suggested, shouted, that protection was possible. I wanted to know why, when, and how these kinds of efforts succeed or fail. I was motivated by the idea that research could help answer these questions and even contribute to the protection of people living in the direst of situations. The choice of Colombia as a research site was dictated by the question, then, rather than the reverse.

I had lived in Central America but had never been to Colombia and knew little about the country, except that it was probably not an easy location in which to do research. I started learning all I could, became drawn to the place, and realized research could be quite feasible and enjoyable, as long as one uses common sense, or does not *dar papaya* (literally to "give papaya"). I found a beautiful country with warm, humble, thoughtful, determined people and, thankfully, great coffee and rich chocolate. What started as my doctoral research became a journey of discovery that led to the findings presented in this book. It was a true education, full of new experiences, treasured memories, and fast friends. It would also hold my first experience with tear gas and encounters with unbearable heat and unimaginable carsickness, among other pleasantries.

I realized early on in my research that I would have to keep a list of all the people that helped me along the way because I was racking up and continued to take on many, many debts of gratitude. In this sense, this book is the result of a true and broad collaboration. However, any remaining errors are, lamentably, my own.

I first express *mis sinceras gracias* to all those who shared their precious time, knowledge, and histories with me and invited me into their homes or stores for a *tinto*, *aguapanela*, or *arepita*. Not only did they offer friendship and fascinating, hilarious, and somber tales and insights, but they also genuinely looked out for my well-being and helped me get to where I needed to go. This book would be nothing without them. I was also received warmly during my shorter time in the Philippines, which was similarly eye-opening.

I was fortunate at Stanford to have an amazing group of advisors. My dissertation committee of David Laitin, Terry Karl, Ken Schultz, and Jeremy Weinstein gave me a combination of healthy skepticism, constructive criticism, and frequent encouragement that pushed me to do better. I could not have overcome many of the research hurdles without them. Other faculty also gave instrumental guidance. Karen Jusko was incredibly helpful with breaking down research design issues and I also had many enlightening conversations with Alberto Díaz-Cayeros, Beatriz Magaloni, Jim Fearon, Josh Ober, Steve Krasner, and Mike Tomz. I am especially grateful to Eliana Vásquez, for our conversations and her unwavering enthusiasm and support, and to her family. I also thank my undergraduate advisors Barbara Walter and David Lake at UC San Diego for helping me first get started in political science research.

My peer group of fellow Stanford Ph.D. students were good friends and commiserators throughout. I thank Claire Adida, Mike Albertus, Leo Arriola, Rik Bhavnani, Thomas Brambor, Matt Carnes, Darah Cohen, Luke Condra, Roy Elis, Alejandro Feged, Joe Felter, Brodie Ferguson, Desha Girod, Bethany Lacina, Natan Sachs, Jake Shapiro, and Jessica Weeks for suffering discussions with me, serving as sounding boards, and giving great feedback. My colleagues at the Josef Korbel School at the University of Denver also provided encouragement and helpful comments on various later drafts: Debbi Avant, Erica Chenoweth, Rachel Epstein, Cullen Hendrix, Danny Postel, and Aaron Schneider. Thanks also go to all my other friends and colleagues at Stanford, Princeton, the University of Denver, and elsewhere for their support.

I thank Robert Dreesen, my editor at Cambridge University Press, for believing in this project and his guidance in the publication process. I also thank Brianda Reyes, Sarah Lambert, Anand Shanmugam, and Julia TerMaat for their editorial assistance and the three anonymous peer reviewers of the manuscript, who provided valuable criticism and insights. I thank Marcela Vega Vargas, a talented Colombian artist, for masterfully channelling my vision in her wonderful illustration of the cover image.

I am indebted to Mauricio García Durán and Teófilo Vásquez of the Centro de Investigación y Educación Popular (CINEP), Fabio Sánchez Torres of the Universidad de Los Andes, Jeff Villaveces at the United Nations (OCHA), Sol Santos, Nathan Cruz, Zakia Shiraz, and Grant Miller for their facilitation of data, sage advice, and friendship. I also thank Padre Mauricio Uribe at the Universidad Sergio Arboleda for his encouragement, wonderment, and polite driving.

A number of individuals both in Colombia and in the United States were also extremely supportive and helpful. These include Gloria Inés Restrepo, Esperanza Hernández Delgado, Hernán Molina, Luis Emiro Valencia, Camilo

Echandía, Marcela Palacios Garzón, Leslie Wirpsa, Mariana Puerto, Fredy Barrero, Andrés Casas, Janice Gallagher, Adan Griego, Julie Sweetkind-Singer, Julia Simarra, Estella Duque, Zephyr Frank, Jon Bellish, Santiago Dávila, Christian Caryl, and Dani Powell.

This book was greatly enhanced by excellent research assistance by Liz Carolina Garzón, Marie Claire Vásquez Duzán, Juan Jurado, Daniela Uribe, Anjali Menon, Jenna Rodrigues, Kate Castenson, and Natalie Southwick.

A number of organizations also provided great insight and assistance during my research. These include the Asociación Campesina de Antioquia, the staff at FOR-Colombia, the Corporación Júridica Libertad, and the Taller de Vida. I also received invaluable assistance and support from various offices in the Government of Colombia. These include the High Advisory for Reintegration, the Colombian Vice-presidency's Human Rights Observatory, and the Ministry of the Interior. In the Philippines, I am grateful for assistance from Catholic Relief Services and The Asia Foundation.

During my research I was honored to present my project as it evolved at the Instituto Fedesarrollo, the CEDE seminar at the Universidad de Los Andes, and CERAC, all in Bogotá, as well as the Department of Political Science at the University of Maryland – College Park, the American Political Science Association Annual Conference, and Stanford's Workshops in International Relations and Comparative Politics. The feedback I received from these presentations greatly steered my thinking.

I am grateful for funding support from the Dwight D. Eisenhower/Clifford Roberts Fellowship, the Smith Richardson Foundation World Politics and Statecraft Fellowship, the Stanford Goldsmith Writing Award in Dispute Resolution, the Stanford Diversity Dissertation Research Opportunity grant, the Stanford CICN Research Grant, the Stanford Graduate Research Opportunity award, Stanford's FSI O'Bie Schultz Dissertation Travel Fellowship, and Princeton's Bradley Foundation Research Fellowship. I received support as a Postdoctoral Fellow at Stanford and Princeton through the Empirical Studies of Conflict program (ESOC), for which I am also grateful.

Lastly, I am thankful to my family. I am thankful to my parents, Sue and Ron, for instilling in me the good sense to be able to complete this work with sensitivity and insight and without harm. I also know that my "Colombian journey of discovery" caused them at least a few sleepless nights and for that, I am sorry. I am appreciative of my brother, Ben. Through the highs and lows, you were always there with a smile on your face, maybe not always following whatever I might have been droning on about as a struggling student, but always nudging me to keep going. Thanks. You are an inspiration.

Abbreviations

ACIA	Integral Peasants Association of the Atrato Region
ACR	High Advisory for Reintegration/Colombian Agency for Reintegration
ACVC	Peasant Farmer Association of the Cimitarra River Valley
AFP	Armed Forces of the Philippines
ANA	Afghan National Army
ANUC	National Peasant Association
ARMM	Autonomous Region in Muslim Mindanao
ASOPROA	Association of Small- and Medium-Scale Producers of Eastern Antioquia
ATCC	Peasant Workers Association of the Carare River
AUC	United Self-Defense Forces of Colombia
CAFGU	Citizen Armed Force Geographical Units
CDF	Civilian Defense Forces
CINEP	Center for Investigation and Popular Education
CNAC	National Confederation of Communal Action
CNRR	National Commission on Reparation and Reconciliation
COCOMACIA	Community Council of the Peasant Association of the Atrato Region
CPP	Communist People's Party
CPR	Communities of Populations in Resistance
CRIC	Cauca Regional Indigenous Council
DANE	National Administrative Department of Statistics
DAS	Administrative Department of Security
ELN	National Liberation Army
EPL	Popular Liberation Army
EZLN	Zapatista Army of National Liberation
FARC	Revolutionary Armed Forces of Colombia

FATA	Federally Administered Tribal Areas
FMLN	Farabundo Martí National Liberation Front
FSA	Free Syrian Army
IGO	Intergovernmental organization
ISAF	International Security Assistance Force
ISIS	Islamic State of Iraq and Syria
JAC	Community Action Board
LCC	Local Coordination Committee
LRA	Lord's Resistance Army
M-19	Movement of April 19
MAQL	Quintín Lamé Armed Movement
MAS	Death to Kidnappers
MBNC	Bolivarian Movement for a New Colombia
MILF	Moro Islamic Liberation Front
MNLF	Moro National Liberation Front
NATO	North Atlantic Treaty Organization
NDF	National Democratic Front
NGO	Nongovernmental organization
NPA	New People's Army
PCCC	Colombian Clandestine Communist Party
RUF	Revolutionary United Front
SDA	Special Development Area
UP	Patriotic Union Party
ZOP	Zone of Peace

I

Introduction

Civilian Autonomy in Civil War

They've got me pissed with so much gosh-darn questioning
About what color my flag is, if I'm Conservative or Liberal.
They've got me fired-up with so much gosh-darn finding-out
About whether I'm an ELN-er, EPL-er, support the AUC or if I'm FARC.
They've got me worn-out with so much gosh-darn interrogating
About whether I've been opening my gate for the army and
giving them water from my well . . .

I'm a hard-working campesino, poor and very honorable,
I live happily but they've got me wound-up like a vine . . .
Well look misters, I'll answer you all,
I want this to be clear:
I ain't on nobody's side, I do what's right, not what's wrong . . .
So that's why I beg you, and ask you: questions – no more
Don't screw with me anymore!
              –Colombian folk song, "El Campesino Embejucao"[1]
                          by Oscar Humberto Gómez

Me tienen arrecho con tanta juepuerca preguntadera
que qué color tiene mi bandera que si soy Godo o soy Liberal
Me tienen verraco con tanta juepuerca averiguadera
que si soy Eleno, Epelo o siquiera apoyo a las AUC o soy de las FARC
Me tienen mamao con tanta juepuerca interrogadera
que si yo a la tropa le abro la cerca y si le doy el agua de mi manantial

---

[1] Translated to English by the author. A *campesino* is a farmer or peasant. *Embejucao* is derivative of the Spanish word *bejuco*, or vine, and is taken to mean wound-up like a vine, enraged or worked-up. The ELN, EPL, and FARC are guerrilla groups. The AUC are right-wing paramilitaries.

Yo soy campesino trabajador, pobre y muy honrao
vivía muy alegre pero me tienen embejucao ...
Pues miren señores a todos ustedes yo les contesto
y quero que quede muy claro esto:
yo no soy de naide, hago el bien, no el mal ...
así que les ruego, suplico y pido: ¡ya no más preguntas,
no me jodan más!

One day in the early 1970s in the village of La India in central Colombia, residents were warming up for a soccer match on a field that was not much more than a clearing in the forest. As one of the referees that day recalled, a ragtag group of guerrillas in *campesino* garb and boots appeared out of the jungle and asked if they could join.[2] Short on players with few people living in the area, the villagers welcomed them. It was not long before an army patrol arrived. None the wiser that there were guerrillas in the mix, the troops asked if they could also join the game and they all ended up playing a friendly match (of course, the villagers eventually won). At the end of the game, one group of "campesinos" said goodbye rather quickly and left through the jungle. For several years, the villagers continued to play the occasional game against the army, who remained none the wiser.

Historically, communities like La India have been intertwined with various armed actors with close, often benevolent relationships and information flows. This is possible because insurgents sometimes fit the mold of the idealized benevolent guerrilla hailed by classical theorists like Mao Zedong (1961) and Che Guevara (1961): noble, disciplined fighters defending the people and pursuing justice.[3] Governments, as counterinsurgents, are similarly advised to protect the population (Galula 1965). But this is not always the case. At some point in La India, things began to change. Conflict intensified and armed actors became more hostile and violent toward the civilian population.

There has been a similar turn of events in the rest of Colombia and in many other conflicts around the world. Beginning in the second half of the twentieth century, civil wars have been prevalent, claiming the lives of an estimated

---

[2] ATCC#1, La India, 10/2007. Interviews were conducted anonymously and are designated by community, number of participant, location, and date. In this study, "armed groups" or "armed actors" are terms used interchangeably to refer to any macro-level army in the armed conflict, including "leftist" guerrillas, "rightist" paramilitaries, or the public forces of the government (army, police, etc.). "Towns," "counties," and "municipios" are also used interchangeably to refer to Colombian localities. Interviewee names, some place names, and other potential identifying information have been changed to protect individuals.

[3] According to Guevara (1961, 39), "The peasant must always be helped technically, economically, morally, and culturally. The guerrilla fighter will be a sort of guiding angel who has fallen into the zone, helping the poor always and bothering the rich as little as possible in the first phases of the war." He continues, "The line should be soft and hard at the same time: soft and with a spontaneous cooperation for all those who honestly sympathize with the revolutionary movement; hard upon those who are attacking it outright, fomenting dissentions, or simply communicating important information to the enemy army" (81).

16.2 million people (Fearon and Laitin 2003). Indeed, most of the world's killings and human rights violations occur in conflict settings and most victims are noncombatants (Sivard 1993), with civilians comprising four out of every five of Colombia's war victims (GMH 2013). Rebels can be abusive (Weinstein 2006), states use mass violence (Valentino 2004), and, with changing conflict conditions, civilians come to face the predicament of the *campesino embejucao* of the song: caught in the crossfire, "*entre la espada y la pared*," or "between a sword and a wall." They can be stigmatized in the "fog of war" and accused of collaborating with the enemy (Kalyvas 2006). In Colombia, they must additionally deal with the problems of coca, youth recruitment, and displacement from their lands, among other maladies. And, like the *campesino embejucao*, most civilians facing less-than-benevolent armed groups just want to be left alone.[4] What are people in this predicament to do and what chances do they have? Are they helpless, inactive, and consigned to a fate of abuse, as many accounts describe?

I argue to the contrary that civilians are not necessarily passive or powerless. They are actors with agency whose ability to respond to the dangers of conflict derives from social cooperation. Villages with different social relations deal with increasing pressures and violence differently. This is illustrated by returning to the village of La India as the conflict worsened and contrasting its experience with that of the nearby village of San Tropel, just to the west over some low hills. In 1998, paramilitary forces that had by then arisen in the region brutally executed twelve woodcutters in San Tropel and dumped their bodies in the Carare River (El Tiempo 2009).[5] Just a short time later, in 2001, this same group was preparing to kill eleven residents of La India, but did not because a community organization that had been formed there to deal with the problems created by the conflict, the Peasant Workers Association (ATCC in Spanish), came to the civilians' defense and advocated on their behalf.[6] The eleven people lived. Though this is but a single episode, it is emblematic of many similar events in this community (I explore these communities in detail in Chapter 7).

This raises a puzzle: given similar pressures, why were residents of La India able to act but not those of San Tropel? And why were the people killed in San Tropel, but not in La India? More broadly, how common are these kinds of actions? How do they affect armed groups and how can we tell if they affect levels of violence? It is not obvious that unarmed civilians in civil wars can protect themselves against heavily armed combatants, and yet some civilians do. The attention of both journalists and scholars has concentrated on the many victims of civil conflicts – "If it bleeds, it leads." Yet in line with a

---

[4] Popkin (1979), Kriger (1992), and Kalyvas (2006) suggest that macro-actor goals are not civilians' primary concern. According to Nordstrom (1992) on Sri Lanka and Mozambique, civilians are often not even familiar with macro-actors' goals, "Civilians often had difficulty distinguishing sides, especially according to ideological considerations of just and unjust. Indeed, many of the victims of war – torn from comfort and community, family, and home, too often wounded or bereaved – do not know what the conflict is about or who the contenders are" (265).
[5] Heard of by ATCC#2, La India, 10/2007.   [6] ATCC#3,4, La India, 10/2008.

corollary that "If it's nonviolent, it's silent," few accounts examine how the people who are not victims survive. Millions of people have been displaced from the countryside in Colombia, but many have been able to remain as well.

The topic of this book is how civilians can retain their autonomy, or self-rule, in the face of armed groups and protect themselves.[7] Civilians may flee violence or seek protection from an armed group, but these options can be dangerous, unavailable, or unappealing, since many would prefer to stay in their communities. Facing this dilemma, their alternative in autonomy is to actively avoid participating in the conflict between the contending armies to avoid its damaging effects and gain even a small degree of certainty in their daily lives.[8] However, in changing, complex environments and with but one life to live, following this course is difficult for most individual civilians. Even when many civilians might share such preferences and together be more effective in gaining protection, fear creates collective action problems in confronting combatants. Some residents may receive benefits from relationships with armed groups, or armed groups may seek to penetrate and control communities – to divide and rule. Social cooperation and organization is therefore the key to help civilians overcome fear, manage their own communities, and deal with armed group pressure in an enduring manner. The narrower question of autonomy and protection from armed groups therefore links to the broader question of what capacity civilians have for social cohesion and cooperation in war settings – the question of social capital (Putnam 1993; Buonanno et al. 2009 related to crime). While civilian strategies for autonomy can and do arise specifically as a response to deal with armed conflict, preexisting bases of social cooperation are a helpful catalyst.

In Colombia and other countries there are many notable examples of local organizations for autonomy and organizational actions for protection in wartime. A review of these cases reveals they are more common than one might believe. To give an initial sense of their breadth in Colombia, according to one survey, more than 500 local officials (mayors and governors) held dialogues

---

[7] The concept of autonomy has been previously introduced in UNDP 2003, Sandoval 2004, and Tarrow 2007. According to the UN report, "Autonomy of citizen movements vis-à-vis the armed organizations and indeed the State itself ... but not neutrality has allowed them to keep themselves apart from the armed confrontation. They have avoided taking sides in favor of one or the other band, but always show themselves to be on the side of the population. Since armed groups attempt to involve them in the conflict, they have claimed their right to survive. That way any initiative from a group is replicated in another, and any position is communicated equally to all. They have also earned themselves a degree of autonomy with respect to central government. As one activist put it, 'What's on the line are our lives, not the government's life.' Therefore they look for alternative ways of handling the conflict, beyond the desires and recipes of the national government. They know that they cannot sit around waiting to act until the government has organized its grandiose 'negotiations' with armed groups."

[8] I make no normative judgment about the righteousness of either participating in "liberation" struggles or defending the establishment, "la patria."

with armed groups during the peak years of conflict (El Tiempo 2001a).[9] To more precisely illustrate the prevalence of civilian autonomy organizations and actions, I classified community cases based on the criteria of being local and grassroots-based (i.e., at the community level), "apolitical," based on social cohesion and organization (not individual), and nonviolently seeking protection from violence (from one or more groups).[10] Across Colombia, more than fifty locations formally organized for self-protection from armed groups since the early 1990s.[11] Figure 1.1 shows a map of these civilian organizations by their *municipio*, or town. These cases are found in many regions of the country and vary according to types of strategies implemented and the number of people, villages, and areas involved.[12]

Civilian autonomy in conflict settings is also found more broadly around the world than might be expected. Figure 1.2 shows a map of cross-national protective actions by civilian organizations in conflict conditions that were classified

[9] However, few public officials wish to publicly admit to such dealings. Interactions varied from mere intimidation and conversations under pressure to communication, small-scale humanitarian accords, peace communities, constituent assemblies, and voting. As Gilberto Toro of the Federation of Municipios observed, "While the state is impotent in guaranteeing local governability [stopping abuses of the civilian population] we are going to have desperate mayors turning to new ideas."

[10] These cases may include idiosyncratic actions and social processes as well as formal organizations created to promote local peace. A case is considered "apolitical" if, in its beginnings, it does not have apparent, formal, sustained relationships with macro-political actors, such as the public forces or armed groups. However, some communities are eventually co-opted by or integrated with the state. Some but not all of these cases confront conflict environments with multiple macro-actors. The communities that are identified are not believed to have formal relationships with any macro-political actors, but from afar it is difficult to tell by which group(s) they may feel threatened. Inferences about the number of armed groups these communities face are found in Table 1.1.

[11] I classified cases from secondary sources through a broad and admittedly nonsystematic search since there is not usually standard language to describe these experiences (i.e., many more "silent" cases might exist). These codings are therefore not comprehensive and possibly omit many actions. In some cases the limited information and context available in the reporting also present challenges in assessing the nature of events and social cooperation, possibly producing classifications that are inaccurate. The resulting collection of cases are examples of collective actions but are *not* precise analyses of the effects of civilian strategies, which would require much more labor-intensive measurements – such as those found elsewhere in this text.

[12] While the autonomy movements do not encompass every village within each municipio where they are located, the number represents roughly 10 percent of municipios with the presence of at least one armed group at the peak of the conflict or about 20 percent of the smaller set of municipios that were affected by conflict for extended periods during the 1990s and 2000s. A number of these organizations are profiled in the United Nations Development Program's Good Practices website database, a catalog of over 250 community experiences intended to disseminate examples of and lessons from how different civil society actions and organizations have "overcome" the armed conflict. Some of these are user-submitted. Though the database is still surely missing many experiences and movements, 51 of these profiles explicitly mention the aim of "autonomy." Greater detail on the diversity of actions taken by communities is contained in the history and case study chapters ahead.

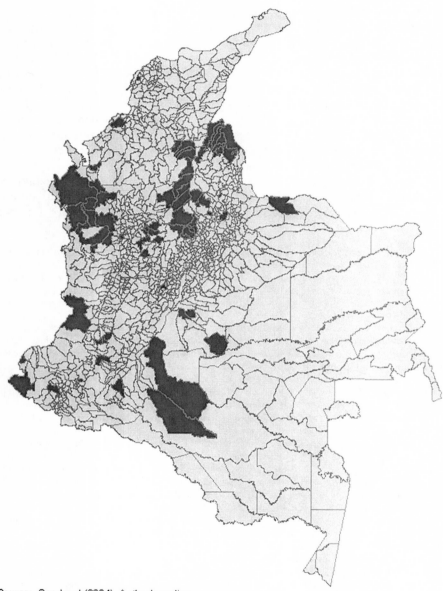

Source: Sandoval (2004), Author's coding

FIGURE I.I Map of formal civilian autonomy organizations in Colombia

similarly to the Colombian cases (Table 1.1 at the end of this chapter contains further details on these examples).[13] These fourteen countries with civilian

---

[13] Many but not all of the countries where these cases are found fit the accepted national level definition of civil war of at least 100 annual battle deaths for each party to a conflict and at least

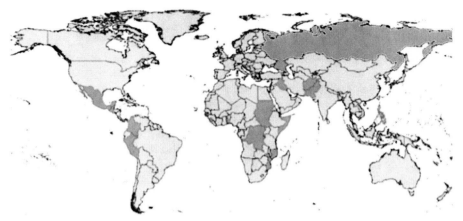

FIGURE 1.2 Map of civilian autonomy in civil war around the world.
Source: Author's coding.

autonomy actions comprise around one-quarter of countries that experienced civil wars since 1980 (including only some communities from these countries). Instances of protective actions and organizations are found in Asia, Africa, the Middle East, and Latin America. In some countries, there are only a few press reports on one or two isolated communities, such as the profile of a single village leader in Dagestan, Russia, who negotiated a path for his community between Russian counterinsurgents and Islamist militants (Greene 2010). In other countries, there are cases that are more deeply profiled in the budding anthropological literature on this topic and involve many communities. Studies of the Peace Zones in the Philippines identify at least ninety-one communities that organized with the help of the Catholic Church to opt out of the conflicts between the Philippine military and communist and Muslim rebel groups (Santos 2005, Hancock and Mitchell 2007). There are cases as diverse as the religiously motivated and superstition-based Naprama movement and Jehovah's Witness communities in Mozambique (Wilson 1992) as well as strategies of avoidance as found in Guatemala's Communities of Populations in Resistance (CPRs, Falla 1994).

Examples of armed resistance for autonomy are also included in Table 1.1, although they are not the emphasis of this study.[14] Cases of local armed

1,000 total annual battle deaths among all sides (Fearon and Laitin 2003). Cases in countries falling short of this standard were included because their locales still suffered what would reasonably be considered civil war conditions and contestation.

[14] There are additional cases of apparent armed resistance in Colombia and other countries but these are excluded because their origins are not entirely bottom-up. Rather, they are political and "pro-government militias" allied with the state. Examples from Colombia in this category include the Convivir self-defense forces, the village-based peasant soldiers program (*soldados campesinos*), and paramilitary groups.

resistance range from the Rondas Campesinas studied by Starn (1999) and Fumerton (2001) in different regions of Peru to Iraq's Anbar awakening of Sunni tribes (at least in their beginnings) to Muana's (1997) description of the origins of the Civilian Defense Forces (CDF) in Sierra Leone. In Chapter 9, I more closely review instances of civilian autonomy from the conflicts in Afghanistan, Pakistan, the Philippines, and Syria.

Many of these cases are highly organized and have been publicized, but there may also be more subtle, underreported kinds of civilian social cooperation and strategies. Given this variety, it can be hard to tell whether and which social organizations and collective strategies explain differences in resilience to violence across communities. This task is further complicated by possible reverse causality and selection biases since, if conflict harms social cooperation, then social relations and civilian strategies may be solely derivative of the powerful armed groups, with no independent success at suppressing violence. Any observed existence of civilian collective action or impact would then be epiphenomenal, or merely due to existing in peaceful places. Alternatively, many civilian self-protection processes largely exist in stateless, conflict-ridden areas, which could also make them more predisposed to suffer violence. Given these research challenges, I address three interrelated research questions:

(1) Where and why do local social organizations arise?
(2) What strategies do such organizations permit communities to use to deal with civil war violence?
(3) Why and under what conditions do armed groups change their behavior toward (organized) civilians?

To study the question of civilian autonomy in civil war, I use multiple social science methods, from statistical tests to interviews and case studies from the Colombian conflict. This process involves the careful construction of counterfactual scenarios of what would have happened, what the armed groups would have done, had civilians not used a given strategy or taken a given action. I find that some kinds of civilian social arrangements, organizations, and strategies can reduce civil war violence, suggesting that civilian autonomy occurs more broadly than originally believed. At the same time, and with reason, there are also limitations on where civilian organizational processes succeed – they are not a panacea. By exploring these conditions, I find that, along with successes, communities experience challenges and failures. While some organizational processes appear to affect certain kinds of violence and conflict dynamics, organizations are also more likely to buckle under extreme levels of combat and overall have few discernable effects on the intensity of the fighting between belligerents themselves.

In the rest of the chapter, I first present my main argument about the importance of civilians' social capital, organizations, and strategies for limiting civil war violence and delimit its scope. I also briefly summarize the research findings in support of this argument. I then situate this study in existing literatures and indicate how they have so far only obliquely addressed the questions surrounding civilian autonomy. I then preview the research design and methods. Lastly, I preview the chapters to come.

THE ARGUMENT

My main argument is that there are conditions where civilians can use social processes to reduce violence perpetrated against them. The field of conflict resolution usually pays most attention to state actors, nonstate armed groups, and national-level peace negotiations. By contrast, this argument is grounded in civil society (sometimes referred to as "Track II") in considering why civilian bystanders succeed or fail in organizing opposition to state oppression or to a potentially harmful insurgent movement. Since armed actor coercion of (and violence against) civilians has been theorized to stem from divisions within civilian communities (Kalyvas 2006), I argue that social cohesion affords civilians greater chances to overcome fear, break the "law of silence" and revive communication, and implement collective strategies for protection.

In situations where communities face multiple armed actors or even a single abusive group, compliance and alliance do not guarantee protection. It is here that cohesion and collective strategies can help communities achieve autonomy, or maintain democratic decision-making power over outcomes *for* the community *within* the community, without influence from outside armed groups.[15] Violence can be reduced through *institutional* solutions to avoid participation in the conflict, manage the internal order of communities, limit the inroads of armed groups, and demand accountability from these groups.

With three outcomes to explain in this book, I develop a three-part "civilian autonomy theory" that links civilian organizations to strategies and then to security. First, variation in the social and demographic landscape and technical assistance from external actors (be they the government, churches, or NGOs) propels some communities to organize more easily than others. Second, cohesive, organized communities can make collective decisions about how to best deal with the various dangers of civil war conflict. Although civilians may commonly align with dominant armed groups or displace, in addition to these standard strategies, I pay special attention to strategies to retain autonomy in the midst of multiple armed groups. These can include what can be termed "weapons of the weak" (Scott 1985) for conflict settings to deal with conflicts and divisions within civilian communities as well as "weapons of the *not-so-weak*," such as overt protest and actions by nonviolent community guards. The selection of strategies is shaped by an interaction between civilian

---

[15] These arguments were first published as my doctoral dissertation (Kaplan 2010). My main interest and assumption is that civilian responses to violence are usually instrumental, intentional, and with strategic forethought. However, they can certainly also be emotional, cathartic processes or be born out of frustration.

preferences, social cohesion, and the past and prospective threat environment, and some strategies are more assertive and thus potentially more effective than others. Third, the strength of civilian organization, selected strategies, and armed group incentives jointly determine substantive outcomes such as levels of violence. In sum, it is the unity of civilian centrists that helps impede and isolate violent "extremists." This theory is stated in general terms to pertain both to the case of Colombia and be adapted to explain patterns in other conflicts.

A main task of this theorizing about autonomy is to specify civilian mechanisms that generate protection. I show how different civilian actions reduce violence by affecting armed actors' behavior, capabilities, or ways of thinking. I take a moment here to foreshadow the strategies and mechanisms that I identified through reading and fieldwork and elaborate on them in greater depth in Chapter 2.[16] The multiple kinds of violent threats civilians face call for multiple solutions. Subject to the constraints of available ideas and imperfect information about levels of danger, civilians may thus select different kinds of autonomy strategies in different places as they organize and adapt responses to different types of violence.

These autonomy mechanisms can be grouped according to their level of formalization and depth of cooperation. First, there are cohesion and solidarity mechanisms, which more resemble ad hoc coordination in that some are less premeditated or enduring. These can include preexisting social harmony, which means fewer conflicts among neighbors to exploit, or the common knowledge among residents that allows them to collectively and spontaneously protest aggression and resist armed groups' attempts at domination.

Second, there are formal organizations and mechanisms that are based on deep and sustained cooperation and intentionally oriented for protection. Civilians can actively promote ideational norms among residents against aiding armed actors (a so-called culture of peace), develop local conflict resolution processes (so civilians do not seek policing by outside actors), develop early warning systems to avoid combat, dialogue with armed groups and investigate suspected enemy collaborators for them, and link with external nongovernmental organizations (NGOs) and international governmental organizations (IGOs) to "go public" to protest aggression and shame armed actors. As one man told me in reference to these kinds of strategies, "Creating peace is an everyday process."[17] Some strategies are more contentious toward armed actors than others, and some formally organized communities that use these

---

[16] The terms "strategy" and "mechanism" are interchangeably used to convey processes that affect violence. However, a mechanism is a causal process whereas a strategy is a plan that is chosen by an agent. Some mechanisms that affect violence, such as preexisting cooperation, are not strategies that civilian agents can actively choose, but are still mechanisms that affect armed group violence.

[17] ATCC#3, La India, 10/2007.

strategies may publicly opt out of the conflict and declare their territory and population off limits to combatants.

With this articulation of strategies, I argue for a more nuanced view of how civilian communities act. Formal, public protests have a role to play, but peace and stability do not always require banning or expelling armed groups from territory and may not depend on singular, publicized events. There may also be other, less visible strategies. A main observable implication from both the covert and overt kinds of mechanisms is that greater organizational capacity should predict less violence after accounting for other factors that predict violence.

Even as this work shifts focus to civilians and their agency, civilians' actions cannot be divorced from armed groups, whose motives and incentives, preferences and choices are key for explaining violence visited upon communities. Armed groups coerce or abuse in part because they suffer little consequence, have poor information, or have not considered other ways to achieve their goals.[18] In theory, by making killing more difficult or even costly and by reducing mistakes in targeting and costs of governance, civilian cohesion and the strategies it enables should reduce violence. It becomes more difficult for competing armed groups to seed violence through social divisions or for commanders to tolerate organizational abuses. Civilians may induce armed actors to change behavior because of what I refer to as the "sensitivity" to their reputations and legitimacy, by incorporating new ideas, or by affecting internal group politics.

These armed actor motives provide insight into when civilians' efforts are likely to succeed, suggesting a broad but delimited set of conflict conditions and armed group preference profiles. Communities should be more likely to affect violence and civilian livelihoods in areas where armed groups might have incentives to commit violence but hold preferences that are relatively more flexible and, with the imposition of only small costs, can be persuaded to change their behavior. This may occur, for instance, when armed groups have what I call "live and let live" preferences and even in some cases "abusive-coercive" preferences. They may not be Guevara's "guiding angels" but are more concerned about limiting civilians' defections than winning their full-fledged support. Groups may also be so inclined when they do not completely depend on civilians for their resource bases. In contrast, civilians should be less able to avoid violence in cases where groups are highly resolute in killing or winning, such as cases of genocide (or "draining the sea" to get to the insurgent "fish").[19] These scope conditions for autonomy add a dose of realism to the

---

[18] Violence can also be irrational and random. My focus is on systematizing how civilians may on average influence the "rational" behaviors of armed groups.

[19] Armed resistance groups during the Holocaust and other genocides are noteworthy exceptions (Semelin 1993, Tec 1993). In Colombia, examples of armed civilians fighting off armed groups include the towns of Don Matías in Antioquia (Ivan García 1994) and Rionegro in Santander (El Tiempo 1996).

discussion by not postulating civilian success as inevitable. They are found to varying degrees within Colombia as well as other countries.

A related question to what impact civilians' organizational efforts have on violence is where their organizations come from. Some forms of social cooperation and organization can be stimulated as a response to violence and serve as bases for mobilization. Others can exist prior to the onset of conflict. I draw on collective action theories and literatures on protest and resistance to theorize about when civilians will coordinate or organize spontaneously "now out of never" (Kuran 1991) to cope with violence. I explore the social conditions associated with the prevalence of organizations across towns and take organizations to reflect a degree of cooperation.[20]

The sources of organization are an interesting topic in its own right and are also helpful for validating a causal relationship between organization and violence. This is because, in an alternative process to civilian autonomy, armed conflict may damage social relations instead of spurring civilian responses. With organizations surviving and existing in peaceful areas, researchers could be susceptible to bias in the selection of cases for study, making an observed negative relationship with levels of violence spurious. Since I argue that civilians have independent effects on violence, I additionally argue that conflict does not on average disrupt social relations or censor the selection of autonomy strategies.

To the extent that civilian organizations and their strategies are not merely derivative of (epiphenomenal to) conflict dynamics, they merit consideration as an additional explanatory variable. Indeed, by accounting for prior levels of conflict through a historical statistical analysis, I find that conflict does not necessarily disrupt social relations and can even reinforce them. The case studies in Chapter 8 reveal examples of exogenous stimuli for organizations in towns with histories of conflict. Some organizations may also exist in unfavorable conflict dynamics and take on lives of their own, persisting even as dynamics change. However, consistent with the success of civilians' strategies being conditioned by armed group actions, cohesive communities and strong organizations can protect but, under pressure, their resilience will be put to test.

Colombian Social Organizations as Platforms for Civilian Autonomy

One Saturday morning in August of 2008, I saw the central role of organizations in vivid relief. I was sitting in a plastic chair in front of a store on a dusty lane in the village of La India, idly chatting with a new acquaintance from the

---

[20] Communities face challenges to mobilization because they may have few resources to offer selective benefits, have difficulty using the law to enforce contracts given state weakness, and cannot use coercion since they espouse nonviolence. Many organizations persist and maintain membership because they provide social benefits and opportunities for social interaction and exchange. In some cases this may be because the organization is the only "game in town."

community. Suddenly, a woman ran out into the street bawling at the top of her lungs. Wailing with sorrow, she dropped to her knees, hands covering her face, and shrieked, "They killed him, they killed him!"

In an instant, seemingly the entire village came out onto the street and surrounded her, including the man I was chatting with, who ran to join the growing crowd. These friends and neighbors encircled the crying woman five people deep, practically giving her a big group hug, asking about what happened and showing concern. Feeling like an outsider and challenged to interpret the scene, when the man eventually returned I asked, "Who? Who's been shot? What's happening?"

The woman had received a cell phone call from her son, who was working in the fields nearby. He had been shot, apparently by a local criminal gang (*pandilla*). He said, "Mom, I've been shot, and I'm dying."[21]

What happened next was even more remarkable, as I saw the village swing into action and saw the community process of the local farmer association – the ATCC – that I had heard about play out before my eyes. With all the commotion, the vice-president of the association quickly arrived at the scene. When he found out what was going on, he immediately jumped on a motorcycle and sped off to make the two-hour trip to the nearest police station to get help, report the crime, and push the authorities to capture the assailants. As he passed me, he turned his head and we briefly made eye contact. Behind his stoic expression – like the one often worn by campesinos – I felt there was also a message, as if he meant to say, "Sometimes, this is what we have to do here. It's not happy, but we do it."

The collective spirit to console the woman and protect the community made an impression on me as I realized this is what communities like La India have done for years. When transporting my argument to Colombia, it applies first and foremost to formal "peace" organizations, such as the ATCC organization in La India. But a key insight from the argument is that civilians also take important actions outside of formal, well-known organizations that were designed or named specifically to promote peace, such as "peace communities." Taking a step back, it is apparent that many of the peace organizations are built on the foundations of smaller, more basic community organizations and social unity. I therefore consider several additional measures of rural community organization. These include the highly organized Indigenous and Afro-Colombian populations, economic cooperative associations, and land reform councils (ANUC), though the principal source of variation I study are local village or neighborhood councils of campesinos (mestizo peasants) known as *juntas de acción comunal* (Community Action Boards) across Colombian municipios (towns).

---

[21] I was not able to determine which group was responsible (whether it was a neo-paramilitary criminal band) or what the outcome was for the young man.

The most common form of rural organization in Colombia, the juntas are the main forum through which residents coordinate to solve local problems and provide public goods. They were formed beginning in the late 1950s to bolster the countryside after a bloody conflict known as *La Violencia* (The Violence) but were later largely left to their own devices. The juntas were intended to foster reconciliation and "coexistence" but were not specifically designed to undertake protective strategies *during war*. Nevertheless, I theorize that juntas affect violence because they embody the high levels of coordination and social capital necessary for a community to implement more complex autonomy (or other) strategies and procedures to preserve the community in the face of conflict.[22] Examining the presence and functioning of juntas presents a convenient way of tackling challenging research design issues because they are more simply measurable and comparable than larger, irregular autonomy organizations, vary across many geographical units, and predate the recent period of armed conflict.

The analysis of the junta councils yields several notable research findings. After controlling for combat and contention among armed groups, a variable representing juntas has a negative effect on violence. On average, if a town were to move from no juntas to the 75th percentile in junta coverage, it would produce an approximate 25 percent reduction in selective killings, but mainly when the conflict intensity remains moderate. Ethnic minority populations also appear to suffer less violence, but the evidence on other social organizations suggests they are less helpful. The juntas are found, if anything, to be more prevalent in historically conflicted areas, including those areas that were affected by the brutal La Violencia conflict during the 1950s.

The case studies in Chapters 7 and 8 show that juntas helped cement social relations and later were catalysts for communities to maintain social unity and stand up to armed groups. In the ATCC zone, juntas were key subunits of an information-gathering, coordinating, and pacifism-promoting network. In other towns in Cundinamarca, the juntas appear to have played more subtle but still important roles for dealing with armed conflict. Histories from these towns also show that while the juntas were effective at buffering communities they were also weakened prior to the onset of conflict by factors such as clientelism. This suggests a prominent role for the legacies of juntas in addition to the juntas themselves.

Since directly measuring autonomy and predicting strategies prior to their occurrence is complicated, my analysis focuses on the prior characteristic of organization. Organization enables a variety of strategies that could account for differences in levels of violence across towns, of which autonomy is only

---

[22] The relevant "social capital" of local organizations such as juntas can take the forms of shared preferences and reduced intracommunity conflict, participation, and information networks, which can affect outcomes of violence through several mechanisms. These organizations may also reflect a stronger collective identity.

one. Organization may have general benefits for reducing violence above and beyond what individuals are capable of, regardless of conflict conditions. But organization can also stand in for collective choices to flee or ally, in addition to enabling autonomy. To isolate the link between organization and autonomy, I also analyze the effects of community organization under the conditions of threats by multiple armed groups, where autonomy is most expected.

Scope of the Argument

My argument is delimited by several bounds of scope that clarify the concept of civilian autonomy and the conditions for when cohesion, organization, and autonomy strategies are likely to help avoid violence. To begin, I focus my attention on collective, localized, ongoing processes at the community level in conditions of civil war. Collective processes are prioritized because individuals have limited choice sets facing violence. Localized processes are prioritized because they are principally aimed at dealing with the specific, immediate problems a community faces and are more geographically delimited than general, broad-based peace "movements."[23] Ongoing community processes are elevated over specific actions because actions must generally be sustained over time to continue to keep violence from visiting the community since armed groups can return. In this framework, protest events are but one of various strategies that an organized community may employ.

The study also focuses on the rural sector. In rural areas the state tends to be less present and the physical and membership boundaries of communities are blurrier, making autonomy strategies both more necessary and likely. Collective strategies and movements for protection and autonomy can and do occur in urban slums, but urban areas have clearer lines of armed group control, better information flows, and the possibility of more forceful responses by state forces if conflict spikes, and armed groups operate more clandestinely.

I acknowledge but do not emphasize the role for civilians' preferences over political affiliations or particular strategies. When civilian communities hold strong preexisting preferences for or against a given armed actor these preferences can affect their choices. However, evidence suggests these ideological preferences tend to be weak relative to the preference for doing what it takes to survive when under threat – they have no "dog in the fight." Though I discuss and measure the preferences of residents of different communities, I assume civilians' preferences in violent situations are not static ideologies but instead tend to be influenced by armed groups (similar to Kalyvas 2006). I see

[23] Civil society peace actions such as region- or nation-wide marches, symbolic votes, protests, etc. can certainly still play important roles for resolving civil conflicts and reducing violence (for instance, general arguments by Sharp 1973 and Sharp and Paulson 2005, anti-ETA protests in Spain by Funes 1998, and nonviolent protest in Colombia by Cante and Ortíz 2005 and García Durán 2006).

the main limiting factors for civilians to respond to armed actor aggression as organizational capacity, cohesion, and coordination, rather than preferences to do so. To the extent that preferences influence civilians' prospects, I argue it is the variance in residents' preferences that matters – either social unity or disunity, which can influence civilians' capacity to work together and keep armed groups out.

I refine my argument by identifying certain types of organizations as more effective at reducing violence through autonomy than others. A critical organizational characteristic is whether organizations attempt to remain apolitical relative to the interests of macro-armed and -political actors. If civilian organizations or communities hold political stances, they can be stigmatized or targeted for perceived alliances. Indeed, this alternative depiction of organizations has found support in other notable cases such as El Salvador (e.g., land cooperatives were targeted by the army, see Wood 2003). Given the risk of stigmatization, I assume communities or organizations that have delimited aims, act for self-defense, and do not pursue larger political projects (including state takeover) will have the best chances for protection through autonomy strategies, since their claims to political neutrality will be more credible.[24] For instance, I find that the relatively apolitical juntas reduce violence more than legacies of land reform councils, which may sign a community as espousing leftist platforms (Chapter 5). A community may be targeted if it is seen as a rival or contender for power (in the case of land reform councils, by right-wing paramilitary groups).

I concentrate primarily on *nonviolent* civilian strategies to deal with armed groups. Social movements (Tarrow 1994) and nonviolent resistance (Schock 2005, Chenoweth and Stephan 2011) have been shown to be effective at pressuring states to respect rights and overthrow autocratic regimes, but relatively little attention has been paid to how these tools can be used during armed conflict or to pressure nonstate actors. Yet civilians' nonviolent strategies during war merit attention, first, because they are more prevalent than armed local civilian resistance strategies in Colombia (though there certainly are noteworthy examples of effective armed resistance for self-defense and autonomy, including the indigenous Movimiento Armado Quintín Lame; Peñaranda et al. 2006). These civilian groups are differentiated from the armed actors of a conflict by acting for self-defense, with no wider goal of state takeover. In the

---

[24] Communities and organizations that aim to be apolitical often still advocate for community development. Advocacy for development can blur the line of a community's "political" position when rural peasants incorporate anti-neoliberal platforms and rhetoric into their organizing, as they sometimes do, since they resemble the political platforms of many insurgent groups. This may increase risks since armed actors may associate these positions of residents with their stances in other policy domains including, for example, whether they have explicit links with or sympathies for other macro-political actors. However, when simply staying on one's land becomes political and grounds for being targeted, the situation begins to approximate genocidal conditions as there may be little a community can do given an armed actor's extreme preferences.

case of armed strategies for autonomy, this criteria effectively excludes political paramilitary projects that either from their inception or in due course aid the state with counterinsurgency.[25] Second, focusing on nonviolence avoids the ambiguity and ethical dilemma of whether armed civilians are still "civilians." Armed resistance can certainly be an important strategy for maintaining autonomy, though by directly participating in hostilities and forgoing the status of "noncombatant," civilians can become legitimate targets of armed groups (permissible targets under International Humanitarian Law).

My main interest is understanding the ability of civilians to reduce violence against their communities and protect human rights. Yet civilian social processes may also fulfill many other functions during conflicts. These can include increased cooperation and participation, improved governance, economic development, and less tangible results such as the psychological benefits of inspiration and empowerment (within the community and as a symbol for other communities), and a sense of security, hope for the future, belonging, identity, community, etc. I set these benefits aside for others to study because, even if they are realized, their value and the value of civilian autonomy strategies could ultimately be questioned if they fail to reduce violence. While there may be many senses in which civilian movements promote peace, here peace is conceived of as the extent to which violence is reduced.

I mainly study the effects of social processes on violence against civilian community members and do not deeply explore outcomes for the broader armed conflict or for armed groups. It would be helpful to know whether and when local initiatives affect larger dynamics of conflict such as onset, termination, the spread (or displacement) of violence to other communities, or the intensity of fighting between armed groups. However, since some conflict dynamics are largely a byproduct of interactions between the armed groups themselves, only certain civilian mechanisms might have influence, by affecting armed groups' resources or capacities, for example. There are also measurement challenges to detect these effects with the available granularity of measurements at the local level. Even so, some parts of the study have implications for the broader conflict and I later discuss some pertinent examples, such as how autonomous communities can assist with the demobilization of combatants.[26]

Lastly, and to reiterate, civilians' success at protecting themselves also depends on the conflict conditions and armed group preferences. Cohesion

---

[25] Some armed actors build their own civilian organizations or cadres as support networks, such as the FARC's Movimiento Bolivariano por la Nueva Colombia (MBNC) militias and Unión Patriótica (UP) political party. With the criterion of being apolitical, I distinguish forms of organization where initiative is rooted in civil society.

[26] The ATCC has provided guarantees for local troop demobilizations (ATCC#3, La India, 10/ 2007). The Nasa Indians have also used nonviolent methods to stop FARC attacks on police posts (El Tiempo 2001b).

and community processes are expected to be able to deal with up to moderate levels of contestation and at least moderately amenable armed group types. Communities are more likely to be overrun in the midst of heavy fighting or when facing highly resolute or ruthless groups.

CURRENT PERSPECTIVES ON CIVILIANS AND CIVIL WARS

This study engages and bridges several academic literatures. I first review studies of violence in civil war and how civilian behavior has been portrayed in these studies. I then review the contributions of studies on civilians in other kinds of conflict settings short of civil war yet where the state is absent. Lastly, I contrast these studies with the anthropological literature on community resistance to armed groups (originating mainly on Colombia). I highlight how the study of both violence and social movements can be advanced if these literatures better engage with each other and how this study works toward that goal.

The Literature on Civil Wars

The turn toward micro-level analysis of violence in the recent literature on civil wars provides a strong foundation for analyzing the effects of civilian institutions and autonomy. Rather than focusing on the normative and legal aspects of the human rights regime and rights violations, these works have espoused positivist arguments to account for what actually happens in conflicts. For instance, Valentino (2004) argues that massive violence in the form of "draining the sea," or targeting civilians to deprive rebels of support, is a common strategy in counterinsurgency. Weinstein (2006) argues that rebel organizational structures can enable or limit abusive behavior toward civilians, even in zones of complete control.[27] Kalyvas (2006) argues that, as a result of the "identity" problem of outing enemy supporters in the "fog" of irregular wars, armed actors use "selective" violence to coerce support. There have been several valuable quantitative studies on the patterns of conflict and violence in Colombia by authors such as Restrepo et al. (2006) and Sánchez Torres (2007). These studies all share the common thread of placing primacy on macro-actors in armed conflicts and how their decisions and behaviors affect war onset, rebel recruitment, violence, and war termination. The insights from these works mean it is now essential to control for these factors in any analysis of civilian-based explanations of armed conflict. Yet these existing explanations leave unexplained variation in violence – how does violence vary within the same conflict conditions and among the same armed groups? How does violence vary within areas where states are weak?

---

[27] Azam (2006) provides another explanation for violence in zones of control, arguing that warlords may also have incentives to victimize their own civilians, first for plunder and second to suppress wages and lower the opportunity cost of recruitment.

The role of civilians in this literature is eclectic, though civilians are seen as primarily integrated with armed groups, with limited independence. Little is said about how civilians deal with and diminish violence. Many works have studied the challenge of rebel recruitment in civil wars including Popkin (1979), Taylor (1988), Lichbach (1994), and Humphreys and Weinstein (2008). These works analyze the collective action problem rebel groups face in inducing civilians to join them and become combatants – to mobilize for violence. Explanations for participation range from ideology to selective enticements to coercion. Even if civilians are not recruited directly into the rebel ranks, they may still provide aid to armed groups in the form of resources (Wood 2003) or information (Kalyvas 2006).

Studies on civilian participation in conflicts share some similarities with this study but also exhibit important differences. Similar to my arguments, Wood's study argues civilians' risky choice to support rebels is also a form of agency. In her study, based in El Salvador, the civilians' aid to guerrillas was rooted in the guerrillas' benevolence toward the peasants (by pursuing the revolutionary goals of liberation and political autonomy in relation to landholders) and largely observed in areas of complete guerrilla control. With these differing conditions from those that I focus on, Wood arrives at a distinct form of civilian agency that is neither autonomous nor protective.[28] In another study, Petersen (2001) emphasizes the role of strong communities in how people are "pulled into rebellion" to form resistance movements. By contrast, I consider how communities avoid rebellion (e.g., how to stay at what he calls the "zero" position when it is the safest option). On Colombia, Salazar and Castillo's (2001) theoretical models describe when civilians will either aid a dominant armed group or displace, but nothing more.

In the context of civil wars, Kalyvas is one of the main scholars to systematically incorporate civilian processes into the production of violence. He highlights and emphasizes the mechanism of denunciations by *individual* civilians (for personal or ideological reasons) to explain selective violence by political actors as a "joint process" over any civilian *collective* action aimed at opposing such divisions.[29] His theory does make a place for what he calls civilian "local committees," which he sees as "small information processing groups" that *can* screen denunciations by individuals and veto selective killings. However, he does not deeply theorize about or measure this process.[30]

---

[28] Wood also studies the demilitarized community of Tenancingo, which might be considered a case of civilian autonomy though it is not clear whether this effort was organized from the bottom up.

[29] However, coercive violence is not always well-targeted, "There is evidence that political actors are successful in generating deterrence via selective violence *in spite of* killing many innocent people" (Kalyvas 2006, 109).

[30] According to Kalyvas, "Local, usually village-based committees handle and screen information for armed actors. ... In exchange for monitoring and information, local agents obtain a valued immanent good: the power to rule over their communities" (Kalyvas 2006, 110).

The details are vague concerning where these committees arise, how they collect information, the nature of the principal–agent relationship with armed actors, and whether they are necessarily relegated to the role of "agents."[31] Kalyvas only argues that these committees' effectiveness is determined by territorial control – they persist only in areas of contested control through the fear of "double defection" (with his few examples limited to completely contested areas).[32] The committees are rendered unnecessary in these zones though, since armed groups are unable to use selective violence as they cannot sufficiently protect informants to encourage denunciations. Implicit in his discussion is that committees often cooperate (collaborate) with only one side in the conflict, with little chance for enduring autonomy, neutrality, or "fence-sitting" as conditions change (or what he calls "hedging," or "double-dealing"). In this book, I point to a greater diversity of civilian-combatant relationships.

To summarize, although the field has examined why civilians join armed groups and why they support them with manpower, resources, or information, explanations for violence tend to omit civilians as autonomous actors. Their organizational processes to avoid conflicts or ability to protect themselves are discounted. They are generally assumed to be powerless and usually for good reason: they are unarmed and are subject to coercion by often ruthless armed combatants (Kalyvas 2006, Weinstein 2006). A realist perspective would therefore assert that civilian nonviolent tactics and even armed resistance are futile. By describing civilians as "caught in the crossfire," many accounts equate them with helplessness and subject to various forms of suffering. If help comes from the international community, it is often too little or too late, and sometimes

---

[31] As one village committee's behavior is explained, "The village's solidaristic reputation was endogenous to its relatively peaceful behavior during the war and that the fear of mutual denunciations led the otherwise contentious villagers on a path to cooperation" (Kalyvas 2006, 294). However, this is an incomplete account of which villages can manage committees. He asserts that, "There is no significant variation in local practices and institutions of factional accommodation or types of factional and individual interaction in the villages of the Argolid" (297). But, it is not clear how these are measured. His litigiousness measure could represent well-functioning courts as well as discord and there are no other measures of institutions or inter-actions within villages. While he notes "avoiding a vicious cycle was a key concern of local leaders" (295), some of whom were "credited ... for managing the village's fortunes success-fully" (296), the mechanism is simply described as "Diplomacy" (297). This relationship between committees and conflict could also be unique to Greece's social landscape.

[32] In Kalyvas's anecdotal cross-national examples of committees, the three zones of contested control are blended together even though they have different predictions for violence and civilian capabilities. While he acknowledges challenges in determining control (236) from secondary sources, the committees are nevertheless lumped in zone 3, which could be inaccurate (242). Further, in the examples of committees in Greece there is no explanation of variation in village committees *within* zone 3. Eleven villages are coded with examples of mutual deterrence (293) of at least 20 villages coded as existing in zone 3 in at least some time period.

even counterproductive (Luttwak 1999, Kuperman 2000).[33] It is puzzling for these theories that in some instances, civilians are not mechanistically part of the landscape of battle, but rather are calculating agents that seek to foil armed actors.

The Literature on Civilian Institutions

Related to the studies on subnational (dis)order is a growing body of works in political science that has shifted attention from states and armed actors to analyze "informal" institutions. These studies document subnational protection schemes and conflict resolution by civilians and civil society in the contexts of riots and interethnic conflict, without recourse to the state. Scott (1985, 1992) describes the everyday resistance of peasants against their landlords and elites in the form of "weapons of the weak" and "hidden transcripts" in Malaysia. Fearon and Laitin (1996) describe how interethnic cooperation, not conflict, is actually the norm and highlight in-group policing institutions that limit interethnic spirals of violence. Varshney's (2002) study of Indian cities argues that enduring associations are sturdier than ad hoc relationships and communication to deal with rumors and quell interethnic riots.[34]

These informal institutions for resolving disputes and providing order where the state is absent (Ellickson 1991) play important and prevalent roles across Latin America (Levitsky and Helmke 2006). This study is therefore certainly not the first to pay close attention to the savviness of civilians. It departs from these works, however, with its different scope of analyzing strategies in the arguably more dangerous context of civil war settings, where communities may face multiple armed groups and a different set of violence-related problems.

The Literature on "Peace Communities" and Civilian Autonomy

Diverging from the literature on civil war violence, a growing philosophical and anthropological literature on peace movements has identified "peace communities" as a local collective strategy to avoid and end conflicts (García Durán 2005). Many of these strategies to avoid violence involve opting out of the conflict by carving out a geographically defined area that is off limits to

---

[33] However, this is not to say that interventions never happen or are ineffective. Kuperman shows that even a small intervention during the Rwandan genocide could likely have protected thousands of Tutsi civilians. Indeed, the small UN peacekeeping force in Kigali was able to employ some strategies that were successful in protecting Tutsis threatened by the Interahamwe, including harboring them in the city's soccer stadiums (see the film *Ghosts of Rwanda*).

[34] In contrast to Varshney, while "associations" may have explanatory power for understanding riots, my theory does not predict such organizations are necessarily resilient enough to deal with armed groups (though for some moderate forms of violence they can be). Indeed, I find cooperatives and ANUC land reform councils do not consistently reduce violence and instead posit even more intense forms of cooperation may be required.

armed actor hostility (Hancock and Mitchell 2007; Anderson and Wallace 2012).[35] These studies point to some apparently successful responses to violence and displacement, though with origins in anthropological and advocacy traditions, research has tended to be either normative or descriptive. Ethnographic and advocacy works on different communities include Nordstrom (1997), Amnesty International (2000), Hernández Delgado (2004), Sanford (2003, 2004), Bouvier (2006), and Hancock and Mitchell (2007), while Lederach (1997, 2003) adds a religious and spiritual perspective on these movements. Much of the discourse on these movements draws on the concept of "peacebuilding," which has origins in post-conflict rebuilding of communities (Lederach 1997 and 2005, Pearce 1997, Bouvier 2009, USAID 2009). The application of this approach to communities in the midst of conflict has emphasized education and promoting a "culture of peace" and the common Colombian refrain of "*convivencia*," or "coexistence," as end goals. These goals are noble but can also be vague, ostensibly suggesting a linear process that may oversimplify how to arrest complex conflict dynamics.

It is thus a challenge to gauge how prevalent these civilian-led efforts have actually been or how successful they have been at protecting civilians. While human rights and peace activists and some scholars embrace civilian efforts to "resist" and "create peace" in the face of adversity and hail such bravery, scholars such as Kalyvas (2006) and Luttwak (1999) would argue that any apparent effectiveness on the part of civilians is largely a result of armed actor permissiveness and is epiphenomenal, or derivative of conflict dynamics. No empirical research to date has attempted to rigorously adjudicate this debate.

Part of the problem is that despite anecdotes of effectiveness research remains undertheorized. There may be many local movements in the name of "peace," but it is not clear how such movements can be compared to distinguish mere rhetoric from strategies and effects. This leads to conceptual questions about how to define a comparable set of organizations and recognize autonomy organizations. Given these first-order issues, it is also not surprising that the causal mechanisms civilians may use *during* conflicts, or processes by which organized civilian resistance might affect substantively interesting outcomes, have not been precisely specified.[36] There has been an incomplete consideration of the interests and motives of armed groups and how civil society might affect their incentives for using violence. As a result, the

---

[35] Sometimes also referred to as "Humanitarian Spaces," these areas often pursue policies of neutrality.

[36] However, some NGO and International Organization (IO) programs have tried to consolidate and standardize approaches (European Union, Redepaz, Constituent Assemblies, Middle Magdalena Program for Peace and Development [PDPMM], Suippcol, United Nations Development Programme, etc.).

causal "force" of civilians has not been made falsifiable or pitted against the explanations of violence previously reviewed in this section that are rooted in the macro-politics of armed actors.

Additional issues with the state of research on civilian autonomy organizations stem from the body of cases that have been studied. First, while the high-quality anthropological work on various cases offers many lessons, the cases have not always been methodically or self-consciously chosen, leading to possible selection biases (i.e., overlooking unorganized, highly violent, or demolished communities). Second, many of these cases involve nonstandardized geographic units of analysis, which complicates making comparisons and measurements both across these cases and possible control cases of counterfactual communities that did not organize for autonomy. Third, cases have been used to build theories of behavior, but these theories have then rarely been tested on out-of-sample cases with either qualitative or quantitative methods to assess generalizability of findings (King et al. 1994). In sum, these works have not risen to Kalyvas's challenge that they are rarely independently or lastingly effective.

In this book I aim to go beyond both the buoyancy of activists and the vagueness of scholarly pessimism to analyze the mechanisms of civilian autonomy processes and the evidence relating these processes to outcomes of violence. I synthesize the best elements of the violence, institutions, and peace literatures to supply theoretically grounded empirical answers on when and how civilian autonomy is possible. The rich body of case studies on "autonomy" inspired my shift in perspective toward civilian agency to argue that other variables and actors matter in addition to "Weberian" state presence, armed actor control, and wealth. From the informal institutions literature I incorporate a theoretical approach for how civilians' institutions solve problems in anarchy. From the civil war studies I import the causes of violence, armed group behavior and preferences, and competitive hypothesis testing. Yet I focus on the *opposite* collective action problem from that of rebel recruitment – civilians seeking to limit violence and end civil wars.

In the end, this study is not a critique of the legal and normative field of human rights scholarship but rather an extension toward analyzing causal mechanisms and conditions for success. Going beyond the rhetoric is important because political actors may not have incentives to follow normative prescriptions and rules as talk can be cheap. Like studies of the empirical effects of human rights treaties (Simmons 2009) and trade regime issue-linkage (Hafner-Burton 2009) on compliance with human rights norms, I put subnational human rights mechanisms to realist scrutiny. By arguing that civilians and their institutions can independently affect their own livelihoods in the "crossfire," but only under certain conditions, I embrace the tension between collective action and opportunity structure approaches (Taylor 1988 and Lichbach 1998). I conclude the viewpoints of human rights activists and more structure-oriented civil war scholars are both partially correct.

RESEARCH DESIGN AND METHODS

The research pitfalls in the literature point to careful research design as essential for credibly addressing the controversy of civilian autonomy and responding to realist critiques of civilian strategies. As I elaborate in Chapter 4, I test my theories across multiple units of analysis by integrating quantitative techniques with fieldwork and qualitative analysis, bringing methodological structure and rigor to the question of civilian agency. Tests are from Colombia and with emphasis on the years from 1990 through 2005. This is an especially relevant period since the conflict and civilian peace movements intensified during this time, but the study is also closely grounded in the historical context of the preceding years. The design accounts for alternative (structural) hypotheses of violence to isolate the marginal protective effects of civilian organization.

This study has two quantitative components that fuse many disparate subnational datasets. I first use statistical analysis to test for a relationship between different civilian organizations and violence across the standardized geographical unit of municipalities and examine the conditions where this relationship holds. I then analyze the determinants of civilian organizations as proxied by junta councils, including the prior violence of La Violencia as a causal factor. This helps shed light on possible selection bias and circular relationships, and suggests they are not great threats to valid inference.

In the case study component, I compare five "towns" from two different case sites in different regions to include a diversity of experiences. The case analyses reflect over 200 interviews with a wide variety of respondents, including ex-combatants, and contain careful process tracing of history. A first case is the formal organization from the introductory anecdote of the ATCC in the department of Santander, which serves as a plausibility probe. I trace how the ATCC's investigatory institution deals with the problem of denunciations using a within-case dataset and compare it with counterfactual unorganized neighbor communities.

To select additional "out-of-sample" cases, I use statistical matching techniques to settle on the rural municipios of Bituima, Vianí, and Quipile from the department of Cundinamarca, not far from the capital of Bogotá. These cases embody a quasi-experiment since they contain variation in their levels of junta organizations but otherwise share similar characteristics. The qualitative analysis depicts over sixty years of small-town Colombian history from La Violencia through the present day. It showcases the texture of campesino life as well as perspectives from ex-combatants on cross-community differences and armed group decision-making.

PLAN OF THE BOOK

This book is written for readers with general interests in civil conflict and human rights. However, some chapters contain relatively more social science detail about the analysis of civilian autonomy than others. Readers interested in the general argument and cases of the book should pay most attention to Chapters 2, 3, 7, 8, 9, and 10. Readers that are especially interested in the analytical approach may additionally benefit from Chapters 4, 5, and 6.

Chapter 2 further develops civilian autonomy theory to explain the degree that communities retain self-rule in the face of competition among armed groups in civil wars. I elaborate on the three-part theory that links civilian organizations to strategies and then to outcomes of violence, highlighting the decision-making of both civilians and armed groups.

Chapter 3 provides context for the study by reviewing the historical processes and events since the 1950s that shaped social capital and armed conflict violence in Colombia. I explain the origins and politics of social movements for peace such as the peace communities and review how the junta village councils in Colombia came to be central forms of civilian organization in the context of the conflict.

Chapter 4 describes the integrated, multimethod research design for the next four empirical chapters and shows how such an approach can both be implemented safely in potentially risky settings and help overcome various threats to inference. I discuss how the large-n quantitative methods provide an overview of the impact of community organizations on violence while qualitative case and interview methods provide additional depth. I also describe my field research process and preview the data sources I collected during fieldwork.

Chapter 5 contains a quantitative analysis of how civilian communities and their organizations affect civil war violence. I measure the presence of these organizations across Colombian municipalities with a unique dataset on the local junta councils. When tested against extant explanations for violence including the balance of military control and lootable natural resources, I find these councils (as well as Indigenous and Afro-Colombian minority group organizations) have salutary and significant effects on levels of violence.

In Chapter 6 I analyze why junta organizations emerged where they did across Colombian towns. I address the potential concern that the influence of the armed conflict on the councils themselves could invalidate the finding that juntas reduce violence. Historical analysis and data from the La Violencia conflict of the 1950s show these councils are in fact more likely to be found in areas with social capital *and* that experienced past violence. I use statistical matching procedures to help identify "matched" pairs of neighboring towns with different levels of junta councils ("nesting" these cases within the larger statistical analysis). These cases (from the department of Cundinamarca) are analyzed in Chapter 8.

Chapter 7 analyzes the rural organization known as the Peasant Workers Association of the Carare River (ATCC) to better understand whether and how specific autonomy "mechanisms" function to protect civilians. The Carare civilians constructed a local institutional process to investigate threats against suspected armed group collaborators to clarify the "fog of war" and reform civilian preferences to participate in the conflict. I analyze a unique within-case database I created on threats and killings and find that the local institution itself proved to be a critical factor for both explaining and limiting levels of violence. Neither the creation of the institution nor its effects were merely the results of the capabilities or choices of armed actors.

In Chapter 8, I qualitatively explore the approaches that communities quietly innovated (or failed to innovate) to deal with armed conflict violence in the small, impoverished Cundinamarca coffee-growing towns of Quipile and its neighbors to the north, Vianí and Bituima. Though only a few hours from Bogotá, these cases suffered from state absence and guerrilla pressure. The stronger junta councils and levels of community cohesion and organization in Bituima and Vianí relative to Quipile allowed their populations to better resist and cope with the pressures from the FARC guerrillas (and from the army, and later, paramilitaries). The findings highlight strengths and weaknesses of the quantitative analysis and point to new hypotheses about how local politics and clientelism can shape the capabilities of civilian organizations.

In Chapter 9, I explore additional instances of civilian autonomy from out-of-sample cases from around the globe. I assess support for the theories I developed in Colombia among additional out-of-sample communities of Colombia's contested FARC demilitarized zone of the Macarena region, among Zones of Peace communities that have pursued autonomy in the Philippines, among communities in Afghanistan and Pakistan seeking to avoid counterinsurgent–Taliban crossfire, and among communities in Syria caught between government and rebel forces. These cases show that the book's main argument is not culturally bounded and in fact supersedes cultural differences as an explanation for violence.

The last chapter, Chapter 10, synthesizes the contributions of the book for the study of human rights, conflict processes, and order in weak states. I provide an overview of why, how, and when armed groups will change their behavior in response to civilian actions or cross-community differences. I also outline a research agenda for studying civilian behavior in conflict settings and discuss policy implications for protecting human rights. Lastly, I reflect on the normative implications of this research and how NGOs and external actors can ensure they "do no harm" in working with embattled civilian populations.

TABLE 1.1 Cross-national examples of civilian autonomy in civil wars

Country	Year(s)	Armed or Unarmed?	Number of Localities	Sources	Brief Description	Number of Armed Actors
Afghanistan	2006	Unarmed	1–3	Gall and Wafa 2006; Suleman and Williams 2003	Some local towns, tribes peacefully resisted Taliban (and NATO), Musa Qala district of Helmand Province; Jaghori District of Ghazni Province.	Multiple
Afghanistan	2009	Armed	Unknown	Gall 2009	Villagers in some [Helmand] districts took up arms against foreign troops to protect their homes or in anger after losing relatives in airstrikes.	Multiple
Afghanistan	2009	Armed	1	Gopal and Rosenberg 2009	A village in Nangahar in eastern Afghanistan rose up against the Taliban, in response both to Taliban violence and abuses as well as an entreaty of development resources from the Afghan government.	1
Afghanistan	2009	Armed and unarmed	1	Jaffe 2009	U.S. entreaty to insurgents and village elders in Kamdesh village, Nurestan, to encourage them to develop a plan to manage local security affairs in the midst of a withdrawal of U.S. forces from region to more populated areas.	1

(continued)

TABLE 1.1 (*continued*)

Country	Year(s)	Armed or Unarmed?	Number of Localities	Sources	Brief Description	Number of Armed Actors
Colombia	1980s	Armed	Multiple	Houghton and Villa 2005	Quintín Lame Indigenous self-defense group in Cauca, other sporadic local examples.	Multiple
Congo-Uganda	2009	Armed	2+	Gettleman and Schmitt 2009; Bavier 2009; Gettleman 2009a	After Ugandan Lords Resistance Army (LRA) rebels were pushed into Congo, some terrorized villages started self-defense committees armed with shotguns and slingshots to protect themselves near Dungu. Also wider movement in larger town of Faradje, but also displacement.	1
Greece	1944	Unarmed	~10	Kalyvas 2006, citing Frangoulis	Local village committees vetoed violence from both rebel and German armies.	Multiple
Guatemala	1982–1993	Unarmed	2–4	Stoll 1993; Falla 1994	Communities of Population in Resistance (CPRs) of displaced civilians remained in disputed territories hiding from the government.	Multiple
Iraq	2006	Armed	20+	Al-Ansary and Adeeb 2006	Tribes in Anbar Province defended villages from Sunni insurgents, requested government armaments.	1

Kenya	1960s	Unarmed	Unknown; Kiambu	Mau Mau local councils were said to veto violence.	Barnett and Njama 1966	Multiple
Lithuania	1941–1952	Unarmed (?)	Multiple	Some towns tried to remain neutral during World War II.	Petersen 2001	Multiple
Mexico	1992	Unarmed	1+	In Chiapas, Acteal/ Las Abejas religious community's peaceful movement against state and paramilitary oppression; nonviolent pacificism separated them from Zapatista National Liberation Army (EZLN) guerrillas. Nonviolence in response to paramilitary pressure and Acteal massacre.	Tavanti 2003	Multiple
Mozambique	1989–1993	Unarmed	Multiple	Jehovah's Witness peace zones; Naprama movement against Renamo rebels.	Wilson 1992	Multiple
Pakistan	2008	Armed	Multiple	Lashkar militias resisted Taliban violence, especially in "lawless" FATA region; U.S. considered an "Anbar" tribal strategy for the Pakistani tribal areas along the Afghan border.	Perlez and Shah 2008a; Gettleman 2007	Multiple
Pakistan	2008	Armed and unarmed	2+	Neutral/ peace zone in town of Buner, near FATA, "The villagers in Buner say they would prefer to handle the Taliban on their own, rather than have the	Perlez and Shah 2008b	Multiple

(continued)

TABLE 1.1 (*continued*)

Country	Year(s)	Armed or Unarmed?	Number of Localities	Sources	Brief Description	Number of Armed Actors
					heavy hand of the army come and do it for them. . . . A new peace committee composed of elders and politicians passed a resolution declaring Buner a zone free of both the army and the Taliban." Also nonviolent negotiations by councils in Landi Kotal.	
Pakistan	2009	Armed	1	Masood 2009; Khan 2009	Tribal leaders in Bannu, Sertelegram, and Kanju in Swat who had armed against Taliban were attacked and killed. Before Taliban could kill survivors, villagers came out with guns to fight them off.	1
Pakistan	2009	Armed and unarmed	1 district, many villages	Tavernise and Ashraf 2009	1,000+ villagers in the Dir District armed to fight off the Taliban after they attacked a mosque with suicide bombers, killing thirty.	Multiple
Peru	1982–1997	Armed	~4,000	Starn 1999; Fumerton 2001	Rondas Campesinas repelled Sendero Luminoso, coopted by government.	1

Peru	1982–1997	Unarmed	Unknown	Starn 1999; Fumerton 2001	Some Rondas Campesinas did not arm; they opted out of conflict in some regions, resisted joining government counterinsurgency programs.	Multiple
Philippines	1988–2004	Unarmed	91+	Coronel-Ferrer 2005; Santos 2005; Hancock and Mitchell 2007	"Peace zones" were declared to peacefully resist first NPA and government forces and then MNLF, MILF, and government forces in Mindanao and other regions.	Multiple
Russia	2010	Unarmed	1	Greene 2010	Village leader in Sulak in Dagestan dialogued with army and Islamist insurgents to avoid participating in conflict.	Multiple
Rwanda	1994	Unarmed	Multiple	Doughty and Ntambara 2005	Highly cohesive Muslim communities and other minorities resisted/did not participate in genocide; tried to protect themselves and Tutsis.	1
Sierra Leone	1990s	Armed	Multiple	Muana 1997; Humphreys and Weinstein 2006a	Civilian Defense Forces (CDF) arose in local villages to repel Revolutionary United Front (RUF) rebels, later coopted by the government.	1
Somalia	2008–2009	Armed	Localities in Dusa Marreb	Gettleman 2009b; Gettleman 2009c; Raghavan 2010	Sufis around the town of Dusa Marreb armed against incursions by the extremist Islamic militant movement, the "Shabab."	1

(continued)

TABLE 1.1 *(continued)*

Country	Year(s)	Armed or Unarmed?	Number of Localities	Sources	Brief Description	Number of Armed Actors
Sudan	2007	Unarmed	Unknown	Gettleman 2007	Some neutral towns mediated conflicts between Arab tribes, "The wali, or governor, of South Darfur called a peace conference and urged neutral tribes to mediate a cease-fire."	Multiple
Sudan	2009	Armed	Multiple	Snapp 2010; Heaton and Fick 2010	"Arrow Boy" militias against LRA incursions.	1
Zimbabwe	1970s	Unarmed	Unknown	Kriger 1992	Civilians avoided aiding both ZANU rebels and government forces; some committees vetoed violence.	Multiple

2

A Theory of Civilian Decision-Making in Civil War

"Many people wrongly think it is [just] the Association that should come to the defense of each individual, but it should be the opposite."
– Resident of La India, Santander, 1995 (ATCC Archives)

"The guerrilla respects the thinking of the Association [ATCC]. There's no reason why it should disappear. On the contrary, it should be strengthened."
– FARC Commander, 2001, near La India, Santander
(ATCC Archives)

"The mentality of the armed groups has changed a lot and we respect certain things."
– Paramilitary Subcommander, 2001, near La India, Santander
(ATCC Archives)

One Saturday morning in La India, an elder conciliator invited me to join him at the Adventist mass. Since the church had a strong influence on the ATCC's nonviolent approach, I jumped at the chance. From the main street, we walked a few minutes through a small wooded area and came upon a clearing and the church. I watched as the congregation greeted each other, then we entered and sat in a pew in the front row. As the service began, the people sang hymns and read along from the prayerbook. I quickly lost my place, however, so I quietly nudged my companion to ask him where we were. So as not to disturb the songs, he whispered, "I don't know." Since he was following along and skimming the pages with his finger, I quizzically asked, "What do you mean you don't know?" He looked over at me sheepishly, shrugged his shoulders, and said, "I don't read." His reply was stunning, and was an epiphany for how impressive the mobilization of the ATCC and other communities around Colombia truly was. Indeed, how is it that ordinary people like this elder conciliator are able to confront violence? The answer is a story of organization.

Civil wars are not fought in social vacuums. They are fought in social landscapes. These landscapes are often variable, with notable social differences from one town or village to the next. My central argument is that these differences shape how civilians cope with civil war conflict and, in turn, how they are treated by armed actors. In this chapter, I outline a theory of when, how, and why variation in cross-community characteristics, such as organization, affect outcomes for civilians in civil war settings.

Civilians tend to be viewed in limited ways, as either collaborators or victims of armed groups. In contrast, I argue civilians have greater latitude as agents and explain how differences in civilian organization and cooperation determine their ability to implement protective strategies to retain autonomy, or self-rule. I further explain why and how these strategies can be effective under conditions that might normally invite violence, whether these are zones of contested territorial control or confrontation with armed groups with weak disciplinary structures. I show how these civilian strategies can affect armed group behavior and discipline, and also explore their limits to do so.

I explore the full range of civilians' available choices, but primarily focus on collective strategies designed to retain autonomy and self-rule in the face of competition among multiple armed groups in civil wars. The concept of autonomy is adapted from the goal of communities that have declared themselves "peace communities" or "resisting" communities. More specifically, autonomy means maintaining democratic decision-making power over outcomes *for* the community *within* the community, without influence from outside armed groups. I also subsume under this concept the more tangible results of being able to keep the community in place and resist forced displacement as well as mitigate violence against residents. Self-rule can encompass decision-making abilities and the *realization* of decisions. In the realm of justice, community autonomy means the community (and not other actors) retains decision-making power over whether individuals should live or be sanctioned or killed. I refer to "de facto" autonomy, then, as the ability of civilians to shield themselves from the effects of external actors and therefore see their own decisions implemented, enforced, and respected.

The drive for autonomy stems from the great uncertainty civilians face in their daily lives in conditions of civil war. With only one life to live, one mistake or one random act can spell doom. Under the peaceful conditions known to most residents of the developed world, political order is sustained by a hegemonic macro-political actor – usually the state – that guarantees security, often in the form of a "social contract" where security is exchanged for support and taxation (Tilly 1992). Order can break down and residents may face insecurity when this actor is either repressive or abusive (e.g., Valentino 2004) or under anarchy when other political actors compete for power. This absence of order and rule of law most often occurs in "weak" or "failed" states (if the state were strong, there would be no problem of civil war).

An option to make daily life more certain and increase chances of survival is to turn to indigenous – meaning local – organizations. Since armed actor coercion of civilians has been theorized to stem from divisions within civilian societies (Kalyvas 2006), I argue that social cohesion among civilian communities affords them greater chances to keep armed groups out and implement collective strategies to retain autonomy than acting individually. I develop a general three-part civilian autonomy theory that links civilian organizations to strategies and then to outcomes.

First, variation in the social and demographic landscape and technical assistance from external actors (be they the government, church, or NGOs) propel some communities to organize more easily than others. Second, cohesive, organized communities can make collective decisions about how best to deal with the dangers of civil war conflict. In addition to the standard strategies of alignment with macro-actors these can include more subtle "tactical" responses, or "weapons-of-the-weak" (Scott 1985), to deal with discord within civilian communities as well as more forceful "weapons-of-the-*not-so-weak*" tactics, such as overt protest and actions by nonviolent community guards. Civilian preferences, social capital, and the (past and prospective) threat environment all interact to determine strategy selection. Third, the strength of civilian organization, selected strategies, and armed group incentives jointly determine substantive outcomes such as levels of violence.

The existing literature on micro-studies of civil war raises the possibility of civilian agency but does not contain answers. Kalyvas suggests in his study of selective violence that local committees can play an important role in limiting violence against civilians but admits that, "[W]e *know little about how they actually operate*. Perhaps their most important feature is that they often have a role in determining what violence is visited on the locality in which they operate, but how this power is wielded varies" (2006: 110; emphasis added). Weinstein (2006) examines how rebel organization affects governance structures toward civilian populations, and argues that abusive groups invite resistance or cause civilians to flee. But he says nothing about when these choices will be made or how civilian "agency" occurs. As this body of scholarship stands, it is like having a model of democratic participation without a theory of the participants – the voters. Yet as Kalyvas (2006) has stated, civil wars are "highly endogenous processes," opening the possibility that armed actor choices may partly result from civilian moves as well. In the rest of the chapter, I explain how civilians come to cooperate, how they act collectively, and when armed groups will be affected by their actions.

THE ADVANTAGES OF COMMUNITY COHESION AND ORGANIZATION

To retain autonomy, I argue that civilians can act strategically and effectively, even in the harsh conditions of civil war violence. But, for a hope of mounting protective strategies, communities must first be able to cooperate. Lone civilians, like lone soldiers, are unlikely to be effective in complex and changing environments and against military organizations. An individual may have trouble, for instance, assessing the conditions of the conflict, committing to not collaborating if most of his neighbors are collaborating, or credibly convincing an armed group that he is not a collaborator. He or she may also face risks for blowing the whistle about threats or acts of violence. In contrast, groups of civilians are more likely to have the capacity to deal with complex and changing environments. They have more information and options, longer time horizons, and can pool risk (see Ober 2008 on epistemic communities of Ancient Greece). In this section, I explain the sources of and variation in communities' cohesion and organizational potential.

From an organizational standpoint, communities face the risk that armed groups may peel off individual community members from a pacifist cause by offering selective incentives, either in the form of payments or the application of violence to settle feuds. Peaceful residents of communities seeking to collectively avoid or minimize the effects of the conflict must face the tyranny of the few "extremists," militants, or collaborators from the various sides in the conflict – those who, by virtue of picking up weapons, exhibit a greater willingness to use violence. So the question becomes: how do civilian organizations keep their residents from giving in to the temptations to participate in the conflict and fracture the community? This challenge faced by civilians is the *opposite* collective action problem to that of rebel groups' recruitment efforts. In sum, it is the unity of civilian centrists that helps impede and isolate violent "extremists."

Challenges to Collective Action

When communities are threatened with violence, most residents are better off if they can act to stop or reduce it.[1] Individuals would generally prefer to protect their communities and remain in their homes than choose displacement. Yet there is a reason why organized responses to civil war violence are not ubiquitous: there are considerable challenges to collective action given its risks, the high costs of retaliation, and short windows of time for coordination.[2] These organizational pitfalls reflect a civilian's dilemma that is similar to the challenges of collective action discussed by Olson (1965).

Most individuals want to stay put, but do not have strong incentives to defend their communities on their own since they are unlikely to succeed and armed actors might respond with further violence. Participation in community defense may preclude safely fleeing to refuge, making hesitance on the part of individuals quite rational. In these situations, fear can be both pervasive and

---

[1] Some individuals may still benefit from or take advantage of the conflict for personal gain.
[2] The challenge of rebel recruitment has been cast as a related collective action problem under fear in civil wars.

devastating to cooperation. Under the "law of silence," residents stop communicating out of the fear that they will be ratted out to an armed group for even discussing the situation.

To act, individuals require certainty that they can count on their neighbors. Despite fear, two types of communities are well positioned to act collectively and implement strategies to avoid violence. First, communities of residents with *homogenous* interests for remaining in the community to protect their livelihoods will mobilize relatively easily (Olson's "privileged" groups). These kinds of communities may organize precisely because the residents all highly value protection and avoiding displacement and because their similarities help them agree when choosing collective strategies. Many residents of rural communities, for instance, possess a keen sense of "belonging" (*pertenencia*), or identification with their homes and communities, and cannot envision new livelihoods elsewhere. Because of common interests, civilians will participate even with little knowledge about the preferences of their neighbors.[3]

Second, social explanations of collective action as discussed by Marwell and Oliver (1993) suggest even some communities with *divergent* interests are able to organize. In these communities, although some residents may be risk averse and require high certainty that a resistance movement will be successful, they can be spurred to organize insofar as individuals' choices are interdependent and influenced by the strength of community leadership and by what other members do.[4] In this case, first movers with the strongest preferences are likely to form a critical mass that reassures the rest of the community that the project will succeed.[5] The minority with strong preferences for defending the community in the face of violence may be unable to successfully organize alone. But they are likely to move first and successfully mobilize others when they either (1) are able to persuade their neighbors or compensate them with selective benefits so they join in or (2) believe their actions alone will inspire confidence in their neighbors. Chwe (2001) argues that communication and the ability of the community to generate "common knowledge" (or, in this case, a culture of resistance) is crucial for reassuring more reluctant residents (see related models

---

[3] Forced displacement can have a homogenizing effect on civilian preferences within a community if, when civilians consider whether to return to their lands, less resolute residents are separated from their more resolute neighbors.

[4] This could reflect a prisoner's dilemma, with individual displacement as a form of defection. It may be converted into a cooperation game depending on "tipping points": Civilian leaders would hope to spark a pattern of participation whereas armed actors seek to cauterize participation and deactivate civilian organizations to achieve displacement on the cheap. The last people to join in the community effort may determine whether the effort succeeds or fails because their allegiance can eliminate armed actor inroads into the community and provide information about the community's unity.

[5] Applying Marwell and Oliver's terminology, the public good of community defense has an "accelerating" production function where "successive contributions generate progressively larger payoffs" (63).

by Kuran 1991 and Lohmann 1994).[6] The creation of common knowledge and even greater reassurance can be facilitated by social capital, network links, and repeated interactions among individuals.

Social Capital and Pathways to Organization

The civilian's dilemma points to social capital as a key explanation of cooperation. This is because privileged groups with homogenous preferences for collective action tend to be rare. The importance of civil society as a counterbalance to formal (state) institutions has been noted by Bobbio (1988) and Cohen and Arato (1994). The related concept of social capital – the vibrancy of civil society – was originally explored at the local level by Putnam (1993), and has been expanded and adapted to many different forms and contexts (Almond and Verba 1963 studied the related concept of civic political culture; see Rubio 1997, Sudarsky 2007, and Kaplan and Nussio 2015 on social capital in Colombia). The notion of strong horizontal relationships among residents is particularly applicable to the context of rural communities in civil war. Social ties help residents decide what is best for their community, to launch organizations that survive over time, and to directly affect levels of violence by preventing armed groups from seeding dissent among them. I later describe how conflict-relevant civilian social capital in Colombia comes from three main sources: existing natural bases for networking and reciprocity, preexisting organizations, and technical assistance for cooperation provided by external actors. Further, even acts of violence can promote coordination and the homogenization of preferences, depending on the severity and timing.

Certain demographic and geographic configurations foment strong social ties and reciprocity within civilian communities better than others (Petersen 2001). Population size, population density, and network links among residents including natural bases such as shared ethnicity or ties from economic complementarities may aid the implementation of collective strategies. A village's relative isolation may also promote close intracommunity social relationships (Humphreys and Weinstein 2006a). For instance, in Colombia, colonizers and homesteaders that migrated to "wild" areas (after experiences with armed conflict) tend to have long-running reciprocal relationships and especially deep commitments to stay on their lands (Legrand 1986). In less developed areas, social interaction is also supported where favorable geography lessens costs of intracommunity transportation, communication, and exchange through

---

[6] Strong links between individuals may encourage participation, but weak links may speed up information transmission (Chwe 2001). This information can be transmitted through rituals, the strength of interpersonal relationships, a common spoken language, strong leaders, communication technology, and technical support from NGOs including church networks. Once an organization has been established, institutional arrangements may be created to prevent reneging on commitments to defend the community. These are likely to include positive inducements since moral stances against violence often rule out coercion.

The former community store and cooperative of the ATCC came to be used as a meeting space, La India, Santander, Colombia, 2007.
Photograph by Oliver Kaplan.

features such as rivers or footpaths. By contrast, if a community is close to large cities or international borders, there may be more exit options and therefore fewer close relationships, likely making local organizations weaker and displacement less costly. Clear property rights and titles to land may also both promote cooperation by preventing disputes between neighbors over property boundaries and instilling stronger preferences to organize to avoid displacement.

Prior experiences of cooperation among residents in other issue domains may also translate into cooperation in the face of threats and violence when the conflict comes to town. Civilians may rely upon interpersonal relationships and authority structures of preexisting local organizations when assessing how to deal with an armed group and how many individuals might participate in a collective strategy. Examples of these kinds of organizations and experiences include local junta public goods councils, committees formed to deal with cattle rustling, indigenous tribes, agricultural cooperatives, or experiences with political party mobilizations. With these foundations, some communities are said to possess particularly strong cultures of organization and resistance (in Colombia, such communities are informally described as "*berracos*," or "toughies").

External actors can also serve as focal points that help communities communicate and coordinate when facing armed groups. For instance, NGOs and churches can support communities in their efforts to respond to conflicts by providing them with "technical assistance" including ideas about how to organize or what strategies are available. They can also provide accompaniment and a forum – a safe physical space – for meetings and communication.[7]

Finally, the threat environment may stimulate or impede the formation of social capital and organization (what could be termed the "endogenous" formation of social capital). An absence of violence may mean there is little reason for increased civilian organizing. Strong interests among armed actors to commit high levels of violence may preclude any civilian social capital or resistance actions. Similarly, under intense conflict conditions, leaders of community organizations may also be directly targeted with repression in an effort to weaken these structures. Moderate levels of violence may therefore most stimulate intensified social relations and a collective response by civilians since there is both enough reason ("demand") to unify and tolerable risks for first movers.[8] Moderate violence may also increase the ability of civilians to act collectively by producing sorting within civilian communities where less resolute civilians leave the community. The result may be increased homogeneity of preferences among the remaining residents to protect themselves.

The Added Value of Cooperation and Organizations

The essential feature of organizations for the theory of civilian autonomy is that they embody intense, institutionalized forms of cooperation among individuals. This helps civilians in two ways. First, cooperation can mean fewer divisions within a community that armed groups can exploit and act as a mechanism of protection. Second, as institutions that operate in conditions of subnational rather than international anarchy, community organizations help civilians engage in "repeat play" (Keohane 1984).[9] Because organizing on the spot in the midst of a conflict is possible but difficult, preexisting organizations that have already solved collective action problems empower civilians in several different ways.

First, well-functioning organizations can withstand the loss of any single individual and live on. They therefore have the ability to maintain decision-making

---

[7] NGOs that have provided such assistance include the Inter-Church Justice and Peace Commission (Justicia y Paz), the Middle Magdalena Peace Program (PDPMM), and the Network of Peace (Red de Paz).

[8] Under such circumstances, civilian responses would be partly though not entirely endogenous to the moves of armed actors.

[9] They play a similar subnational role as international regimes, which are "Sets of implicit or explicit principles, norms, rules and decision-making procedures around which actors' expectations converge" (Krasner 1982, 57). These frameworks define liability and decrease costs of information and transactions.

procedures that endure over time and are not ad hoc. Second, organizations can aggregate information from many people and places to understand security conditions and bases of civilian support, and they have sufficient lead time to deliberate and make decisions before armed groups arrive. Third, organizations can tap collective memory and knowledge and develop best practices for dealing with particular threats as they arise. Fourth, organizations have bureaucratic capacity to implement collective strategies to maintain internal order within communities. Fifth, organizations can act as figureheads for communities and interface, advocate, and negotiate with external actors and other organizations.

Civilians' initiatives to bargain or negotiate are frequently attributed to the strength of a single popular leader instead of organizations. While some individuals may be capable of undertaking effective nonviolent actions, such individuals do not materialize out of thin air. They are usually produced by especially cooperative and visionary communities. Community leaders are frequently emboldened to advocate for their community's interests when they have the support of a broad section of their members (and leaders themselves may also shape incentives of residents to support the common good). With broad support, leaders' positions are also likely to carry greater weight with armed groups.

A community planning meeting at the 25th (26th) anniversary celebration of the founding of the ATCC, La India, Santander, Colombia, 2013.
Photograph by Oliver Kaplan.

I argue that organizations with three main characteristics are the most helpful for protecting communities. First, organizations will be effective if they have decision-making experience, with clear lines of authority and procedures for aggregating preferences and incorporating new information. Second, broad and legitimate organizations should be more effective. Organizations that are all-encompassing of a community's population are more likely to be recognized and respected as the community's decision-making body by residents and as the community's figurehead by outside actors. They may also be inclined to act in moderation, as Kant's liberal theory of "perpetual peace" would expect (1970). Broad organizations also suffer from fewer "spoilers" who might seek to undermine the community for selective benefits from armed groups. Third, organizations that are "apolitical" relative to macro-actors have greater chances for successful protection. Politically oriented organizations may be polarizing or be more easily "stigmatized" by armed actors. They may be seen as threatening for their politics or as tacitly supporting enemies and therefore quickly become targeted (e.g., labor or land reform movements, or local arms of political parties). By contrast, organizations that remain local, represent local interests, and are cautious in their entanglements with larger political movements are less likely to alienate armed actors.

CIVILIANS' CHOICES AND PATHWAYS TO AUTONOMY

After organizing, what can civilians do to protect themselves? "Resistance" – *"resistencia!"* – is a common mantra but it can be conceptually vague. What does it mean? Resistance against whom, how, toward what goal? In what way would resistance affect armed groups and provide protection? How can resistance be evaluated empirically at the micro level? Going beyond the resistance mantra requires a testable theory with clearly specified mechanisms.

From a realist perspective in which material power determines outcomes, nonviolent tactics and even armed resistance implemented by organized civilians should have little success against more powerful armed actors. This section argues to the contrary that civilians can still have agency and avenues to affect their livelihoods and perhaps the strategic situation in a civil war, even when they are less (militarily) powerful than armed actors.

I first enumerate the general *strategies of alignment* available to civilian communities in relating with armed actors and explain how these strategies are selected.[10] I then proceed to explore the special case of the strategy of opting for "autonomy" from the armed groups in greater depth, including the *tactics, or specific mechanisms,* civilians use to deal with threats. I also explain why and

---

[10] These strategies may not reflect a community's first preference and may instead be chosen out of necessity (Kalyvas 2006, Mason 1996).

when certain "bundles" or sets of tactics are likely to be chosen by different communities and over different periods of time.

Civilian Selection of Strategic Alignments

Civilians facing the threat of violence in armed conflict are primarily concerned with survival, although they would also like to protect their property, economic prospects, standards of living, and social relations. A main choice civilians make to balance these interests is how they position themselves (politically) in relation to competing macro-level actors. Hirschman's (1970) "voice-exit-loyalty" framework provides a productive way to think about the variety of responses available to civilians. Organized civilians have a number of alignment strategies from which to choose: do nothing or flee (exit); ally with a macro-actor (loyalty); and autonomy (voice), or actively avoiding alignments, reducing civilian participation in the conflict, and demanding accountability through various armed and nonviolent mechanisms.[11]

Prior scholarship has suggested that civilians' alignments are primarily endogenous to, or a result of, armed actor preferences and pressures. I do not dispute that armed actors' choices and strategies greatly shape the options open to civilians.[12] It is only logical that armies are advantaged in their ability to coerce civilian support through force. Nevertheless, I argue that existing accounts and portrayals of civilians are incomplete, with important variation in the selection of civilian strategies left to be explained by community-level factors. Short of sudden attacks against the population, civilians may carefully deliberate about their options before implementing responses to violence.[13]

Civilian cultural or political preferences can also influence alignment decisions. Civilian preferences may tip a community toward (or against) allying with ideologically close (or distant) macro-actors as balances of control shift. For instance, communities with leftist or socialist preferences rooted in poverty may be naturally inclined toward guerrillas and their ideological goals.[14]

---

[11] Sometimes referred to as neutrality. Stoll (1993) as well as Kalyvas talk about allying with both sides, or "double-dealing," as a strategy.

[12] This parallels how elites can structure available choices for voters in voting models.

[13] Forward-looking armed groups would like to quash civilian threats to their hegemony. In equilibrium there must be some uncertainty on the part of armed actors (rooted in civilians' collective action problems) about how civilians might respond that conditions the oppressiveness of their strategy to root out potentially hostile civilian movements before they arise. Or, armed actors, in trying to organize communities or hold meetings with them to gain control, may "tip their hands," giving communities much-needed *time* to coordinate amongst themselves. Civilian movements face uncertainty because they do not know what the armed actors do not know about them and may miscalculate armed group preferences.

[14] Despite facing dangers from government forces, the peasants in Wood's (2003) account of the civil war in El Salvador were naturally inclined to support the FMLN as a result of their economic oppression, desire for justice, and contact with Liberation Theology.

In contrast, other types of communities, such as those that are either isolated or founded around ethnicity, may be accustomed to local political autonomy and have stronger preferences for maintaining such a position even when armed groups arrive and contest their territory.[15] So, depending on the conflict dynamics, civilians' preferences may either speed or slow civilian alignments with macro-actors.

Civilians' most basic strategy is to "do nothing." In other words, regardless of organization, civilians have no collective strategy. While this choice is most likely observed because of a failure to organize, even organized communities may decide not to align or implement specific policies to maintain their independence if these choices incite greater repression or if they are unfamiliar with available tactics. Under threat and with no strategy, the displacement of civilians may occur "drop by drop" (*gota a gota*) as residents flee one by one to separate destinations. This displacement can further inhibit future attempts to organize if there is no one left to count on, a reality not lost on preying armed groups.

Aside from doing nothing, organized communities may be advantaged in being able to coordinate a *collective* exodus from dangerous territory in a more orderly process. Peasants in El Salvador developed the *guinda* system to prepare temporary shelters and evade government troops (Todd 2010), similar to the avoidance strategies of some communities in Guatemala (Falla 1994) and Kenya (Barnett and Njama 1966). Families can be kept together as they arrive in a safer location that is ready with supplies and assistance from neighbors, NGOs, and/or the government, as the ATCC helped absorb and resettle residents who fled combat in outlying villages (CNRR 2011, 418). This collective strategy may be used with an eye toward later facilitating a more rapid and orderly return to the territory if and when conflict conditions improve, as the communities along the Cacarica river in Chocó eventually did, forming the CAVIDA network of humanitarian zones (CINEP 2003, Justicia y Paz 2003). Unfortunately, resorting to the "do nothing," individual displacement, or collective displacement options has been all too common in the history of the Colombian conflict as many people have been killed or displaced from their

---

[15] Shared preferences for autonomy may arise from a variety of sources. First, residents that share certain socioeconomic characteristics may naturally tip toward autonomy. For instance, recipients of land parcels may unite for common defense of their properties. Preferences may be strongest among lower middle-class communities that are not so poor as to look to guerrillas to promote their grievances or get involved in the coca economy nor so wealthy as to look to paramilitaries for protection, as large cattle ranchers have (even though levels of organization may vary within these groups). Second, culture may play a role. Residents' pervasive religious beliefs may make them more inclined to try nonviolent strategies and increase the likelihood that residents share autonomy preferences (for instance Evangelicals and Seventh-Day Adventists). Lastly, activist NGOs and religious institutions such as churches can plant the seeds for organized resistance by providing technical assistance and acting as focal points for coordination.

homes (perhaps consistent with Colombia's generally low levels of community social capital as observed by Sudarsky 2007). Today, there are many ghost towns in Colombia, as Sepúlveda Roldán (2004) illustrates in his portrayal of the microcosm town of Saiza in Córdoba.

Civilians may also ally with an armed actor for protection from that actor as well as from incursions by a nearby enemy army. This is often a tacit bargain or social contract where support in the form of material provisions or information is exchanged for protection and the maintenance of public order.[16] Where the presence of the army is strong, most communities side with the government for protection from insurgent groups. Armed groups also often force peasants into the "bargain" of paying protection taxes (*vacunas* or vaccination payments) in exchange for "protection." In an illustration from Putumayo, Colombia, the *cocalero* movement allied with guerrillas for a time to resist government counterinsurgency pressure and aerial pesticide spraying to continue producing their coca crops (Ramírez 2001). This alliance strategy can risk future retaliation if the balance of control later shifts and a new armed actor becomes dominant.

The final alignment strategy communities may select is autonomy from all armed actors in their region, or self-rule.[17] According to Sandoval (2004, translated from the Spanish), "Autonomy is that which is determined from within . . . one cannot conceive of peace with justice as a paternalistic gift of two powerful actors that supposedly agree . . . Autonomy is independence when facing armed actors" (187). The motive for pursuing autonomy is frequently to gain independence from the "alliance" bargain described earlier to avoid complications with enemy groups who would punish real or perceived defections. Autonomy strategies may therefore be especially common after shifts in the military balance of control, when civilians are signaled and stigmatized as supporters of the formerly dominant power (and when that power also remains close enough to exact revenge). As such, autonomy strategies often involve formal declarations of centrist political positioning for increased credibility.[18] However, while the term "autonomy" has been frequently adopted by communities and scholars alike, what it means for influencing behaviors has received scant critical and theoretical attention.

---

[16] This strategy and its incarnations are discussed at length in Mason (1996) and Kalyvas (2006).

[17] The language and rhetoric of autonomy can present some confusion. Autonomy is claimed by many communities because it is softer and less threatening than claiming "neutrality," which is more positional and less about civilian decision-making. This is why formal declarations of autonomy can reflect the implementation of autonomy policies and tactics although the conceptual fit may be loose: groups that do not use the language of autonomy may implement its mechanisms and groups that use the rhetoric may see autonomy as a goal but not implement many policies to that end.

[18] Declarations themselves may be considered a tactic. Declarations of autonomy can be antagonizing to armed groups if they fear that other communities view the toleration as a reason to "hold out" too. However, declarations may serve as a useful tool to gain outside attention or clarify which community members are "in" and which are "out."

Autonomy in conflict settings has often been seen as synonymous with "neutrality" or nonalignment. The difference may be semantic, but for conceptual clarity I see autonomy as a broader concept since it does not require positional decisions and can be an ideal that is sought even in the face of a single abusive group (whereas neutrality is often a relational concept vis-à-vis other actors). Autonomy can be conceived of as independence in decision-making and the freedom from violence required to sustain it.

Autonomy is a general strategy as well as an end goal that a community may try to reach through various "autonomy strategies" or *tactics*. Autonomy can include more subtle, internally oriented, community-building strategies (weapons of the weak) and other cost-imposing strategies on armed groups (weapons of the not-so-weak) that may not be contingent on being neutral or declaring neutrality. In other words, neutrality is only one of the various tactics a community may select to attain autonomy, and there are also strategies to seek autonomy that do not involve neutral positioning. In the next section, I explore more deeply the special case of seeking autonomy and the various tactics employed to maintain autonomy.

Civilians' Selection of Bundles of Tactics to Reduce Violence and Maintain Autonomy

Autonomy-seeking strategies are usually adopted by civilians as a response to multiple armed groups, when each group is worried about losing civilian support to the enemy and willing to use coercion to halt the erosion. When multiple armed groups "signal" and stigmatize civilians as collaborators, communities may seek to credibly commit to not having allegiances to enemy groups and incentivize armies to desist from violence.[19] Communities may act collectively to demand greater accountability when facing a single aggressive armed group as well.

In some rare cases, communities may be relatively cohesive and well armed, making deterrence through force an option. In other organized but unarmed communities, a number of other nonviolent mechanisms can be implemented to reduce levels of violence. Some are based around loose, spontaneous coordination of actions and preferences while others are implemented and sustained

---

[19] The "fog of war" and the inability of civilians to commit to not take sides and collectively deter armed actors are the main pathways to the coercive violence perpetrated against them. These problems stem from two different principal-agent monitoring problems when armed actors are working to consolidate control of a given territory. One is at the group level between civilian groups and either the rebels or the government (or paramilitaries). Without control of an area, armed actors cannot perfectly monitor what "side" a group of civilians is on – whether certain residents of a community are aiding their enemies or if civilian leaders are working to stop them. The other is among civilian group leaders, who may not be able to perfectly monitor and limit the defections of their constituents to exit the community or aid armed groups.

through deeper, ongoing forms of cooperation. Some actions are taken in direct response to specific incursions by armed groups: a displaced community may return to its lands, an indigenous group may confront and protest against armed group kidnappers *en masse* to rescue victims. Other actions are more of a daily, routine variety – social unity, managing information about conflict conditions, dissuasion of youth from participating in armed groups. For either set of tactics, civilian cooperation is a catalyst and the aim is to manage the costs and benefits to armed groups of using violence. The tactics work by dealing with social divisions to make using violence more difficult, providing armed groups with benefits so they are more judicious in their uses of violence, or directly imposing costs on armed groups for using violence.

What follows is a description of the logic behind six of the most popular tactics I identified through site visits, although other tactics may exist that are not yet publicized. I argue that communities mix and match these tactics to select bundles of policies for their specific needs. The tactics are additive (though not necessarily linearly) and increasing in their contentiousness and their probable effectiveness. I then theorize about the decision process for selecting various tactics, which involves similar considerations to those already mentioned for the selection of the broader alignment strategies.

The principles of the Peace Community of San José de Apartadó, Antioquia, Colombia. Photograph by Oliver Kaplan.

First, civilian organizations can promote what has been called a "culture of peace." More concretely, they can attempt policies to change the distribution of preferences among (and incentives that shape) the civilian population of a community from belligerence to pacifism, making civilians less easily seducible by armed actors. Armed groups often have incentives to peel off civilian allies to gain informational or logistical advantages over their opponents. Unfortunately, when this same pressure exists from multiple groups, civilians become fearful of being implicated and killings can spawn desires for revenge. Trust among civilian residents can break down, begetting even more killings. "Preference-changing," culture-of-peace policies can lead fewer civilians to collaborate with armed actors and, when implemented in an even-handed way,[20] can reduce the incidence of "valid" threats and violence against actual civilian enemy collaborators. Cultures of peace can also limit groups' available manpower by impeding recruitment.

Preference-changing, culture-of-peace policies can be implemented in at least two ways. First, leaders can collectively promote ideational norms among residents to influence their preferences and persuade them against participating in the conflict – against seeking selective benefits from aiding armed actors. This can involve appeals to the inherent value of nonviolence or be rooted in religion or the good of the community. Appeals may also be made to logic and history. For instance, educational programs about the dire consequences of spirals of violence sparked by defections can be enough to help community members coordinate on nonparticipation for fear of personal harm. Second, civilian leaders can manipulate the levers of social incentives – pressures and rewards – to convince residents to forgo the possible gains of selective benefits armed groups. Communities with elders (e.g., Indigenous elders) or leaders who are especially revered may have the most power to award special responsibilities, promote social acceptance, or threaten potentially devious residents with social ostracism. Such measures along with paths to leadership and recreational activities can be especially important to persuade youths not to join the ranks of armed groups.

If successful, these coordinated preference-changing efforts can yield an added benefit: reassurance among residents in the form of common knowledge that mitigates possible intracommunal security dilemmas. Similar to the collective action process described earlier, an individual's choice to desist from participating in the conflict is linked to the choices of neighbors. Individuals do not want to be the only ones "losing out" if everyone else is dipping into the benefits provided by armed groups (or alternatively may want protection if everyone else is denouncing and has an armed actor patron). If civilians see that they are not losing protective advantages or selective benefits relative to their peers they will be less interested in collaborating and denouncing.

---

[20] I.e., not biased toward or against any macro-actor.

In theory, a culture of peace is minimally "contentious" in that it imposes few direct costs on armed actors and so should run relatively low risks of retaliation. In fact, armed actors may not actually be aware that a community has an intentional policy of this nature. They may only find that it is harder to find good informants or material aid. Though a positive step toward peace, this mechanism's impact is limited without other tactics that clarify information for armed actors about residents' behavior because people could still be falsely accused of collaboration and then violently sanctioned.

Second, strong communities can implement local conflict resolution processes to minimize the degree to which civilians go to outside actors to police problems of local order. In areas of weak state presence where judicial courts are largely absent, civilians may bring disputes between neighbors over issues such as property boundaries, debts, or livestock trampling crops to armed actors to gain an advantage through coercion or violence (such disputes can occur even when social capital is high). The acts of delinquent youths or common criminals can similarly balloon into larger problems without a system of justice. These conflicts give armed actors an excuse to get involved in a community's affairs and they often exploit these divisions to gain information about and purge their suspected enemy collaborators, even though accusations by locals are often false and for personal gain (e.g., Kalyvas 2006). If the community can implement procedures to successfully resolve disputes before they reach armed actors, they can short-circuit cycles of informants and killings.

Third, communities can establish local investigatory institutions that leverage civilian advantages in local information to clarify accusations by armed actors against suspected enemy collaborators. For a variety of reasons, civilians may be accused of participation in the conflict and threatened because of the "fog of war." For instance, armed groups may misinterpret observed activities of civilians as providing material aid to their enemies or they may receive false denunciations for the reasons mentioned in the preceding paragraph. By "vouching" for *falsely* accused suspects but not confirmed collaborators, a civilian transparency process can reduce indiscriminate violence. This is especially true if it is costly for armed actors to monitor and police civilians and their reputations or popular support suffer for killing wrongly accused enemy collaborators (see next section and Chapter 7).[21] Transparency about civilian actions can also de-incentivize participation in the conflict if it increases the probability that civilian collaboration with an armed group will be identified and punished. Investigatory procedures are usually established through

---

[21] I resist using the term "innocent" to describe individuals in this situation, since the inverse ("guilty") can disregard the contextual risks that war creates. It suggests that other victims are somehow culpable and that targeting them may be justifiable, when it is instead preferable to resolve such cases without resorting to violence. However, some communities use this shorthand in their everyday discourse when referring to rights violations.

dialogues with armed groups and convincing them of the benefits of allowing civilians to bear the costs of (credibly) policing their own communities.[22]

Fourth, communities can protest and "go public" to denounce aggression and abuses and shame armed actors. This tactic relies on the dissemination of messages to affect armed groups' reputations not only in the eyes of the government and international actors (Keck and Sikkink 1998) such as the United States, but also in the eyes of other civilians and communities who may be influenced about whether or not to support a particular actor (alluded to in prior works such as Petersen 2001 and Weinstein 2006; see Hafner-Burton 2008 on the mixed effects of NGO shaming of governments for human rights abuses). Communities may engage in marches or other symbolic acts and link with external NGOs and IGOs to help magnify the wrongdoings to a wider audience.[23] One tactic is to call out armed groups on their contradictions and hypocrisies. For instance, armed groups that at least marginally value ideology (political, religious, or other) and claim to be the "defenders of the people" among their goals may be susceptible to communities' use of rhetorical traps to impugn the group's legitimacy for acts of violence (these rhetorical traps may additionally serve as a form of moral persuasion; see Guerra Curvelo 2004).[24]

The threat of publicly protesting an armed group's misdeeds may also be used so that protests stay "off the path of play." The option of protesting may provide increased leverage in quieter forms of bargaining over protecting civilians with would-be aggressors by, for example, allowing the group(s) to save face.[25] The choice to actually "go public," then, may be made under bargaining failures after more conciliatory overtures toward armed groups are not reciprocated. Protest can bring important gains in protection to a community but can be highly contentious and confrontational toward armed groups. Since protest may anger armed actors and provoke greater repression if it fails, this strategy requires high degrees of cohesion and commitment among the civilian population.

A variant of protesting seen in Colombia as well as some other countries is the declarations of neutrality that set a community's territory off limits to

---

[22] Dialogues can also mitigate problems of private information about capabilities, increase trust, and possibly humanize the civilian community in the eyes of armed groups.

[23] Churches and NGOs such as Peace Brigades and Fellowship of Reconciliation have engaged in a practice known as "accompaniment" to maintain enduring observer presence in threatened communities. They can then immediately report on threats or rights violations to media outlets, foreign governments, and international organizations and raise the costs of attacking a community by introducing the possibility that a foreigner or city-dweller might be harmed. See Mahony and Eguren 1997.

[24] Although verifying the impact of this mechanism requires further study, Ball (1998) finds support in his study of El Salvador and argues it should not be underestimated.

[25] Using the reputational lever may also affect the internal politics of armed groups by empowering more restrained factions over other factions.

armed groups (a "peace zone"). When balances of power are unstable or may shift, demarcating territory aims to avoid retribution by shunning entanglements with an out-group. This can also help attract broader attention from outside the community. The act can furthermore be seen as an attempt to proclaim the unity of the civilians and signal that if the group tries to divide or coerce the population it will fail.

An additional protest variant is the use of massive nonviolent manpower to force armed groups to concede to specific actions. Communities may use the sheer number of unarmed people to confront and overpower a few armed combatants. They may persuade combatants to concede through moral appeals. If the combatants instead prefer to fight, they must decide whether to commit a massacre. The protestors may even be able to physically stop the troops if they try to attack. On several occasions, the Nasa Indigenous Guard, consisting of around 500 unarmed community members who carry symbolic staffs, have appeared at guerrillas' and kidnappers' hideouts to pressure these groups to release residents who were taken captive (Wirpsa 2009).

Fifth, organized civilians may devise early warning systems to help civilians avoid being caught in the crossfire of combat between armed groups. Information and emergency procedures may be set up within the community or through dialogues with combatants to either convince them to fight outside the boundaries of civilian settlements or temporarily displace or shelter residents until fighting has subsided.

Sixth, communities may attempt local-based armed resistance against external armed groups to protect residents. This strategy employs a logic of deterrence to directly impose (or threaten to impose) military costs on armed groups for abuses they may commit. This strategy has been implemented in several example communities both within Colombia and abroad, but many communities across many conflicts do not arm because it entails great risks. Creating a local defense force requires high degrees of cohesion and coordination, not to mention manpower (though civilians may be advantaged in their local knowledge of the social and physical landscape). Many rural civilians are farmers, not soldiers, and have little military experience.[26] Furthermore, resistance with arms can forfeit a community's legitimate claim to being noncombatants. Lastly, if civilians miscalculate their capacity relative to existing armed groups, arming – a form of hostility toward armed groups – may lead to harsher retributions and unacceptable levels of casualties. Since civilians reside in stationary villages, they can become sitting ducks if they are outgunned.

The bundles or combinations of tactics that communities might employ can be ordered according to their differing degrees of costliness, aggressiveness, or "contentiousness" toward armed actors (the concept of contentiousness is

---

[26] The choice to arm may additionally depend on the availability of weapons and balance of firepower held by the armed groups, whether there is a tradition of armed self-defense in the community, and even possibly on gender balances and the role of women in the community.

discussed by Tarrow 1994 and McAdam, Tarrow, and Tilly 2001 and applied by García Durán 2006a to Colombia).[27] I argue that civilians look both internally within their communities and organizations and externally toward their environments when selecting strategies, reflecting the collective action-opportunity structure framework (CARP-SPOT) elaborated by Lichbach (1998). Civilian organizations select tactics of differing levels of "contentiousness" after consideration of both the organizational potential they have for implementing them and the risks they face from armed groups should they mount contentious, cost-imposing strategies that fail. The choices can be conceived of as falling along a continuum of stylized ideal strategies, where civilians calculate whether to "go public" or pursue less contentious "backroom"-style negotiations and appeasements.[28]

In addition to any calculations about costs and benefits of various strategies, the repertoire of strategies available for any given community will in many cases be determined by the epistemic constraint of the availability of *ideas* about different strategies. Communities can only choose and implement strategies they know of and about which they have information to assess prospects for success. The tactical repertoire may therefore be shaped by brainstorming and creativity among community members themselves, or may come from knowledge about which strategies have been used in other places, what their requirements are, and how they have fared. Indeed, I am only able to list here the general strategies that I have been able to identify during my research and, naturally, other effective strategies could be improvised in the future. The choice of a bundle of multiple tactics may be further constrained if some strategies are mutually exclusive. For example, if a community decides to arm against outside groups, this precludes a philosophy of nonviolence and attempting to convince armed groups of wishes to be left alone as nonparticipants.

Optimally, communities choose the strongest bundle of policies they can manage to implement for the greatest possible amount of protection without provoking a more violent response (i.e., where the marginal benefit of the decline in violence of the next incremental tactic equals zero). In other words, they decide based on an assessment of expected utility – the probability of success and the expected benefits if they are successful relative to alternative outcomes. Although I argue that a calculation process underlies decision-making, some communities may be predisposed to naturally prefer particular tactical approaches because of risk aversion or risk tolerance and cultural factors including ideas about nonviolence or the inherent value of resistance (what Wood 2003 calls the "pleasure of agency").

---

[27] This presumes that more contentious strategies are generally more effective at reducing human rights abuses or the odds of displacement, conditional on a given level of armed actor threat. The sensitivity to costs imposed by civilians' strategies may vary from the government forces to illegal armed groups.

[28] Kernell (1986) develops a similar decision framework in the realm of presidential politics.

TABLE 2.1 *Examples of civilian organizational strategies and tactics by contentiousness*

(by increasing levels of hostility)

Contentiousness of Civilian Strategy	Strategy set	Examples
Low	Displace (individually)	San Francisco and Angelópolis (Antioquia), Saiza (Córdoba); many others
	Ally	Peasant Soldiers and Informant Network programs, coca growers in Colombia, Rondas Campesinas in Peru, FMLN supporters in El Salvador
	Displace (organized/ collectively)	*Guindas* in El Salvador, CPRs in Guatemala, ATCC, Cacarica
	Early warning systems	COCOMACIA, ATCC
	Peace culture, norms of nonparticipation in conflict	ACVC, ASPROBRAS, ASOPROA
	Declare autonomy, negotiate with armed groups	ATCC, some Indigenous groups, *ACIA* (Chocó Afro-Colombians)
	Declare autonomy, bar passage of armed groups in territory, shaming	Peace communities of San José de Apartadó, San Francisco de Asís, Cacarica; COCOMACIA
	Declare autonomy, direct unarmed confrontation and protest	Nasa Indigenous Guard
High	Armed resistance	Quintín Lame Armed Movement, Rondas Campesinas (Peru), CDF (Sierra Leone)

Different strategy bundles are shown in Table 2.1 along a continuum of their "contentiousness" toward armed actors in terms of the costs they impose and the benefits they provide. The community examples provided are only roughly classified based on qualitative knowledge of the types of strategies they have chosen.

More subtle tactics are commonly attempted first. If they should fail, communities may then vociferously protest or arm as a last resort, when they feel no other options are available. According to this theory, a community will select the most contentious tactic bundles when highly organized, when there is external support, and when there is moderate armed group pressure. Civilians may also be more inclined to try contentious actions when there is a relative mismatch in capabilities that favor the civilians relative to armed groups (perhaps if armed groups are scattered) and they have high confidence of success. By contrast, when armed group pressure is extremely high, contentious autonomy actions may be attempted but will be difficult to sustain or may lead to retaliation, and quieter strategies may be more prudent and prevalent. By their nature, some of these strategies are more visible to the rest of society (and therefore social science researchers) than others.

Some tactics are also more effective for responding to particular types of violence than others. Institutional solutions for information management and intra-communal disputes may work best for problems with denunciations to armed groups. Advocacy and early warning systems may work best for extricating a community from the crossfire of combat. By contrast, these mechanisms may be less relevant for cases of abusive behavior, where armed groups may instead primarily be influenced by their legitimacy being put in jeopardy or by more aggressive responses. In the next section, I outline the conditions under which armed groups are influenced by these strategies.

EXPLAINING VIOLENCE: CONDITIONS FOR DE FACTO AUTONOMY

This section explains how civilians' strategies interact with the conflict environment and armed groups' strategies to determine outcomes of interest such as violence. When civilians' strategies are successful at mitigating violence, I refer to it as "de facto" autonomy. In addition to avoidance strategies, I outline the scope conditions for civilians' ability to affect the behavior of armed groups and militaries with strategies that address specific causes of violence. Armed actors are brought back into the discussion by analyzing the variety of preferences they hold under differing conditions. This leads to several observable implications for empirical testing about when violence is likely.

I argue that for armed groups to be influenced by organized civilian communities, they must both have incentives to use violence (or civilian resistance would be moot) and be sufficiently flexible in their motives for violence to be open to civilian influence.[29] I call this a group's *sensitivity* to civilians. Existing theories provide a helpful starting place for the discussion of sensitivity, although taken individually, they do not provide a complete depiction of when armed groups might respond to or be impeded by civilians.

I cull three central factors from existing theories about how armed actors fight for their survival in the face of threats of external pressure and internal disintegration. First, a group's founding institutions, ideology, and norms of

---

[29] For instance, armed actors may exhibit a middle range of preferences where they would still derive benefit from killing civilians but could also be persuaded not to. If they choose not to kill, they may bear only a small net loss if they can be assured they are not losing civilian support.

behavior not only serve as recruitment planks but also shape its attitudes towards violence and the place of civilians (internal group characteristics). Second, the relative dependence of an armed group on civilians with respect to its resource base will determine both its discipline and concern for its reputation (in interactions with other actors). Third, a group's time horizons and security situation, which are closely related to territorial control, will affect its tendency to cooperate for the gains of repeated play with a community (situational factors).

These three factors can combine and interact to produce hybrid groups and conflict conditions with various sensitivities to civilians. For armed groups to be responsive, they cannot solely be interested in maximizing expropriations from civilians or violence as an end in itself. Groups of this nature will mostly be influenced when they are met with force. However, this does not mean that less extreme groups with moderate preferences over these pursuits will necessarily have few motives for using violence. These factors can further interact with each other. For instance, a group's ideology may determine its resource usage, and resources may degrade group norms, and both of these may determine how much groups want to expand their territorial reach or contest control.[30] After first reviewing each of these factors, I illustrate how this argument applies to several archetypal armed groups in the civil war literature by highlighting their interests and expected sensitivities to civilians.

Internal Armed Group Characteristics

Armed groups vary in their governing institutions (Arjona 2014), and an armed group's susceptibility to civilians can vary based on its ideological beginnings (Weinstein 2006) and its institutions. A group's early goals and attitudes toward violence may shape its violent behavior – for instance, whether armed groups pursue genocide and abuse or place weight on protecting populations. Members of some groups may come from civilian communities and retain familial ties and loyalties to these communities, even if they become more opportunistic and involved in illicit economies. Group norms may guide the discipline and restraint of members and determine how much weight they give to civilians' moral arguments about the use of violence.

These base dispositions and ideologies toward using violence can be sticky and persist over time, even after resource or conflict-event "shocks." Group members' particular beliefs about violence may endure in the group to reinforce and revive them at different points in time. Group norms may also shift as the composition of a group changes. This is increasingly seen as conflicts

---

[30] For most groups, these traits are not as static as they may commonly be viewed. They can change over time and the salience of different concerns can be activated based on new considerations or strategic situations. Groups may also not be monolithic and can simultaneously consist of ideologues, opportunists, abusive criminal elements, etc.

internationalize and foreign fighters that hold other ideologies and norms mix with local fighters with closer ties to communities (Bakke 2014). In some instances, civilians can exploit these divides to "nudge" armed groups toward rights-respecting norms (Kaplan 2013b).

Resource Bases and Dependence on Civilians

The mix of an armed group's resources can affect both its concern for legitimacy and its discipline and ability to improve its behavior. Civilians can provide essential goods to armed groups (relative to their opponents) including food, water, cellular phones, etc. Groups may also use civilians as sources of information and manpower, for instance as recruits or labor for extractive resource production. Beyond civilian inputs, groups can support themselves with resources from external backers, diasporas, cash crops (coca, poppy), natural resources (oil, diamonds, etc.), kidnapping, and extortion. A greater balance of voluntary civilian inputs means groups depend more on civilians for their survival. This can produce a greater concern for their legitimacy and reputation within a single community or among nearby communities that may be watching. Even resource-intensive groups may want to avoid bad reputations if notoriety draws outside intervention or creates political problems for external patrons.

Groups that are resource-poor tend to emphasize ideology over selective incentives in their recruitment strategies. Such groups will therefore attract fewer opportunist recruits who might be rewarded through pillaging and will develop stronger disciplinary structures, although some bad apples may remain (Weinstein 2006). Some of these groups may not be averse to policing abusive troops but do not because they lack the minimum incentives or necessary organizational structures and capacity. In some cases, civilian pressure can provide these incentives for reform.

Situational Factors

Sensitivity may also be shaped by the conflict settings armed groups find themselves in and their preferences for controlling or conquering territory. Kalyvas (2006) argues groups have incentives to use violence when they are contesting control of territory (also referred to as the control-collaboration theory). The intensity of conflict, a group's level of security, and pressure from opponents may shape how patient armed groups are in waiting for the gains of repeated interactions with civilians versus taking the immediate gains of targeting suspected enemy supporters or extorting communities. According to ancient Chinese philosopher Sun Tzu (2005), soldiers in hostile territory – "desperate" or "death" ground – will fight especially hard. Groups in such situations or those that place high value on victory may be prone to coerce civilians. But groups may have varying preferences over attaining victory and may care relatively more about not losing what ground they hold and avoiding losing out to enemy groups.[31]

Armed groups may have incentives to use selective violence, but also may place less value on the gains they would obtain through the use of violence. For instance, if a group already has an expansive base area, the marginal strategic gains of controlling new areas may be low. When armed groups are able to reap lootable resource profits on the black market, protecting their bases may be relatively more important than bearing the costs to take new territories. In these cases, civilians may be able to increase the group's security on the cheap by providing information and reassurance that they are not collaborating with the enemy. In sum, when there are stalemates, there is little interest in winning a war, or the costs required to win are high, preventing defections to the enemy can become a compromise measure for armed groups short of winning the full allegiance of civilians.

Sensitivity to civilians is distinct from the use of violence against civilians and can be measured prior to acts of violence. It can be thought of as how armed groups experience costs (either material or moral) for using violence – an elasticity of how responsive they will be if civilians decide to pressure them. Groups sometimes use violence because it is cheap, easy, or simply a "default" behavior and how they are used to operating (Kaplan 2013b). Sensitivity combined with pressure from civilians can tip the behavior of armed groups in circumstances when violence is a means to an end rather than an end in itself. This can be hard to observe, however, because acts of violence (or their absence) are binary events that either occur or do not occur and therefore usually reveal little about the preferences of armed groups, such as their resoluteness or the utility they gain from committing the acts. Some acts of violence may be much more valuable to them than others. This raises the question of whether armed groups are just on the tipping point between killing and abstaining from killing, or they are set to kill no matter what. They may choose to rule by fear because it is cheap or because they do not have alternative considerations or roadmaps for how to interact with the population. But they could be induced to act differently.

I now show how some of these factors combine to produce armed groups with different sensitivities to civilians according to existing categories in the literature. How frequently groups actually hold these sensitivities is a separate empirical question.

The Sensitivities to Civilians of Some Archetypal Armed Groups

I outline the sensitivities of groups that are genocidal, economically motivated, ideological, and hybrid. A first type of armed group may have strong

---

[31] An implicit assumption of Kalyvas's theory is that armed groups are continuously trying to expand their reach and gain more territory, for whatever ends.

preferences to target or kill the civilian population and derive little benefit from civilian support. Such groups could be considered "ideologically genocidal" and will be insensitive (inelastic) to civilian overtures. In general terms, these groups could be defined as having extreme interests and are capable of and willing to use a "final solution" to achieve them (Valentino 2004). They may pursue ends such as ethnic cleansing (identity-based targeting), but also resort to annihilation of populations to defeat an enemy at all costs or to obtain economic benefits that are obstructed by civilians (e.g., to gain land through displacement for illicit crop cultivation, African palm plantations, or megaprojects such as dams). Since these "genocidal" groups target civilian organizations, avoidance strategies or direct force may be the approaches with best hope for influencing they (e.g., Jewish resistance in Nazi-controlled areas in World War II; Tec 1993).

Strictly economic groups such as cartels or purely economically motivated rebel groups can be similarly inured from civilians, but for a slightly different reason. "Opportunistic" groups permit abusive violence through indiscipline as a selective reward for their members (Weinstein 2006). Groups like drug cartels do not necessarily harbor animosity toward civilians and are not necessarily trying to defeat opponents or the state militarily, but neither greatly depend on civilians for support or their livelihoods. As pure criminals, cartels have no compunction against killing if civilians get in the way. This is seen in the recent extreme violence perpetrated by cartels in Mexico. With these groups, avoidance strategies or meeting them with force may be most effective (as the CDF forces countered the looting RUF rebels in Sierra Leone). It is primarily when these groups' support is threatened that they might be responsive to civilians.

On the other end of the spectrum are groups that are strictly "ideological" and promote the liberation of the people in the traditions of Mao and Guevara. These groups will measure their use of violence to a greater degree, making civilians' organized autonomy strategies less necessary. Where these groups reign, civilians can use the dominant strategy of allying with an ideological group for protection to avoid punishment. These groups most commonly meet resistance from civilians under conditions of shifting control. These less abusive ideological groups or benevolent state actors will proactively respond to the population and incite little resistance, and so will not likely be influenced by civilians.

A primary type of group I identify as meeting the sensitivity conditions for effective civilian autonomy movements is what could be called "hybrid opportunist." These groups may partially depend on civilians for resources but also benefit from other resource bases. They may be shaped by ideological beginnings, resource shocks, *and* interactions with civilians.[32] So while they may

---

[32] Weinstein mainly theorizes about governance in zones of complete control, where whether or not bargains are struck between rebel groups and communities derives primarily from armed group characteristics. I argue that groups are more malleable and that there can be learning and that dynamic relationships can be reshaped by civilians.

have incentives to use violence or permit abuse, they may also be varyingly susceptible to organized civilian strategies and able to reform. These groups may be poorly organized and permit their members some selective "pillaging" benefits but may also be susceptible to having their cover blown, which would bring the intrusion of authorities. Within hybrid opportunist groups, ideologues may at times overpower opportunists, or vice-versa.

A key insight from the identification of the hybrid opportunist groups is that even Weinstein's economic groups can seek a veneer of political legitimacy. Although Weinstein suggests these groups will be out-competed by more economic groups and wither, it is not clear how frequently this occurs in the real world, and he gives little indication about the actual prevalence of these different groups. Three important examples may be the cocaine-trafficking FARC "revolutionaries" and the "anti-subversive" paramilitaries in Colombia, and even the heroin-trafficking but religious Islamist Taliban in Afghanistan.[33]

This argument about armed group sensitivity does not make civilians epiphenomenal (ineffectual) or make the production of violence a tautology (i.e., that belligerents commit violence when they have incentives to commit violence) because armed groups can still have incentives to use violence. The theory is falsifiable and would be weakened if groups with sensitive preferences ended up using violence against organized communities as much as unorganized communities even in moderate conflict conditions. It would also be undermined if violence were used for some other motives that civilian organization fails to effectively address.

Civilians' Levers

I argue that civilian-sensitive armed actors can be induced by organized civilians to reduce acts of violence. Armed groups in civil war often face a strategic dilemma that creates incentives to commit violence. Even when armed groups are well-intentioned, uncertainty about civilian allegiances due to the "fog of war," private information, and civilians' collective action problems may lead to violence, especially if the costs of using violence are low. Furthermore, armed groups' predatory tendencies or organizational pathologies can lead to abuse. Still, despite these incentives to commit violence, I identify two ways in which civilians' strategies can affect armed group calculations: inducing cooperation between enemy armed groups to not kill civilians and marginally but significantly raising the costs of killing.

First, civilians may attempt to shift armed groups' "cooperative" incentives. This may encompass situations where there is joint interest among the armed actors to preserve or not directly target a civilian community. This does not

---

[33] Ironically, these groups all frequently ban drug use in their territories but also participate in the illegal drug trade.

mean that an armed actor alone has no interests in committing violence against civilians. They might, dependent on the choices of their rivals. Rather it reflects a logic where coercion of civilians is like an arms race spiral. The question is whether the groups pull back from the brink of more and more violence. Groups would like to be able to sustain "if you won't, I won't" kinds of agreements, but lack credibility and reassurances. In the face of this kind of "security dilemma," civilians can reassure groups and boost trust by, for example, conducting their own investigations, which decreases the cost of policing to armed groups. In addition, civilians may provide other joint benefits through the linkage of other issues to the nonabuse of civilians, including assistance in negotiating ceasefires, demobilizations, etc.

Second, civilians can attempt to manipulate "uncooperative" or unilateral incentives. These are incentives that matter for a group to reduce killing *regardless of* what their enemy is doing or whether civilians may be perceived to be defecting. For instance, if abusive armies face reputational costs for their acts from NGO monitoring, commanders might be willing to invest in organizational reforms even though they may entail costs (the costs can be multiplied if there is a prospect of being brought to justice when the conflict ends). Preventing societal divisions is another way of increasing costs. With a culture of peace it becomes harder to find informants and more likely that targeted, denounced people are wrongly accused of collaborating with the enemy. Finally, and not to be underestimated, there are the malleable ideas and default attitudes that armed groups may hold about the use of violence.

SUMMARY

This chapter has outlined a theory of civilian behavior in the risky conditions of civil conflict to explain how and when civilians can protect themselves. It emphasizes the role played by organization and social capital. I specified civilian mechanisms that require and are facilitated by cooperation for communities to maintain autonomy when facing shifting constellations of armed groups. As illustrated, many mechanisms fall short of the risky option of arming and can alter outcomes for civilians through their influence on armed groups' behavior. I also considered the conditions under which armed actors might be most receptive to or influenced by civilian entreaties or pressures.

For civilian communities, their level of organization is both a catalyst and a constraint that explains the puzzle of why we observe some but not all communities acting for autonomy and succeeding in reducing violence. Cooperation can arise from many sources both internal and external to a community and both independent of and endogenously from the armed conflict. Some types of organization may be more helpful than others and will enable more contentious strategies. But even when civilian communities have the desire to survive and protect themselves, they may lack the capacity or knowledge to act. Even where civilian organizations are capable, neither they nor their attendant strategies guarantee civilian protection.

Organization shows promise for providing additional protection under certain conditions, armed group preferences and sensitivities, and configurations of conflict. How broadly these conditions exist in any given conflict is an empirical question that I begin to address in the statistical tests and case studies in later chapters. In the next chapter on the social history of Colombia, I connect the theory developed here to specific social organizations and give an overview of the patterns of the conflict and collective actions to protect civilians.

3

The History of Conflict and Local Autonomy in Colombia

Don Apolinar Moscote (Aureliano Buendía's father-in-law): "The Liberals were Freemasons, bad people, wanting to hang priests, to institute civil marriage and divorce, to recognize the rights of illegitimate children as equals to those of legitimate ones, and to cut the country up into a federal system that would take power away from the supreme authority ... The Conservatives, who had received their power directly from God, proposed the establishment of public order and family morality. They were the defenders of the faith of Christ, of the principle of authority, and were not prepared to permit the country to be broken down into autonomous entities" (104).

Aureliano Buendía: "If I have to be something, I'll be a Liberal because the Conservatives are tricky" (106).

        – Gabriel García Márquez, *One Hundred Years of Solitude*

The first response you will get from an average Colombian when inquiring about the armed conflict is, "It's complicated." And it is true. There are regional dynamics, multiple actors, changes across time, various theories and logics, and hidden narratives and subtexts. Colombia has been in a state of conflict since the early 1960s. The fighting between guerrilla, paramilitary, and government forces, with narco-traffickers thrown in the mix, has had devastating consequences for a large portion of the civilian population. Here I provide an overview of the conflict and civilian mobilizations for peace from the second half of the twentieth century through the present.[1] This overview illustrates the breadth, timing, and regionalization of these trends.

---

[1] This is only a cursory overview of the social and conflict history most relevant to this study. The study of the Colombian conflict is such a large field it has come to be known as *Violentology*. For deeper histories by scholars with far more expertise than I see Pizarro and Peñaranda 1991,

The history shows how a variety of social mobilizations grew in response to rising levels of violence. A look back in time shows there have been various historical iterations of conflict followed by civil society responding and working to oppose violence and repair the damage. The causes of these cycles lay deeper in the country's broader social trends and political history.

Structural factors such as the illicit economy, difficult terrain, and state weakness have shaped the state's approach to the conflict and economic development, but the state's approach to governance has also been shaped by politics. A series of inconsistent choices by elites, driven by political contingencies, produced the social landscape that exists today and set the stage for civilian autonomy. As alluded to in the García Márquez passage and explored by Hartlyn (1988), the tensions between Liberal and Conservative partisans produced various bouts of greater rural inclusion and development depending on which party was in power and how severe governance problems became. When confronting the consequences of the La Violencia conflict and later social issues and conflicts, elites – mainly urbanites little affected by the enduring but localized insurgencies – wanted to do just enough but not too much to address the needs of the rural sector.

Staying "between legitimacy and violence" (Palacios 2006) perpetuated inequality, the exclusion of rural classes, and the concentration of power. The inconsistency among elites combined with narco-trafficking and nascent insurgencies was a formula for persistent rural conflict. The vacillation in rural state-building policies and start-and-stop national-level peace negotiations (García Durán 2006b) were also triggers that seeded desperation among the population and capability for local autonomy. With private institutions such as the Catholic Church also advocating for the needs of peasants, a variegated landscape arose, with some communities stimulated to cooperate more than others. As conditions worsened in the 1990s, civilians that had been left to their own devices for decades began experimenting with different responses depending on their community capabilities.

COLOMBIA'S HISTORY OF CONFLICT

The history of Colombia's conflict can be simply summarized by looking at the national homicide rate over time. The graph in Figure 3.1 shows two significant waves of violence from 1946–2005, with a relatively calm period in between.

The assassination of the Liberal politician Jorge Eliécer Gaitán on April 9, 1948, and the ensuing widespread riots in Bogotá, known as the *Bogotazo*, contributed to the beginning of the period of civil conflict in Colombian history known as La Violencia, or The Violence. It affected large swaths of the

Bejarano and Pizarro 2001, Romero 2003, Leal Buitrago 2006, Duncan 2006, García Durán 2006a, Palacios 2006 and Wills et al. 2006.

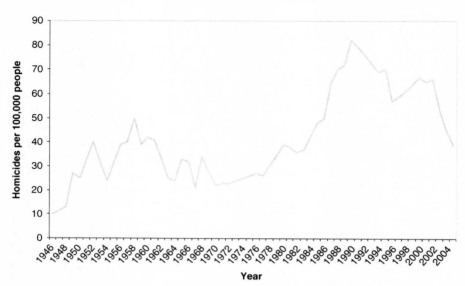

FIGURE 3.1 The Colombian national homicide rate, 1946–2005.
Source: Fabio Sanchez (2007), Colombian National Police.

countryside, resulting in over 200,000 deaths from 1948–1958 (Sánchez and Meertens 2001; Guzmán et al. 1963). The conflict unfolded in several waves throughout the subsequent decades. The conflict has been characterized as neighbor-against-neighbor partisan vendettas between Liberals and Conservatives, which later degenerated into the terrorizing of campesinos by local, clientelist armed bands tied to landholding bosses (*gamonales*).[2] The violence finally subsided beginning in 1958 with the establishment of the *Frente Nacional* (National Front) pact among national elites, which alternated power between the Liberal and Conservative parties, and army operations to eliminate many key bandits (Time Magazine 1964). But the government failed to eradicate emergent guerrilla groups that represented leftist political movements that were excluded from access to power and representation.

The origins of modern-day guerrilla groups are found in these early peasant self-defense leagues. These groups were scattered in different regions that came to be known as the "Independent Republics," including Marquetalia (in southern Tolima), the Aríari region in the Eastern Plains, and Sumapaz in Cundinamarca, southwest of the capital. These areas were targeted by the Army and Air Force in the early 1960s, but holdouts survived. After the bombing of Marquetalia in 1964, Manuel Marulanda organized rebel resistance to the state and, in conjunction with the Communist Party, held the First

---

[2] For additional interpretations of La Violencia and its regional variants, see Guzmán et al. (1963), Henderson (1985), Oquist (1980), Ortiz (1985), Roldán (2002), and Sánchez (2007).

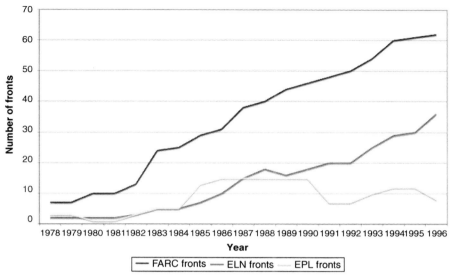

FIGURE 3.2 The growth of guerrilla fronts, 1978–1996.
Source: Echandía (1999).

Guerrilla Conference in 1965. With Marulanda as its leader, the FARC arose as an organization that championed the longstanding "agrarian struggle."

In its early days, the FARC developed focal points for its efforts in the departments of Tolima, Cauca, Meta, Huila, Caquetá, and Cundinamarca, as well as the Urabá and Middle Magdalena River regions. It did not have a national presence until 1982, when the group added the "People's Army" (FARC-EP) to its name, renewed its goals of pressing the causes of marginalized peasants, and doubled the number of fronts. Although its origins were rural, the FARC later expanded to urban areas. Figure 3.2 shows the growth of the FARC over the time. The guerrilla group grew from seven fronts and 850 fighters in 1978, to more than 16,000 fighters in 2000, distributed across sixty-six fronts. Figure 3.3 indicates where FARC attacks were concentrated over the period from 1999–2005. The FARC formed a political wing in the late 1980s called the *Unión Patriótica* (Patriotic Union Party) that ran local- and national-level political candidates as part of a strategy of pursuing "all forms of struggle." In 2000, the FARC renewed its political activities by forming citizen militias as part of the Bolivarian Movement for a New Colombia (MBNC in Spanish) and the Colombian Clandestine Communist Party (PCCC). These organizations espoused communist and anti-imperialist teachings and promoted the formation of cells of spies and infiltrators to support the FARC's armed wing.

Colombia's other major guerrilla group, the National Liberation Army (ELN), formed in 1962, with its first operations in 1965. Modeled after the Cuban Revolution, the ELN was motivated by Liberation Theology and

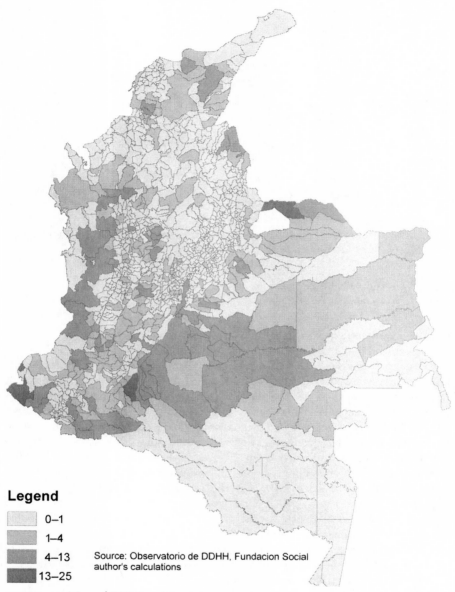

Legend

	0–1
	1–4
	4–13
	13–25

Source: Observatorio de DDHH, Fundacion Social
author's calculations

FIGURE 3.3 Map of FARC activity, 1999–2005

organized around advocating for the poor with the goals of anti-imperialism and forcing the national oligarchy out of power. The ELN grew from 350 members in 1984 to 4,500 in forty-one fronts by 2000, greatly extending its reach across the country (Figure 3.2).

As a consequence of the guerrilla escalation of the 1980s, there were several state-led attempts to negotiate peace. Under president César Gaviria, smaller insurgent groups demobilized, including the Quintín Lame Armed Movement (MAQL), the M-19 (Movement of April 19), and parts of the Popular Liberation Army (EPL). The agreements produced a National Constituent Assembly that led to the approval of a new constitution in 1991, featuring an important set of institutional reforms that included new rights, political decentralization, and greater fiscal control for municipal governments.

Despite these peace efforts, the conflict continued as the FARC, ELN, and factions from the EPL disengaged from the peace process. These different guerrilla groups expanded beyond their traditional roles as intermediaries for the peasants in their interactions with the government and also began financing themselves through illicit activities such as extortion (especially in oil-rich regions), alliances with drug-trafficking cartels, and kidnapping. They began to charge protection taxes on illicit crops, cocaine laboratories, and traffickers (Thoumi 1997). Despite its smaller size, the ELN is responsible for similar numbers of kidnappings and acts of sabotage as the FARC.

On the other side of the conflict, paramilitary groups emerged in the early 1980s after a failed peace process with the guerrilla groups. Their origins are as self-defense groups that were sponsored and financed by large landowners in response to guerrilla transgressions, especially as the guerrillas increasingly targeted these landowners for kidnapping and extortion. The earliest ones arose in the Magdalena Medio (Middle Magdalena) region and along the Caribbean coast, as well as in several other regions of the country. Before long, they morphed to take on some of the counterinsurgency functions of the state and fight the guerrillas. In the process they targeted leftist leaders and people with perceived links to the guerrillas. Thousands of members of the Unión Patriótica party who were stigmatized as being linked to the guerrillas were murdered or disappeared in the late 1980s and early 1990s in what has been termed a politicide, providing the FARC further justification to continue with a militarized strategy (Dudley 2003, Gómez-Suárez 2007).

In 1997, different groups joined together to become the United Self-Defense Forces of Colombia (AUC in Spanish) under the leadership of Carlos Castaño, who had previously founded self-defense groups in the northwestern regions of Córdoba and Urabá. This new group expanded counterinsurgency operations to retake territory that had been held by the guerrillas. It also became involved in the illegal drug trade and introduced new, grotesque forms of brutality into the conflict, including torture, mutilations and quarterings (*descuartización*), and sexual violence. Between 1997 and 2002, many massacres were attributed to groups under the AUC umbrella (Sánchez 2007). When these groups demobilized beginning in 2003, more than 30,000 fighters across thirty-seven blocs and fronts turned in their arms (Oficina del Alto Comisionado para la Paz 2006).

State forces proved insufficient and inadequate to defeat these nonstate actors, but this did not mean they were unimportant actors in the conflict. The Colombian military has had the capacity to protect civilian populations at various times in various regions. Yet the army has not been omnipresent and has also been seen by some as "one more actor in the violence" (Ladrón de Guevara 1998). The public forces have been accused of cases of complicity with narco-traffickers and with paramilitaries, who shared their counterinsurgent goals (Richani 2002).[3] During the peak years of conflict, the office of the Procuraduría investigated, disciplined, and dismissed hundreds of military officials, including generals (Amnesty International 2001). More recently there have been several thousand incidents of "false positives" (CINEP 2007, Human Rights Watch 2015). These incidents involved the killing of peasants and urban poor (predominantly male youths) by state forces and dressing them in fatigues to frame them as guerrilla casualties and increase guerrilla body counts for pay and vacation incentives. While the history of the armed forces has given some residents reason to be fearful, it is a multifaceted institution which has also undergone important police reforms and human rights training, and in at least some cases has prosecuted abusers within its ranks and held them accountable.

The trends of growth of these different armed groups meant rising conflict during the 1990s. The guerrilla groups expanded to have a presence in nearly two-thirds of Colombian towns at the peak of the conflict in the early 2000s. President Andrés Pastrana initiated negotiations with the FARC beginning in 1998, ceding to them a demilitarized zone, or *zona de despeje*, for the talks that was roughly the size of Switzerland in the southeast Macarena region (civilian autonomy within this zone is analyzed in Chapter 9). The negotiations failed in that they did not end the conflict and allowed the guerrillas to regroup and rearm. But the negotiations also exposed the guerrillas' violent nature and generated a greater consensus among the population that a harder line against them was necessary. By the late 1990s and 2000s, with so many armed groups and drug traffickers affecting so much of the country and penetrating multiple levels of government, Colombia began to be discussed as a possible "failed state" (Bejarano and Pizarro 2001, Kline 2003). As a commonly cited symbol of the extent of the threat, mortars fired by the FARC fell inside the presidential palace on the day of President Álvaro Uribe's inauguration in 2002.

The government implemented the Plan Patriota counterinsurgency program to respond to the conflict crisis. The Plan Colombia foreign aid package from the United States came to more than $10 billion was disbursed over more than a decade for areas including training and equipment for the armed forces, counternarcotics programs, development programs, and institutional strengthening. The initiatives helped bring about a gradual de-escalation of the conflict beginning around 2003 with the gradual repulsion of guerrillas and the beginning of the demobilization of paramilitary blocs. Still, the guerrillas' bellicose actions continued and some of the paramilitaries then quietly remobilized and new criminal bands, known as BACRIM, began to appear

---

[3] According to a 1999 State Department human rights report, "Security forces actively collaborated with members of paramilitary groups by passing them through roadblocks, sharing intelligence, and providing them with ammunition" (U.S. Department of State 2000).

Anti-narcotic police back from patrol and seeking respite from the midday sun, La India, 2013.
Photograph by Oliver Kaplan.

(CNRR 2007). Although the Colombian government once again engaged in peace negotiations with the FARC in 2012 and signed an agreement in 2016, the armed conflict has persisted.

The consequences of this long period of conflict in Colombia have been severe for civilians, marked by widespread violence and terror.[4] There have been massacres of tens and sometimes hundreds of people as well as political killings of opposition politicians, social organizers, and labor leaders. At least 220,000 people have been killed in the armed conflict, and many victims have been disappeared and dumped in mass graves (GMH 2013). An estimated 6 million people, representing nearly one-sixth of the rural population, have been forcibly displaced from their homes and communities since 1985, ranking Colombia second only to Syria in the number of internally displaced persons (UNHCR 2010, El Espectador 2015, IDMC 2010, IDMC 2015). The conflict has also contributed to the recruitment of child soldiers (Human Rights Watch 2003) and persistently high rates of inequality and poverty.

---

[4] According to an accounting from the Justice and Peace Law, 2,719 mass graves had been exhumed and over 300,000 people registered themselves as victims of the conflict as of 2010 (El Tiempo 2010).

An obelisk memorial to ATCC leaders who were killed in 1990 in La India, Santander, Colombia.
Photograph by Oliver Kaplan.

All of these factors have added up to great suffering and uncertainty in people's daily lives. These effects can be explained by the increasing contestation among armed groups and narco-trafficking (e.g., Sánchez 2007) but also by state absence, which, in addition to stemming from Colombian politics is also a product of structural factors such as histories of colonization in far-flung areas and the country's mountainous terrain (LeGrand 1986). The expansion of the conflict has, by contrast, only infrequently been associated with the characteristics of specific towns as armed groups broadly sweep over differing neighbor communities.

THE HISTORY OF CIVIL SOCIETY RESPONSES
TO ARMED CONFLICT

Colombia's history has been characterized by much violence, but vibrant sources of social capital remain and have served as crucial bases for collective responses. For instance, Colombia's patterns of colonization have meant some towns have remained independent for much of their history. Isolated, difficult to secure, and neglected, such communities have also created tight-knit social relationships (LeGrand 1986). With these bases of cooperation, some towns were organizing as early as La Violencia to maintain their own security by forming neighborhood watches and self-defense posses to guard against bandits (see examples in Chapters 6 and 8).

In the late 1980s and 1990s, what has been characterized as a broad, nationwide peace movement emerged in response to the spiking violence. Social movements that had previously been centered on social and political protest shifted toward the goals of survival and pressuring the government and armed groups to respect the civilian population and enter negotiations. A graph produced by Mauricio García Durán (2005; see Figure 3.4) shows the number of recorded collective actions for peace over time in Colombia, including national protests, local "peace communities," and other nationwide activities such as the Civilian Mandate for Peace symbolic vote of 1997. García Durán tracks these against increases in the intensity of conflict according to the number of casualty events and kidnappings over time. He finds that since the 1980s there have been many national and local movements of different forms across many parts of the country. His analysis also shows that the prevalence of peace actions tends to increase after spikes in conflict, with the 1997 Mandate for Peace vote as a prime example.

PEACE COMMUNITIES AND FORMAL AUTONOMY ORGANIZATIONS

Like the broader peace movement, the formation of local organizations for protection and autonomy also tends to occur as conflict intensifies. Though regional conflict dynamics vary, many communities' decisions for autonomy were made around periods when paramilitaries arose and contested guerrilla-held zones. As guerrilla groups became more coercive and increasingly abandoned their roles as protectors of and interlocutors for rural populations, peasants looked for other options. The paramilitaries issued many ultimatums for displacement and were feared for their ruthlessness. Various formal organizations formed and adopted strategies in response to displacement through a sorting process where either less resolute civilians fled or whole communities displaced with only the resolute returning to reconstitute.

The trend of community peace strategies can be traced to a number of other contributing factors. First, a variety of social stimuli in the rural sector brought communities together. These included government rural development policies beginning in the 1960s (e.g., ANUC land reform councils and the junta councils, discussed later); Patriotic Union and Communist Party political organizing in the 1980s; and church organizing, which, with the rise of Liberation Theology, increased outreach in rural areas through programs such as Pastoral Social and later peace-oriented organizations such as CINEP, the Middle Magdalena Peace Program (PDPMM), and the Inter-Church Justice and Peace Commission (Justicia y Paz) that provided accompaniment and humanitarian aid. Second, policies such as those embodied by the 1973 Pact

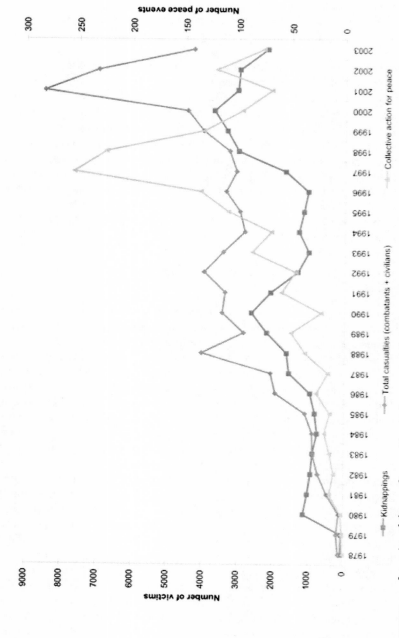

FIGURE 3.4 Intensity of the conflict and level of peace mobilization, 1978–2003.
Source: García Durán (2005), CINEP.

of Chicoral, an agreement between the political parties and large landowners that ended agrarian reform, symbolized the beginning of an era of broader exclusion of rural residents from the political system and reduced state services. This left communities that had been organized by previous rural development programs adrift. Third, the growing connection and communication between small towns, NGOs, and leaders in cities increased the dissemination of social organizing lessons, ideas, and technical assistance. Fourth, the Indigenous rights movement that burgeoned in the 1980s fought for and won legal political autonomy in the 1991 Constitution, which not only aided Indigenous groups but also caused the concept of autonomy to drift to other populations (e.g., Houghton and Villa 2005, Caviedes 2007, and Sánchez and Del Mar Palau 2006 on municipal budgetary autonomy). Fifth, the failures of national-level negotiations and the disengagement of the state left many localities abandoned and unwilling to hold out hope for a broader resolution to the conflict (this was true both during as well as prior to the Pastrana administration; see García Durán 2006a, Bouvier 2009).

The earliest communities to seek autonomy were located in places with both social unity and where armed conflict arrived earliest. Many were in the Urabá and Magdalena Medio regions, and the departments of Cauca, Chocó, and Putumayo. Nascent local movements for protection – not precisely for autonomy – began with marches in response to early displacements. The protests by residents of towns like El Pato are examples of movements that are, at least in name, separate from guerrillas and also against repression by the army (Molano and Reyes 1978). The Indigenous groups' history of resistance to Spanish and colonial institutions and subsequent exclusion from Colombian society, coupled with Indigenous rights movements during the twentieth century, helped them become the first population to advocate for autonomy, establishing an ideal for other communities to emulate. The formation of the Regional Indian Council of Cauca (CRIC) in 1971 was a key antecedent to the Nasa (Paez) community later issuing the Declaration of Ámbalo in 1985, demanding respect of their autonomy from the guerrillas and other armed groups (Houghton and Villa 2005). One of the earliest campesino autonomy movements can be traced to the ATCC of La India in Santander, analyzed in Chapter 7, which formed spontaneously in 1987. Impressively, these communities include some of the more poor, illiterate, and marginalized populations, with few apparent organizational capabilities.

Some early programs and NGOs supported these communities in their struggle. Key organizations include the Middle Magdalena Program for Peace and Development (PDPMM), founded in 1995 by Father Francisco de Roux, and the Jesuit organization CINEP, which promoted the formation of the first peace communities along the Atrato River in the department of Chocó in 1998. These and other NGOs such as Redepaz (Peace Network) have worked to consolidate and standardize community-organizing procedures and promote peace communities more broadly. As Sandoval (2004) shows, formally organized communities arose in many parts of the country (Figure 1.2 in this volume).

Formal autonomy organizations take a variety of forms and actions. They are commonly broken down by ethnic background due to cultural differences in forms of organization (many communities have mixed populations which for present purposes are considered as campesino). Later, I describe some of the most prominent communities to provide a sense of who they are and how they behave. The institutional rules and declarations for many formally organized communities for autonomy are contained in Villarraga (2003).

First, there are the extremely organized and well-known Indigenous group autonomy movements. Colombia has more than eighty Indigenous groups comprising roughly 3 percent of the population (approximately 1.4 million people in 2005). These communities are organized around *cabildo* councils and spiritual authorities such as shamans (Kaplan 2013c). Many have been affected by the conflict entering their territorial reservations and, rooted in their communities' unique cosmovisions and "life plan" documents, many have organized in various ways in response. They have carried out many discrete protective actions with success. Indigenous groups have rescued kidnap victims from armed groups, resolved internal conflicts through systems of Indigenous justice, and protested *en masse* against the taking of towns (up to even holding guerrilla soldiers and evicting army troops).

The Nasa (Paez) Indians in the department of Cauca are especially well organized. Their nonviolent Indigenous Guard, composed of thousands of volunteers who carry symbolic staffs known as *bastones*, have rescued kidnap victims from the FARC, including the kidnapped Paez leader and mayor of the town of Toribío (Forero 2005). Four hundred members of the guard marched for two weeks over the Andes to the rebel camp where he was being held and persuaded the FARC to release him. Several Indigenous groups are also known for their massive protest marches against the conflict and neoliberal economic policies, and in support of Indigenous culture.

Afro-Colombian communities have also innovated their own movements for autonomy from the conflict. Afro-Colombians comprise about 26 percent of the national population (Colombia has the third-largest Afro-descendent population in the Americas after the United States and Brazil). Their initiatives have been mainly concentrated in the departments of Chocó, Valle del Cauca, Nariño, and Antioquia, where their populations are greatest. The Law of the Black Communities (Law 70 of 1993) helped cement Afro-Colombians' access to their collective territories and formalized their community councils, or *consejos comunitarios*. This has helped them to manage their own affairs and provided grounds for organizing. ACIA (2002) is one of the largest Afro-Colombian autonomy organizations with more than 120 villages with 45,000 residents along the Atrato River in the Pacific department of Chocó. These villages have procedures to peacefully resolve community conflicts and comprise an information and early-warning network, among other policies.

Campesino communities have fewer formal organizations and are more variable in composition and policies. The organizations commonly have origins in farmer associations and village junta councils. Perhaps the best-known campesino autonomy organization both in Colombia and internationally is the "peace community" of San José de Apartadó (Hernández 2004, de Sousa Santos and García 2004). This community of displaced returnees in the northwestern Urabá region of Antioquia received accompaniment from NGOs and the Catholic Church, and the Inter-American Court of Human Rights issued precautionary measures to protect the population. Still, this community also suffered the murder of more than 200 residents. Rooted in faith and pacifist ideas, the community's declaration for peace includes the policies that residents will not participate in violent activities, not allow firearms, and not collaborate with armed groups or provide them with information. The community also implemented more extreme policies including a "rupture" with state institutions for lack of responsiveness in investigations of abuses by paramilitary and state forces (Recorre 2007). Since there are many studies on this case and some difficult measurement issues, I do not study it closely here.

The ATCC in Santander (Chapter 7) is a similar association of campesinos though it has distinct policies and institutions. In addition to its investigation procedures and network of information-gathering village councils, it has taken various actions of civil resistance to counter the aggression by armed groups in recent years. In 2001, 800 residents protested for two days against being displaced from their homes. Similarly, after a man was killed and quartered in 2004, hundreds of people again went to protest (CNRR 2009).[5] Rural campesino municipios have also used "constituent assemblies" to coordinate citizens on participating in local politics and supporting mayors in blocking armed actors from involvement in municipal affairs (Sandoval 2004). As I discuss later and in the case studies, individual campesino junta councils have also taken on some functions of the more formal organizations dedicated to "peace" and "autonomy," including methods of dispute resolution.

Throughout these movements, women have played integral roles alongside men in advocating for the autonomy and protection of their communities. Many women have suffered violence during the armed conflict, been widowed, and also served as combatants. However, their work for autonomy is also widespread. Many of my interview respondents were women of all ages, and they offered unique reflections on peace and conflict. But, more than that, they also sought to navigate the conflict as participants in junta councils, as leaders of these councils, and as mayors of municipalities in conflict zones. Within the ATCC, women have served as conciliators alongside men to defuse threats of violence. Women are the backbone of autonomy-seeking organizations, such as the Afro-Colombian COCOMACIA, and they carry the symbolic *baston* staffs as part of the Nasa's nonviolent Indigenous Guard. In quieter ways, women have strived to keep their families intact and inculcated norms of peace and

---

[5] ATCC#3, La India, 7/2008.

A community planning exercise near La India, Santander, Colombia, 2008.
Photograph by Oliver Kaplan.

nonviolence to steer their children away from the conflict. In many communities, women also form back-channel information networks that share news about the war and efforts to organize against it. Although the gendered aspects of seeking autonomy are not the focus of this study, the specific contributions of women to peace in Colombia cannot be overstated.

As is evident, formal organizations for autonomy are impressively diverse. They have many names: peace communities, peace laboratories, zones of peace, no-conflict zones, humanitarian zones and spaces, sanctuaries, territories of nonviolence, constituent assemblies, and peace experiences (León 2004, Sandoval 2004, Páez Segura 2005, Rettberg 2006, Bouvier 2009). The unique origins and nomenclature of these organizations is part of what makes them interesting to study and compare. They also present difficult classification issues for determining what constitutes a peace community since they are also diverse in terms of their mechanisms, composition, political alignments, legal status, rhetoric, and geographic extent. For formal organizations that often have formal declarations of autonomy-oriented policies, there are still many ambiguities about their policies and how well they are implemented. This creates a complication for social scientists because if these organizations cannot be compared or even categorized and classified, how can one identify which mechanisms are operating or what are plausible counterfactual cases? Other political actors in Colombia and elsewhere have had similar difficulties interpreting the nature of these organizations.

The Carare River, La India, Santander, Colombia.
Photograph by Oliver Kaplan.

The Politics of Autonomy and Neutrality

Autonomy movements have arisen as responses to pressure from armed groups in conditions of state absence. Armed actors have responded in diverse ways, with movements being received and respected differently at different times by different armed actors.

The Colombian state's position toward civilian autonomy movements has been two-sided. Subnational accords with illegal armed actors are seen as an affront to state sovereignty and are technically "illegal" in Colombia.[6] Parts of the government including the Colombian military have had little patience for "peace communities." As an example of this attitude, former Defense Minister Jorge Alberto Uribe is quoted as saying, "There cannot be Peace Communities without the presence of the Public Forces" (Navarrete-Frías and Thoumi 2005,

---

[6] Military#1, 2, Bogotá, 8/2009. The term "neutrality" has been politicized in Colombia, so one cannot necessarily draw conclusions about the actual stance of a community from the use of the word. Former President Álvaro Uribe, as governor of Antioquia and later as president, supported what was called "active neutrality," which in reality meant that communities could be neutral, as long as they sided with the government. This may partly explain why communities with practices of noninvolvement in the conflict have come to favor the more acceptable term of "autonomy."

El Tiempo 2005). Based on my conversations with certain military officials (colonels and generals), I found some suspicion of civilian peace and autonomy movements on the part of the military, in part because the military expects and prefers full allegiance and cooperation from the population.[7]

Still, autonomy organizations have been tolerated by the government in a number of regions, and the Indigenous group movements are tolerated even more widely (because of their constitutional legitimacy). Other parts of the government have more explicitly aided local communities' initiatives for peace, including the Social Action Agency's Peace Program, the office of the Human Rights Defender (*Defensoría*), and the Colombian Vice-presidency's Human Rights Observatory's reporting on community peace initiatives (Vicepresidencia 2001). More recently, there has been evidence of an evolution in views toward local peace communities, neutrality, and autonomy. In a groundbreaking statement in 2013, President Juan Manuel Santos asked for forgiveness from the San José de Apartadó Peace Community in Urabá for the previous stigmatization of its residents by government and military officials, saying, "We do not agree with phrases or attitudes of stigmatization [of] those who search for peace and reject violence... we consider that every defender of peace and human rights should be praised and protected. For this, we ask for forgiveness. I ask for forgiveness" (Presidencia 2013).[8] Santos not only acknowledged the suffering of the community and the "mistake" of "unjust accusations," but even went so far as to praise the community as a positive example for peace, noting that such local models are indispensible for national-level peace. Although his remarks may have only garnered momentary attention, they essentially validated the entire Colombian nonviolent peace movement in one fell swoop.

The state's perspective is of course different than that of the communities, who originally selected their organizational strategies precisely because of state absence and anarchy. The state's differing perspective is a result of differing interests and its sporadic rural presence (and thus limited information). But the interests of the state have some overlap with those of communities. Many communities want the *full* and *permanent* presence of the public forces and other state institutions, and have at various times called for the army, the police, and the Human Rights Defender (*Defensoría*) to protect them. This distinguishes these movements from the broader question of political autonomy since

---

[7] As this chapter and Chapter 2 show, communities' policies are diverse, and it is not clear if all autonomy strategies are viewed as threatening or futile or if only certain aspects are disliked. It is also unclear how well different military officials understand and have analyzed the details of these communities' policies and whether their judgments are based more on general preconceptions.

[8] Remarks translated from the Spanish by the author. Santos's statement is noteworthy as coming from someone who previously served as the Minister of Defense in the 2000s, when atrocities were committed by all parties to the conflict.

most communities proclaim their apparent willingness to relinquish their autonomy stances (at least in the realm of security) if the state could sustain its institutional presence and deliver good governance. They seek a beneficial and secure social contract. At least in Colombia, such communities have primarily advocated for protection and have not called for enduring political autonomy or separatism, as is sought by insurgents in some countries. However, because of the state forces' sporadic presence in the daily lives of rural communities, they are somewhat less relevant than other armed actors for the study of civilian autonomy in Colombia.

Paramilitary blocs and guerrilla fronts have at different times blatantly transgressed against formal autonomy organizations, often due to increasing contestation or resource interests. Even though armed groups of some regions are known for being repressive, the influence of civilian organizations and strategies is understudied, with no controlled tests to verify whether these repressed regions are unique in their conflict conditions or types of civilian organizations. The Colombian guerrilla groups tend to be centralized, have greater conformity across fronts, and have peasant origins, so they may exhibit less variation in their treatment of civilians (Gutiérrez Sanín 2008). Still, they can differ in their commanders, local dynamics, resource bases, and recruits. The greater variation among the blocs of the more decentralized paramilitary groups and their general suspicion of civil society makes them more variably influenced by social organization. These stylized facts are examined as testable hypotheses in Chapter 5.

JUNTA COUNCILS AND THEIR RELEVANCE FOR VIOLENCE

As the principal local organization across Colombian communities, junta councils have a surprisingly long yet surprisingly *un*-storied history. I argue that the politics behind the juntas makes them appropriate for the study of local responses to armed conflict. In the discussion that follows, I review their origins, growth, and politics and show why they have (re-)gained a discreet though important role in the present conflict in Colombia.

The idea and initiative to encourage the formation of local councils emerged in 1958 at the end of the brutal La Violencia conflict (Law 19 of 1958). The destruction was a warning to the incoming National Front unity government of the pernicious impact of interference in communities by bands and outsiders. As an early publication on juntas characterized this history, "The violence that tormented the nation during many years clearly demonstrated the need to change the situation that affected the local communities" (Triana y Atorveza 1966, 19).

For the government, local councils were "a response to the climate of internal conflict." They were viewed as nonmilitary pacification and a way of encouraging reconciliation and economic development from the bottom up in violent as well as peaceful areas (Ministerio de Gobierno 1993, 13;

Edel 1969).[9] As such, the juntas were a distinct break from prior community organizational forms of the period before La Violencia, when development policy was more top-down and did not consider local-level community interests. The past paternal-yet-distant relationship between the national government and local communities not only failed as a model of community development, it also failed to integrate the country given that the Colombian state had limited reach into its vast mountainous, rural hinterlands. The juntas embodied not just a strategy for economic development, but also an alternative form of state-building. The Colombian state could not quickly and easily increase its capacity in the wake of La Violencia's devastation, but it could quickly encourage capacity from the bottom up and then establish links of communication and coordination, and incentivize development through matching project funds.

The juntas as an organizational form were not imposed by the state. Rather, the state created and encouraged a legally recognized *vehicle* that communities could freely adopt – it attempted to institutionalize local councils. Virtually any community could be organized into a junta and recognized by the government. Although juntas are sometimes thought of as a local level of government, they clearly fall in the realm of local civil society. According to law, they are defined simply as "Civic nonprofit corporations composed of the neighbors of a place, who unite efforts and resources to meet the most important needs of the community" (Art. 1, Decreto 1930, 1979). It was intended that juntas would help a community solve its own problems rather than look to the government and keep communities informed about government programs (Fals Borda 1960). Juntas select their own development projects and rely on voluntary contributions of labor and cash from their own residents (which may then be matched by state funds). Juntas are involved in providing public goods for economic development such as building roads, schools, and housing, as well as cultural and social events such as festivals.

With the start of the communal action program, the number of juntas grew rapidly. The government did promote juntas in some areas that were affected by violence, but in most cases, communities decided to start a junta themselves. According to the 1993 government census of juntas, 78 percent (23,690) of the juntas were formed by initiative of the community. In contrast, only 12 percent were formed by "promoters" (3,525; e.g., government staff or Peace Corps), 2 percent (568) were formed by the initiative of national officials/authorities, and another 2 percent (587) were formed by the initiative of local/municipal politicians (Ministerio de Gobierno 1993).[10] As Cubides (2006) notes, since

---

[9] The government also implemented a separate, more targeted Civic Military Action program (at the suggestion of U.S. advisers) to provide short-term aid to some of the most war-torn communities (Rempe 1999).

[10] Unfortunately, it appears the micro data from this remarkable study has been lost to eternity.

TABLE 3.1 *Formation of junta councils in Colombia, 1960–1993*

Year	Juntas
1961	1,000+
1966	9,000*
1970	16,108
1974	18,000*
1980	30,007
1987	34,842
1993	42,582 (inventory; 30,362 in census)

+ Estimates in Edel (1969)
* Estimates in Bagley (1989)
Source: DIGIDEC 1993.

many formal kinds of rural organizations met their demise during La Violencia, the slate was clean for new forms to take root, "By more or less *spontaneous* fashion, new independent organizations began to arise" (emphasis added). Indeed, as shown in Table 3.1, the number of juntas has grown steadily since the program began fifty years ago, with two-thirds of existing juntas created by 1980. The 1993 inventory found that nearly 2 million Colombians were active members of juntas in their communities (of a population of roughly 40 million; the mean size of a junta is forty-five people).[11] According to Bagley, although juntas became increasingly common, their numbers belied variation in their functioning, "By the late 1960s, half of rural villages had juntas, although many remained *inactive* for years" (Bagley 1989, emphasis added).

The history of juntas suggests there are four main reasons why juntas can contribute to limiting violence in the Colombian conflict. First, juntas have become reasonably widespread, including in historically conflictive areas, yet are not everywhere. This distribution is helpful for making analytical comparisons since it has meant that some areas with recent conflict have juntas while others do not (or have weak ones). Second, the national politics of the alternating National Front governments – both their goals and tensions – contributed to the political positioning of juntas as independent (apolitical) and generally centrist. This has meant that today they may have a degree of freedom in decision-making (and even autonomy) when dealing with armed groups. Third, and more specifically, by being democratically elected, juntas reflect broad-based and unifying *local* collective action. This allows juntas to clearly

[11] There can be a maximum of one junta per village or neighborhood. According to Article 36, juntas must at minimum have eighty affiliates/members in Bogotá, sixty in other urban areas (forty in urban areas of commissaries), and twenty-five in rural areas (twenty in rural areas of commissaries, which were nonincorporated departments).

represent their communities in relations with outside actors and limit the number of spoilers who can disrupt their processes. Fourth, juntas have proven they are adaptable through their ability to take on new functions and endure over time. More specifically, when faced with armed conflict they have been able to consider new strategies such as those previously discussed that surpass their original mandates.[12]

Anecdotal evidence suggests that juntas have indeed been players in the armed conflict today and that there are a number of ways in which they can impact conflict dynamics. First, some of the juntas' own activities are important for reducing the social divides that might invite intrusions by armed actors. For instance, in addition to the role of juntas in development projects, another important function is to provide local order by adjudicating local disputes or, according to the legal articles, "Seek harmony in interpersonal relations of the community to achieve an environment that facilitates its natural development" (Sec 300, 1987, Art. 11). This task appears to have been widely pursued by juntas since, according to the survey of juntas in 1993, 87 percent of juntas (26,474) had a conciliation committee.[13] Second, juntas have become the organizational building blocks for larger, more formal, and more cohesive organizations that more openly advocate for civilian protection and autonomy with specific reference to the armed conflict (e.g., "peace communities," "humanitarian spaces," etc.). For instance, the farmers' association of ASOPROA in eastern Antioquia was formed through the coordination of various junta leaders in the midst of conflict in 2002. Though not denominated as a "peace community," with united junta leaders, the association adopted various community-strengthening measures to "protect human rights" and avoid the dangers of multiple armed groups.[14]

---

[12] Based on these characteristics of juntas, I conclude that juntas are better positioned than other historic organizations, such as the at-times radical and even militant ANUC land reform councils, to be relevant for reducing violence.

[13] Although the primary function of conciliation committees is to adjudicate ambiguities in the implementation of junta rules, in many cases they have been adapted to deal with other forms of intracommunal conflict as well, or what in Colombia is called "conciliation in equity" (interview, AC#1, leader in the junta movement, Bogotá 8/2008).

[14] According to a document on this association, "The violence reached its highest peak and generated an unprecedented humanitarian crisis in the region that demolished everything that had been built. The leaders noticed there was a very fragile system of organization, only of community juntas, very atomized (*de grupo*). It was necessary to build a system of organization with a higher profile and greater coverage of regional character ... With a very diminished group of promoters that were left and a few juntas comunales in the middle of 2002 an association began to form, holding meetings, crystalizing the idea and bringing in other communities. It wasn't easy, the region was very militarized and the meeting sites were chosen with much caution; even though nothing illegal had been done, there was much fear that the army would find the leaders meeting ... The communities have achieved a certain level of ... independence regarding the management and denunciation of problems or situations ... Interlocution with authorities of every level, [and] ... directly denouncing violations before national and

Third, there are various examples of juntas themselves playing important roles in the crossfire for protecting residents and asserting autonomy since the 1980s (Cubides 2006).[15] Cubides and others view juntas as occupying a special place in the landscape of the conflict, "The juntas are the only [organizations] that seem to be above all suspicion for the contending [armed] groups ... Each armed group has wanted to adopt the JACs, coopt them, ensnare them in their mobilization strategy, but none have been able to completely succeed" (Cubides 2006).[16] For instance, as the conflict escalated in the early 2000s, the government sought to co-opt the juntas as part of the "Democratic Security" plan. And, although some juntas were variably influenced by the government, armed actors, or political bosses, national junta leaders decried this policy and its inherent risks to and encroachments upon them.[17] They advocated for the juntas to remain independent and not take part in the conflict.[18]

In sum, the implications of the history of juntas for their present-day abilities to blunt the effects of conflict are tantalizing for students of human rights and peace studies and deserve careful assessment. Chapter 5 tests *empirically* whether preexisting organizational structures such as juntas help civilians effectively coordinate when conflict comes to town.

SUMMARY

Social movements for peace in Colombia are accounted for historically as a response to the spread and intensification of conflict. They are also the results of particular social landscapes and trends in rural organizing that were shaped by a diverse set of prior causes and motivations, including politics. The national and sometimes local-level tensions that determined the evolutionary course of different social organizations, such as the juntas, provide crucial context for

international human rights organizations ... has permitted the wide improvement in security conditions of the communities that were directly affected by threats from one or other of the contesting [armed] groups, in this way recovering the confidence for team/ group work" (ASOPROA 2006; translated).

[15] A#1, Anolaima, 3/2009.

[16] As Cubides elaborates, "In zones controlled by the guerrilla, in disputed zones, or even in zones controlled by paramilitaries, [the juntas] in contrast are the only form of civil society power. They fill a gap. They are indispensable as forms of authority."

[17] El Tiempo. 2004. "Comunales Preocupados Por Politización Y Amenazas" (Juntas Worried About Politicization and Threats). *El Tiempo*, December 7, 2004.

[18] As one leader asserted during this period, "The juntas will be neither army informants nor instruments of armed groups like the FARC .... This message that they don't involve us in the war is also directed at the paramilitaries and ELN." As the article continued paraphrasing, "The junta leaders arriving from remote villages lamented why they are neglected in development plans but included in plans to involve them in the armed conflict. ... Popular power should stem from the autonomous will of the people and not from the pressures of armed actors. They oppose being used for war" (El Tiempo. 2002. "No Les Serviremos Ni A Uribe Ni A Las Farc" ["We Won't Serve Uribe nor the FARC"]. *El Tiempo*, July 29, 2002).

testing hypotheses and relationships over long periods of time. The political battles among national-level elites along with the varying social landscapes from town to town explain why the juntas' ties to the central government weakened over time and why some juntas remained more vibrant than others. These patterns positioned these organizations for autonomy within the armed conflict.

With many existing works on Colombian history, my argument that Colombian social history witnessed competing political visions is not an innovation. But connecting it to the conflict-relevant social landscape, the behavior of civil society organizations, and the prospects for local autonomy today is. As Romero (2008) observes, urban-rural divides persist even to the present day. My field observations and the case studies of subsequent chapters indicate that urban zones are experiencing greater security but rural areas are still neglected and face resurgent criminal "bands." It is under these conditions that civilians seek to manage and adapt their organizations for autonomy.

The history reviewed in this chapter is helpful for understanding the empirical chapters that follow. The history is first informative for interpreting what juntas may do to help civilians deal with violence. It also suggests there may be a relationship between organizations and the *reporting* of information on indicators such as violence. Lastly, a deep understanding of long-term trends and historical events can help disentangle circular relationships (e.g., between social organization and violence) by pointing to how factors can be measured before the circular relationships became entrenched. In the next chapter, I elaborate on the methods I use to study questions of civilian autonomy and how Colombian history guides the application of these methods.

4

Living to Tell About It

Research in Conflict Settings

ATCC LEADER: Oye Gringo, do you hear that? Listen ... They're coming for you.
ME: Who?
ATCC LEADER: La Guerrilla! ... (laughter)
                                    – Heading upriver from La India, Santander, Colombia, 8/2009

One of the aims of this study is to bring methodological structure and rigor to the question of civilian agency. In this chapter, I outline my multimethod empirical strategy for studying the question of civilian autonomy. The chapter serves as a guide for the next four empirical chapters. I start by describing the broader research design of the study and how the different methods and pieces of evidence fit together. I also discuss the different choices and trade-offs of particular methods and their benefits and limitations. The design deals with the issues of reverse causality between the impact of civilians and armed groups as well as possible bias in case selection. I then describe the research process and preview the data sources I collected during eleven months of fieldwork in Colombia spread over four years.

The research design seeks to understand the central counterfactual question of whether armed groups would have used more violence if not for civilian autonomy strategies and the organizations that enable them. The empirical work is useful for theory building, but its main purpose is to test clearly stated and falsifiable implications of theory. The use of multiple methods in a subnational study in a single (post-)conflict country is beneficial for providing deep and comparative understanding. While no single test or method alone provides conclusive answers for the outcomes being investigated, each method plays an important role in inquiry. The combination of quantitative analysis, purposive case selection, and fieldwork aims to push the methodological boundaries of civil war studies. Taken together, the approaches tend to point toward the same conclusions and paint a coherent picture of civilian behavior.

This research embodies an interplay between inductive theory building and deductive theory testing. When I began this project, I was principally engaged in building theories. I had little initial knowledge about the potential security concerns that could have made this work infeasible or the details or effectiveness of civilian organizational processes. I began my fieldwork interviewing a broad cross-section of subjects from many communities and with diverse experiences to gain background on civilian choices and formulate my research questions.

I then carried out a plausibility probe of the apparently successful case of the ATCC. Within this community case there is theory building based on initial observations and initial validation – that some organizations effectively protect civilians at least some of the time. I also found opportunities for theory testing based on additional data collection and new units of analysis such as individuals, villages, and events. From this initial research, I gained a sense of the variation in civilian social cohesion, organizations, and strategies across formal autonomy organizations, such as "peace communities," and learned about the role of junta councils.

With a theory in hand about organizations, juntas, autonomy, and armed groups, I sought to generalize it to a broader universe of cases by collecting necessary additional datasets (e.g., on organizations like juntas) and visiting new cases in additional field trips. The additional case studies from Cundinamarca are "out-of-sample" cases, which is to say they are unknown, unstudied cases and not cases from which hypotheses were derived (though they are "nested" among the large-n universe of cases). After tests with these new cases, I again transitioned back to the inductive mode of research. Some inaccurate predictions in these cases – for instance due to the effects of clientelism in weakening organizations – suggest refinements to my theory. Such refinements of theory can then be better tested in future research.

WHY THE CASE OF COLOMBIA?

Why study civilian autonomy in a single-country study and why study Colombia? To begin, violence and social organizing are micro-behavioral phenomena that occur at that level. The Colombian civil war also provides a good opportunity to gain a systematic understanding of the choices of civilians since there are widely varying experiences across local communities. A substantial number of communities have overtly implemented autonomy strategies to resist violence and displacement, while others have either implemented more covert processes or been forcibly displaced. In Colombia, like in other countries, there can be drastic differences in social cooperation even from one town to the next, with certain towns benefiting from idiosyncratic and socially beneficial historical events.[1] Variable conflict conditions, levels of violence, and types of armed

---

[1] Some examples of pockets of highly cooperative communities include Las Gaviotas in the eastern plains (Romero 2009), the highly cooperative Afro-Colombian community of Sanquianga (Cárdenas 2008), the Palenque of San Basilio (De Friedemann 1979), and the religiously founded town of Jericó (Jericho; Otis 2010), to name but a few.

groups are also found across these towns. The Colombian case also has many high-quality subnational datasets. As I later illustrate, this has payoffs as it allows for sophisticated comparative methods to select cases for qualitative study. Lastly, I chose to do research in Colombia because its increasing physical security allowed broader access to case sites and because of my Spanish ability.

A potential concern with a single-country study is whether the context of the Colombian conflict is unique, causing findings not to generalize to other settings. For instance, a problem for inference could be that the phenomenon of civilian autonomy in Colombia is broad enough to be studied there but not in many other locations. Colombia is unique in some regards. For a middle-income country, it has a relatively strong legal system. Its war has also been relatively long-lasting, with at times relatively stable and slow-moving conflict dynamics (though punctuated by periods of rapid change and intense fighting).

Yet, similar to other conflict-ridden parts of the world, Colombia is a relatively capable state with weak reach into the periphery. The law is unevenly enforced, if at all, in large parts of the country and illegal armed groups dominate (O'Donnell 1999; Palacios 2006). Some of these areas have high levels of poverty and receive few state services.[2] Colombia is a nominal democracy, however there is high inequality, clientelism, and corruption, especially in the countryside. Colombia's war is certainly not the only one that has economically motivated armed actors and illicit crop cultivation. Colombia may have been an outlier in levels of foreign aid, but it is not clear if it has had relatively great NGO involvement or international attention beyond the drug issue.

Comparative data helps put Colombia and its conflict in context. Sudarsky's (2007) analysis of the 1998 World Values Survey shows that 50.5 percent of Colombian respondents were active members in voluntary organizations (when religious organizations are excluded), putting Colombia in the lower half (middle quintile) of a set of twenty-seven developed and developing countries (and according to Inglehart et al. 1998, a Catholic tradition is correlated with low interpersonal trust).[3] This description is consistent with an uneven social landscape with low overall "civicness" but also pockets of social cooperation.

Similarly, though comparing conflict intensity across countries can be messy, Colombia's conflict falls in the upper-middle range for countries in civil war. It is ranked 86 out of 114 conflicts for total battle deaths and 68 out of 114 conflicts for total battle deaths per capita. However, after accounting for the conflict's long duration, it is lower for average annual battle deaths per capita, ranked at 30 out of 114 conflicts (for conflicts from 1945–2002, based on Lacina 2006 data). This makes Colombia neither the least nor most intense of conflicts. These data give reason to believe that Colombia is not such an outlier on important variables that some of the findings here cannot generalize. Colombia

---

[2] The impoverished Pacific department of Chocó is frequently categorized as one of the poorest places in the Americas.

[3] However, this comparison set may undersample developing countries where conflicts are prone to occur.

naturally shares greater similarities with some country-conflicts than others, but its generalizability is supported by the additional countries classified as having autonomy actions in Chapter 1 and those studied in greater depth in Chapter 9.

THE FRAMEWORK FOR SUBNATIONAL ANALYSIS

The analytical framework in this book allows for the subnational comparison of hypotheses for outcomes of violence and social cohesion against alternative explanations with both quantitative and qualitative methods. I combine a large-n statistical overview with analysis within and across cases. The qualitative and quantitative analyses both draw on a broad array of original and existing data, and I triangulate data from multiple sources and perspectives on the same concepts, such as violence. I use this data to test implications of theory across time and space using several units of analysis, ranging from cross-national examples down to individual events of threats and violence. Topics I consider include: How do individuals view the conflict? How do villages behave? Which municipios are least likely to suffer violence? How do different armed groups and fronts behave?

The different methods have different advantages, with some able to speak better to particular outcomes than others. The large-n methods alone can suffer from the problems of missing data, insufficient control variables, omitted variables, and measurement error. The quantitative methods are most useful for establishing correlations between relatively easily measurable concepts such as social organization and violence, testing for conditional effects, and sampling on a broad distribution of cases. However, with limited availability of this historical data, the methods are not very suitable for measuring or testing civilian strategies since they are often hidden, change rapidly, or are difficult to categorize. Quantitative methods are challenged to distinguish cooperative autonomy mechanisms from alliance or fleeing strategies.

Qualitative methods alone can be subject to problems of selection bias, interpretation, forgetting, and replicability. The case studies are useful for the process tracing of decision points, mechanisms, accurate measurement, and identifying idiosyncratic details not easily observable from a distance or across many cases. The case studies can give faithful accounting of the details of particular communities, but can only be more broadly representative if they are carefully selected. Analysis of only few cases may also not be helpful for assessing causality if there are many potential causal variables. In sum, any one of these methods alone would provide an incomplete picture of behavior. Next I explain how the methods are joined to deal with selection issues and trace decision-making.

The Choice to Use Historical Data

This study is based on historical sources of data and qualitative fieldwork. A historical approach is taken since social landscapes are the product of long-term historical trends and events. Further, with the concerns surrounding selection bias and reverse causality, a long view of history helps incorporate social landscapes prior to the occurrence of violence. This book encompasses over sixty years of Colombian history, focusing on 1990–2005 but going back to the 1940s. As with all historical studies, there can be challenges in collecting data on certain events long after they have occurred. With the passage of time, memories can lapse and relevant people and sources can disperse.[4]

Studies undertaken in the midst of conflict can avoid some of these problems but collecting reliable data during conflict entails other challenges and trade-offs. Such studies are usually best able to describe conditions and generate theory. They are challenged at collecting candid data from subjects, testing theory with methodically selected cases, and porting hypotheses to new samples or units of analysis.[5] Such insights are valuable but can be subject to the conundrum of testing the generalizability of findings, where it is difficult to gauge their reliability and how far they reach. To balance these concerns, I opted to conduct research in areas that had recently emerged from conflict.

An alternative method I do not use is surveys because I felt it was important to measure variables before the start (expansion) of conflict, rather than contemporaneously. Surveys can also be too blunt for understanding the details of complex strategic interactions. Even in post-conflict, it seemed participants would not have enough confidence to reveal their true preferences, decisions, histories, or reasoning. Furthermore, the sensitivity of some questions and the unpredictable security situation across the country could have impeded random sampling or sampling enough units.

To test the effects of juntas and other organizational variables, I analyze observational data on violence by armed groups from 1990 through 2005. Beyond reasons of data availability, these years are also the most relevant time period for study of the emergence and impact of autonomy organizations since many were formed during or immediately prior to this period, and there are also examples of junta activity, renewal, and increasing self-governance. This era in Colombia also saw an apex of violence and combat that affected much of the country. It encompasses the height of paramilitary violence with the AUC expansion and the implementation of the Plan Patriota counterinsurgency campaign. The later years then saw a de-escalation beginning around 2003 with the gradual repulsion of guerrillas and the beginning of the demobilization of paramilitary blocs. Some of the paramilitaries then quietly remobilized and new "emergent" bands began to appear (CNRR 2007). These years are a tough test but are also when we might detect an effect of juntas on violence.

---

[4] However, researchers may be able to access clusters of relevant subjects in refugee camps or demobilization centers.
[5] Field experiments, which are growing in use and popularity, can mitigate some of these issues but also have ethical considerations.

Joining Methods to Deal with Selection Bias Issues

Understanding how cases are selected for study is important for gauging external validity and making inferences about other contexts. Bias from selecting on the dependent variable (violence) could arise from looking at well-known, organized communities because the independent variable (organization) could be correlated with violence in unknown ways. Social organizations could, for instance, exist in more violent areas (or not), which would bias against observing an effect on violence. Alternatively, organized communities could have initially faced less violence than other communities, possibly contributing to their very survival and the later emergence of formal autonomy organizations (with prior violence being correlated with future violence). This encapsulates the related problem of reverse causality, where the effects of conflict could weaken or destroy social organization, causing social organizations to survive and persist only in relatively peaceful places.

The options for selecting cases can be limited for several reasons. Especially in conflict settings, our attention can be drawn to noteworthy cases, while wide-ranging fieldwork is costly. In developing countries, where conflicts tend to occur, there is also usually poor historical and quantitative data to more broadly sample additional cases (though this is improving). A second issue is selection bias from limits on researcher access to sites. At the time of the fieldwork for this study, Colombia was not a post-conflict country, but could rather have been classified as a "conflict" country. A main limitation in field research is the risks of entering conflict and guerrilla-controlled zones.

I use a number of strategies to deal with selection and reverse causality issues. The power of analyzing many cases (large-n) is the overview it provides to understand where particular cases fit within the broader universe of cases. I use standardized units of analysis by looking at violence and the coverage of juntas and other organizations at the municipio level, with over 1,000 municipios in Colombia. My complete sample permits the inclusion of the full range of variation on the dependent variables. It also helps construct valid counterfactuals to compare cases of organized, "resisting" community cases with "nontreated" (unorganized, no autonomy strategy) cases – the "dogs that did not bark." I do this by controlling for potential confounding factors (e.g., conflict dynamics) that might cause any observed relationships between social organization, civilian strategies, and violence to be spurious.[6]

Data for these variables come from numerous micro-level governmental and private sector sources that provide multiple measures of social cohesion and organization and violence. Though it can be hard to come by historical data on social indicators in developing countries going back much before 1990, I was

---

[6] I attempt to control for a variety of preexisting characteristics of municipios. The inclusion of time-invariant historical measures of different organizations precludes the use of fixed-effects to deal with unobserved heterogeneity.

able to assemble data on independent variables from prior to the spike in conflict around that time (indeed, I found several studies and censuses had lamentably been lost or destroyed!). For example, data on the junta councils comes from a rare dataset published by the Colombian census bureau along with qualitative reports from interviews I conducted with members of the juntas movement. Linking data on historical conflict from La Violencia to the variables on the subsequent growth of organizations helps address reverse causality concerns by at least accounting for the distribution of junta councils across towns.

My case selection methods join the quantitative and qualitative approaches of the study. The narratives of the selected cases are a key element of the book. Like some other studies, they use structured, focused comparisons (George 1979) to trace decisions and outcomes, meaning all of the cases are studied with similar (causal) structures and data collection procedures. But, in contrast to other narratives on civil war experiences, this study's narratives try to do something different. The narratives, based on difficult and potentially dangerous fieldwork, are embedded in a larger quantitative overview.

In Chapter 6, I use the quantitative data to identify neighbor towns that are matched on relevant characteristics (covariates) that might contribute to violence, including conflict dynamics, but have differing levels of organization. Within these quasi-experimental comparisons, any differences in outcomes should be attributable to the variation in the difference in the "treatment" of social organization. In other words, at least within a zone, key differences between cases should not be attributable to broader regional historical factors or conflict conditions because they are largely the same. In this way, the matching is an additional solution for avoiding spurious inferences due to reverse causality. There are clear expectations about how these different communities should have behaved during the conflict, and the qualitative variables I collect on those cases can be sensibly compared with the indicators from the large-n datasets. The close link between theory and empirics allows for the identification and systematization of *new, unknown* strategies and social processes from previously overlooked cases.

I selected case sites in recent post-conflict areas both for safety and because in the midst of conflict, interview respondents would be harder to recruit and perhaps less candid. Gaining access to combatant perspectives would also be more difficult. The zones in Santander and Cundinamarca had guerrilla presence until fairly recently, but were safely controlled through government actions to regain territory under Plan Patriota by the time I arrived.[7] While visiting areas of past

---

[7] There is a risk of bias from not being able to access some long-term guerrilla strongholds that had not yet been secured by the military. However, several of the zones I study had guerrilla presence for decades and my quasi-experimental design helps minimize this concern (as does the analysis of FARClandia in Chapter 9). Additional case studies of other communities as they become safer in the future can further assuage concerns of selection bias based on safety criteria. The fact that the sites I visited were safe enough to visit at the time may set these cases apart from other zones that continued to have conflict, but there is little else I could do about this as a researcher.

rather than ongoing conflict may introduce possible selection bias due to limits on where a researcher can safely venture, the zones I study were not quite beacons of tranquility and some persisted with low-level conflict and violence. I interviewed many subjects who were currently threatened or had been previously, as well as previous kidnap victims. In some of the zones I visited, people were killed before, during, and after my visits (by either the military or criminal bands). There were also written threats in the form of pamphlets from armed bands. Nevertheless, I strove to minimize this potential form of bias by talking with civilians from zones with ongoing conflict in safer sites as well as interviewing combatants.[8]

This research design and case selection process is helpful for structuring information for later analysis, but it made the process of data collection relatively difficult because information is easier to come by in some cases than others. Prior scholarship that has examined accessible cases has suffered from case-selection bias: well-known peace organizations are well known because they are good at managing and disseminating information and data. This is the case with the ATCC, where the rich sources of historical information available attract scholarly attention. However, in the ATCC neighbor areas and the other case-study sites there were no local formal civilian or human rights organizations that consistently monitored the consequences of the conflict, and the civilian organizational responses to deal with those consequences were also subtler. The result was much less available data. Studying the full spectrum of cases thus called for modified data collection procedures for the "unorganized" portion of my sample. I return to this issue later in the discussion of interview procedures and in Chapter 8. Compared to the data-rich conflict environment and formal process of the ATCC, studying the other towns also meant reduced expectations for the detail of analysis that could be undertaken.

The case matching research design also made the task of identifying potential differences between towns through fieldwork even harder. If I employed my matching techniques well, and by virtue of the selected towns being neighbors, they should in many ways not be that different (putting my measure of junta councils to a true test!). Furthermore, because of how the cases were chosen, as a researcher I had little background knowledge of these towns and had virtually no acquaintances or research contacts before I selected them and arrived in the zones. While not knowing what to expect made it all a surprise and very exciting (and at times nerve-wracking), it also meant networking to get information would be slower and created an even greater need for creative and precise data collection tools. For instance, I had to devise some new, comparable qualitative measures of cohesion and violence, such as counts of machete fights, which are described in Chapter 8.

---

[8] It is conceivable that respondents that left these zones could have distinct views (compared to an average remaining resident) related to the reasons why they decided to leave. There is not much a researcher can do to mitigate this concern other than to try to include respondents with a variety of reasons for their departures (personal security, economic prospects, family reasons, etc.).

THE CASE STUDIES AND FIELDWORK: "TO THE VILLAGES!"

I visited and interviewed subjects from many locations, but the majority of my qualitative evidence focuses on five core case "towns": the ATCC, its neighbor villages, and the Cundinamarca towns of Bituima, Quipile, and Vianí.[9] I began my fieldwork for the project in 2007 and made multiple short trips to Colombia through 2009 (with follow up visits in 2011 and 2013, and work in the Philippines in 2012). The daily lives and social relations of some of these communities are astonishingly similar to the caricatures of Gabriel García Márquez's novels – small and insular, and with many interwoven familial relationships (though as García Márquez's novels also attest, this does not necessarily make them cooperative or amiable). People meet at the village store, or sit around in plastic chairs and chitchat and drink (many!) beers, perhaps while playing games of *tejo*.[10] Farmers help neighbors harvest coffee or sugarcane. Women wash clothes in the stream or nurse their babies together. Coffee growers come to the town center for meetings, and some residents come for Sunday mass. Many residents are related to each other as some kind of cousin or in-law. With the slower pace of life, information and gossip about others and about newcomers abounds.

My research involved work in cities but mostly involved extensive work in the *campo*, or countryside – in town centers, in *corregimientos* (rural sectors), in small villages, and at lone houses. My contacts and guides were enthusiastic and adamant that I go "*a la vereda*" or "to the village" to get the true perspective of the campesinos, and I found that getting the views from different parts of these municipios was invaluable. For many people, taking me to the village was a point of pride: a place they own, where few outsiders go, with guarded secrets, and a sacred, serene, tranquil lifestyle compared to the bustle of the city. These visits served both to find examples of collective action for autonomy from the "affirmative" (autonomous) towns and, perhaps more crucially, to verify that there were few or no collective actions from the "negative" towns, such as Quipile, which required more extensive visits. Reaching these sites involved many and only occasionally comfortable modes of transportation: planes, taxis, buses, *chivas* (country bus), jeeps (actually, Willys, as Colombians refer to them), motorcycles, *bestias* ("beast," or mule), *lanchas* (motor canoe), and unbelievably steep mountainous hikes in *pantaneras* (rubber mud boots) on what some might call trails.

An ongoing concern was how a "gringo" like myself could safely access these regions. In my fieldwork preparations, I would analyze the security situation with existing data and news reports and identify at least one local contact. I would then ask the questions of whether I could get there safely (i.e., will I get

---

[9] I say "towns" in quotation marks since these rural areas include villages that surround the town centers.

[10] Tejo is a popular game in Colombia in which players score points by tossing iron discs at packets of gunpowder that are set in clay basins and explode when hit.

Campesinos playing a game of *tejo* in a village in the ATCC region, 2008. The game involves tossing metal discs at small packets of gunpowder.
Photograph by Oliver Kaplan.

kidnapped right away?) and whether people are likely to talk to me. I was fortunate to be accompanied in most of my travels by church leaders and priests, NGO staff members, or local residents. For security reasons, I did not stay in zones for long periods at a time (more than three weeks or so) because word travels fast and, before long, everyone came to know there was an American in town. In my research process I would visit, then leave to reflect and analyze, and then repeat. This reality may have limited access to information and understanding of especially deep social relationships. However, on follow-up visits I would return with more focused research questions and broader comparative lenses through which to view the communities.

Even with my precautions, I still encountered some complicated situations that required spur-of-the-moment judgments. In one instance, I was leaving La India at the end of a field visit and my acquaintances helped arrange a ride for the stretch of dirt road to Cimitarra in a friend's car, from where I would catch the night bus back to Bogotá. It sounded faster and better than the last bumpy school bus of the day, so I waited for the car to arrive. When it came at dusk, a gregarious man got out and said hello and shook everyone's hands. Yet I opened the passenger door only to see a revolver lying on the seat. A series of panicked thoughts raced through my mind: Who is this guy!? And why does he

A motorcanoe (*lancha*) heading upriver from La India, Santander, Colombia on the Carare River, 2007.
Photograph by Oliver Kaplan.

have a gun!? Should I get in, or stay another night!? I looked to the others, who did not seem concerned, and not wanting to offend, I anxiously got in and the driver tossed the gun to the back seat. Once moving, I casually asked him about it, and he said he had it because he was a city councilman and, as I had been warned, robberies on the road were common after dark. His answers were hardly reassuring, but we thankfully made the journey without incident. Although planning is key, one can only prepare so much for these dilemmas.

Interview Techniques

As part of my fieldwork I interviewed more than 200 people. Most were civilians from the core case-study towns as well as residents or former residents from many more communities in both rural and urban settings.[11] I ended up interviewing between fifteen and forty-five residents in each town. The civilians comprised a broad cross-section of individuals, including campesinos,

---

[11] Some but not all of these interviews are incorporated into this text. Some were conducted for background purposes to understand the variety of Colombians' general experiences with social organization and conflict.

A bus ride in eastern Antioquia, Colombia.
Photograph by Oliver Kaplan.

Indigenous group members, Afro-Colombians, women and men, and youths (over 18 years old). These people often had various roles: farmers, business owners in the town centers or corregimientos, leaders of formal organizations, local junta leaders, national officers of the acción comunal (junta) movement, and even former coca growers. There were also victims of various kinds of violence: torture, kidnapping, forced displacement (some of the displaced persons had lost everything and were living day-to-day), widows and people who lost family members in the conflict, and even people who were under death threats at the time. I also interviewed members and regular participants in community organizations and juntas as well as nonparticipants in communities with formal organizations or juntas.

Beyond regular community residents, I also interviewed "elite" subjects as diverse as current and former mayors, city councilmen, municipal officials (Human Rights Ombudsmen and Defenders – *Personeros* and *Defensores*), members of churches, NGO workers, government officials, and current and former police and military officers, as well as former guerrillas and paramilitaries. Community leaders and elites were invaluable for gaining historical overviews of the communities. It was also helpful to contrast elite responses with nonelite responses to see how daily life and experiences from the villages at times differed from "official," more central accounts.

A *chiva* bus in Pensilvania, Caldas, Colombia, 2009.
Photograph by Oliver Kaplan.

Interview subjects were recruited in several different ways in hopes of obtaining broad and representative viewpoints. First, I would "snowball," asking one person to recommend other people to talk with who might be knowledgeable about a certain topic, hold a different opinion on a given subject, or have been involved in community affairs at a different period in time. The right introduction was essential for entering a community, arranging initial interviews, and gaining trust.[12] Prior planning and networking was crucial, as these introductions were only possible with the help of many people, including representatives of organizations such as the Catholic Church, NGOs, and fortunate acquaintances I made in Bogotá. At times, gaining trust was additionally aided by participating in community events, joining in soccer games (though playing poorly), or drinking unfortunate amounts of liquor and beer to become "part of the tribe."

Second, in some instances, quasi-random interviews were possible. For instance, on market day I was able to speak with villagers who by chance came into town and ate at a restaurant where I was loitering. At various large,

[12] I had been told before I began fieldwork that, being an American, people might think I was a CIA agent. In at least one instance, this concern was dispelled with irony when I saw a teen walking down a village lane with a "CIA" ball cap on one of my early field visits.

community-wide meetings I was able to speak with people who happened to have had time to stay afterward. Sometimes I was able to meet the guys who happened to be having drinks at the corner store.

All interviews were conducted in Spanish by me and were anonymous, which is one reason why respondent descriptions are vague. As a researcher, I sought to present myself as objective and impartial. I was there to understand histories and protection processes, but not to make value judgments regarding other end goals, particular sides in disputes or conflicts, or people's past behaviors. Most interviews were conducted in the private settings of a person's home or an NGO office, though if a person consented and felt comfortable, the interview sometimes took place at a more public place like a café or a corner store. Interviews varied in length, with some lasting only thirty minutes and others involving multiple sessions lasting hours. While most interviews were with lone individuals, some interviews were with groups of subjects who consented to collective discussions. All interview notes were written by hand and no recording devices were used. In addition to helping protect the identities of subjects, this technique also helped make subjects feel more comfortable. This meant writing in shorthand, though I would write out important quotes word for word and ask subjects to repeat if necessary.

Participants in interviews were almost always excited to share their stories with me. Whether they were tales of desperation or inspiration, most people wanted to be heard and have a voice. Some subjects were fearful or had been previously traumatized and spoke in hushed tones, and conversations required extra empathy and calm for comfort. Some potential subjects declined to participate. Other individuals were ebullient and, even if it could have been risky to share certain details with me, were adamant that I report every detail as a testament to their community's strength, what they suffered or endured, or the truth about atrocities and victimizers. Some were also adamant that I attribute the stories to them by name (which I of course could not and did not do). Despite the possibility of censoring out of fear or danger, I found that people were surprisingly open, perhaps because I was a foreigner, or perhaps because of appropriate introductions by trusted mutual acquaintances.

The interviews were semi-structured. I began my research and interviews with a loose plan of standard interview questions and topics of interest, seeking information that would be helpful for qualitatively understanding key variables and trends. At the same time, I let conversations evolve depending on the insights provided by the subjects.[13] To minimize danger or potential trauma to subjects, I asked general questions about communities and trends rather than

---

[13] In gaining consent and explaining the purpose of my project, I described my interests in general terms to avoid guiding subjects' answers from the start. I told them I was interested in social relationships in the midst of conflict settings and how different towns experienced the years of conflict.

questions about specific or personal events. Subjects who felt comfortable would at times volunteer more personal information or anecdotes. In some cases, I introduced hypothetical scenarios and asked subjects to respond about what would have happened or what people would have done in X or Y situation. Some questions were tailored for each case based on the local history and context. As my thinking and knowledge as a researcher evolved and grew, I adapted my interview approach to ask about relevant and comparable phenomena from town to town to assemble qualitative measures such as the prevalence of *macheteras* (machete fights), *bazaars* (fairs), and responses to cattle theft, which I did not know to ask about when my fieldwork began. In discussions of social organizations I invited subjects to comment on both positive and negative aspects.

I faced two principal challenges in grounding interviews for useful comparisons across space and over time. First, there was the risk that interview subjects might fixate on more current and accessible *ex post* conceptualizations of social conditions and explanations for violence. While I was interested in information on outcomes, what I really needed were *historical* assessments of *pre-conflict* conditions and independent variables. It was also hard for some civilian subjects to clearly remember details of brief events that occurred in times of stress five years prior, ten years prior, or even earlier.

To deal with these issues I used two different interview techniques. First, I asked subjects to think about different periods of time by prompting them not only with years, but also by grounding questions with reference to specific national events, local events, and personal events. Second, instead of interviewing only current long-time residents, I also interviewed people who migrated to towns at specific times in the past, people who left towns at specific times (and were living elsewhere), or returnees who moved away from regions at specific times and maybe only recently moved back, after the conflict had subsided. These kinds of respondents were helpful for pinpointing information at specific moments in time and describing pre-conflict characteristics since time in the town effectively stopped for them when they left or began when they arrived. Finally, interviews with certain elderly residents provided descriptions of La Violencia based on their own recollections or from stories told to them by their parents.

A second challenge of cross-town comparison stems from the inability to visit many different research sites given the rough terrain, poor roads, and potential safety concerns in parts of rural Colombia. I was able to overcome these limitations with some craftiness in interview strategies. I first maximized geographical coverage of interview subjects by leveraging interviews with people at meetings they would attend in town centers or Bogotá. For instance, I interviewed victims of forced displacement in cities that had come from a wide variety of rural towns across all parts of the country. In cities and towns I was also able to interview people who came from dangerous settings that I might not have been able to reach easily.

In addition to the challenge of gaining geographical breadth, I was also concerned about the *comparability* ("anchoring") of observations and interview responses across towns and villages. For instance, even if people from many different villages or towns were to get together in the same room, they might not have a basis for comparing or ordering their communities on dimensions of interest to a social scientist because the community each person knows best is his or her own. By visiting different towns I was able to make some of my own comparative judgments, but it can also be challenging for an outsider to make accurate comparisons, especially with limited mobility and time and arriving in the post-conflict period after causal processes of interest have occurred.

As a solution, I sought out peripatetic individuals who had broad geographic familiarity from traveling across or living in different villages or towns. These key respondents included people who for business or other reasons had traveled extensively within the broader region surrounding their community, such as merchants, bill collectors, agronomists, drivers, priests, etc. As I elaborate on later, ex-combatants were also often more mobile than the civilian population and could provide further insight into cross-town differences. I also encountered people who had recently moved to a case-study town from one of the neighboring case towns and so had familiarity with both. Lastly, some archival documents contain dialogues with residents of multiple villages.

The interviews were varied and yielded mixed though generally insightful accounts. Some people were minimally informed about local history or had little experience with conflict and social organization and could only provide basic background information. Other respondents were keen students of social organizing, local politics, and civil war dynamics. Some were enthusiastic about community processes and organizations, while others dissented and were embittered, perhaps because they felt excluded from a process or program, disagreed with decisions, or had personal issues with leaders, among other reasons.

As a consequence of the larger research design, interview recruitment and information-gathering processes differed slightly between communities with formal organizations like La India with the ATCC and other towns with no formal organizations or NGOs. These latter towns did not have the same kind of centralized collective memory or central point of contact from which to network. Interviews and data collection were therefore more scattershot.[14] Further, since violence suffered by civilians in areas with no organization (or few juntas) can be prone to inaccurate reporting and a relative underreporting

---

[14] The effects of socialization and experience were also evident in formally organized La India. ATCC respondents were more self-conscious of social and conflict processes than those from Cundinamarca, having pondered many explanations for their lot. In the Cundinamarca towns it was less common that any single person would directly attribute broad and abstract factors such as the unity or division of populations as an explanation for different outcomes. Perhaps this was because they tended to only hear about individual events of violence and were less exposed to collective discussions, news, ideas, and narratives.

A game of mini-soccer (*micro-fútbol*) in La India, Santander, Colombia.
Photograph by Oliver Kaplan.

bias, enhanced qualitative measurement techniques were required for comparability.[15] The potential existence of subtle protection mechanisms in the non-formally organized cases also created the need for adapted techniques to discern their effects. Inferences from areas without formal organizations are still possible, but less complete reports make it harder to construct relevant "counterfactual" cases to understand how social variation relates to threats and killings.

Interviews with Ex-Combatants

Discussions with ex-combatants contribute a valuable additional perspective. Interviews with ex-combatants involved slightly different procedures and techniques (and bias concerns) and merit a separate discussion. I fielded twenty-eight total interviews with ex-combatants, with three-quarters from guerrilla groups and one-quarter from paramilitary groups, and including three

---

[15] I rely upon standard indices of violence in the large-n analysis with the hope that, if there are similar reporting biases across municipios, a large enough sample will average them out and that control variables can account for them. However, in any particular handful of cases, there are greater risks of mismeasurement, and police statistics and press reports could be inaccurate if residents do not report incidents out of fear.

Loading coffee in Pensilvania, Caldas, Colombia, 2009.
Photograph by Oliver Kaplan.

female participants.[16] These were the later interviews I conducted, in August 2009, having already selected and visited case zones and heard the perspectives of civilian residents.

I was aided in the recruitment of subjects by the Colombian government's High Advisory for Reintegration (ACR; now the Colombian Agency for Reintegration), which helped me identify and schedule interviews with geographically relevant ex-combatants – individuals that operated in or around my case-study areas – that dispersed after they left the conflict and were living in the capital of Bogotá. The majority of these interviews were conducted in ACR field service centers and were done so voluntarily, anonymously, and in private.[17] While the setting could have affected the subjects' openness or candor, the responses seemed open and truthful. For instance, the location of the interviews did not keep subjects from giving detailed accounts of interactions with civilians, recalling gruesome atrocities, or criticizing the demobilization program.

---

[16] There were two additional interviews that were incoherent and not used. Approximately eight other subjects were invited to participate but did not show up for interviews.

[17] I was certain to emphasize to subjects that their participation was voluntary and was in no way related to their receipt of government benefits.

Obtaining ex-combatant perspectives was prioritized over military and police perspectives because these latter accounts tended to be less relevant or informative. The case-study zones were conflict zones in a weak state and, even with the state forces' periodic patrols, there tended to be little permanent state presence and inconsistent state contact with the campesinos of the far-flung villages of the countryside. It is also difficult to identify military and police personnel that served in a particular zone at a particular time in the past because troops rotate in and out of zones as part of their tours of duty. Despite these considerations I was able to obtain several accounts from current and retired military officers.

The transience of the ex-combatant population combined with the ACR's limited information in its individual profiles meant I could only geographically target subjects with moderate precision. The armed group fronts, blocs, and zones represented in the sample are summarized in Table 4.1. I was fortunately able to track down ex-combatants that had operated in my case-study areas even though it had sometimes been from five to ten years since they had demobilized. Two-thirds of the participants came from fronts or blocs that were involved in my case-study regions. The rest operated in other parts of Colombia but still provided valuable comparative insight.

The group of subjects comprises those people who were enrolled in the ACR's reintegration program and showed up at the service centers to participate in the study. This obviously excludes combatants who had not yet demobilized, been killed, or ex-combatant no-shows.[18] Nevertheless, the sample still includes a range of subjects in terms of their experiences in the conflict and attitudes toward their former patron armed groups. Subjects include individuals who never wanted to be in the conflict as well as individuals for whom it was their life (i.e., defectors as well as captures).

The quasi-random recruitment of ex-combatant subjects yielded a variety of interviewees according to their roles and ranks within the armed groups and their experiences with civilian populations. The participants ran the gamut from informants, to "*rasos*" or foot soldiers, to middle commanders. Some were merely collaborators who did not wear uniforms and kept their places as civilians living in their communities. Others were soldiers whose principal work was to serve as interlocutors with civilians and organize meetings with them. Still others spent almost all their time camped in the mountains or jungle seeking out enemy forces and had almost no contact with civilian populations. Some subjects had experiences in several different fronts or blocs as they rotated across different regions of the country. This was especially true among

[18] Ex-guerrillas and paramilitaries arrived in the demobilization program through different processes. Guerrillas were frequently captured or fled and turned themselves in to state authorities. Most ex-paramilitaries participated in the formal "complete" demobilization of paramilitary blocs beginning in 2003 (for information on this process and the number of demobilized from each bloc see Oficina del Alto Comisionado para la Paz 2006).

TABLE 4.1 *Characteristics of ex-combatant interview subjects*

Guerrilla Front (F) or AUC Bloc (B)	No. of subjects	Departamentos/Municipios where operated in	From case-study zone?
F42	8	Cundinamarca: Viotá, Pulí, Quipile, Vianí, Bituima	Yes
F22	2	Cundinamarca: Quipile, Vianí, Bituima	Yes
B Omar Isaza	1	Caldas: Pensilvania, Samaná	Yes
F47	4	Caldas: Samaná Antioquia: Nariño	Yes
F9	2	Caldas: Samaná	Yes
B AUC Puerto Boyacá	2	Santander: San Vicente de Chucurí Boyacá: Puerto Boyacá	Yes
F27/ F Antonio Navarro	1	Meta	No
F Urbano	1	Bogotá/ various fronts	No
AUC/ ACB/ ACCU	2	Casanare	No
BCB	2	Bolívar Nariño: Tumaco	No
F22 (urban)	1	Bogotá	No
F24	1	Santander: Barrancabermeja	No
ELN	1	Nariño	No

former FARC guerrillas. In the Cundinamarca case towns, the bulk of information from ex-combatant interviews is from former guerrillas. Unfortunately, little is known about the paramilitary groups that arrived there later because they were more clandestine and informal, short-lived, and did not formally demobilize. Instead, they disintegrated and disappeared.

The ex-combatant interviews followed a more structured progression. I began most of these interviews by asking general questions to make the subjects feel comfortable, gain their confidence, and get to know their background.[19] What are they doing now? How do they feel about the demobilization program? Where are they from? How long ago did they enter the reintegration program?[20] I then asked them general questions about their experiences:

---

[19] More than in the civilian interviews, the ex-combatants preferred not to talk much about their personal experiences, either because they preferred not to look back on their former lives or because they feared possible stigma for their actions. For these reasons and for my interest in general information about particular groups and blocs I had no reason or interest to ask questions about personal behavior.

[20] Analysis of these comments was expanded upon and published in two related studies (Kaplan and Nussio 2015, 2016).

A banner from the Colombian Agency for Reintegration (ACR) promoting the reintegration of ex-combatants ("We build peace from the countryside"), 2016. Photograph by Oliver Kaplan.

Which front or bloc were they in? For how long? Where did they mainly operate? What was their role in the group?

Some subjects were more open to discussing these themes than others. Of course, I had expectations about how combatants in different areas would view different towns based on my fieldwork, but to avoid tipping them off about my interests or hunches, I would begin with general queries and then probe progressively closer toward my topic of interest. Depending on their cogency and willingness to discuss prior questions, I asked more substantive questions, phrased somewhat open-endedly to encourage free association: Did they notice differences between villages or towns? Was there a lot of combat or pressure from other groups? What was the group's attitude toward using violence?

I would raise the topic of civilian resistance toward the end of interviews if it did not come up previously: Did civilians ever resist their group's control? Did they act collectively? What did they tell the armed group? How did the group respond? Why?[21] I would sometimes conclude with some hypothetical questions such as: What civilian strategies did they think were best from the civilians' point of view?

The inclusion of ex-combatants enriches the study by highlighting their groups' reasons for using violence and transgressing against communities, and other themes. They add textured descriptions of the intensity of conflict to the rough quantitative indicators of armed group activities. Through their mobility the ex-combatants are also able to provide comparative perspectives across towns on civilian characteristics that can be hard to obtain from the mostly stationary civilians. Some ex-combatants were also formerly junta leaders prior to being soldiers and so were able to see issues from both points of view. For some, being in an armed group seems to have reinforced the importance of juntas for protection. Interviews of ex-combatants from areas beyond my case-study zones reveal additional examples of apparent movements for autonomy from armed groups at the village level. Lastly, it was "interesting" to converse with these subjects (especially former guerrillas) about how they viewed gringos.

As valuable as these ex-combatant interviews are, extracting useful information is not without pitfalls. First, the accuracy of ex-combatants' memories was variable since the subjects I interviewed had demobilized between two and twelve years prior to the interviews. I was asking them to recall events from five to fifteen years ago when they were living different lives. Second, it was complicated to temporally and spatially piece together different accounts. Since fronts can cover several municipios, even if subjects were contemporaries from the same front they may not have operated in the same place or even known each

---

[21] I also asked clarification questions during the interviews to confirm whether the subjects and I had mutual understandings of what they were reporting regarding civilian autonomy and advocacy. This was a relative advantage of the interview technique compared with surveys.

other. Further, some units were mobile and moved across wide swathes of terrain, causing trouble in pinpointing where individuals saw or remembered certain events or trends. This was a larger concern for ex-guerrillas, since many were transferred between different fronts during their careers. Third, interviewees had varying capacities to recall their group's interactions with civilians, either because they were less exposed to, less sensitive to, or less observant of civilian issues. Fourth, in a similar vein, the subjects' variable positions in the groups meant some ex-combatants had greater exposure to group leaders and decision-making processes than others. Fifth, ex-combatant reports could suffer from confirmation bias. They might either be inclined to confirm *ex post* that they respected civilians or that civilians had agency to whitewash the darker aspects of their group. Subjects could also dissemble and tell half-truths to confirm what they expected I, the researcher, wanted to hear (social desirability bias).

Ex-combatants' *ex post* justifications for their actions can be unreliable. Like any such reflections, they are not complete, definitive accounts of decision-making and require further confirmation. Still, there are also reasons to believe in the validity of these accounts. Many subjects were able to recall certain autonomy events in great detail. Further, they did not solely recall civilians advocating for their rights but instead also distinguished many regions where civilians were subjugated. Some accounts are also corroborated by civilians' stories, archival documents, and secondary sources with interviews conducted by other researchers studying other questions. In general, when I encounter ambiguity or contrasting accounts – about levels of control, attacks, violence, and explanations of behavior and decision-making – I try to show the different versions and indicate levels of uncertainty and doubt. This transparency includes examples from their statements that do not support my theory.

Participant Observation

Participant observation during visits to communities was also an important part of understanding social differences across towns. I spent many months in small towns and gained insight into the daily lives of residents. I was also able to attend specific events and meetings. I observed village, junta, and cooperative meetings and saw the struggles and successes of various decision-making processes. I saw trainings of junta leaders. I saw how villagers interact with NGOs and international organizations. I observed protest marches and funerals, and attended church services. It was often informative just to see who would and would not show up to these meetings and events – who and how many people would seek assistance from village leaders, organization leaders, or mayors? Who would go out to work in the fields? I could also observe features such as how the local economy functioned, how much common knowledge and communication there was between residents, and how close together the houses were.

Participant observation in the post-conflict settings I studied from 2007–2009 pointed to obvious social and attitudinal differences between towns. It also provided intangible validity to the statements made by interview subjects. However, a problem with post-conflict observations is that, though it is safer than conflict zone research, they are *ex post* to the causal relationships of interest. The state of the world one can observe is "contaminated" by the very experiences of conflict itself. Any such observations are therefore only moderately helpful for measuring differences that existed between communities before armed groups arrived.

In the Archives

A last set of data is from various archives. I accessed documents from government archives, community archives, and personal collections of individuals involved in the acción comunal movement. The ATCC's musty, dusty, rat-filled community archive was a particular treasure trove of information (and, yes, rats!). It contained personal journal entries; verbatim meeting minutes from civilian organization meetings; verbatim transcripts of meetings between civilians of organized and unorganized communities and various armed groups; original documents and acts; and correspondence between the community and armed groups, government officials, and international organizations. These documents hold special validity because they were not recorded for the purposes of posterity or academic research, but rather to hold potentially deceitful actors to their words. They provide a snapshot in time and let us reconstruct particular moments in history. They also provide a glimpse inside the heads of armed group leaders, highlighting their interests, approaches, decisions, and rhetoric toward communities (at least inasmuch as they would communicate to civilian communities in private settings). The archival data show consistencies with both civilian and armed group testimonies and thus serve as a useful validity check for potential reporting biases in some interviews (and some *interviewers*!).

Secondary Sources

The case-study analyses are supplemented with existing secondary sources and news reports. A goal of using these sources is to obtain adequate coverage of events in *both* organized and unorganized case towns. Violence data based on press reports, fieldwork, secondhand sources, and existing datasets was compiled, coded, and geo-referenced and then matched to case-study towns and villages.

SUMMARY

This chapter has sought to transparently present the methodological choices, challenges, and contributions of this book. Civilian autonomy is a question that is ripe for careful research design to critically scrutinize the claims of "peacebuilding." Reflection on methods is also important given the reality of studying a conflict setting and because the topic involves sensitive issues, subtle strategies, and "hidden transcripts" (Scott 1992). Since understanding civilian agency requires understanding civilian organizational problems and institutions, I measure and compare social characteristics, organizations, institutions, strategies, and conflict processes. I map problems of violence that civilian mechanisms aim to solve and then empirically link them to outcomes.

The larger design holds several advantages. It controls for hypotheses of violence and tests these hypotheses across standardized units of analysis. To reduce selection bias, the design samples broadly across these many units, including organized, unorganized, violent, and peaceful communities. The historical context of the cases is used to assess complications from reverse causality. The case selection procedure joins the different methods and helps structure information. And, since field experiments are often not practical in conflict settings, it is helpful that the cases that are identified for study simulate experimental conditions. Overall, the design embodies a triangulation of many methods, data sources, and viewpoints to provide both breadth and depth of knowledge.

The different methods have different roles. I lay bare some of the limitations of these methods and the sources of potential biases and mismeasurement. Quantitative methods are good for an overview and verifying broad correlations but are less able to test hidden strategies and are subject to measurement error. Qualitative methods allow for the careful process tracing of history to provide both the top-down view of the armed groups' perspectives on civilians as well as the civilians' bottom-up opinions and observations of armed groups. However, qualitative cases can be susceptible to selection bias and problems of making broader inferences.

This study's integration of methods means the whole is greater than the sum of its parts. Yet, even with the technical and social scientific aspects of this study, I have sought to breathe life into it and not lose the texture of the setting and culture in which I worked. The social science is needed, but it must not be forgotten that my subjects are real people and many have suffered torture, loss of loved ones, trauma, and displacement, and have still persevered.

The empirical chapters ahead apply these methods to test implications of theory. In the next chapter, I provide a statistical overview of the relationship between autonomy-enabling social organizations and violence across Colombian municipios.

5

How Civilian Organizations Affect Civil War Violence

"In conflict zones, there always has to be someone there in the community to advocate for the community."

—Ex-FARC combatant (Exc#9), Bogotá, 8/2009.

Even as the La Violencia conflict still raged in some parts of Colombia, a small team of sociologists went to study the municipality of Chocontá, Cundinamarca in 1959. They focused on the small village of Saucío as a microcosm of a new community development program that held the promise of social repair (Fals Borda 1960).[1] The now-famous early account of the "communal action" program starts with the parable about the construction of a new school for the community. Desperate for a better educational facility for their children, residents of the village first joined together to hold a bazaar (fair) to collect donations, but they got burned when local authorities squandered the funds. With little to show for their efforts, decaying cooperative traditions, and a mistrust of authorities, the village formed a junta (board) in a second attempt to complete the project.

A promoter (technical advisor) arrived to help break the community's inertia, and reach consensus on the need for the school. As a catalyst (Fals Borda 1960: 51), the promoter helped form the junta, broker with authorities, and train community leaders in organization, bookkeeping, and project management. But the promoter's stay was only temporary, since he was too costly to keep around for long (52). The decisions came from the people, with the junta taking the lead and dedicating the school when it was completed the next year. The Saucío junta next set its sights on electricity and road projects (33). An agricultural cooperative also sprang from the junta, including a store that provided credit and maintained the shared tractor and sewing machine (43).

---

[1] Translated and paraphrased from Fals Borda (1960) by the author.

The communal action in Saucío was credited with producing "a resurgence of collective energies that otherwise would have been left dormant" (Preface). In his description of an awakening, Fals Borda notes the junta helped form a collective identity and ethos – "a liberation of the traditional campesino." With newfound pride and independence (60), the campesinos were no longer "submissive and unsophisticated." Instead, when the farm boss would pass, "they would no longer take off their hats and salute with reverence and fear" and would "act with dignity, and demand and command." As one resident said, "We no longer need mayors who are only concerned about collecting our taxes" (60).

Communal action also altered the social order within the community as well as the community's relations with other actors and institutions. It was credited with "reducing the brawls in stores and rowdy weekend drunks to only those marginal individuals outside of communal action." The beer bottle began "losing its social prestige" and the junta provided "healthier avenues for the expression of prestige" (61). The junta also embodied a challenge to institutions, such as the Catholic Church, that resisted social change or that had a "cultural monopoly." The scholars emphasized the resulting "*autonomy*," which "implies recognizing the talents and efforts of the people, united, that as a general rule have been ignored by the dominant classes."

The precursors for confronting the armed conflict are evident even in this early study. The authors show how the junta of Saucío contributed to community order and managed the community's autonomy against outside actors. Little did they know the juntas would continue to serve in this role for decades to come, and against different and more lethal armed actors. This chapter empirically tests observable implications of the theory from Chapter 2 about the protective roles of civilian organizations such as juntas – like Saucío's – in conflict settings with statistical analysis across the universe of Colombian towns. The chapter aims to be accessible to readers without backgrounds in statistics. The statistical models and other technical information are included in an appendix (see Tables 5.1 to 5.7) for readers interested in those details.

This book argues that civilians themselves, through their varying *cohesion and local organizations,* can impact real-world outcomes and explain variation in violence. Local civilian *organization* is essential for reducing violence because individual civilians, similar to individual fighters, have little recourse and are ineffective when navigating dangerous, complex, and changing environments such as those of a civil war. The key empirical challenge to assessing this argument is overcoming the identification or "measurement" problem of separating the impact of civilians on civil conflict from the reverse – whether conflict destroys or stimulates social organization, and whether social organization dampens or accelerates violence. Past studies of civilian movements have had limited generalizability because of the problems of few cases (small-n), case selection bias, nonstandardized units of analysis, and the poor accounting of reverse causality.

For the analysis of how local civilian organization affects civil war violence, I exploit data across counties (municipios) on various community organizations in Colombia including the village or neighborhood juntas councils through which residents coordinate to solve local problems and provide public goods. This is because their existence is broad enough and their history is long enough to attempt to distinguish causal relationships. Juntas are theorized to affect violence because they proxy the high levels of coordination and social capital necessary for communities to implement more complex "autonomy" (or other) strategies to preserve themselves in the face of conflict. Because the presence and functioning of juntas are more simply measurable and comparable than larger or more formal autonomy organizations (such as "peace communities" or farmer associations) and their presence and effectiveness vary across many localities, they offer a convenient way of getting leverage on the challenging research design issues. Data on these councils comes from a rare dataset published by the Colombian census bureau as well as interviews I conducted with members of the juntas movement.

As an implication of my theory, the main tests I conduct on the effects of juntas focus on forms of selective violence. After controlling for combat and contention among armed groups, I find that a variable representing juntas has a negative effect on violence. In other words, organized civilian communities on average tend to suffer fewer effects of violence than unorganized communities. The next chapter adds confidence to these results by showing that the formation of civilian organizations was unlikely entirely a result of earlier patterns of conflict. The findings provide insights about general civilian behavior in civil war and the recent wave of civilian resistance to the armed conflict in Colombia that accelerated in the early 1990s.

In the sections that follow, I first conduct a basic analysis of conflict-related drivers of violence. Second, I analyze the effect that the juntas of campesino (mestizo) communities have on violence when accounting for the conflict-related drivers. I also examine the violence-reducing effects of highly cohesive Indigenous and Afro-Colombian populations and other organizations. Third, I conduct some additional tests to better understand the scope of the juntas' effects on violence. Fourth, I review the history of the outlier case of the town of Belén de Los Andaquies to contextualize the findings. I conclude with a summary of findings and possible avenues for further research.

THE JUNTA COUNCILS' IMPACT ON VIOLENCE

Universe of Cases and the Unit of Analysis

To test the effects of juntas, I analyze data on violence by armed groups from 1990 through 2005. Beyond reasons of data availability, these years are also the most relevant time period for study of the emergence and impact of autonomy organizations since many were formed during or immediately prior to this period and there are various examples of junta activity, renewal, and increasing self-governance as discussed in Chapter 3. As such, these years are a tough test but are also some of the more likely years when we would detect an effect of juntas on violence.

I use the municipio, or county, as the relevant unit of analysis (municipio-year). This is in some ways not the ideal unit, as there are lower levels of geographical division in Colombia that might more aptly represent "communities." It may also gloss over some important differences between urban and rural areas or between the county seat and peripheral villages for certain municipios. However, the municipio is the lowest unit for which broad and reliable data is available on the dependent and independent variables of interest (in other chapters I test implications of my theory at lower levels of analysis). Municipios also still allow a much finer-grained analysis than Colombia's thirty-two departments. The sample of municipios is heterogeneous. Some are highly populated, some are nearly empty. Some are vast, some are small. The mean area of the municipios is 1,174 sq. km and the mean population for 2005 is 38,530 people.

The Dependent Variable

To measure violence against civilians, I use the annual civilian homicide rate for municipios as the dependent variable, measured as homicides per 100,000 residents. I use two sources for this data. First, I use data from the Colombian NGO CINEP, which is based on independent press reporting from twenty-six national newspapers and includes only armed conflict violence – "political" homicides – and not those due to common crime. This source is advantageous because it has broad coverage across the country and is arguably unbiased. Although only events that are reported in the press are recorded and many events are surely absent, this source should still permit relatively accurate comparisons across municipios. According to this data, 7 percent of political homicides are attributed to the ELN, 11 percent to the military, 15 percent to the FARC, and 67 percent to paramilitaries (Figure 5.1).

I also use data collected by the Colombian National Police. This data has coverage in all municipios with police presence and reporting should not depend on the (inconsistent) presence of press reporters. However, it also depends on people reporting crimes to the police (and that the police report this data) and it is a "catch-all" statistic that covers more than just conflict-related killings. In addition to including deaths from common crime such as murders resulting from brawls and robberies, the police data also includes deaths of noncombatants at the hands of all armed actors, including the guerrilla groups, paramilitaries, the police, and the armed forces (excluding combatant deaths). While the data certainly includes episodes of selective violence, some of the violence counted as homicides is more indiscriminate in nature, including civilian deaths from combat, massacres, acts of terrorism, and

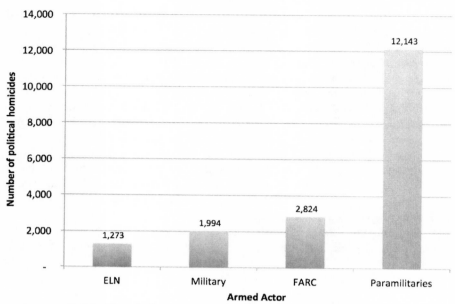

FIGURE 5.1 Political homicides by presumed perpetrator, 1990–2005.
Source: CINEP.

land mines. The map in Figure 5.2 shows that while violence is fairly widespread, there are also areas of calm.

A Conflict-Based Model of Violence

I first analyze when and where armed actors will have strategic incentives to contest territory and commit violence. I do this because the ability of civilians themselves to affect violence is most likely observable after conflict variables are controlled for. Further, any relationship found between civilian organization and violence could be spurious if highly organized communities suffered less violence than other communities because they faced less pressure from armed groups. In the next section, I add other civilian-related variables to the analysis. One of the main conflict-related explanations tested with this data from Colombia is Kalyvas's (2006) theoretical arguments and empirical conclusions (based on other countries) about how the balance of territorial control affects violence.

In brief, Kalyvas's research suggests that much of the violence against individual civilians in civil wars is a result of battles for territorial control among armed actors (the control-collaboration model). Violence is strategically and selectively used against enemy collaborators to coerce support among the civilian population. Violence is both used to gain control of territory and is also the result of the dynamics of territorial control. According to his logic, violence is produced "jointly" by the main mechanism of denunciations of enemy

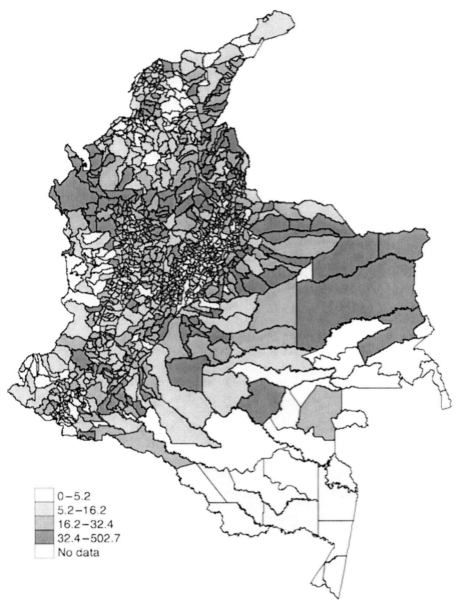

FIGURE 5.2 Map of mean annual political homicide rates by municipio, 1990–2005.
Source: CINEP; Author's calculations.

collaborators to the armed actors by civilian informants. These informants only risk implicating a neighbor for one group if they are confident their patron will be able to protect them from retaliation from the enemy group. Denunciations and therefore selective violence are thought to be most commonly carried out by the stronger armed actor in zones of dominant but incomplete control. In contrast, violence is relatively low both at the front lines where control is evenly contested, and in areas where one army or the other enjoys complete control. This theory predicts an upside-down "U" relationship between violence and the military balance of control.

Examining this relationship with statistics at the micro level can be labor-intensive if not altogether impossible. Kalyvas (2006) uses a survey methodology to classify variations in the military balance of control based on the responses from civilians about the presence of armed groups near their homes. He traveled vast areas of the Greek countryside to code civilian perceptions of control during that country's civil war and finds evidence to support his theory of selective violence. Kalyvas and Kocher (2009) use existing U.S. government surveys of hamlets for a test on the Vietnam War. This data collection technique is prohibitively difficult in the case of the *ongoing* conflict in Colombia, but existing data can be used to approximate the balance of military contestation. I use data graciously provided to me by the Colombian Vice-presidency's Human Rights Observatory, economist Fabio Sánchez of the Universidad de Los Andes (see Fabio Sánchez 2007), and press-based data from the Jesuit research center CINEP.[2] My initial analysis of conflict takes into account both the magnitude and balance of armed actor activity in predicting violence. A variable for Total offensive actions (attacks) captures the magnitude of armed activity in a municipio in a given year by all armed actors occurring *between* two or more actors. This variable is constructed as the counted sum of a variety of belligerent activities.[3] This variable and the results of the regression analysis are described in the appendix.

Variables for economic resources are also included as explanations for violence. Resources may represent strategic interests for armed groups and therefore the intensity of contestation and incentives to commit violence against civilians. Resources may also predict abusive, undisciplined armed actor organizations (Weinstein 2006). As Colombia is known to have drug cartels and cocaine production, I include a variable for the area of coca cultivated in each municipio-year in hectares based on United Nations aerial survey data (United

---

[2] Sánchez's data comes from information from both the Colombian Government and the nonprofit organization Fundación Social (Sarmiento Anzola 1998).

[3] To measure the military balance of control, I include a squared term of the Total offensive actions by the various armed actors in the specification since Kalyvas's theory would predict an upside-down "U"-shaped curve explaining selective violence. I also devise a second way to measure the military balance of control by creating a variable based on the proportion of attacks by each armed group "side" in a given municipio-year. This variable is used in the police data regressions because the higher counts of attacks make it a more feasible proxy.

Nations 1998–2006). In some models I also control for oil infrastructure, since armed groups have been known to siphon and sell oil on the black market at contraband gas stations, and a count of the number of mineral mines in each municipio (East View Cartographic 2002).

I also include a number of additional control variables. To control for variation in demographics across counties, I include variables for population, population density, and the percent of population from minority groups from the 1993 national census. The percent of households with dirt floors and the adult literacy rate (1993), also from the census, are used as interchangeable measures of socioeconomic status (SES) and poverty.

To account for geographic variation, I include a measure for rough terrain since Fearon and Laitin (2003) find cross-nationally that mountains are a proxy for rebel group activity and areas where rebels can hide. I measure rough terrain as the elevation above sea level of the county seat of each municipio and in some specifications as the standard deviation of elevation in meters. To account for isolation and state strength, I include a measure of the distance of each municipio from its departmental capital and measures for a municipio's lengths of rivers and paved road access (DANE 2000; and created from GIS VMAP data). Region indicators (dummies) are included to account for region-specific variation and department effects are also tested. Lastly, a one-year lag of the homicide rate dependent variable is included to account for serial auto-correlation of homicides in municipios and year dummies are included to account for national trends in violence over time.

The results lend some support to Kalyvas's balance of control theory from the Colombian case (see Table 5.2 with CINEP data and Table 5.3 with Police data). They show that the total offense and balance of control variables both affect violence at statistically significant levels ($p < .01$), with marginal improvement in the amount of variance explained (r-squared = .34). Total offensive activity is significant and positive in all models and, on average, every additional action is associated with an increase of about 2.5 in the homicide rate. Nearly half of all municipio-years experienced at least some offensive activity. This suggests that magnitude of combat itself could be capturing some of the incentives for violence against civilians reflected in the balance of control theory.

The area of coca cultivation has a statistically significant and positive effect on violence in most police models, even after controlling for combat. On average there is an increase of four deaths per 100,000 residents for every additional 1,000 hectares of coca cultivated (the municipio with the most coca has 15,000 hectares). This is consistent with the narrative in Colombia about the harms associated with coca. Many civilian *cocaleros* (coca growers) are viewed as tacit participants in the conflict and have regular interactions with armed group and drug cartel buyers, increasing the risk of homicide. Other variables that predict important strategic interests and contestation are discussed in the appendix.

Overall, these models suggest that the conflict variables reasonably approximate the strategic incentives of armed groups to commit violence.

Testing the Explanation of Social Organization and Social Capital

Civilian autonomy theory suggests communities in civil wars might gain protection through several mechanisms if they are organized versus if they are not. The relevant counterfactual to assess whether juntas reduce violence is that, given two similar municipios with similar conflict histories, a municipio with more juntas should suffer less violence. A community achieves a degree of "de facto" autonomy if it suffers fewer than expected civilian killings given the local configuration of conflict. This leads to a first hypothesis:

H1: *Municipios with higher densities of local junta councils should have lower levels of homicides, all other things equal.*

To measure the variation in the presence of juntas across municipios, I use data on the number of juntas in a municipio in 1985 as published by the Colombian census bureau (DANE 1985 and DANE 1987).[4] As a measure from a single point in time, this variable will best explain variation in violence across municipios as opposed to across time. Of the 990 municipios that existed in 1985 there is data on juntas for 967 of them. The 1985 data shows there were 18,458 total juntas. Information from the 1993 junta census shows that 27 percent were in urban sectors and 72 percent were in rural sectors (implying that if juntas are found to have an effect, it is likely occurring in rural areas).

To approximate the extent to which local communities (with specifically rural villages and small towns in mind) are covered by juntas across counties, I calculate an indicator of *juntas per capita* by dividing (normalizing) the number of juntas in each municipio by its census population in 1985. For ease of interpretation of this indicator, the fraction is multiplied by the mean size of a junta of forty-five members to estimate the percent of "communities" that have juntas out of the (imagined) number of those that could (hence, "Juntas Per Communities").[5] The Juntas Per Communities measure ranges from a low of zero percent to high of 48 percent with a mean value of 6 percent. The distribution of this measure of juntas is mapped across municipios in Figure 5.3.

---

[4] While published in 1985, the initial collection and compilation of this information on junta councils may have occurred a few years earlier. Although I could not find earlier data, there are two references to a juntas "registry" or "directory" produced in 1978 and 1981, respectively. Since I could not access these sources, for the purpose of this analysis, I refer to 1985 as the time of the final count. However, to the extent that the measurements were taken earlier, it would mean they are even less contaminated by the growing violence of the 1980s.

    Ministerio de Gobierno and DANE. 1978. *Registro Juntas de Acción Comunal.* Bogotá: DANE, as cited in: DANE. 1982. *Indicadores Socioeconomicos de Desarrollo Rural en Colombia,* Bernal E., Alejandro (coordinator). Bogotá: DANE. There is also a reference to a "Directorio Nacional de Juntas de Acción Comunal-1981" in: DANE. 1993. *Las Estadísticas Sociales en Colombia.* Bogotá.

[5] The use of an estimate of villages from 1970 (DANE 1971) to create a Juntas per Villages indicator yields similar results, but it has more missing data.

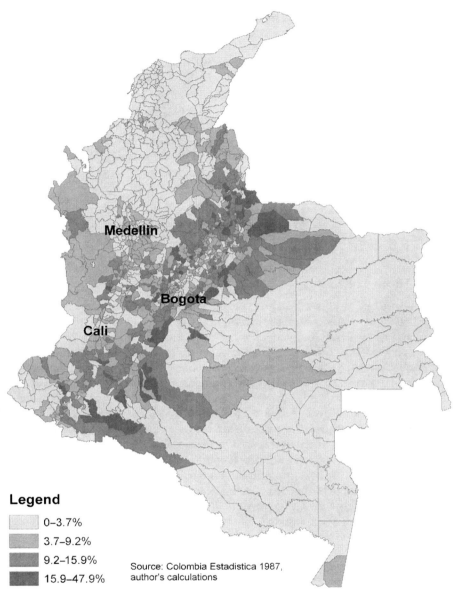

Legend

0–3.7%

3.7–9.2%

9.2–15.9%   Source: Colombia Estadistica 1987,
             author's calculations
15.9–47.9%

FIGURE 5.3 Map of juntas per communities by municipio.
Source: DANE 1987; Author's calculations.

The strongest evidence for my hypothesis on the effect of civilian organization would be a direct, negative correlation between juntas and homicides after controlling for conflict variables. But the theory of armed actors' sensitivity to civilians suggests it is more likely that the effect of juntas will be attenuated at high levels of conflict. Juntas should affect violence in some regions and moments in which violence might plausibly be in the interests of armed actors for coercion or other ends. They may do this through autonomy mechanisms that manage the costs and benefits to armed actors such as vouching, normative beliefs for avoiding the war, and resolving community conflicts. However, juntas are less likely to affect violence in areas where armed groups are fighting especially hard for objectives or have strong interests in targeting the population. This implies an additional hypothesis to be tested:

H2: *The effect of juntas on homicides is conditional and will* interact *with and be attenuated by the level of armed actor combat and contestation, as represented by the total number of attacks and the balance of attacks.*

Direct Effects of Juntas

There are strong results for a direct effect of juntas on violence. Analysis using CINEP violence data shows a significant, negative bivariate relationship between juntas and the political homicide rate in Model 1 of Table 5.2. Results from the regression models in Table 5.3 using the police homicide rate show that the Juntas per communities coefficient is also negative once the intensity of combat and balance of control are controlled for (significant at the .05 level). Figure 5.4 (based on Model 4 of Table 5.2) shows the significant substantive effect the junta councils have on violence: based on the mean values for the CINEP homicide rates. A change in the level of juntas from 0 to 0.11 (to the 75th percentile) can lead to an average estimated decrease of 25 percent in the homicide rate, reflecting a modest but significant degree of protection for most communities. As expected, the conflict-related variables account for a relatively large share of the variation in violence in the models, but the Juntas variable still has a small amount of explanatory power above and beyond the base model variables and conflict indicators (moving the r-squared about 0.02, or about one-third the change compared to the change from the introduction of the conflict variables).

Additional tests in the appendix contain more refined tests of the effects of juntas. For instance, the juntas are also effective in areas where multiple groups are operating and potentially endangering the population. In these tests, the sample is restricted to municipios with at least one or two attacks in a given year and municipios where both guerrilla and government/paramilitary actions were registered (not shown). These tests lend support to the theory that juntas represent a vehicle for protection through autonomy strategies since these are the most likely conditions where juntas are representing and implementing the autonomy protection strategies theorized in Chapter 2, and not just strategies of aligning with dominant actors.

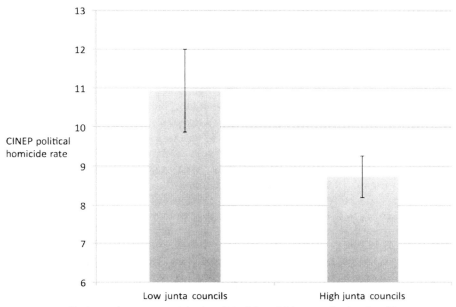

FIGURE 5.4 Estimated mean municipal political homicide rates by levels of junta councils, 1990–2005. Low Junta councils is the 0 percentile; High Junta councils is the 75th percentile (0.107); Error bars indicate 95% confidence intervals; Estimated based on Model 4 of Table 5.2 (CINEP data).

A key issue that could affect the reliability of these results is reporting bias, a risk not just in this study of civilian organizations, but for all studies of civil conflict. It is possible that the presence or absence of social organizations like juntas can lead to a reporting bias. If juntas are stronger in rural, isolated communities and CINEP news and police coverages are weaker in those places, it could produce the negative relationship that is observed.[6] A similar finding could arise if people rely on juntas instead of the police in places where juntas are strong (as a result of state absence or fear of entanglements) and these juntas do not report to the authorities. On the other hand, if communities with juntas are more organized than those without juntas, they may be *more likely* to report homicides to the police. If this were true it would actually bias against results confirming my theory that juntas suffer less violence.

I gauge the severity of this problem and address it in several ways. First, evidence from Cubides (2006) corroborates that juntas tend to be key reporting sources. Cubides mentions the following example:

In 1997, in a zone that had been recently dominated by the guerrilla, a unit of the army's elite forces was annihilated. The only civil power acting in the zone to register the dead and the survivors was the local junta. The media sought the official story and came back

---

[6] The homicide rates from the CINEP and police datasets are correlated at r = 0.3; see Table 5.7.

to the junta's president, the only one who could give public faith to what happened. The junta was the only organization to manage to survive in the middle of the war zone and with the tacit recognition of both sides.

As this episode shows, if juntas help communities retain autonomy and increase information flows about acts of violence relative to communities without juntas, counts of violence could appear to be highest in areas with juntas. This would bias against finding any violence-reducing juntas effect.

Second, comparisons of these large-n data sources with qualitative data I collected from the ATCC case and the Cundinamarca towns (see Figure 8.2) also suggest organized communities are *more* likely to report violence. Third, underreporting bias that could lead to spuriousness should be partially accounted for in the statistical tests that control for and subset cases based on "ruralness" and state presence with the inclusion of the variables of distance from department capital, paved roads, and population.[7]

The junta measure's inaccuracy may also mask a larger junta effect on violence. This could be for two reasons. First, some juntas that were likely measured in the dataset appear to be shells today, existing mainly in name (as found in some of the Cundinamarca towns in Chapter 8). Juntas may be inactive because they successfully met communities' public goods needs or because of clientelist depredations. This would weaken any observed "treatment effect" of juntas (i.e., they are measured as having a violence-reducing effect even though in reality they are inactive or clientelist). Second, if juntas are underreported in some areas where they actually exist, it means some cases that actually got the treatment of juntas are classified by mistake as part of the control group that does not have juntas (meaning if the junta effect holds, these towns should suffer less violence). This would cause the mean violence of the "control" (low junta) group to drop closer to the "treatment" group's because the juntas are actually reducing violence but are not observed as doing so.

The Juntas: Organizational Effects or Favorable Conditions?

I consider three additional factors that might undermine the suppressive effect of juntas on violence related to community homogeneity and coexistence: the La Violencia conflict, inequality, and polarization. To test an additional implication that juntas resulted from earlier violence, I also add a dummy (zero or one) variable reflecting the severity of La Violencia to the estimates of present-day violence to account for an area's unobserved, or omitted, "historical propensity for violence."[8] I coded dummies for whether or not a municipio experienced "high levels" of violence based on historical information in

---

[7] Additional tests exclude department capitals and municipios that are within 20 kilometers of the capitals from the sample. Other control variables such as government officials per capita and the presence of police stations and inspections (administrators) should also help to account for reporting biases to official sources.

[8] This is similar to pulling this latent "propensity" out of the regression's error term.

Guzmán et al. (1963) and Roldán (2002) on the La Violencia period from 1948 through 1963. There are dummies for the first wave of violence and the second wave of violence (1954–1958), as well as remnant violence after the peace accord was signed and the National Front government was installed (1958–1963).[9] I also coded additional dummies from Guzmán reflecting whether or not a municipio was the headquarters of any local bandit bosses during the entire episode (1948–1963) as an additional indicator of conflict and disorder. Consistent with historical accounts, municipios in the central departments of Tolima, Cundinamarca, Huila, Boyacá, Santander, Caldas, Antioquia, and Casanare tended to suffer high levels of violence while the departments of Nariño and Cauca in the southwest and Magdalena (today spanning Cesar, Bolívar, Magdalena, and Guajira) in the northeast suffered very little violence (Figure 5.5).

Experiencing La Violencia appears to be significantly and *positively* associated with greater violence today. This points to a serial correlation in violence and suggests La Violencia is working to account for a municipio's latent propensity for conflict. But, the observed effect of the junta councils *is not washed out*; it remains significant and negative. This suggests that even after correcting for a possible selection bias in the distribution of juntas due to a circular relationship between violence and social organization, juntas continue to work to suppress violence in the 1990–2005 period. In an additional test of only La Violencia municipios, the significant and negative effect of juntas persists, arguing against juntas solely reflecting some kind of post-Violencia "learning" effect about how to get along (not shown). It also hints at a "reversal of fortune" of sorts (e.g., Acemoglu et al. 2002), where areas that were previously violent during La Violencia were *revitalized* upon an increase in coverage of juntas. I return to the effects that La Violencia may have had on junta formation in the next chapter.

Inequality is one of the first factors to which analysts attribute Colombia's social and armed conflict woes. By distribution of land and income, Colombia has historically been one of the most unequal countries in Latin America and the world (Lorente 1985). Albertus and Kaplan (2013) show this inequality has persisted in part because of poorly implemented agrarian reforms. Could juntas mainly be reflecting *minifundios* (small farms) and equal social relations? Could degrees of inequality produce qualitatively different armed groups and incentives to use violence? Could inequality impact conflict beyond mere levels of poverty? I examine these questions by using municipio-level variables for GINIs of land area and land value estimated based on the cadastre (land registry) by Offstein (2005) for the late 1980s.[10]

---

[9] A designation of "highly violent" does not necessarily mean that all parts of a municipio experienced violence. Results are similar using data on La Violencia coded by Oquist (1980).

[10] The GINI is a commonly used estimator of what proportion of land is held by a given proportion of the population. These measures are missing data for several departments, including the department with the most municipios, Antioquia.

FIGURE 5.5 The geography of La Violencia
Source: Compiled by author based on Guzmán et al. 1963, Roldan 2002.

The land value GINI is not a significant predictor of violence regardless of whether the juntas councils are included in the estimation, suggesting it adds little explanatory power above and beyond the other conflict and societal variables in the models (Table 5.4). However, the GINI land values do washout the significance of the junta councils (land area GINI has no effect). This suggests that juntas are somewhat correlated with inequality. Still, while juntas may be more likely to be formed in areas with minifundios, the junta councils are a better predictor of violence than inequality in these models and the entirety of their violence-reducing effect cannot be reduced to background levels of equality. This issue is taken up again in the following chapter on the origins of juntas and in the case studies.

I account for the amount of political unity or discord across municipios immediately after La Violencia when the first juntas were being formed. I constructed an indicator of the political polarization (Polarization) in the vote for president in the National Front government in the 1962 election.[11] This variable is not a significant predictor of subsequent violence in the 1990s and 2000s (even though violence has been directed at leftist social movements) and the juntas effect persists. This is perhaps because the conflict has been of a less partisan nature and the juntas or the indicators of economic stratification may capture more important aspects of social unity.

Conditional Effects of Juntas

Testing Interactions with Conflict Intensity. To check the limits of the effects of juntas I test for an interaction effect between Juntas per capita and Total offense. The interaction is statistically significant using the police data, as both the constitutive terms and the interaction term are significant ($p<.05$; Table 5.3 Model 6) and in the predicted direction. The estimate of Juntas is negative, suggesting that it is working to decrease homicides, while Total Offense and interaction terms are positive. Together, these effects suggest the violence-reducing effect of juntas weakens as conflict intensity increases (Figure 5.8). The significant relationship between juntas and homicides is not conditional on

---

[11] Polarization in a municipio is calculated based on the following formula: $1 - (\%\text{Conservative Vote} - \%\text{Liberal Vote})^2$. Using this data to measure political polarization in 1962 can be problematic because of the rule under the National Front pact that the presidency alternate parties from term to term. Still, there is some variation in voting that can be exploited. Although 1962's presidential election was supposed to automatically go to a Conservative and was in fact won by Conservative León Valencia, Liberal candidate López Michelsen made a rogue run for office as part of the Liberal Revolutionary Movement (MRL) party. Votes for Michelsen were annulled but were still tallied and summed to 24 percent of the ballots. This amount certainly does not reflect a balanced vote but should still be able to provide a relative estimate of polarization in many parts of the country. Unfortunately, this municipio-level indicator cannot say much about political preferences at the village level.

the intensity of combat when using CINEP data (though is nearly conditional for paramilitary violence; Table 5.5 Model 3).

Testing Interactions with Political Ideologies. To examine how the junta councils perform in conditions of ideological stigmatization (and against the kinds of hybrid armed actors that may target enemy collaborators based on such stigmatization), I constructed a variable to indicate the fifty-three municipios where Communist Party or Patriotic Union Party (leftist) mayors were elected between 1988–2000. Partly a result of the FARC's "all forms of struggle" approach that mixed political organizing and the use of force, the politicians and organizers of these splinter movements were perceived as leftist rebel supporters and were exposed and therefore targeted by right-wing armed groups (a "politicide"; Gómez-Suárez 2007). They also contributed to the stigmatization of the communities that voted for them. Many civilians of these communities became perceived as leftists and were also left open to politically motivated retaliation. However, in line with civilian autonomy motives, I test whether the juntas might have a mediating effect on violence in these historically "leftist" areas by interacting the juntas variable with this partisanship variable.

While a Patriotic Union legacy itself correlates with higher violence (an ideological effect of the anti-UP stigma), and some junta leaders have been targeted, the juntas dampen this effect (a countering-stigma effect; Table 5.5 Model 5). This effect is consistent with the juntas' general efforts to keep communities impartial in the conflict and dampen violence due to political stigmatization (or other forms of collaborator stigmatization). This finding further speaks to the theoretical scope conditions for civilian autonomy, suggesting that particular types of armed actors such as the "hybrid" groups can be influenced by local social organizations to keep from using violence (e.g., groups with particular political motives for violence that lack ideological restraints against using violence). By staving off politicide, or at least limiting its effect on the general population, the power of the juntas may also be relevant for countering mass killings and genocide.

Effects of Juntas on Additional Conflict Outcomes. I tested several additional dependent variables of other manifestations of violence to get a clearer picture of the scope conditions for when juntas and the strategies they enable may defuse violence. I use data on forced displacement from the NGO CODHES (Consultancy for Human Rights and Displacement). I also test indicators of massacres (events where four or more individuals are killed at once) from both Colombian government and CINEP data. Regression results (not shown) indicate some possible massacre-reducing effects of juntas but little relationship with displacement (though the act of displacement also involves response behavior on the part of civilians).[12] This suggests that, consistent with

---

[12] The relationship between juntas and massacres may be sensitive to model specification, as juntas is negative and significant using Zero-Inflated Negative Binomial or Logit models, and so may forestall massacres. Juntas is positively associated with displacement data from

both theory and the interaction effect encountered earlier, juntas are decreasingly effective as conflict conditions intensify or armed actors have strong motives for killing.

The Effects of Juntas Over Time. The conditional nature of the effect of the junta councils can also be explored by looking at how the juntas' effectiveness varies over time. A key implication is that junta effectiveness should vary sensibly with the facts of Colombia's historical conflict patterns. To see the juntas' trend, I regressed the Juntas and conflict variables against violence in a series of annual cross-sectional models. The Juntas coefficients are plotted by year in Figure 5.9 with 95 percent confidence intervals.

This analysis illustrates the varying capacity and limits of civilian cooperation. The nationwide effect of juntas is found to be negligible during the early 1990s, which can plausibly be explained by the relative calm and low levels of conflict. At this time, the guerrillas were expanding and paramilitary groups were still being conformed, so conflict conditions may have been either too calm to spark civilian responses or not yet sufficiently widespread to observe a juntas effect. A strong, significant, and negative juntas effect is observed from 1995–2000. This period saw escalation in armed group presence and combat. Juntas may have worked to protect residents through organizational learning and possibly the diffusion of best practices over time. There was then a period of severe brutality until the paramilitaries demobilized in 2003–2006, during which time the juntas' effectiveness again appears to have diminished. There are several possible reasons: armed groups became more opportunistic and cartel-like, less political, and fought harder; juntas and other organizations became increasingly targeted beginning around 2001, likely diminishing their organizational capacity (El Tiempo 2004); and the state increased its reach through Plan Patriota, making social organizational strategies less necessary in secured areas.

This interpretation of the events is supported by the trend in violence directed against the juntas themselves. I coded the killings of junta leaders based on the press reporting data compiled by CINEP. For the eleven-year period from 1996–2006 there were 423 events with 546 victims, indicating the juntas themselves were not immune to violence.[13] Killings spiked around 2000–2001, suggesting a change in the nature of the conflict that corresponds with the reduced effect of juntas on violence. If juntas are directly targeted, it becomes

---

the Presidency's Social Action agency. This data is based on registration of displacements in receptor municipios for government social benefits and is viewed as an underestimate, raising questions of data reliability. Reporting bias could be present if registration is correlated with community organization.

[13] This is surely an undercount, though perhaps less so than counts of violence against the general population because there is likely better reporting from organizations and about semipublic figures.

harder for them to protect their own populations.[14] This timing also corresponds with an increase in the intensity of conflict and the FARC modifying its political strategy, which likely further endangered junta leaders with both armed groups.

Junta Effects by Armed Groups. Another way to explore the conditional effects of juntas is to disaggregate the conflict homicide rate for armed groups in the conflict as they may have different reactions to the juntas. I created variables for killings of civilians by the guerrillas and paramilitaries based on which actors are "presumed responsible" for the acts in CINEP's press reporting data (for many cases, no perpetrator is identified). The junta effects are strongest for predicting homicides by paramilitaries, with no significant effects associated with violence by guerrillas (Table 5.5; paramilitary effects are significant at $p < .05$ even when land value GINIs are included in the model).[15] I also tested whether the violence-mediating effects of junta councils were stronger after the AUC paramilitary umbrella group formed in 1997 (the interaction between the Juntas variable and a Post-1997 dummy variable is negative though not significant). Consistent with these results and with the temporal trends in the reductions in violence, the juntas indeed helped mediate violence during the height of the paramilitary surge.

A plausible interpretation of this result is that the juntas are more effective in protecting against and credibly signaling to out-groups that enter communities seeking to purge enemy collaborators (paramilitaries surged in the 1990s and dislodged guerrillas in many areas; the army surged post-2002). The paramilitaries' default may be to target juntas, historical Patriotic Union party strongholds, and other social organizations, but they may be more susceptible to influence in areas where juntas push back against them or where they feel they can safely delegate some order-maintenance responsibilities to juntas. The largest effect of juntas on violence would then appear to come from paramilitaries improving their treatment of civilians. This could be consistent with the guerrillas being more disciplined overall or having greater general affinity for the peasants or better baseline information to identify enemy collaborators in rural communities. In such circumstances, guerrilla behavior should not be more greatly influenced or "reformed" by strong local councils.

Further support for these possible differences in armed groups' attitudes toward the juntas and civilian communities is found in additional data and

[14] For instance, see: "Por ser de izquierda, asesinaron a líder comunitario en San Vicente del Caguán" ("For Being of the Left, a Community Leader Is Killed in San Vicente del Caguán"). 2008. *El Tiempo*, December 15, 2008.

[15] These differences should be considered with caution since there is underreporting in the press data, with many acts with unidentified perpetrators and likely more inconsistent coverage of guerrilla killings relative to paramilitary killings since paramilitaries are usually stationed closer to towns. However, as noted, various control variables should help account for such reporting biases. Further, a social capital interpretation is consistent with interview accounts of paramilitaries attempting to build juntas in some areas where none exist to consolidate territory.

historical evidence. When the data I compiled on killings of juntas leaders is broken down by armed groups, one sees there are many more victims at the hands of the paramilitaries than the guerrillas. This finding is consistent with the different approach that the FARC took toward the juntas. A news report in El Tiempo (2002) with the headline "The FARC Stalk the Juntas Comunales" describes a document recovered in an army raid that outlines a new FARC "popular power" political strategy to weaken state institutions from the bottom up. They planned to attack the political system by threatening governors, mayors, and city councilmen. They would then win over the population and control politics by having the junta movement replace the elected officials they forced to flee. This turn of events greatly worried the national juntas umbrella organization, the National Juntas Confederation (CNAC). CNAC's human rights advocate responded, "We don't want to fall into the trap where if we don't obey we'll be displaced or killed ... the FARC wants to intimidate us and we want to strengthen participatory democracy and local development, but based in respect and tolerance."

This suggests three conclusions. First, the FARC is generally more amenable (than the paramilitaries) to respecting civil society and civilian organizations.[16] This may mean that the juntas were mainly effective in gaining autonomy in the conflict by protecting communities from incoming paramilitary forces. Second, although the FARC (and likely paramilitaries) became more and more opportunistic it still valued local political support. Third, the increased "political" competition over the juntas is consistent with its leaders being more directly and violently targeted and with the waning effect of juntas over time. This rising FARC pressure is confirmed in case studies and ex-combatant interviews in later chapters.

Overall, juntas appear to decrease violence on average in conditions of moderate conflict intensity and, in some cases, may also be able to reduce violence at more severe levels of conflict. That juntas decrease violence after controlling for resources and coca cultivation, the severity of armed combat, and the balance of control provides some reassurance they are effective in at least some regions where armed groups might have incentives to kill. These results fit with the theoretical expectation of the third part of my theory about the conditions for "de facto" autonomy. They suggest that social organizations can be effective under many conflict conditions but have the best chances for reducing violence among hybrid armed groups and moderate conflict conditions.

---

[16] According to a FARC bulletin, the guerrillas seek to work with the juntas, saying "[The Communal Action movement] strikes out on an independent path, outside of the politicking and corruption of chiefs and bosses. Modernizing the Communal Action and making it a democratic participative alternative will contribute all its long history to the design of the New Colombia" (Boletín informativo del Comité Temático de las FARC-EP N° 11).

ADDITIONAL SOCIAL ORGANIZATIONS

Percent of minority population. I include the percent of a municipio's population that is of Indigenous or Afro-Colombian descent both as a control variable for the effect of the Juntas variable and as an indicator of organization in its own right. First, minority group population is an important control variable since Indigenous and Afro-Colombians form juntas less frequently than (mestizo) campesinos and their unique local councils and organizations are not included in the tally of juntas in a municipio. Without this measure, the effect of Juntas per capita would be increasingly underestimated as the minority population increases. Second, the dense social ties among minority group populations imply they may be an additional relevant indicator of civilian organization in conflict settings. This points to a third hypothesis:

H3: *The greater the proportion of minority populations in a municipio, the lower the homicide rate, all other things equal.*

The minority population variable has a significant and strongly negative effect, suggesting that a large presence of Afro-Colombian and/or Indigenous minority groups in a municipio reduces the homicide rate, all other things equal (Table 5.3). This could be due to such groups existing in fringe areas of the country where armed groups may have little presence. However, these groups actually tend to reside in more conflictive zones and the result stands after controlling for combat activity, geography, and population density. A possible interpretation consistent with the juntas finding is that these minority groups, through their ethnic identities and intragroup ties, have strong community cohesion and organizational structures that help them deal with conflict. For instance, the Afro-Colombian *consejo comunitario* and Indigenous cabildo organizational structures were essential for winning rights to territory as well as legal autonomy of local decision-making, beginning in the late 1980s and early 1990s and continuing through today. The same organizations have also been known to play important roles in preserving order in the community ("Indigenous justice") as well as managing interactions with outsiders, be they regular visitors, the army, or illegal armed groups (see Guerra Curvelo 2004, Wirpsa et al. 2009).[17] In a different study, I find that Indigenous communities with stronger shamans suffer relatively less violence than Indigenous communities with weaker tribal authority structures (Kaplan 2013).

Evidence on participation rates across ethnic groups is consistent with the interpretation that the organizations of minority groups help them limit violence. As shown in Figure 5.6, based on my calculations from 2005 census data, the Indigenous population in the rural sector participates in communal organizations at *three times* the rate of either mestizos or Afro-Colombians.

---

[17] Though unlikely, there could also be reporting bias for homicides if these groups or municipios underreport homicides to the police because they have their own justice procedures.

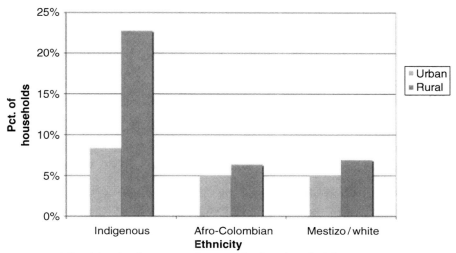

FIGURE 5.6 Participation in community organizations by ethnicity, 2005
Source: Author's calculations based on 2005 census.

Indeed, when the percent indigenous population variable is separated out from other minority groups, the estimated reduction in violence is even greater, all other things equal.

I also examine several additional organizational forms that are important in rural Colombia for their possible effects on violence. Since these additional organizations are theorized to be less useful for seeking civilian autonomy per the organizational characteristics developed in Chapter 2, they resemble a "placebo" test of the junta councils. First, I include a measure of the number of economic cooperatives existing up through the year 1976 from the *Directorio Nacional de Entidades Cooperativas* (DANE 1978). This count includes cooperatives for agriculture, transportation, credit, and mutual aid. In contrast to the junta councils, cooperatives are not found to significantly reduce violence across rural municipios and their effect is even positive in some cases (Table 5.4; this measure does not disaggregate between types of cooperatives). This could mean that cooperatives reflect robust social capital ("cooperation") but still fail to protect civilians. It could also mean that cooperatives could be targeted for being viewed as excessively political or Communist, be insufficiently inclusive of community members to implement broadly effective protection policies, or be found in target-rich areas that are not captured by other measures. To the extent that cooperatives do reflect cooperation, the findings could indicate there is something unique about the junta councils as organizations that make them more effective.

Lastly, I consider the potential role of ANUC (National Peasant Association) land reform councils as indicated by the prevalence of their land invasions during the 1970s (from Zamosc 1982). As mentioned earlier, although the ANUC councils were not as widespread as the junta councils, for a time they were a central organization for economic development in certain parts of Colombia. I find the ANUC councils indicator does not appear to reduce or significantly affect recent violence. This is plausibly explained by their gradual disappearance or their being more political and more easily stigmatized (as leftist) than the other kinds of social organizations tested.

In sum, as "placebo" tests, the cooperatives and ANUC councils proved to be like sugar pills – they look like juntas but do not have the same effects because they have different and less useful intrinsic characteristics. This is consistent with Cohen and Arato's (1994) perspective on the boundaries that constitute civil society organizations, as entities such as economic cooperatives and land reform councils are born from civil society but are not a part of it. The results on these organizations provide added support for the uniqueness of the juntas' (and ethnic minority communities') ability to unify residents to seek autonomy.

LEARNING FROM AN OUTLIER: THE CASE OF BELÉN
DE LOS ANDAQUIES

The data indicate that the municipio of Belén de los Andaquies in the department of Caquetá is the biggest outlier in junta councils per capita (2.47 juntas per 45 residents). The extreme juntas value for this case does not exert great leverage in the analysis because it is well predicted (it suffered an expectedly low amount of violence given its many juntas). But the case presents a good opportunity to learn about the validity of the juntas indicator from qualitative confirmation since there should be a strong expectation of vibrant juntas and collective actions for protection.

In my fieldwork I was fortunately able to interview a resident from the rural area of this town.[18] She confirmed that the town historically had strong juntas, which were still active in the 1990s. The juntas there were responsible for many public works before the guerrillas came. In one instance, a junta organized the town to build a new water tank after the first one was swept away in floods. Many residents pitched in and they held a *bazaar* (fair) and fiesta to raise funds, with people donating money, a roasted pig, *sancocho* (traditional Colombian stew), etc. (Molano et al. 1994, 186).

There are several stories behind the origins of the town's strong juntas. First, the town had an active priest in the 1960s named Juan Salateo who would visit the villages in the countryside and helped organize them to cooperate and build public works for the community, such as chapels. Second, according to one interpretation, the juntas were adopted early and easily as a carry-over from the

[18] Bel#1, Bogotá, 2/2009.

culture of *caciques,* or chiefs, that organized society among the previous Andaquies Indigenous group (the group died out in late 1800s, though some residents have indigenous features from intermixing, or *mestizaje*). Third, colonist settlers escaping La Violencia from Huila were reportedly very cooperative in founding the town in the shadow of state neglect (Tulio Rodríguez 1982, aptly titled *Forgotten Municipios*). As my subject summarized, the town was historically "peaceful and united."

During the more recent years of armed conflict, the junta leaders played an active role in advocating for their communities and dialoguing with armed groups. For instance, they would attempt to recover youths who had been forcibly recruited and would sometimes try to conciliate and reverse death threats (mainly issued by the FARC guerrillas) against members of the community. In the villages, the junta leaders also played the role of conciliator to resolve disputes between neighbors over issues like property lines (*linderos*) or disagreements among cheating couples, etc. There was also a notable collective act of resistance when the guerrillas tried to attack the police station. The townspeople came out dressed in white and protested by forming a human chain to hold off the impending attack (interview; Sandoval 2004 citing El Tiempo).

The complete picture is more varied though and not quite so rosy. Even with the examples of advocacy and autonomy, some junta leaders had to displace from the municipio under threat (although many junta leaders were able to remain). The guerrillas also exerted pressure and manipulated the juntas in some ways. In a report in Molano et al. (1994, 187) that contrasts with what I found earlier, the juntas did what guerrillas told them to and "the guerrillas organized everything in that town," from forcing residents to hold a bazaar and tejo tournament to repair roads to holding a beauty pageant to fund a bridge. In sum, while there is strong anecdotal evidence that the level of social organization in Belén de los Andaquies corresponds with the junta measure and helped civilians assert their autonomy in the face of armed conflict, neither is social organization invincible to high levels of coercion. Some of the insights from the case of Belén de los Andaquies, including the importance of the church, are explored more broadly in the next chapter on the origins of juntas and corroborated in Chapter 8.

CONCLUSIONS

The juntas in Colombia not only helped to repair social relations after the devastation suffered during the 1950s, but have also persisted to become important civilian organizations in the conflict today. Beyond their immediate role in public goods provision, juntas are also shown to play a role in dampening violence in the armed conflict in Colombia. They signal that variations in characteristics across communities such as the strength of civil society matter for conflict outcomes, even after controlling for variation in armed conflict. Tests of juntas as well as other social organizations in Colombia help refine our understanding about the degrees and characteristics of civilian cooperation that are most helpful for limiting violence. There is also some evidence that the effects of juntas are conditional on and mediated by the intensity of conflict conditions and different types of violence.

This research shows that civilian-based explanations of violence are complements to the macro-actor explanations from the existing literature. The analysis also provides an out of sample test for Kalyvas's preeminent model of violence against civilians. Despite issues of measurement error and incomplete data, these tests show promise for extending the balance of control explanation of violence and measuring it in new ways. However, this explanation for violence in the Colombian context is found to be relatively weak compared to measures of raw levels of armed contention (offensive actions) in an area. More broadly, this chapter contributes a methodological framework for evaluating the impact of civil society initiatives for peace building.

These conclusions also deserve a note of caution. The results are not meant to be an explanation of the various strategies that civilian communities might select to attain autonomy or the impact of specific strategies. These findings can only hint that juntas effectively allow for civilian autonomy of decision-making as a strategy (independence, opting out). Since conciliation councils appear to be widespread in juntas, a plausible interpretation of these results is that juntas keep local conflicts between neighbors from spiraling to reach the macro-armed actors, thus reducing denunciations even in zones where armed groups have incentives for coercive killing. It is also possible that juntas provide a platform for dialogue and negotiations with armed groups. It is plausible, however, that in some areas juntas may be the vehicle through which civilians *ally* with particular macro-armed actors to preserve their communities.[19] Precise junta-based mechanisms are studied more carefully in the case study chapters.

Overall, juntas have shown to be "sticky," persisting over time, implying that such organizations may represent effective interventions for solidifying local stability and order in the longer term. These implications for policy raise an inevitable question – if juntas are so effective, why does not every community already have a strong junta? This question of where juntas arise is closely intertwined with whether their effects are derivative of conflict conditions. The next chapter analyzes the factors that drove the formation and growth of the junta councils. It deals head-on with the possibility that juntas are only passive and largely shaped by the conflict and casts doubt on this as an explanation for the correlations found here.

---

[19] For instance, according to Ramírez (2001), the juntas of coca-growing civilians in some municipios of Putumayo and Cauca seem to have tacitly allied with guerrilla groups and other coca purchasers in the mid-1990s to protest government fumigation of crops, civilian harassment, and violence. Ramírez and Mitchell (2009) also show that these communities later took more autonomous positions.

Appendix

This appendix describes the measurement of variables and statistical tests in this chapter in greater detail.

Additional Information on the Units of Analysis

This study accounts for long historical processes in violence and social capital, meaning some measures of the independent variables are from many years prior to the violence. This creates a concern for specifying the unit of analysis because Colombian political geography changed over the timeframe of study – since 1985 when juntas are measured to the present. In that window, about 10 percent of existing municipios in the sample were split to create new jurisdictions. In 1985, there were 990 municipios. Today, there are nearly 1,100 (DANE 2007). This could be problematic since it could cause indicators measured in 1985 to not correspond with indicators measured later on (e.g., if a measure of juntas is taken in 1985 and the municipio subsequently splits, measurements of homicides, attacks, and even population will be underestimated because they will be attributed in part to the offspring municipio).

I minimize the extent to which changing geography and splits in municipios affect the results by remerging the variable values for "mother" and "daughter" municipios where possible (DANE 2000; slight discrepancies exist between the count of municipios in the census and the administrative data). This is simplest for daughter municipios that were created from only one other municipio since when new municipios are created from multiple municipios, it is nearly impossible to know which daughter characteristics should be attributed to which mother municipio. To address this issue, in some cases I created quasi-mega-municipios that merged values of the connected mothers and daughter(s). I say "quasi" because some of these "mothers" were always separate and never actually existed as conglomerate entities. For these few cases I had to merge municipios that existed in 1985 because they had multiple overlapping splits. The municipios of Bagadó, Tadó, Condoto, Nóvita, Istmina, and Lloró in Chocó and Santa Ana, Plato, Chivolo, Ariguaní, Pivijay, and Fundación in Magdalena and their daughters are each taken as single municipios. As an additional check, I also ran specifications with only those municipios whose boundaries remained intact in the subsequent twenty years.

Additional Information on the Juntas Per Capita Variable

For the data from 1985 to be relevant today, one must assume some amount of path-dependence – that the distribution of juntas in the past is correlated with juntas today. Although using data on juntas that is measured much prior to the dependent variable may entail a trade-off in accuracy of measurement of (correlation with) juntas today, it has advantages for dealing with endogeneity. Data from 1985 is a reasonable compromise for balancing these two goals. Although the absolute count of juntas may differ from other published counts, the measure still likely has relative validity across towns.

Census population counts for certain municipios appeared problematic compared to population censuses from other years and population estimates from the National Planning Department. Because these figures produced extreme outliers for the juntas per capita variable, they were reestimated based on the additional sources. For 1993, population data for Cabrera in Santander and Recetor and Chameza in Casanare were abnormally low and were recoded. For 1985, extreme population data was recoded for Chita, Cienaga, Combita, Chiquiza in Boyacá, Toribío in Cauca, Uribia in Guajira, Fuente de Oro in Meta, Mosquera in Nariño, Charalá in Santander, and Lérida in Tolima. The statistical results remain robust whether these cases are included or excluded from the sample. Because this measure is sensitive to counts of population, I also test additional specifications based on population data from the 1993 census and averages of the 1985 and 1993 censuses. Although the 1985 data may be more accurate because it is contemporaneous with the measurement of juntas, the 1993 census is generally considered more reliable for most other statistics.

Figure 5.7 graphically displays the distribution of juntas by this measure, which is bimodal.

Additional Information on Control Variable Measures

Sanchez's dataset includes the following measures as reflecting offensive initiative by an armed actor: confrontations initiated by the group, ambushes, attacks on installations, terrorist bombings, other terrorist acts, incursions on populations, assaults on private property, roadblocks, harassment, robberies, and illegal roadblocks. The activities plausibly reflect initiative and control through the ability to act freely, although some of the activities are perhaps aimed more at civilians than enemy armed groups (however, incursions,

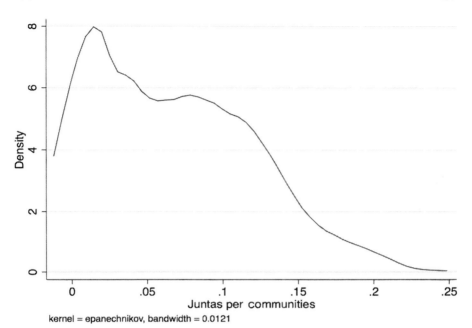

kernel = epanechnikov, bandwidth = 0.0121

FIGURE 5.7 Distribution of juntas in Colombian municipios.

robberies, and roadblocks are relatively few compared to the other categories). Government actions only include attacks.

The measure of total offensive actions *excludes* more blatant activities against civilians such as homicides, political homicides, displacement, massacres, and kidnappings (indices that might reflect the dependent variable of homicides). This measure of balance based on total observed events may be partially endogenous to control to the extent that armed groups use actions to consolidate power. Nevertheless, this does not preclude the measure from being a relative guide for levels of control, for instance, if these attacks can be roughly mapped to Kalyvas's zones of control – that most areas with none to few attacks are completely controlled by a given group (e.g., either the state or the guerrillas), areas with low to moderate attacks exhibit dominant but contested control, and areas with many attacks are the front lines of battle (where indiscriminate violence against civilians may occur but there is little selective violence). These data are validated in an analysis of the relationship between land reform and insurgency by Albertus and Kaplan (2013).

Data on elevation was taken from the 1985 Divipola. Missing data was filled in by the author from geographical information at www.fallingrain.com. Other tests (not shown) use standard deviations of elevation calculated for each municipio to account for variation in rough terrain.

The Carribean Coast dummy includes the departments of Guajira, Cesar, Atlántico, Magdalena, Bolívar, Sucre, and Córdoba; the Pacific Coast dummy includes Chocó, Valle del Cauca, Cauca, and Nariño; the Central Andean dummy includes Antioquia, Caldas, Risaralda, Quindío, Tolima, and Huila; the Eastern Andean dummy includes Norte de Santander, Santander, Boyacá, and Cundinamarca; the Eastern dummy includes Arauca, Casanare, Meta, Caquetá, and Putumayo; the Amazon dummy includes Guainía, Guaviare, Amazonas, Vaupés, and Vichada.

The summary statistics for the dependent and independent variables are displayed in Table 5.1. A comparison among municipios above and below the median level of the Juntas variable helps to highlight some basic relationships among variables. First, consistent with expectations, the high-juntas group suffers a lower mean level of violence than the low-juntas group. Second, some other variables (population, population density, and cooperatives) appear to substantially differ across the groups of municipios, suggesting these are important factors to include in the analysis since they may be associated with both the development of the juntas as well as violence (Table 5.6). Lastly, missing data is not a large concern. For most of the models, 929 of 990 possible cases enter the regression, with only about sixty to seventy cases missing data, or about 7 percent of the sample.

Statistical Results

To test the effect of junta councils on violence I specify a panel regression model with municipio-year data, with some variables varying across time and space and others only varying cross-sectionally (time-invariant). I test GLS models with random effects:

Homicide Rate$_{it}$ = a + BHomicide Rate$_{i,(t-1)}$ BTotalOffense$_{it}$ + BTotalOffenseDummy$_{it}$ + BBalance of Control$_{it}$*BTotalOffenseDummy$_{it}$ + BBalance of Control$^2_{it}$*BTotalOffense-Dummy$_{it}$ + Bz + e

The estimates of the effect of juntas are generally consistent across specifications, including when using robust standard errors and errors clustered by municipio. The effect of juntas is significant after controlling for roads, rivers, mines, oil, socioeconomic status, and population variables. The effect is also robust to removing outliers with high juntas such as Belén de los Andaquies, outliers with high homicides or massacres, only municipios with positive counts of armed group attacks, the department of Antioquia (which may have under-reported junta counts), and for small municipios with populations of less than 30,000. The effect is somewhat sensitive to population estimates used for assessing junta coverage, however. The estimates using 1993 population are less statistically significant although still negative. The effect of juntas is also seen in a propensity-score matching model, where the homicide rate for cases above the median level of juntas is 24 percent lower (Table 5.6).

In additional robustness models, I tested the Juntas variable interacted with year dummy variables as well as muncipio fixed-effects (dummy variables for each municipio). These models are helpful for reducing the influence of possible omitted variables. These tests face limitations, however, given the time-invariant structure of the cross-sectional variables in the models. In some of these tests, the results for the Juntas variable are consistent and exhibit a significant and negative correlation with violence (however, in some specifications the Juntas variable is not significant). Overall, these models provide some additional confirmation of the results, but are not conclusive.

The effect of juntas on violence may be understated. First, the use of a lagged dependent variable of homicides to control for time trends can suppress the coefficient of the Juntas variable if juntas have the effect of reducing homicides in the past as well as in the present. The long-term effect (i.e., the effect of juntas that does not act through the lagged homicide rate) using CINEP data in Table 5.2, Model 4 is represented by a B of -28.17, which is actually 38 percent larger than the short-term effect.[20] In the long run, then, the juntas reduce homicides by up to 20 percent on average.

It is possible that the correlation could be susceptible to alternative interpretations. However unlikely, I examine two possibilities here: mismeasurement and only effects on criminal homicides. First, rather than reflecting the importance of communal organizational processes, it is possible that the juntas variable reflects levels of urbanization, development, state strength or reach, or proximity to cities, which all could reduce violence. This is not likely, however, because much of the variation in state strength should be captured by the geographic and demographic variables of elevation, rivers, population, population density, SES (dirt floors and literacy rate), coca cultivation, and distance to departmental capital.[21] In alternative specifications (not shown), junta results are robust to the inclusion of indicators for state strength for 1995 of the number of police stations in the county seat and locations of military bases, as well as an indicator of government officials per capita.[22]

Second, it is also possible that the observed effect of juntas could just be limiting criminal homicides among neighbors, and not by armed groups (which would not be so terrible). This is difficult to parse with the police homicide data. Even if this were the case, it still could be considered an important effect of juntas since some scholars argue that all civil war violence is, at its root, local. Still, this interpretation is unlikely, since homicides track closely with levels of combat and juntas interact with levels of offensive activity.

---

[20] The long-term effect is calculated using the formula: $B_{x_1}/(1-B_{lagDV})$. If the lagged variable has no effect (B=0) then short-run effect equals the long-run effect. As B of the lag goes to 1, the long-run effect goes to infinity. In Table 5.2, Model 4, $(-20.423/(1-.275)) = -28.17$.

[21] See Fearon and Laitin (2003) for cross-national arguments about state strength and civil war. See Collier and Hoeffler (2004) for arguments about poverty and related grievances.

[22] Only the government officials per capita is statistically significant (and negative) after the other controls are included.

TABLE 5.1 *Summary statistics*

Variable	Observations	Mean	Std. Dev.	Min	Max
Political homicide rate (CINEP)	14,745	9.75	28.18	0	502.74
Total offense (CINEP)	14,995	0.66	1.87	0	49
Total armed actions (1998–2005)	8,040	2.43	6.21	0	134
Police homicide rate (1998–2005)	7,864	67.77	86.14	0	2,034.26
Coca area (ha.; 1998–2005)	8,040	110.10	843.63	0	22,732.4
Number of junta councils	1,005	18.48	21.43	0	187
Juntas per communities	941	0.07	0.06	0	0.48
Pct. minorities	998	0.06	0.19	0	0.99
Cooperatives	1,005	1.99	11.13	0	262
ANUC raids (land invasions)	1,005	0.88	2.87	0	38
Population (1993)	983	33,556.90	182,199.00	584	4,900,000
Log 1993 population	983	9.47	1.06	6.37	15.41
Elevation (m)	993	1,222.86	912.01	0	3,657
Std. dev. elevation	995	340.56	246.37	1.07	1,560.98
Distance to dept. capital	993	121.69	97.85	0	850
Pct. Dirt floors	974	0.23	0.18	0	0.93
Literacy rate	998	0.67	0.15	0	0.87
Population density	998	115.04	480.93	0	10,609.10
La Violencia	983	0.40	0.49	0	1

	N	Mean	SD	Min	Max
Churches	953	4.64	22.94	1	622
Paved road access	961	0.39	0.68	0	1
Polarization	740	0.50	0.36	0	1.00
Land area GINI	857	0.68	0.14	0	0.98
Land value GINI	857	0.66	0.13	0	0.91
Total guerrilla attacks (1985)	994	0.36	1.76	0	39.00
Year municipio founded	1,005	1858	109.28	1525	2002
Villages	725	25.91	19.52	2	207
Patriotic Union	1,005	0.05	0.22	0	1.00
Caribbean region	1,005	0.12	0.32	0	1
Pacific region	1,005	0.15	0.35	0	1
Andean region	1,005	0.25	0.43	0	1
East Andean region	1,005	0.35	0.48	0	1
Eastern region	1,005	0.07	0.26	0	1
Amazon region	1,005	0.03	0.17	0	1

TABLE 5.2 *Models of CINEP political homicide rates, 1990–2005, by municipios*

	(1)	(2)	(3)	(4)
Political homicide rate	0.360**	0.332**	0.324**	0.275**
(1-yr lag CINEP)	(10.82)	(9.56)	(7.23)	(8.64)
Juntas per communities	−20.248**	−12.514*	−16.472*	−20.423**
	(−3.89)	(−2.11)	(−2.15)	(−3.47)
Total offense (CINEP)			4.743**	4.486**
			(9.74)	(11.91)
Total offense^2 (CINEP)			−0.103**	−0.079**
			(−5.79)	(−4.67)
Log 1993 population		−0.062	−2.214**	−2.320**
		(−0.16)	(−4.54)	(−5.66)
Elevation (m)		−0.002**	−0.002**	−0.002**
		(−3.50)	(−2.77)	(−3.10)
Distance to dept. capital		0.004	−0.010**	−0.003
		(1.05)	(−2.58)	(−1.07)
Pct. Dirt floors		3.099^	−1.208	−0.010
		(1.66)	(−0.55)	(−0.01)
Population density		−0.001**	−0.001^	−0.000
		(−2.77)	(−1.70)	(−1.29)
Pct. Minorities			−4.718*	−2.029
			(−2.26)	(−1.23)
La Violencia			−0.770	−0.134
			(−0.94)	(−0.23)
Coca area (ha.)			0.002	
			(0.61)	
Constant	7.383**	8.155^	26.195**	29.173**
	(13.86)	(1.74)	(4.42)	(6.40)
Region effects	Yes	Yes	Yes	Yes
Year effects	Yes	Yes	Yes	Yes
Observations	14,115	13,950	6,503	13,935
R-squared	0.14	0.17	0.26	0.21
Municipios	941	930	929	929

Robust t-statistics in parentheses; Errors clustered by municipio
** $p < 0.01$, * $p < 0.05$, ^ $p < 0.1$

Population density, SES, and regional effects should also be decent controls for crime. More strongly ruling out this interpretation, I find consistent results in additional tests when excising rates of common crime by using CINEP's political violence data.

Discussion of Control Variable Results

A puzzling result is that, after controlling for combat and population density, poverty or income as measured by the percent of residents with dirt floors and literacy rates is associated with decreased homicides in the police data. This subnational finding potentially contradicts Collier and Hoeffler (2004) on their claims about poverty and civil war onset. It is possible that poverty is proxying areas that are less strategically vital to the armed groups (or poorer communities report less to the police). Alternatively, from a collective action point of view, poor populations might rely more on each other and have greater community cohesion or place greater importance on communally provided public goods, even after accounting for the presence of juntas.

An indicator for rough terrain is included because it may reduce the mobility of armed groups and thus combat activity. The elevation variable is negative and significant, suggesting that living in mountainous terrain affords civilians some degree of protection (the standard deviation of elevation is not significant in the CINEP specification). Interestingly, the effect of this variable is robust after controlling for combat variables. This suggests that mountainous terrain could be a proxy for some other explanation that reduces violence. For instance, in Colombia, mountains may be a proxy for state strength since the high-up cooler climates were settled first, with many low-lying zones colonized only recently. It is also possible that mountainous terrain could reflect some amount of social capital among residents, since communities in mountainous areas may be more isolated than their lowland counterparts and so have to rely more on each other (for similar arguments about paved roads in Sierra Leone, see Humphreys and Weinstein 2006b). Alternatively, mountains may alter the way combat unfolds – armed groups may have much more sporadic presence or civilians may be able to hide more easily when combat breaks out.

The presence of oil pipelines in a municipio does not have a statistically significant relationship above and beyond the conflict model, even though oil is known to be a lootable resource in Colombia. The absence of this relationship could be because oil infrastructure has been increasingly secured by the state and multinational corporations (MNCs). The presence of mines (gold and emeralds, for example) has a significant and negative effect on violence. This could be because these areas are also more secured, have labor unions, or involve MNCs.

Estimating the Conditional Effects of Junta Councils

The Juntas variable in interaction with Total Offense has a moderate impact on homicide rates. Since interaction effects can be difficult to interpret, I assess the average marginal effect of juntas on violence conditional on the level of offensive activity graphically in Figure 5.8 (based on Model 6 of Table 5.3). A main question is whether the negative effect of juntas is significantly different from zero for *relevant* values of attacks from the sample data. On average, juntas have a dampening effect on violence conditional on there being about nine or fewer offensive events in a municipio in a given year, although this negative effect can only be distinguished from zero with 95 percent confidence when

TABLE 5.3 *Models of police homicide rates, 1999–2005, by municipios*

	(1)	(2)	(3)	(4)	(5)	(6)
Homicide rate (1–yr lag)	0.367** (33.26)	0.299** (27.37)	0.368** (32.73)	0.297** (26.46)	0.293** (25.97)	0.296** (26.43)
Juntas per communities			14.743 (0.76)	-37.562* (-1.99)	-42.982* (-2.24)	-52.568** (-2.66)
Log 1993 population	0.148 (0.14)	-9.516** (-8.66)	0.106 (0.09)	-10.374** (-8.83)	-10.680** (-8.43)	-10.316** (-8.78)
Population density	-0.001 (-0.57)	0.005* (2.25)	-0.001 (-0.46)	0.005* (2.55)	0.005** (2.62)	0.005** (2.61)
Elevation (m)	-0.008** (-5.76)	-0.008** (-5.54)	-0.008** (-5.43)	-0.006** (-4.54)	-0.006** (-4.52)	-0.006** (-4.62)
Distance to dept. capital	0.009 (0.77)	-0.003 (-0.27)	0.010 (0.86)	-0.006 (-0.57)	-0.000 (-0.04)	-0.007 (-0.60)
Pct. Minorities	-44.279** (-6.31)	-58.818** (-8.71)	-44.669** (-6.29)	-58.220** (-8.41)	-53.228** (-7.51)	-58.443** (-8.45)
Pct. Dirt floors	-46.642** (-7.61)	-62.899** (-10.63)	-46.746** (-7.59)	-59.827** (-10.04)	-58.344** (-9.19)	-59.648** (-10.01)
Total offense		2.520** (14.77)		2.439** (13.91)	2.473** (13.97)	1.917** (7.01)
Offense dummy		23.094** (6.10)		21.806** (5.67)	22.006** (5.68)	22.534** (5.84)
Balance of control		52.154** (3.17)		50.599** (3.03)	50.981** (3.04)	53.605** (3.20)
Balance of control^2		-61.486** (-4.22)		-58.813** (-3.99)	-59.176** (-3.99)	-62.190** (-4.20)

	Model 1	Model 2	Model 3	Model 4	Model 5	Model 6
La Violencia					4.864* (2.35)	5.038* (2.46)
Coca area (ha.)	0.000 (0.27)			0.004** (2.62)	0.006** (3.68)	0.004** (2.65)
Mines					-3.563* (-1.96)	
Oil pipeline					4.675 (1.30)	
River length					-5.604** (-3.14)	
Paved road access					2.292 (0.92)	
Juntas * Total offense						5.715* (2.49)
Year effects	Yes	Yes	Yes	Yes	Yes	Yes
Region effects	Yes	Yes	Yes	Yes	Yes	Yes
R-sq between/ overall	.77/.28	.77/.34	.78/.29	.77/.34	.77/.34	.77/.34
Observations	6,748	6,748	6,510	6,503	6,447	6,503
Municipios	964	964	930	929	921	929

z-statistics in parentheses

** $p < 0.01$, * $p < 0.05$, ^ $p < 0.1$

Model 1: Base model

Model 2: Base model plus conflict variables

Model 3: Base model plus juntas

Model 4: Base model, conflict variables, and juntas

Model 5: Base model, conflict variables, La Violencia, juntas, mines, oil, rivers, and roads

Model 6: Base model, conflict variables, La Violencia, juntas, and juntas interacted with armed actions

TABLE 5.4 *Models of additional organizations, 1990–2005, by municipios*

	(1) CINEP homicide rate	(2) CINEP homicide rate	(3) CINEP homicide rate	(4) CINEP homicide rate	(5) CINEP homicide rate
Political homicide rate (1-yr lag CINEP)	0.274** (8.65)	0.268** (8.10)	0.232** (5.98)	0.212** (5.65)	0.263** (6.84)
Juntas per communities	−19.930** (−3.37)	−21.320** (−3.56)	1.992 (0.36)		−24.166** (−3.52)
Pct. Minorities	−2.057 (−1.25)	−1.418 (−0.81)	−2.136 (−1.27)	−2.276 (−1.33)	0.163 (0.08)
Cooperatives	−0.042** (−3.12)	0.312^ (1.82)			
ANUC land invasions	−0.011 (−0.12)	−0.030 (−0.25)			
Total offense (CINEP)	4.487** (11.88)	4.634** (9.81)	3.728** (10.48)	3.772** (10.92)	4.055** (11.36)
Total offense² (CINEP)	−0.077** (−4.60)	−0.073* (−2.33)	−0.065* (−2.19)	−0.062* (−2.09)	−0.075** (−4.62)
Log 1993 population	−2.158** (−4.93)	−2.268** (−3.80)	−1.227** (−2.93)	−1.483** (−3.66)	−2.090** (−5.35)
Elevation (m)	−0.002** (−3.10)	−0.001** (−2.76)	−0.002** (−3.82)	−0.002** (−4.01)	−0.001* (−2.40)
Distance to dept. capital	−0.003 (−1.13)	−0.005^ (−1.66)	−0.004 (−1.33)	−0.005 (−1.46)	−0.002 (−0.54)
Pct. Dirt floors	0.016 (0.01)	−0.083 (−0.05)	−0.993 (−0.56)	−1.304 (−0.75)	0.941 (0.53)

Population density	-0.007*	-0.001*	-0.001^	-0.000
	(-2.15)	(-2.09)	(-1.79)	(-1.34)
La Violencia	-0.056	0.070	0.175	0.035
	(-0.09)	(0.13)	(0.30)	(0.06)
Land value GINI		1.901	1.019	
		(0.60)	(0.31)	
Land area GINI		0.220	1.339	
		(0.07)	(0.40)	
Polarization				0.247
				(0.24)
Constant	29.121**	19.331**	22.251**	26.042**
	(4.99)	(4.14)	(4.87)	(6.12)
Year effects	Yes	Yes	Yes	Yes
Region effects	Yes	Yes	Yes	Yes
Observations	12,840	12,195	12,600	10,890
Municipios	856	813	840	726
R-squared	0.219	0.167	0.152	0.216

t-statistics in parentheses; Errors clustered by municipio

** p < 0.01, * p < 0.05, ^ p < 0.1

Model 1,3,4,5: All municipios

Model 2: Rural municipios (>20 km from Department Capital)

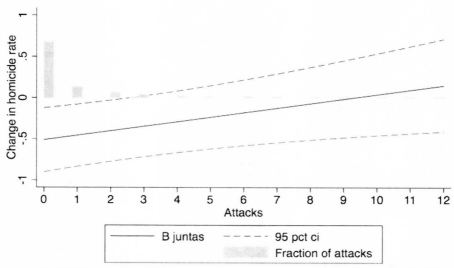

Effect of a 1 percentage point increase in junta coverage (0,48); Mean homicide rate is 68/100,000

FIGURE 5.8 The conditional effect of juntas on the homicide rate by levels of conflict

there are two or fewer attacks. Conditional on there being nine or fewer attacks, the average marginal effect of a percent increase in junta coverage on violence ranges from reductions of –0.53 (at zero) to –0.02 (at nine). Even at two attacks (B = –0.41) this is a nontrivial percent change relative to the mean homicide rate, as discussed earlier.

Since the effect of juntas is conditional, it is possible that juntas may have different effects at different levels of armed conflict. For levels of attacks greater than 2.8 but less than about 41, the conditional effect of juntas is not statistically significant because zero is within both of the upper and lower bounds of the confidence intervals (for this range of attacks it cannot be distinguished from zero). When there are 41 or more attacks, the mean conditional effect of juntas flips positive suggesting that juntas are no longer effective at providing protection at such a high level of attacks and actually increase violence. But what is the substantive importance of this result in relation to the actual distribution of attacks across cases? How prevalent are these different effects? The long tail of the distribution of attacks indicates that the positive effect of juntas on violence only holds for less than 1 percent of the sample with a high severity of armed conflict. It is not theoretically obvious why juntas might be measured as increasing violence at extremely high levels of contestation.

The distribution of attacks speaks to the substantive importance of the conditional effect of juntas. It has a long tail, with most municipios suffering few (registered) attacks per year. Approximately 55 percent of the municipio-year cases had zero attacks, about 15 percent had one attack, 8 percent had two

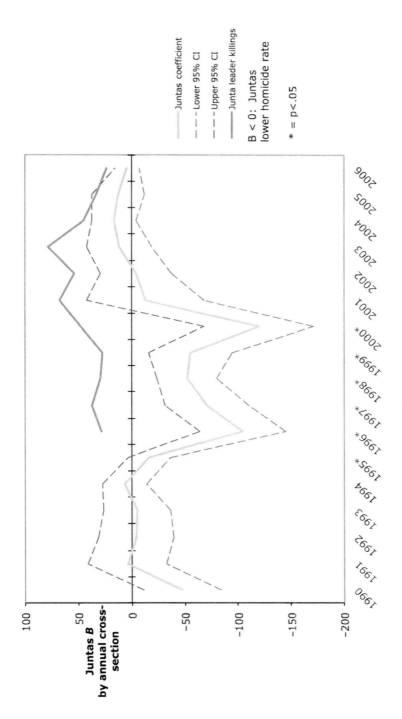

Legend:
——— Juntas coefficient
– – – Lower 95% CI
–·–·– Upper 95% CI
——— Junta leader killings

B < 0: Juntas
lower homicide rate

* = p<.05

Year

Juntas *B*
by annual cross-
section

Source: CINEP political homicide
data and authors' calculations

FIGURE 5.9 The effect of juntas on violence over time

TABLE 5.5 *Models of killings according to armed group perpetrators*

	(1) Paramilitary homicide rate (CINEP)	(2) FARC homicide rate (CINEP)	(3) Paramilitary homicide rate (CINEP)	(4) Homicide rate (CINEP)	(5) Homicide rate (CINEP)
Political homicide rate (1-yr lagged DV)	0.217** (7.55)	0.157** (4.59)	0.218** (7.61)	0.279** (8.86)	0.269** (8.24)
Juntas per communities	−21.737** (−6.03)	−0.814 (−0.59)	−17.785** (−5.41)	−16.308* (−2.48)	−15.956** (−2.86)
Pct. Minorities	0.052 (0.04)	0.911* (2.57)	0.332 (0.24)	−2.044 (−1.25)	−2.436 (−1.54)
Cooperatives				−0.041** (−3.05)	−0.043** (−2.76)
ANUC land invasions				−0.010 (−0.12)	−0.016 (−0.18)
Total offense (CINEP)	1.966** (7.36)	0.461** (5.03)	1.675** (4.08)	4.477** (11.74)	4.388** (11.83)
Total offense^2 (CINEP)	−0.038** (−4.48)	−0.003 (−0.52)		−0.079** (−4.62)	−0.076** (−4.82)
Log 1993 population	−1.376** (−5.77)	−0.265** (−3.57)	−1.230** (−5.34)	−2.147** (−4.93)	−2.246** (−5.13)
Elevation (m)	−0.001* (−2.35)	−0.000 (−1.42)	−0.001* (−2.22)	−0.002** (−3.10)	−0.001** (−2.66)
Distance to dept. capital	0.000 (0.21)	−0.000 (−0.14)	0.000 (0.23)	−0.003 (−1.13)	−0.004 (−1.45)

	(1)	(2)	(3)	(4)	(5)
Pct. Dirt floors	0.575	1.177**	0.605	0.011	-0.562
	(0.53)	(3.38)	(0.55)	(0.01)	(-0.35)
Population density	-0.000^	-0.000	-0.000^	-0.000	-0.000
	(-1.68)	(-1.38)	(-1.74)	(-0.48)	(-0.53)
La Violencia	-0.289	0.153	-0.205	-0.192	-0.157
	(-0.75)	(1.20)	(-0.53)	(-0.33)	(-0.27)
Juntas * Total offense			-251.676		
			(-1.45)		
Post-1997				2.252**	
				(3.33)	
Juntas * Post-1997				-6.543	
				(-0.90)	
Patriotic Union					10.907**
					(3.18)
Juntas * Patriotic Union					-94.363**
					(-2.72)
Year effects	Yes	Yes	Yes	No	Yes
Region effects	Yes	Yes	Yes	Yes	Yes
Observations	13,935	13,935	13,920	13,935	13,935
Municipios	929	929	928	929	929
R-squared	0.12	0.08	0.12	0.20	0.22

t-statistics in parentheses; Errors clustered by municipio

** p < 0.001, ** p < 0.01, * p < 0.05, ^ p < 0.1

TABLE 5.6 *A matching model of the effect of juntas*

	(1) Probit Juntas per communities
Political homicide rate	−0.003**
(1-yr lag CINEP)	(−6.64)
Pct. Minorities	−0.479**
	(−4.95)
Cooperatives	0.027**
	(2.66)
ANUC land invasions	0.023**
	(4.14)
Churches	−0.088**
	(−11.99)
Total offense (CINEP)	0.034**
	(2.64)
Total offense^2 (CINEP)	−0.001
	(−0.79)
Log 1993 population	−0.205**
	(−9.15)
Elevation (m)	−0.000^
	(−1.75)
Distance to dept. capital	−0.001**
	(−7.43)
Pct. Dirt floors	0.327**
	(3.56)
Population density	−0.005**
	(−18.97)
La Violencia	0.113**
	(3.84)
Region effects	Yes
Year effects	No
Pseudo R-squared	0.31
Municipios	899
Observations	13,485

z-statistics in parentheses; Juntas is split at the median of 0.062
** $p < 0.01$, * $p < 0.05$, ^ $p < 0.1$

PANEL B *Average treatment effect of junta councils on CINEP homicide rates*

Variable sample	Treated	Controls	Diff	T-stat
Unmatched	7.52	11.72	−4.20**	−8.84
CINEP Homicide ATT	7.52	9.83	−2.31**	−3.25

TABLE 5.7 *Pair-wise correlations of conflict variables and juntas*

	Juntas per communities	CINEP Hom Rt.	CINEP total attacks	CINEP Guerrilla	CINEP Para-military	CINEP Gov't	Police Hom Rt.	Total attacks	Guerrilla	Para-military	Gov't
Juntas per communities	1.00										
CINEP Hom Rt.	-0.06	1.00									
CINEP total attacks	-0.03	0.29	1.00								
CINEP Guerrilla	-0.04	0.19	0.73	1.00							
CINEP Paramilitary	-0.06	0.23	0.47	0.39	1.00						
CINEP Government	-0.02	0.26	0.94	0.49	0.24	1.00					
Police Hom Rt.	0.01	0.43	0.28	0.16	0.16	0.27	1.00				
Total attacks	0.00	0.24	0.69	0.45	0.26	0.69	0.34	1.00			
Guerrilla	0.02	0.22	0.57	0.41	0.20	0.55	0.28	0.91	1.00		
Paramilitary	-0.04	0.12	0.22	0.20	0.29	0.15	0.14	0.41	0.23	1.00	
Government	-0.01	0.20	0.69	0.38	0.20	0.73	0.32	0.86	0.61	0.23	1.00

attacks, 6 percent had three attacks, etc. Only about 7 percent of municipio-years suffered ten or more attacks. So, in about 80 percent of the sample (51 percent of the sample suffering at least some armed activity), the juntas decrease violence to some degree (with 95 confidence). Figure 7.1 of attacks (CINEP) for the ATCC profiled in Chapter 7 and the Cundinamarca towns in Chapter 8 (Figure 6.4) show they suffered this level of low to moderate intensity for most of the 1990s and 2000s, with a few years registering extremely intense fighting. Other parts of the country, such as zones in the departments of Arauca and Casanare and the Urabá region, were heavily contested by armed groups and suffered many more attacks.

6

Why Some Communities Are More Organized than Others

> "Community organization in Nariño (Antioquia) is pretty weak ... Altruistic solidarity is scarce for collective needs like the construction of roads, schools, and health centers ... the juntas are greatly decayed."
>
> – Henao Delgado and Arcila Estrada (1993, translated)

> "Jericó (Antioquia) ... sprung up in the 1850s and its founding fathers were picky. They didn't allow miners, cowboys and roughnecks to take up residence and allowed in only those considered decent, God-fearing people. Missionaries built convents and schools. The town is now home to four museums ... a library, a cultural center, a botanical garden."
>
> – Otis (2010)

The previous chapter showed that different levels and forms of social organization can reduce levels of civil war violence suffered by civilians. Intertwined with this relationship are the questions of where social organizations come from and where they are likely to arise. This chapter addresses these questions and does so for three main reasons. First, knowing where social organizations arise in a developing country is itself an interesting question, with implications for social and economic development. I find that geographic, demographic, and social factors all play roles in the formation and spread of local junta councils (qualitatively, I also consider promotion efforts by government personnel and private actors).

Second, understanding the causes of juntas helps deal with the threat to valid inference of reverse causality – that junta councils might only exist and survive in historically peaceful places. Introducing the indicator of the violence suffered during the La Violencia conflict of the 1950s shows that juntas were actually more likely to be formed later in the 1960s and 1970s in areas that suffered relatively more violence in the prior conflict, easing concerns of spurious correlation. These statistical tests along with a close reading of Colombian history between the period of La Violencia and when juntas are measured – both up to 1960 and from the 1960–1985 interim period – show that conflict conditions were low and relatively stable through most of the country. The tendency for juntas to be formed in historically conflicted areas was therefore not likely disrupted during this period.

Third, with a better understanding of junta origins I am also able to unite the statistical analysis with the case studies to better rule out confounding explanations. An ideal research design to study this question would be an experiment that randomly assigns juntas to communities. While we cannot go back in time and rerun the history of junta formation, the statistical techniques in this chapter can be used as a tool to simulate these experimental conditions by more precisely matching sets of towns with similar *likelihoods* of having juntas (treatment) but that in reality developed quite different patterns of social organization. I elaborate on this method of case selection and argue that it can be an appealing option for researchers in the field of political science when facing constraints such as time, safety, or resources that preclude the use of other methods such as random case selection.

After outlining this method I apply it to select a set of towns for qualitative study of social organizations, civilian autonomy strategies, and violence. To preview this method, I statistically match towns on observable indicators and then select neighbor towns with similar conflict histories to help minimize issues with unobserved variables. I arrive at sets of towns in case study sites in the departments of Cundinamarca and Caldas (discussed in Chapter 8). Given the dangers of fieldwork in a country like Colombia that is still experiencing conflict, the case selection techniques balance representativeness with safety and help assure that the research findings are not vulnerable to unmeasured global factors that might affect all these towns similarly.

EXPLAINING THE FORMATION OF JUNTA COUNCILS

If juntas as an organizational form seem to correlate with reduced violence, a natural question to ask next is why some communities decide to organize juntas and others do not? This section tests various social and structural explanations for variation in juntas per capita across municipios. As noted previously, while juntas are sometimes encouraged by actors external to the community, they are most frequently the creations of the communities themselves. Juntas are often the product of networking in the absence of state provision of services. They should therefore be found to arise in areas with strong social relations and social capital (of course, effective juntas are also an *indicator* of cohesion). Variation in political geography and demographics can be crucial determinants of these intracommunity relations, as can shortages of and demand for public goods.

A municipio's population is a strong determinant of its coverage of juntas. Less populated municipios are much more likely to have more juntas per capita than more populated municipios (population density has minimal impact once population is controlled for; see chapter Appendix). The number of villages in a municipio from the 1960 agricultural census (DANE 1962) also strongly and significantly predicts a larger number of juntas. This could indicate the possible number of communities that could form juntas.

Geographically, there is a fairly strong relationship ($p < 0.1$) that municipios that are closer to department capitals are slightly more likely to have more juntas per capita. Juntas tend to be more prevalent in municipios in the Eastern region followed by the East Andean region. An indicator of rough terrain (standard deviation of elevation) is similarly significant, reflecting zones where settlements are more broken-up. Surprisingly, whether or not there is paved road access to a municipio is not a significant determinant of juntas once these other factors are controlled, even though isolation might create greater demands for community self-reliance.

The results for indicators for poverty and socioeconomic status (percent of households with dirt floors; literacy rate) suggest that *poorer* communities (in 1993) tend to have a greater density of juntas (although juntas may have affected economic growth). This speaks for a needs-based, demand-driven explanation of junta formation. Wealthy communities likely have more private goods or get public goods more easily from the state.

A variety of indicators of civil society strength are also strong predictors of juntas. The number of churches in a municipio's county seat (Catholic or other denominations, Sarmiento Anzola 1998) is associated with increased coverage of juntas. Consistent with the characterization of Jericó, churches may provide an important form of technical assistance for community organizing, a curious contradiction with the World Values Survey finding that Catholic countries have relatively lower levels of social capital. A measure of cooperatives is not significantly correlated with juntas. The percentage of the population of minority groups is also not significantly associated with juntas even though the presence of minority populations may suppress the number of juntas. This could be because, rather than organizing through juntas, Indigenous and Afro-Colombian communities have their own organizational structures, such as *cabildos* or *consejos comunitarios*, which are not counted as juntas.

I also test the impact of land (in)equality on junta formation. Inequality of land values (in 1985) significantly reduces the likelihood of having juntas – they are more prevalent in more equal municipios.[1] This equality finding could reflect greater cooperation because of shared socioeconomic preferences; closer proximity of farms, which aids networking; or that clusters of small minifundios have greater needs for public goods. As I find in tests of violence in

---

[1] The results on polarization, villages, and inequality should be taken with caution since more cases are missing data on these variables.

Chapter 5, the effects of juntas on violence are dampened by inequality but are also more robust than inequality and more strongly associated with levels of violence.

As a check of whether the juntas are more prevalent in areas with preexisting cooperation, I attempt to account for the amount of political unity or discord across municipios immediately after La Violencia when the first juntas were being formed. I again use the indicator of the political polarization (Polarization) in the vote for the 1962 presidential election in the National Front government. I also test the percentage of Liberal votes as a measure of polarization, possibly reflecting holdouts who did not support the National Front (not shown). I find that polarization is significant and negatively associated with juntas, indicating that less polarized (more cooperative?) places went on to form more juntas (although polarization may be overpowered by inequality). Again, as noted in Chapter 5, junta effects remain significant when controlling for prior political polarization (a possible form of social cohesion) as well.

In sum, both social and structural factors predict the formation of local councils in Colombia. In the next section, I elaborate on the relationship between La Violencia and juntas.

THE ROLE OF LA VIOLENCIA AND REVERSE CAUSALITY

Instead of juntas explaining violence, it could be that juntas are endogenous to – shaped by – conflict patterns and are merely an indicator of histories of low violence. To attempt to minimize this possibility, I use a measure of juntas that was taken in 1985, five to ten years prior to the episodes of violence being studied. This should effectively rule out the possibility of a contemporaneous reverse causal relationship: the past distribution of juntas should be highly correlated with the current distribution of juntas, but it should be impossible that violence after 1990 affected the distribution of juntas in 1985 (and violence spread to new areas during this time). However, even with the large time lag between the measures of juntas and violence, the path-dependent nature of both these variables (suggested by both the quantitative and comparative historical analysis) could still potentially bias these results.

The argument goes like this: violence is correlated over time, so violent areas tend to stay violent and peaceful areas stay peaceful; high historical violence (or combat, which act like omitted variables) destroys social relations over time so that juntas only survive in historically peaceful areas; these same areas with juntas are then observed in the future to be relatively more peaceful than their counterparts without juntas for some unobservable reason having nothing to do with the autonomy mechanisms of juntas.[2] In short, historical violence

---

[2] It is also conceivable that juntas could survive in combative areas, but not play an important combat-related role. For example, they may just provide public goods, in which case, even if many juntas exist in combative areas, there would be no observable effect on violence.

might affect both the distribution of juntas observed in the 1985 data as well as subsequent violence, causing the true effect of juntas on violence to be spurious and overestimated. Juntas would then *reflect* peaceful conditions, rather than bring such conditions about.

The severity of this issue depends on how one thinks violence might affect the formation and survival of juntas. If one believes that a history of violence *impedes* the formation or survival of social capital and therefore of juntas, the observed beneficial effect of juntas might be a byproduct of peace (epiphenomenal). This would suggest a reciprocal relationship where low social capital leads to violence, which leads to low social capital, etc. Alternatively, if a history of violence *stimulates* social cooperation in some places – for instance, through necessity or government intervention – and violence is then tamped down, it would lend support to the explanation that juntas are indeed independently benevolent. So, for juntas to be at least partially *exogenous* to the conflict, they must have formed and persisted as much if not more in historically conflictive areas as in peaceful areas prior to the more recent era of conflict (for which they are theorized to causally impact).

To get a true understanding of the impact of juntas, prior violence must be taken into account. I review two episodes of twentieth-century Colombian history to better understand how violence may have affected the process of junta formation and civilian social capital: La Violencia of the 1950s and the subsequent years through 1985, when the juntas are measured. A careful reading suggests that a reverse causal relationship in a (negative) direction that would bias against the junta results is unlikely. First, there is evidence that La Violencia, in addition to reflecting a propensity for violence, increased community cohesion and stimulated the creation of juntas. Second, I find there was relatively little civil war activity that would affect juntas from 1960–1985. Third, I find that conditions that promoted social networking in the absence of the state were important stimuli for the creation of juntas.

La Violencia and the Distribution of Juntas

There is no question that La Violencia was one of the most devastating conflicts in Latin America in the twentieth century. What is less clear is its impact on social relations in Colombia. It is true that many communities were torn apart and there were migrations from the countryside to cities, implying a negative relationship between violence and community cohesion. However, there are other reasons to believe the relationship is positive and, in fact, the historical record favors this account. Information on La Violencia can account for part of the distribution of juntas because the government encouraged juntas to pacify ravaged areas and because some aspects of the violence itself engendered community cohesion.

To statistically measure an area's historical "propensity" for violence and test whether this affects junta formation, I again use the dummy variables

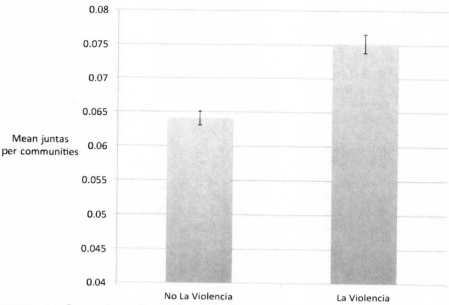

FIGURE 6.1 Comparison of La Violencia and junta coverage

coded based on Guzmán et al. (1963) and Roldán (2002) that are discussed
in Chapter 5. A simple comparison of towns with "high" and "low" junta
coverages in Figure 6.1 shows that juntas are slightly more common in La
Violencia areas. Similarly, the La Violencia variable is significant and positive in
the OLS juntas selection models that predict the distribution of juntas across
municipios. This suggests that places that suffered violence in the 1950s were
actually more likely to have formed juntas that persisted through 1985, not less
($p < .05$). Experiencing La Violencia on average translates into about 1 percent
more juntas per "communities." Only when inequality is included in the
specification does La Violencia no longer significantly predict juntas (though
it retains a positive relationship). This suggests that inequality likely contributed to La Violencia.

An examination of department-level data on the distribution of juntas shows
similar trends. In the early 1960s, juntas were *no less prevalent* in La Violencia
areas ($r = 0.01$) and this distribution of juntas is associated with the juntas
measured in 1985 ($r = 0.69$; calculated based on Ministry of Government
data in Edel 1969). I also find positive correlations between where the
early government promoters were assigned, whether a town experienced La
Violencia, and levels of juntas in 1985. These findings fit with the historical
evidence that juntas were encouraged in areas that had seen significant violence (Bagley and Edel 1980). This finding also argues against the possible

spuriousness of the earlier results that juntas reduce violence and is consistent with considering juntas a policy "treatment."

The perspective that La Violencia increased community organization actually appears fairly consistently within the sparse existing literature. In perhaps the only prior econometric study of juntas, Edel (1971) sampled ninety-six communities with juntas to understand variation in the implementation of community development projects. Contrary to his expectation, Edel found that residents of communities in the sample afflicted by La Violencia actually made *greater* investments in community goods with community-contributed funds (which he views as an indicator of community "effort") during his 1964–1965 time frame.[3] Elsewhere, Edel suggests that not only did communal action occur in areas with legacies of violence, but that it was also beneficial. He claims the reunification of feuding populations around community projects and the isolation of unpopular bandit leaders were frequent results of community development (Edel 1969, 42).

Other sociological reports of the era corroborate several possible reasons why La Violencia may not have been as detrimental for social cooperation as might be expected. For instance, Torres (1963) argues that communal responses to banditry engendered community solidarity where neighbors banded together to defend themselves.[4] Similarly, Guzmán et al. (1963 Vol. 2, 423) observe that community action actually helped to end violence in many areas. Torres also suggests that the violence and guerrilla movements of this time led to a greater desire for economic development and increased people's expectations for upward mobility when peace was restored, which could have increased the appeal of juntas as a solution. These explanations speak to the robustness of the violence-reducing effect of juntas and are also consistent with civilian autonomy theory as an effective *response* to conflict and violence – just as much yesterday as today.

Assessing Armed Conflict from 1960–1985

The period between the beginning of the juntas program in 1960 and the measurement of juntas taken in 1985 was a relatively tranquil period in Colombia's recent history, with a lull in violence (see the homicide rate time series graphed in Figure 3.1). It is therefore unlikely that conflict in this time period affected the subsequent distribution of juntas across Colombian municipios in a prejudicial way. According to Zamosc, the resolution of La Violencia of the 1950s was fairly abrupt: "After 1953 the disturbances

---

[3] However, Edel does not find that the government invested more or was likely to have more promoter staffers in La Violencia areas (in contrast with the correlation I find), though Edel's cases are not a random sample.

[4] Camilo Torres Restrepo was a priest, sociologist, and founding member of the ELN. He became an early martyr of that group.

receded to marginal mountainous areas. This created conditions for a rapid normalization" (Zamosc 2001, 107–108).[5]

The ELN and FARC rebel groups formed in the 1960s, but their activities remained sporadic, limited, and contained by the armed forces. As Zamosc continues, these insurgents faced difficult beginnings, "The guerrillas ... in the hills were unable to recruit for what the peasants seemed to regard as a useless continuation of violence" (Zamosc 2001, 112). The army also routed the communist holdouts known as the Independent Republics in 1964–1965 (in Tolima and Huila departments; Ruhl 1980). According to Ruhl's characterization, the 1970s were relatively calm in terms of guerrilla activity, "By the early 1970s, the army had reduced the guerrillas to more of a nuisance than a serious concern ... Colombian newspapers were praising the armed forces 'final' eradication of the guerrillas" (Ruhl 1980).[6]

The historical record indeed confirms the sporadic presence of guerrilla groups through the 1970s and into the 1980s (see the growth of guerilla fronts in Figure 3.2). The ELN only had three fronts through 1980 (Echandía 1999). The FARC was formed in 1966 but only registered activity in ten municipios (fronts) until a broader expansion as a "people's army" in the early 1980s (Echandía 1999). Furthermore, early paramilitary groups such as MAS (Death to Kidnappers) only formed in 1983 in Puerto Boyacá and had only sporadic influence until the late 1980s. Drug cartels, such as the Medellín Cartel led by Pablo Escobar, also did not greatly expand until the cocaine boom of the mid-1980s. By this time, statistics show that 30,007 juntas had already been created (Ministerio de Gobierno 1993).[7]

Finally, the historical record also shows that the conflict greatly expanded over time from the mid-1980s and onward. Figure 3.2 shows that both the number of guerrilla fronts and the national homicide rate have increased since the 1960s, but these trends really first accelerated in the 1980s. Furthermore, in 1985, the presence of guerrillas was still quite sparse compared to the subsequent growth in activity that would occur over the following two decades. According to data in Echandía (1999), in 1985 only 173 municipios registered guerrilla presence and only 123 had "active" guerrilla presence from 1987–1989, affecting around 15 percent of the country. In contrast, data from 1995 shows 622 municipios had guerrilla presence and 190 had active presence, affecting 20–60 percent of the country (from 1993–1995). This suggests that there were many places that were equally peaceful when the juntas measure was

---

[5] For instance, while there was still some guerilla violence in the early 1960s, Ortiz shows that there were 16,000–18,000 deaths between 1958 and 1965, but that by 1963, violence greatly receded.

[6] This is not to deny that certain parts of Colombia did indeed continue to experience armed conflict, just that it became far less common. For data on events of army "repression" during this period, see Torres and Barrera 1982.

[7] Regression analysis also shows that 1985 data on the distribution of insurgent activity by municipio does not correlate with juntas.

taken and that, where juntas were prevalent, they went on to reduce violence in some of the areas that were later touched by the expansion of the conflict.

This discussion casts doubt on the possibility that the legacy of La Violencia and any post-La Violencia violence significantly affected the distribution of juntas in a way that would raise the specter of biased results due to reverse causality. Colombian history is actually fairly consistent with my theory. Even today, anecdotal evidence suggests that, in certain areas, violence has been the impetus behind many of the social movements to protect human rights.

SELECTING CASES UNDER CONSTRAINTS IN MULTIMETHOD PROJECTS

The statistical analysis of the drivers of juntas was used to choose cases for qualitative study. I outline a new set of procedures to select cases for qualitative analysis in multimethod research projects when flexibility or quantity in choosing cases is constrained. The constraints could include researcher time or resources, safety, missing information, or other factors that commonly crop up in the field of comparative politics and preclude large qualitative samples, randomized selection, or gaining more detailed information on certain cases. The method should be especially useful for the increasing trend of multimethod subnational research designs that involve fieldwork and many potential cases from which to choose (it could similarly be helpful for systematically incomplete archives). This method proves useful here for selecting municipio-cases in Colombia for qualitative study to test the relationships between social organizations and levels of violence in a civil war/post-civil war context where selection is constrained by safety and resource considerations. In the end, I used the model to select six additional towns from two case study areas, which are profiled later in this chapter.[8]

Regardless of the various goals of case-study research, as Geddes (2003) discusses in her chapter entitled "How the cases you choose affect the answers you get," a clear rationale for selecting cases is crucial for minimizing selection bias. Case selection that is based on a statistical (large-n) model of relationships and unit characteristics helps resolve this problem by providing insight about where particular cases lie among the entire universe of cases on observable traits. Fearon and Laitin (2008) call for randomized case selection to minimize researcher bias from selecting cases with which they are already familiar and increase representativeness. This helps limit omitted variable bias but requires the ability to potentially study any case in the sample and cull a large number of

---

[8] I originally selected two additional towns to study in the western department of Caldas, Pensilvania and Samaná, as well as the neighboring town of Nariño in Antioquia. Insights from fieldwork I conducted in Pensilvania are consistent with civilian autonomy theory, but I was not able to conduct similar research in the other towns. These comparisons are therefore not included in this study.

The town of Pensilvania, Caldas, Colombia, 2009. During field visits it was observed that villages in the surrounding countryside exhibited similar patterns of juntas de acción comunal advocating for civilian autonomy to towns in Cundinamarca and other parts of the country. Photograph by Oliver Kaplan.

qualitative cases to achieve representativeness. Lieberman (2005) calls for "nesting" cases within large-n models by selecting cases on the regression line that have wide variation in the independent variable of interest. This strategy allows the researcher greater flexibility and takes into account observed differences between cases but does not mitigate unobserved heterogeneity not measured in the large-n analysis.

The method I outline here aims to balance latitude in selecting nested cases, as may be required by circumstances, with representativeness. Further, it aims to provide guidance in making smart choices given the sometimes overwhelming number of possible cases for study when researchers may not have clear *a priori* impressions of where they lie within distributions of potentially confounding or unmeasured variables. Multimethod projects involving field research components in conflict settings can especially benefit from this method. There are often obvious limitations of safety, costs, or difficulties to traveling to certain regions in the midst of conflicts. Even post-conflict situations can be dangerous, as security situations can change rapidly and be difficult to assess.

It is almost impossible to avoid the critique that any safe place for the researcher risks selection problems and is therefore not likely representative of all cases. But with this method, at least within the realm of "safe" sites, the researcher can have increased confidence that conflict intensity is controlled for and that cases are similar. The method's transparency helps readers make their own assessments of the severity of this issue. This method could therefore be called the method of "living to tell about it," since it allows for safety but also helps assure that the "it" – the story and information collected – will be worthwhile, with representativeness and inferential value.

The main challenge, then, is how to minimize both observed and unobserved heterogeneity biases. Using propensity-score matching techniques with a bivariate dependent variable or picking cases on the regression line can help deal with matching on observable characteristics (Seawright and Gerring 2008). To set up a quasi-experiment, the next step is to choose cases among those with similar propensities for independent variable "treatment" so as to maximize variation on the independent variable(s) of interest (in an Ordinary Least Squares regression framework, this entails minimizing the residuals while maximizing the dispersion on the independent variable; Lieberman 2005). The statistical techniques are really shortcuts that help deal with the complexity of a multidimensional (multivariate) problem of assignment to the "treated" group. It is therefore also helpful to compare the actual variable values across the pool of matched cases to see how closely they each correspond and ensure that great discrepancies in certain *observable* factors are not overwhelmingly driving differences in propensities (since these too could ultimately be correlated with the dependent variable of interest).[9]

Still, there can remain the problem of unobserved bias or global (nonregion specific) explanations for an observed correlation between the independent and dependent variable.[10] Traditionally, omitted variable bias is addressed in inferential sciences in three principal ways: (1) measuring variables (so they are no longer omitted), (2) randomization (so that omitted variables are orthogonal to treatment), or (3) assumptions about how cases can be matched on unobserved variables. When researchers reach the case selection stage of a project they have usually already collected all the large-n measures that are available or thought to be relevant. If they then face a (security) constraint on the number or types of cases they might access, randomized selection may become impractical. At that

---

[9] This procedure has limitations for matching since the calculated propensities are additive combinations of variables that allow for greater differences on some variables to be offset by similarities on others. Exact matching on certain variables is one solution. This matching technique may better stand on its own for large-n statistical use than picking particular cases where the precise values of a particular variable can matter a great deal. Balance tests can be useful for identifying whether, overall, treatment and control were assigned as-if randomly to their respective groups by sharing similar values on covariates.

[10] Since there is matching within the region, these are global factors that might cause the selection of the matched region itself to not be representative of the larger universe of cases.

point, assumptions about unobserved similarities – how cases fit within a given strata of a variable of interest – can be employed to further reduce bias.

A useful assumption is Tobler's first law of spatial analysis, which states that, "Everything is related to everything else, but near things are more related than distant things" (Tobler 1970).[11] Applying this law would call for the researcher to select proximate or neighbor cases. Of course, a researcher might equally apply a different "law" that could provide guidance on how characteristics of units are generally related or stratified.[12] Selecting matching neighbors on the geographic dimension should also have the added advantage for the field researcher of making it easier to transit from one site to another if there is access between them (roads, paths, waterways, etc.).[13] For increased representativeness, *clusters* of pairs of matched cases should vary on the geographic dimension as well, drawing from diverse regions. The researcher may then apply other considerations based on constraints as necessary, such as safety, distance to travel, available case histories, etc., or to stratify or match on additional post-"treatment" (or secondary treatment) variables that do not belong in a selection equation.

The development and application of this method for case selection sets this study apart from prior micro studies on civil war. Few if any studies have selected cases rigorously and transparently to deal with problems of reverse causality or omitted variable bias. Lacking transparency and theoretically grounded procedures, it can be difficult to have a solid *a priori* understanding of the representativeness of the cases chosen by an analyst. Wood's (2003) insightful study of civil war in El Salvador does not use quantitative methods and selects what she deems "typical cases" that also meet the criteria of safety, military contestation, political tractability, and variation in agro-economies. Without a large-n component, however, it is hard for readers to evaluate whether the villages in her comparison set are useful contrasts or are truly representative of all villages and therefore assess tests of her theory. The case selection therefore renders the analysis more useful as a theory-building exercise (she originally began with a different research question but then shifted to studying civilian participation upon visiting her sites). Kalyvas's (2006) book discusses what he deems to be "representative" towns from the Argolid region of Greece. Through the wide-ranging interviews upon which some of his

---

[11] The neighbor criterion could also be incorporated into the regression framework, either through contiguity indicators or latitude and longitude for closeness. Technically, this geographic assumption requires the additional assumption that the likelihood of encountering different neighbors on the independent variable is orthogonal to the dependent variable. In this application, it means that towns with differences in juntas do not happen to cluster together for some reason that is also correlated with violence.

[12] E.g., perhaps a temporal rule, such as towns that were founded in a given period.

[13] With contiguous units, there is the chance of contamination or spillover effects from one case to the other. Hopefully, selecting cases based on variation in the key independent variable limits this problem.

quantitative measurements are based, he assembles a broad coverage of cases, but does not directly confront selection issues or match villages.

Selecting Cases to Study Junta Councils

The main goal of studying cases in depth is to trace the mechanisms that might account for the effect of juntas on violence encountered in the statistical analysis and probe how resilient these mechanisms are to armed group pressure in different settings. The new cases should help answer a number of questions that are difficult to study with large-n data. For instance, do junta mechanisms account for trends in violence, or are these trends accounted for by other explanations? Is the juntas variable a good measure of social capital? Were other organizations besides juntas more important for explaining violence? Did juntas represent community interests, or were they subjugated to clientelist relations? Did juntas align with armed groups or instead implement tactics to maintain their autonomy from influence and violence? Are there confounding factors that keep theorized junta mechanisms from transferring to affect violence? New cases can help uncover additional empirical support for the mechanisms and highlight new, unknown processes (theory building).

In selecting cases, I faced constraints of safety and resources when I opted to conduct research in "post"-conflict Colombia. It is a country with wide variation on civilian movements for autonomy from conflict but has also been known for kidnapping of foreigners. As I would later find out, even the towns I visited that were recently "post-conflict" had security concerns. These were towns that most urban Colombians had never heard of (epitomizing the country's urban–rural disconnect). I was warned of the possibility that informants, militants, or gangs were possibly lying in wait, and found that information travels fast in small towns, so that everyone and anyone would know within days that a *gringo* had arrived.[14] I also learned that not long prior to my visits to some towns and even possibly during them, there were FARC spies on the very bus lines I sometimes used to get in to and out of the case-study regions (fortunately for my peace of mind, I only found this out on the way *back* from my site visits). Youths were killed in nearby villages shortly before, after, and even during some site visits. Militants were still turning themselves in to the town Ombudsmen for demobilization (in one instance, this happened the night before I interviewed one). Propaganda "pamphlets" intended to intimidate residents were also distributed.

Instead of aimlessly setting out into the Colombian countryside, and with time constraints, my approach led me to fewer and more purposefully selected cases. The selection modeling is useful as a way of thinking about which towns

---

[14] Fortunately, many of my contacts were looking out for me and were also plugged in to the local situation (*coyuntura*) or had sufficient prestige to keep undesirable events from transpiring.

were selected into the "treatment" group of having juntas and approximating quasi-experimental conditions. So, in addition to the plausibility probe case studies on the ATCC (Carare Peasant Workers Association), I conduct three new comparisons of matched municipios as theory-testing cases. Since there are 990 municipios in Colombia and many variables to control, I first use the statistical propensity-matching procedures to determine a town's likelihood of having juntas.

To test the first proposition from Chapter 5 that juntas decrease violence, I matched cases on all other characteristics using the propensities and looked for pairs that diverged in levels of juntas. I looked for cases that had relatively equal probabilities of receiving the "treatment" of having juntas from the middle range of propensity scores (support) that were neighbors or in the same department.[15] Selecting cases from this middle range of support should help assure that the cases are fairly typical municipios (expected to have average levels of juntas but actually have more or less) and reduce the likelihood that omitted variables or "noise" are causing observed differences in juntas between pairs.[16] Choosing neighbor towns helps further reduce unobserved differences among towns and also eases passage between towns once in the field.

I was also interested in the histories of armed conflict since I hypothesize that civilian organizations will only be likely to reduce civil war violence in areas that actually suffer from civil war. I further cull from the pool the group of towns that suffered at least some attacks according to the data and manually match cases on conflict dynamics in the 1990–2006 period of the study by both intensity and mix of active armed groups. This measure of conflict intensity is not included in the propensity model because it is "post-treatment" (i.e., it is measured subsequent to the juntas and so does not explain them; it could be considered a second treatment whose propensities could be modeled separately). As an additional assurance, I also restricted the possible cases to those that are coded as having experienced high levels of violence during La Violencia of the 1950s to decrease the likelihood of including places that have been historically peaceful.

To test the second proposition about the possible attenuating effect of the intensity of armed group activity on junta council capability, I matched a second set of cases (in Caldas) with high levels of juntas but *varying* levels of armed group activity in the form of attacks (recall from Chapter 5 that this variable is measured apart from incidences of violence against civilians).

[15] I dichotomize the dependent variable of juntas per capita and use a probit model to identify cases that cluster around probabilities of 0.5. I also consider an OLS model since the actual juntas variable is interval and look at cases that cluster around the mean of predicted values. Comparison sets could be chosen from different propensity strata for generalizability if there is confidence that the model is complete and does not suffer from omitted variables.

[16] For example, pairs at an extreme end of the propensity distribution could have one case that is extremely mispredicted and was expected to receive (not receive) the treatment but did not for some reason possibly correlated with the dependent variable. One can of course still learn from such cases, but they pose a greater challenge to solely examining the comparative statics of a few key variables.

Armed group actions Juntas councils	Low to medium	High
Low *Prediction:*	*No juntas effect* Quipile (Cundinamarca)	*Displacement/violence* ATCC neighbors
High *Prediction:*	*Juntas decrease violence* Bituima, Viani (Cundinamarca) ATCC 1990s	*Weak or no junta effect* ATCC pre-1987; post-2000

FIGURE 6.2 Comparisons of selected cases

Although I could have constructed a second propensity model for attacks, I instead "eyeballed" cases with junta propensities close to 0.5, high levels of actual juntas, and that are in the same region but vary in average numbers of attacks over time. The application of these case selection methods ended up being fairly "blind" for the researcher – I knew little about the cases beforehand and the actual levels of violence do not on the surface strongly support or undermine my hypothesis.[17] The cases I arrived at and their predictions for juntas and violence are shown in Figure 6.2 (and map of Figure 6.3).

As noted in Chapter 4, I spent between two and four weeks in each of these sites interviewing (randomly where possible) past and present junta leaders and members, and members of other relevant organizations. I also interviewed populations of ex-combatants, displaced residents, and church and NGO leaders in the zones and nearby cities. Although these different clusters of case towns may appear close to each other on the map of Colombia, the case zones are different in their subcultures and conflict dynamics, with different armed group blocs, fronts, and patterns of contestation, and are at least a day's travel apart. They should therefore be helpful for assessing the generalizability of theory in different subregions of Colombia.

SELECTING CASES FROM CUNDINAMARCA

There are not many regions in Colombia where the number of juntas varies among *neighboring* municipalities and yet these municipalities also have similar

---

[17] Whether this constitutes "peeking" and should be done is a question worthy of debate. I argue that having an understanding of the dependent variable values from the large-n analysis does not tarnish the case selection as a test so long as one has few *a priori* qualitative understandings about the case that would drive selection.

FIGURE 6.3 Map of case study sites

likelihoods of having high levels of organization and experienced at least some armed conflict. However, in the western region of Cundinamarca, there are a handful of counties that match these requirements. The two small neighboring municipios of Bituima and Vianí both have many juntas for their levels of population in 1985 (90th–99th percentiles). Quipile, their immediate neighbor to the south (as well as the nearby towns of Chaguaní and Anolaima), is measured as having a below-average number of juntas per capita (approximately 25th percentile).[18] Table 6.4 and Figures 6.6 and 6.7 display how the

---

[18] This case would ideally have zero juntas, but I decided it had sufficiently few juntas to be a viable test and thought it more important to geographically match neighbor towns than squeeze slightly more variation out of the Juntas variable. This choice may also help avoid falling prey to possible measurement error in the Juntas indicator if zeros are relatively more likely to be mistakenly measured. The irony was not lost, however, that I may only be able to access and learn about "low" junta cases and their levels of organization by interviewing junta leaders.

cases compare on actual versus predicted values for juntas (Figure 6.8 displays their predicted homicide rates based on Model 4 of Table 5.2). This mountainous region with colonial origins is about three hours west of Bogotá and it has historically suffered from state neglect (poor roads, water quality, health services, etc.). Other than slight differences in elevation, the towns look similar from a distance, with small populations of between seven and ten thousand people and agriculture-based economies (coffee, cane sugar).

These towns are contiguous and share similar geographic settings, all lying between road corridors that radiate northwest and southwest out of Bogotá. However, there are some apparent differences. Vianí and Bituima are two different towns but for analytical purposes I decided to consider them as a group, since together they have similar values on the Juntas indicator, closely match Quipile on important observables such as population and poverty, and were originally a single municipio until Vianí split off. While the analysis of two town centers and municipal administrations in two treatment towns could cause problems for inference (if somehow correlated with both social networks and later violence), Quipile also has several corregimientos (noncounty-seat "urban" areas) that could approach the size of the county seat of a small municipio. By way of comparison, I decided the inclusion of the low-junta town of Anolaima did not make sense. Even though it is in the same region, its level of urbanization means state presence might be greater, leading to different conflict dynamics and a smaller potential role for social organizations.

An advantage of this pairing is its proximity to Bogotá and the feasibility of traveling to the region. Despite this location, it apparently historically suffered moderate to high levels of armed group influence. The towns in the subregion seemed to have experienced similar degrees of influence by the same armed groups, likely due in part to their compact sizes (Figure 6.4). They had been largely dominated by the FARC, and even the same guerrilla fronts, during most of the time period of study. For some periods, paramilitaries briefly extended their reach, and the army mounted counterinsurgency operations over about a four-year period from 2000 through 2004. A key question to be investigated in Chapter 8 is whether the conflict dynamics fit my scope conditions for junta-based autonomy of experiencing the presence of multiple armed groups and ongoing uncertainty about levels of contestation.

These counties should provide a tough test for junta autonomy mechanisms. First, their dynamics of armed group control – possibly switching abruptly from FARC control to army control – may not have created conditions where civil society independence would be helpful. Second, there are no known, formal meta-organizations such as peace communities in these areas. Third, even with the measured historical disparities in junta coverage from one town to the next, as close neighbors, these towns may still share social organization characteristics (because of proximity, diffusion, and possible measurement error), making it unlikely to observe effects based on differences in juntas. Fourth, most of these towns are recorded as having suffered high levels of violence during La

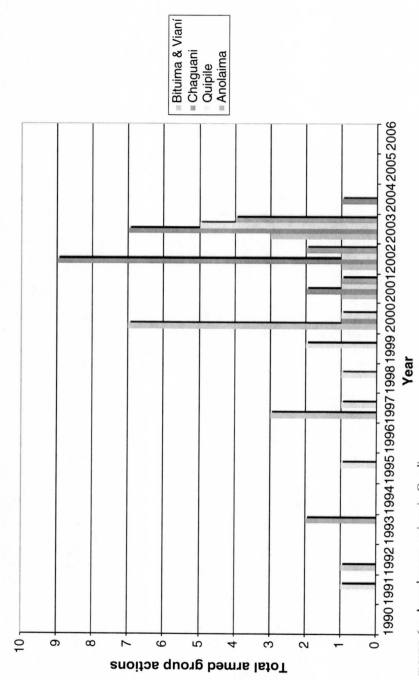

FIGURE 6.4 Armed group actions in Cundinamarca case towns.
Source: Government of Colombia.

Violencia, so any observed negative relationship between juntas and violence should not stem from these areas being historically peaceful. Lastly, a peek at the dependent variable of violence suggests that the high-junta counties actually suffered high homicide rates for some years. This prompted the goal for the qualitative research of verifying the accuracy of the large-n violence indicators, whether all these cases really did suffer similar levels of contestation, and, counterfactually, whether they would have suffered more violence had they fewer juntas. Overall, these towns provide a fruitful contrast with the culturally distinct, highly organized ATCC case of the low-lying Magdalena Medio region.

THE ATCC CASES IN SANTANDER

The ATCC case (Carare Peasant Workers Association) of Chapter 7 was chosen prior to my statistical modeling as a plausibility probe. While this organization spans several municipios, I still try to approximate a match on other community characteristics by comparing the ATCC with nearby neighbor communities. I also exploit within-case variation inside the ATCC to test theories at smaller units of analysis (regions, villages, and incidents) and over time. These "cases" include:

1. ATCC area over time:
   i. Pre-organization (1975–1987)
   ii. Post-organization (1987–2000)
   iii. Post-resurgence of violence (2000–2007)
2. ATCC area vs. grouped neighboring areas (the large villages of San Tropel, Santa Rosa, Miralindo, La Sabana, and other smaller villages)
3. Intra-ATCC comparison of villages and threat incidents.

CONCLUSIONS

This chapter provided a better understanding of the origins and prevalence of the junta councils. In doing so, it helped to confront some of the potential reverse causality and selection bias issues presented in Chapter 5. Beyond the relevance of this analysis for the study of violence, it is also one of the first systematic studies of the historical social and organizational landscape of Colombia. This involved identifying the role that the monumental event of La Violencia played in reshaping Colombian society as well as the importance of inequality as a determinant of social organization.

This analysis explains why, if juntas are so effective, every community does not already have a strong junta as of today. Both social and structural factors influence the formation and persistence of junta councils: they are found to be more prevalent in areas that are less populated, are poorer, have more churches, have greater land equality, are less politically polarized, and received support from promoters. Juntas are also less prevalent (though not significantly) where there are sizable ethnic minority populations, who tend to form their own social organizations. Still, the question is open to further study, as there are several possible additional reasons why juntas are not (active) everywhere. One major reason could be that isolation and limited information and communication has slowed policy diffusion – that only relatively recently did a consensus begin to form among different Colombian campesinos (or churches and NGOs that support them) that organizational structures can make a difference. Juntas were also not originally envisioned as being active or useful in conflict settings (but were intended to prevent conflict recurrence). Instead, the distribution of juntas may have been partly determined by communities' differing needs for public goods provision, or other organizations, such as labor unions, may have filled a collective action gap.

The chapter deals directly with the possibility that juntas are derivative of the conflict through path-dependent processes and plausibly rules this out as an explanation for the observed association of more juntas with less future violence. I find that juntas formed more prevalently in La Violencia zones or at the least were no less prevalent in such zones. The finding conforms to the historical consensus on the effects of La Violencia and of junta development and promotion. For Colombia, at least, this is further evidence that the formation of civilian organizations such as juntas and their effects on violence are not completely determined by the preferences of armed actors, the dynamics of conflict, or latent propensities for conflict.

Lastly, the analysis of selection bias issues aided the development of a case selection methodology that is particularly useful for coping with researchers' constraints, including limited resources or working in conflict conditions. After deploying these techniques in this chapter, the next two chapters discuss the small-n research findings from the selected matched cases. As a product and benefit of this methodology, these cases are not "just so" stories that might be convenient examples of theory (Elster 2000; Bates et al. 2000). They are embedded in a larger explanatory framework and are structured, focused comparisons (George 1979) that take careful measures of key variables. The cases have known variation in variables, but are "out-of-sample" with regard to the cases that were used to theorize about specific protection mechanisms. With their mechanisms unknown beforehand, they help set up civilian autonomy theory for possible falsification.

Appendix

This appendix describes the measurement of variables and statistical tests in this chapter in greater detail.

I model the variables that explain variation in juntas as a simple OLS regression with region effects since panel data on these variables are not available for the time period prior to 1985. The summary statistics for the dependent and independent variables are displayed in Table 5.1 in Chapter 5. The regression results are displayed in Table 6.1, Table 6.2, and Table 6.3, and show that demographic, social, and geographic variables are all significant predictors of junta coverage (to ease interpretation, Juntas per communities is multiplied by 100 and re-scaled to reflect percentages). Table 6.1 is a base model and Table 6.2 and Table 6.3 add additional covariates (though they drop cases). For comparison, the dependent variable for Table 6.2 Model 4 is the raw number of juntas instead of the normalized Juntas per communities variable.

Table 6.3 Model 1 uses a binary dependent variable for the propensity-score matching case selection procedure. This makes sense since, according to Figure 5.7, the distribution of juntas per capita is bimodal despite a long tail. In OLS models of junta formation I consider closeness of cases to the regression line (minimizing residuals). Below, I model a cross-sectional selection equation to explain the likelihood of having juntas.[19] Figure 6.5 displays the distribution of treatment and control cases by propensity quartile and shows that this method is effective at separating "experimental" groups.

---

[19] This model used to select cases is based on the data I had collected up to this point in my research process. The other junta selection models presented earlier were developed later and are more complete. However, the predicted case matches do no vary much among the various models because they share many similar characteristics.

TABLE 6.1 *Models of juntas per "communities" in 1985, by municipios*

	(1)	(2)	(3)
Log 1993 population	−1.863**	−1.896**	−1.770**
	(−10.17)	(−9.98)	(−7.81)
Population density	−0.000	−0.000	−0.002^
	(−0.10)	(−0.20)	(−1.83)
La Violencia	0.850*	0.855*	0.791*
	(2.38)	(2.39)	(2.16)
Elevation (m)	−0.000	−0.000	−0.000
	(−0.29)	(−0.24)	(−0.31)
Distance to dept. capital	−0.003^	−0.003^	−0.004^
	(−1.79)	(−1.78)	(−1.77)
Pct. Minorities	−0.497	−0.487	−1.464
	(−0.41)	(−0.40)	(−1.16)
Pct. Dirt floors	2.078*	2.004^	1.345
	(2.01)	(1.93)	(1.21)
Paved road access			−0.556
			(−1.59)
Total guerrilla attacks (1985)		0.068	−0.224
		(0.66)	(−1.47)
Churches			0.083*
			(2.48)
Caribbean region	0.259	0.260	0.579
	(0.27)	(0.27)	(0.59)
Pacific region	5.146**	5.067**	5.338**
	(4.98)	(4.87)	(4.98)
Andean region	3.186**	3.123**	3.322**
	(3.21)	(3.13)	(3.23)
East Andean region	5.621**	5.560**	5.862**
	(5.61)	(5.52)	(5.68)
Eastern region	8.592**	8.537**	8.828**
	(7.63)	(7.56)	(7.66)
Constant region	20.068**	20.411**	19.324**
	(9.22)	(9.12)	(7.96)
No. Municipios/Observations	929	929	896
R-squared	0.34	0.34	0.34

t-statistics in parentheses
** $p < 0.01$, * $p < 0.05$, ^ $p < 0.1$

TABLE 6.2 *Models of juntas per "communities" in 1985, by municipios*

	(1) Juntas per communities	(2) Juntas per communities	(3) Juntas per communities	(4) Number of juntas
Log 1993 population	−2.899**	−2.825**	−3.255**	7.760**
	(−11.04)	(−9.98)	(−11.32)	(8.09)
Pct. Dirt floors	2.917*	3.927**	3.571**	5.510
	(2.34)	(2.99)	(2.80)	(1.30)
Population density	0.001	0.001	0.001	−0.007*
	(1.22)	(1.45)	(1.15)	(−2.13)
Distance to dept. capital	−0.001	−0.001	−0.001	0.010
	(−0.44)	(−0.46)	(−0.40)	(1.03)
Std. dev. elevation	0.003**	0.003**	0.003**	0.007*
	(3.77)	(3.36)	(2.93)	(2.45)
Pct. Minorities	2.605	2.611	1.759	4.571
	(1.24)	(1.15)	(0.84)	(0.65)
La Violencia	0.121	0.280	0.008	0.215
	(0.30)	(0.63)	(0.02)	(0.14)
Land value GINI			−8.297**	−19.801**
			(−3.66)	(−2.62)
Polarization		−1.277*	−0.892	−2.551
		(−2.17)	(−1.52)	(−1.30)
Cooperatives	−0.015	−0.021	−0.040	−0.181
	(−0.44)	(−0.61)	(−0.84)	(−1.14)
Villages	0.052**	0.052**	0.064**	0.337**
	(4.67)	(4.59)	(5.71)	(9.01)
Churches	0.035	0.037	0.093^	0.509**
	(0.90)	(0.96)	(1.90)	(3.13)
Year municipio founded	−0.000	0.001	−0.000	−0.010^
	(−0.15)	(0.46)	(−0.07)	(−1.83)
Caribbean region	0.151	−0.052	−0.138	5.929
	(0.12)	(−0.03)	(−0.10)	(1.30)
Pacific region	5.210**	5.634**	5.899**	24.550**
	(3.94)	(3.66)	(4.07)	(5.07)
Andean region	4.169**	4.302**	6.582**	24.561**
	(3.24)	(2.83)	(4.62)	(5.16)
East Andean region	6.329**	6.388**	5.613**	22.040**
	(4.91)	(4.19)	(3.96)	(4.66)
Eastern region	10.314**	10.126**	9.094**	15.871*
	(5.00)	(4.43)	(4.32)	(2.26)
Constant	27.898**	25.889**	37.112**	−51.191**
	(6.10)	(5.26)	(7.40)	(−3.06)
Observations	682	585	507	507
R-squared	0.42	0.41	0.51	0.59

t-statistics in parentheses
** $p < 0.01$, * $p < 0.05$, ^ $p < 0.1$

TABLE 6.3 *Junta case selection models*

	(1) Probit Juntas per communities	(2) OLS Juntas per communities
Log 1993 population	−0.457** (−6.04)	−1.781** (−7.86)
Elevation (m)	0.000** (5.14)	−0.000 (−0.11)
Distance to dept. capital	−0.001* (−2.16)	−0.004* (−2.05)
Pct. Minorities	−0.337 (−0.81)	−3.026* (−2.01)
Pct. Dirt floors	−0.153 (−0.48)	0.340 (0.29)
Literacy rate	−0.537 (−0.81)	−4.542* (−2.00)
Churches	0.002 (0.07)	0.049* (2.01)
Paved road access	−0.281* (−2.44)	−0.481 (−1.37)
Population density	−0.005** (−4.43)	−0.001 (−1.23)
La Violencia	0.360** (3.45)	0.796* (2.17)
Caribbean		0.477 (0.49)
Pacific		5.216** (4.92)
Andean		3.136** (3.07)
East Andean		5.847** (5.68)
Eastern		8.659** (7.52)
Constant	4.399** (4.93)	22.946** (7.75)
Observations	896	896
Pseudo R-squared/R-squared	0.21	0.34

z-statistics / t-statistics in parentheses

** $p < 0.01$, * $p < 0.05$, ^ $p < 0.1$

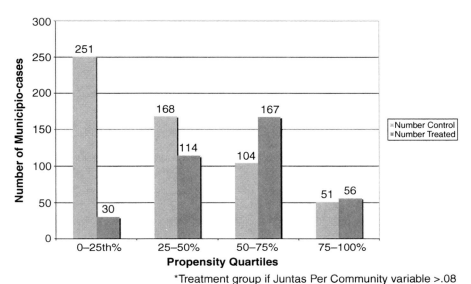

*Treatment group if Juntas Per Community variable >.08

FIGURE 6.5 Distribution of junta-treated and control cases by propensity-score quartile

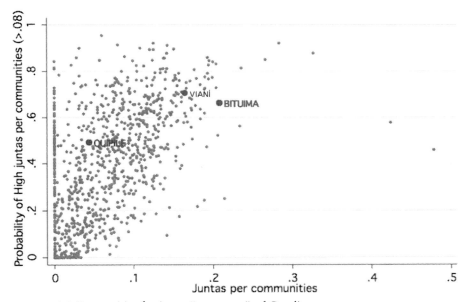

FIGURE 6.6 Propensities for junta "treatment" of Cundinamarca towns

TABLE 6.4 *Characteristics of Cundinamarca towns*

Municipio	Selected Towns			Nonselected Comparison Towns		
	Quipile	Bituima	Viani	Anolaima	Chaguani	Guayabal de S.
Juntas per communities (1985)	4.4%	20.8%	16.5%	0.0%	2.7%	9.4%
Predicted prob. of high juntas "treatment" (if Juntas Per Comm.>.08)	0.52	0.61	0.71	0.31	0.7	0.61
Number of juntas (1985)	9	14	13	0	3	8
Number of villages (1965)	36	14	17	49	25	11
1993 population	10,033	2,932	4,107	12,959	5,080	3,835
Number of city blocks	55	33	36	181	26	37
Elevation (m)	1,443	1,412	1,498	1,657	1,200	1,630
Std. dev. elevation	305.9	209.9	221.3	426.0	472.1	237.3
Distance to dept. capital (km)	82	111	104	71	113	62
Pct. Minority population (1985)	0.1%	0.1%	0.1%	0.2%	0.2%	0.3%
Pct. Dirt floors	32.6%	24.0%	14.2%	13.1%	25.4%	16.4%
Literacy rate	72.0	71.0	75.2	75.1	70.5	77.7
Total churches (town, 1995)	1	1	2	3	2	1
Paved road access (1985)	0	0	0	3	0	0
Population density (1985)	78.4	48.1	60.4	106.2	30.4	65.0
1950s La Violencia	1	0	1	0	1	0

	1900	1772	1853	1882	1700	1845
Year founded	1900	1772	1853	1882	1700	1845
Officials per 1,000 residents	1.1	5.8	2.1	1.2	2.5	0.5
Number of police stations (town)	1	1	1	1	1	1
Number of police inspections (town)	0	1	0	1	1	0
Coca area (ha)	0	0	0	0	0	0
Total AUC actions	0	0	0	0	2	2
Total FARC actions	11	5	4	4	6	13
Total ELN actions	0	1	2	0	1	0
Total army actions	3	2	2	3	11	10
Total armed group actions, 1990–2006 (gov't)	14	8	8	7	20	25
Total armed group actions, 1991–1999 (CINEP)	3	1	2	2	1	1
Total armed group actions, 2000–2005 (CINEP)	4	2	0	3	4	3
Avg. police homicide rate (1990–2007)	42.8	42.1	44.4	54.5	31.2	84.3
Avg. displacement rate (1998–2005)	868	550	831	205	1,029	1,076

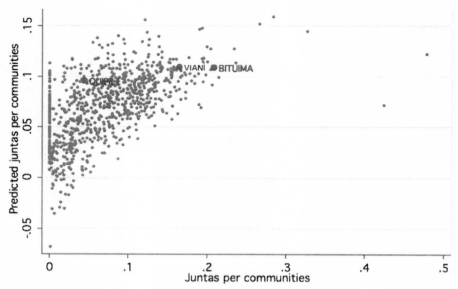

FIGURE 6.7 Predicted junta values of Cundinamarca towns

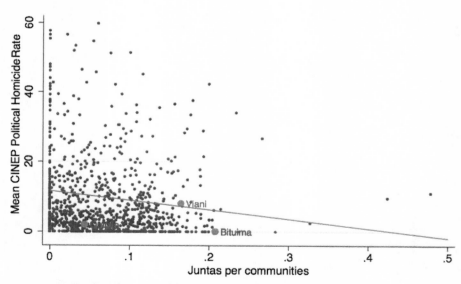

FIGURE 6.8 Predicted vs. actual homicide rates in Cundinamarca towns

7

The Institution of the ATCC

Protection through Conciliation

> *Thank God for the Association. If it weren't for the Association's mediation on*
> *my behalf, I'd be dead now. They're good people. Many accused owe their lives to*
> *the Association.*
>   – Interviewee (ATCC#2), La India, Colombia, November 2007

Late one February night in 1987, a small group of leaders from various
village councils along the Carare River, in the heart of Colombia, met in secret.[1]
They were respected family men who had been in the region for some time and
knew each other well. In the back room of a house, they discussed the pressing
topic of how to respond to a threat of violence against the community, an
ultimatum from multiple armed groups giving residents a choice to displace,
join one of them in the conflict, or be killed. The community had already seen
years of atrocities, and even their small gathering risked great danger – should
anyone have seen them or passed word of their discussion on to any of the
armed groups, they would have been killed.

They were caught between armies, but what were they to do? If they threw
their lot in with the army or paramilitaries, the guerrillas would surely find out
and kill them. And yet, if they joined the guerrillas in hopes of protection, the
paramilitaries would have no mercy. "Well," one man proposed, "we could
find some weapons – take up arms and defend ourselves." Others demurred,
arguing that they were not soldiers, had no weapons, and would easily be
crushed by the standing armies. "What's worse," another said, "we would be

---

[1] This vignette is based on secondary sources and several interviews, some of whom were present in
these discussions (ATCC#3,6,7,8, La India, 10/2007). The contents of this chapter were previously published in Kaplan 2013a.

no better than the armed groups, and then they would have every right to target us."

To manage this problem of stigmatization, the discussion came around to a fifth option. From then on, they would manage their own affairs and would not take any part in the conflict among the armed groups. Unsure how the armed actors would respond, they sought them out in motor-canoes to declare they would neither leave nor take any sides. Surprisingly, after many months of discussions, the various armed groups acceded to the civilians' policies. The result was the formation and survival of an organization called the Peasant Workers Association of the Carare River, or ATCC.[2] Over the following years and decades, the organization ostensibly developed the agency to create physical and political space and deal with the uncertainty and continuing risks of civil war. But was the organization itself really effective over time and across space at providing certainty and security to civilians? How did it function? In what ways is this experience unique? This chapter analyzes the case of the ATCC by bringing methodological structure to Colombia's culturally rich rural communities.

The case of the ATCC illustrates some of the mechanisms through which local organizations, which were found in the statistical analysis to reduce violence, actually function to protect civilians. The ATCC is a good case for studying the phenomenon of civilian autonomy and dispute resolution strategies because it exhibits variation over time (within the case and within its area) on the prevalence of violence as well as the presence and functioning of its institutional procedures. The ATCC's municipios also register above-average historical levels of local junta councils and therefore have experienced less violence than would have otherwise been expected.[3]

Violence against civilians arising from armed groups' exploitation of neighborly disputes has been shown to be pervasive in civil wars. Sometimes the victims of killings have participated in the conflict by collaborating with a rival army. In other instances, suspects are killed when residents make false accusations against their neighbors and denounce them to armed groups to achieve personal ends. This chapter argues that local justice procedures can substitute for state justice to solve these problems in areas where there is a "fog of war" and state presence is weak.

The ATCC experience is remarkable for the apparent effect it has had on violence. Although approximately 10 percent of the population in its region was killed over a twelve-year period leading up to its formation, it was able to negotiate accords and procedural rules with the various local armed groups. The subsequent period from 1991 to 2000 saw an absence of violence during which time there were reportedly no civilian

---

[2] As previewed in Chapter 1, *La Asociación de Trabajadores Campesinos del Carare* in Spanish.
[3] The importance of juntas to the ATCC process is described below.

victims.[4] The evidence suggests it is hard to deny some independent impact of civilian institutions on levels of violence. Neither the acceptance of the accords nor the cessation of violence in the case of the ATCC can be completely explained as resulting from permissive preferences of armed actors.

I make three claims to argue how and why these institutions can manage the "identification" problem common in civil wars, when there are incentives to implicate even upstanding civilians as collaborating with armed actors. First, a civilian institution that is larger than any one person and persists over time can act as an investigatory body to evaluate denunciations by armed actors and send a signal that "separates" (exonerates) pacifist civilians from belligerents. Since individuals may have incentives to misrepresent their private preferences and actions in the "fog of war" (e.g., Fearon 1994), these signals help resolve uncertainty and should make killing more difficult or even costly and reduce mistakes in targeting and costs of governance. Second, civilian norms of non-violence and nonparticipation in the conflict are necessary to minimize the participation of individual civilians in the conflict in the first place. Third, there must be some minimal degree of joint interests between armed actors in not harming civilians so that they will abide by the civilian institutional arrangement.

Evidence for the theoretical argument is based on qualitative and quantitative data collected through field research in 2007 and 2008. I conducted approximately forty-five interviews of ATCC residents in both Bogotá and the ATCC zone, including founders and presidents, as well as residents who were currently or formerly involved in the coca economy, recently migrated to the area from neighboring zones (or traveled the region widely), and had personally been threatened by armed groups. I was also able to access the community archives at the ATCC offices, which contained verbatim minutes of meetings between the ATCC and guerrilla and paramilitary leaders and army officials, and discussions among the ATCC's governing council; diary entries; local census data; and copies of the ATCC's institutional rules. Lastly, to serve as a check for the interview data and expand data coverage, I also accessed existing quantitative data from secondary sources for the ATCC and neighboring regions.

On a methodological note, this case study chapter is careful to be explicit about the various within-case cases it uses to test theories. First, variation in both independent and dependent variables is exploited over time across case periods. Second, I make comparisons between the ATCC area and its adjacent neighboring areas that are not part of the organization (but otherwise experienced similar conflict dynamics). Third, the analysis draws on counterfactual

---

[4] Tragically, as the ATCC's procedures were being consolidated, three of the ATCC's founding leaders, Josué Vargas Mateus, Sául Castañeda, and Miguel Ángel Barajas Collazos, as well as journalist Sylvia Duzán, were assassinated by paramilitaries in the *cabecera* of Cimitarra in 1990.

cases and reasoning. Lastly, I use a within-case dataset at the individual and village levels of analysis to further test explanations for violence.

The chapter proceeds as follows. First, the ATCC case is put in context with a description of its setting and recent history. Second, alternative explanations for patterns in violence are analyzed with qualitative and quantitative data for the region and found to be incomplete. Third, the ATCC conciliation process is analyzed as an explanation for violence using an original dataset of threat conciliations. Fourth, insights about the stability of the ATCC's procedures are put to a further test with data from the most recent period of conflict in the region.

THE ATCC IN CONTEXT AND TRENDS IN VIOLENCE

The ATCC's "area of influence," where its members reside and it exercises decision-making and protective authority, extends across 100,000 hectares of territory (1,200 square kilometers, or about 400 square miles) and encompasses thirty-two villages (with thirty-six local councils). The area is nestled along the banks of the Carare River in a steamy, forested valley crisscrossed by river tributaries. The area lies about fifteen miles from the county seat of Cimitarra, but it cuts across the neglected rural peripheries of six municipios. Today, the ATCC area is home to about 5,000 people, with about 2,000 of them (300 families) residing in the village center of La India.

The Carare region is an ethnic microcosm of Colombia, with a population that includes a small group with Indigenous origins, Afro-Colombians who migrated from the Pacific department of Chocó, and mestizos who migrated down from the mountain towns of Boyacá and Santander. Yet because of its diverse ethnic composition and with few roads, the region had few natural bases for cooperation. The integration of residents came about, in part, through the complementary productive activities of these different groups. The mestizos were farmers, while the Afro-Colombian residents, who had previously lived along the Atrato River, were boatsmen who helped transport goods. The river network was also an important lifeline of communication and exchange: milk, produce, and wood would flow down the river, while cases of beer and other supplies were shipped upriver.

Like many other frontier regions in Colombia, the Carare has historically had minimal state presence. Since armed actors first entered the region more than thirty years ago, its history can be separated into approximately three distinct eras. Across these eras, and even within them, there is variation in levels of violence, the presence and functioning of the institution, and other significant independent variables.

The first period began in 1975, when the FARC and ELN guerrilla groups first moved into the region, and continued through the rise of paramilitaries and the ATCC's founding in 1987. In this crossfire, providing aid to one side often brought retaliation from the other. This bloodiest period saw an estimated 530 to 585 civilians killed through 1987 (more than 10 percent of the population), with 60 percent of those killed at the hands of paramilitary groups and 40 percent by the guerrillas (Restrepo 2005, 72; CNRR 2009).[5] Residents said that it was common to see the bodies of the dead floating down the Carare River. To counter the insurgency, the army implemented *carnetización*, an ID-card monitoring program that required residents to report to a local base every one or two weeks.[6]

When the army presented the residents of La India with the ultimatum at a meeting on February 20, 1987, the ATCC civilians demonstrated strategic thinking in their response. I found that there were real debates among leaders about how to respond to the armed groups.[7] Agreeing that without their land they had nothing, yet not wanting to participate in the conflict, they decided for the "fifth" option – not arming and staying in the zone as unarmed and neutral. Despite initial hesitation, the guerrilla and paramilitary groups each conditionally accepted the civilians' proposal as long as their counterparts did as well.

A second period of consolidation began as the ATCC's institutions and norms were put in place and armed actors became accustomed to dealing with the civilians. There was virtually no conflict-related violence from 1987 until the next millennium. The perception of the effectiveness of the ATCC is reflected in a 1989 journal entry from a former association president where he declares, "Today we have passed two years of living better. There's no war, no thirst, no hunger. Long live the Association" (ATCC Archives). Nevertheless, from around 2000 through the present, violence returned and a third era began for the region. I later analyze this third era as new data for a test of my mediation hypothesis as an explanation for violence.

As a skeptical researcher, the purported vanishing violence seemed suspicious. In interviews, I pressed subjects with questions about violence in this period. Interestingly, in some interviews, people would begin to tell me there *were* deaths and massacres in that time. But, when I would press them harder, asking, "Really, like in 1995?" they would think for a minute and respond, "No, wait, that was earlier (or later)."[8] Overall, my findings confirmed that there were death threats in the 1990s, but few if any conflict-related deaths (though some died in machete fights among drunks or fights over women).[9] Impressive as it seems, only a structured analysis can resolve to what extent this can be attributed to civilian processes as opposed to causes that lie elsewhere.

[5] ATCC#9, La India, 10/2007.   [6] ATCC#3, 6, La India, 10/2007.
[7] ATCC#1, La India, 10/2007.   [8] ATCC#10, La India, 7/2008.
[9] ATCC#4, La India, 8/2008.

TABLE 7.1 *Key variables in the ATCC region, 1975–2007*

Period	Civilians killed	ATCC rules	ATCC norms	Territorial control	Illegal group resources & discipline
1975–1987	530 total victims; Average of 44 victims annually	No rules	Fear; threats; weak norms; civilian informants	FARC dominant, then contested by army and paramilitary	Emeralds, cattle, oil
1987–2000	3 estimated conflict-related deaths; no victims from 1991–2000; selective violence defused/diminished	ATCC; informal accords for investigation of accused	Strong, widespread norms; violent past and new process inspire participation	Contested; then paramilitary dominant but with infighting, continued but sporadic FARC presence through 1995; FARC presence diminishes around 1995 and paramilitary gain complete control	Emeralds, cattle, oil; FARC front received coca funds from central committee; FARC executed some abusive commanders; paramilitaries merged into AUC organization in 1997; coca from 1998
2000–2007	Selective killings resume; approximately 35 conflict-related victims	ATCC, formal tribunal, village delegates	Migrants to the area, youths, and coca growers who did not experience violence or ATCC formation violated neutrality norms and participated in conflict	New contestation; then increasing paramilitary control; then some paramilitary demobilizations and new bands emerge	Emeralds, cattle, oil, coca, coca taxes

EVALUATING EXPLANATIONS FOR VIOLENCE:
THE BALANCE OF CONTROL

This section assesses how various explanations account for the observed trends in violence over time with special attention to the surprising era of the absence of violence during the 1990s. These explanations include: general (national-level) trends in violence and peace negotiations; shifts in territorial control; changing rebel organization, resource bases, and discipline; and increased international human rights advocacy. I assess these hypotheses with various "cases" within the ATCC meta-case. I derive eleven real and counterfactual cases across the ATCC and its neighboring regions (see Appendix B). While I find these alternative explanations do not completely account for violence, I only discuss the territorial control hypothesis in the body of the chapter. The alternative explanations are summarized in Table 7.1 and discussed in greater depth in Appendix B.

Changes in Military Contestation and Control. Kalyvas (2006) argues that much of the violence against individual civilians in civil wars stems from battles for territorial control among armed actors. Violence is selectively used against suspected enemy collaborators to coerce support among the civilian population. Violence is used to gain control of territory and is also the result of contestation for territorial control. Violence is "jointly" produced as civilian informants denounce enemy collaborators to armed actors when they feel protected from retaliation. Such denunciations may arise from war-related motivations, but may also be false and involve local disputes among neighbors.

Denunciations, and therefore selective violence, are thought to be most common by the stronger armed actor in zones of dominant but incomplete control. By implication, neutrality strategies – fence-sitting and double-dealing – are permitted by armed actors for individuals and local committees in completely contested areas, but nowhere else. Neutral civilian organizations might therefore exist only because they reflect a stalemated balance of power, and thus have little independent impact. Institutions to clarify the "fog of war" are thought to get eliminated or be useless where they might be most effective.

Can the ATCC's apparent mitigation of violence be attributed merely to existing in zones of either complete control or evenly contested control (epiphenomenality), rather than in a zone of dominant control (where it might independently affect violence)? To answer this question, I compare the military balance in the ATCC region with that of other regions. Kalyvas operationalizes complete control as when the enemy army has no presence day or night (according to civilian perceptions), dominant control as when the enemy army only has presence at night, and contested control as when the government does not have control at night (Table 7.2). Although there are challenges in applying this standard to assess control, I adapted several interviewing procedures for this task. I asked interviewees from among various villages across the ATCC region the following two questions related to military control: first, "Around

TABLE 7.2 *Predictions of the balance of control theory of violence*

Control description	Control zone type	Violence prediction
Full control by incumbents; adequate security both day and night	1	No violence
Mainly but not fully controlled by incumbents; sporadic covert activity by insurgents	2	Incumbent violence
Balance of forces: incumbent security adequate by day, only marginal at night; sporadic to regular covert insurgent activity at night	3	No violence
Mainly but not fully controlled by insurgents. Incumbent presence marginal at day; regular covert and overt insurgent activity	4	Insurgent violence
Insurgents are the primary authority day and night	5	No violence

year x, which actor had control of the area during the day? At night? Was the control strong or weak?" and second, "Did you have to pay a tax to an armed actor? Which one(s)?"

The ATCC's antecedents should be a textbook case for Kalyvas's theory. The FARC maintained initial dominance in the region through the early 1980s and little violence occurred (the guerrillas had an estimated 500 fighters in 1978; García 1996). Guerrilla control began to erode and they retreated for a time as the army and paramilitaries moved into the department of Santander.[10] As the guerrillas ceded control, they strengthened their offensive against the population as a last-ditch attempt at coercion (García 1996). With the rise of the paramilitaries and army presence through the mid-1980s, all of the elements predicted in a zone of dominant control were present – denunciations, varying degrees of contested control, and selective violence. As one resident put it, "There were people that were seriously implicated by the sapos (frogs, or informants), people that worked for one group or for the other. There was an information campaign and many people were 'marked' by a certain group ... The dark waters of this river are a silent witness to the numerous dead they dumped in there" (Hernández Delgado 2004; translated by author).

My interviewing and secondary sources indicate that in the next period, from 1987 through 2000, the army (and paramilitaries) had increasingly dominant yet still incomplete control (hence the ultimatum).[11] This should have

[10] ATCC#3, 11, La India, 10/2007.
[11] E.g., ATCC#3, 12, Bogotá, 8/2008. Figure 7.7 below shows the balance of threats across villages between guerrillas versus the army and paramilitaries and indicates that a number of villages had continual threats, as well as relatively more threats by a dominant actor.

predicted intense, continued selective violence by the army and paramilitaries, yet in reality violence dropped off dramatically. Although the guerrillas largely withdrew their forces, they remained active in the area (partially confirmed by García 1996). I heard of further examples of guerrillas threatening civilians during the 1990s from camps in the nearby mountains. In almost every interview, when asking whether the guerrillas had left the zone, people consistently responded, "Always, there has always been guerrilla presence here."[12]

Beyond the interview evidence I collected, there are additional signs of guerrilla presence in the mid- and late 1990s. For instance, in a meeting of ATCC leaders early in 1996, one leader noted that, "Three months ago the FARC called the directors of the ATCC for a meeting" (ATCC Archives 1996). The individual went on to make an additional observation about the conditions during this time period in the Carare region, "The armed groups that operate in the region have informants right here and are committing violence for gossip – a problem that the ATCC has to fix, and not the armed groups." They also noted dialogues with the paramilitaries during this period.

The National Commission on Reparation and Reconciliation (CNRR 2011) study provides similar evidence of guerrillas contesting the ATCC region during the 1990s. In a section on "The interference of armed actors in the area of influence of the ATCC," the CNRR study notes that, "From the mid-1990s, armed groups began to gain terrain in the Carare, including the ATCC zone of influence and the corregimiento of La India. This influence meant a permanent tension between the armed actors and the ATCC, which persisted in convincing the campesinos to not plant coca and not interact with armed groups" (CNRR 2011, 179). The section in the CNRR study on "The reign of armed actors, the persistence of violence, and the expansion of coca, 1994–2010" makes particular reference to the guerrillas and notes, "[T]he persistence of the guerrilla, with the 23rd Front locating its base in the mountains of Landázuri and Peñon, projecting toward other places in the Carare" (CNRR 2011, 167). The strategic importance of the Carare region to the guerrillas is also noted in subsequent pages: "The guerrillas continued to have presence in the Carare region ... considering the zone a passing place or a strategic corridor" (CNRR 2011, 171).

Quantitative data from the Jesuit think tank CINEP tends to corroborate these characterizations. In most years of the 1990s, guerrilla groups registered at least some armed activities (Figure 7.1) and human rights violations (Figure 7.2) in or near the ATCC zone (data is missing for 1995).

My interview instrument allowed me to further cast doubt on armed actor control as a determinant of ATCC autonomy and impact. By phrasing the question on control about an "actor" rather than an "armed actor," I did not force respondents to answer with the name of an armed group. Indeed, some

---

[12] ATCC#3, 13, La India, 10/2007.

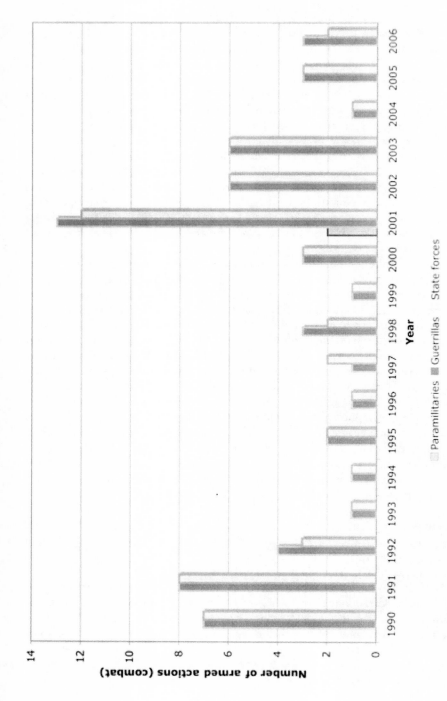

FIGURE 7.1 Armed actions in ATCC municipios, 1990–2006
Source: CINEP, author's calculations.

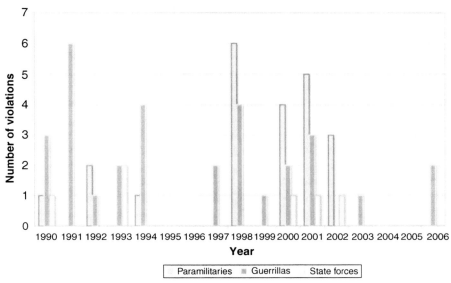

FIGURE 7.2 Human rights violations in ATCC municipios, 1990–2006
Source: CINEP, author's calculations.

respondents naturally responded that the "actor" who had control was in fact *the civilian ATCC.*[13] Furthermore, many respondents noted that they did not pay protection taxes to anyone since the ATCC was able to negotiate an end to this practice in the region.[14] More than once during the 1990s the ATCC civilian leaders were able to brush off the dominant paramilitaries' efforts to install a base in the town of La India by arguing that it would only cause them more problems with the guerrillas.[15]

Perhaps the most important evidence against the explanation of territorial control for patterns in ATCC violence is that *its causal mechanism persisted, but did not lead to violence.* If the balance of control theory were right – that the ATCC could only have thrived under contested or complete control – denunciations, threats, *and* violence *all* should have ceased. It is incongruous with the theory that denunciations and threats continued to occur, but did not lead to the killing of civilians (see interviews, García 1996, Hernández Delgado 2004). The ATCC therefore either persisted for some amount of time in a dangerous zone of dominant control or in other conditions that were nevertheless quite dangerous. Without prompting, one respondent characterized the situation and threats of the 1990s as "selective violence,"[16] while another

[13] ATCC#14, La India, 10/2007.   [14] ATCC#3, 6, La India, 10/2007.
[15] ATCC#10, La India, 7/2008.   [16] ATCC#3, La India, 10/2007.

reported that armed actors' strategies were "psychological" and designed to control through "threats and fear."[17]

In sum, the theory of territorial control appears to explain some but not all periods of violence and its absence in the ATCC region. The patterns of control would have predicted higher selective violence than actually occurred. I next explore how the ATCC dealt with the denunciation mechanism so that it would not lead to violence.

CIVILIAN INSTITUTIONS AS AN EXPLANATION: THE PROCESS OF THE ATCC

Levels of control or violence may indeed contribute to the establishment and persistence of institutions such as the ATCC, but they provide an incomplete picture of the decrease in violence observed after the founding of the ATCC. This leaves open the possibility that it is explained by something inherent to the ATCC. The ATCC has fulfilled many roles and functions for the citizens of the region, including economic development planning, operating a community store, lobbying government officials, and giving civilians early warning ahead of impending battles. Many of these functions can potentially affect the dynamics of conflict and violence in direct and indirect ways. However, the function that most directly affects violence is the institutional procedures the civilians developed to deal with threats from armed actors and resolve disputes over civilian allegiances. This provision of "order without law" (Ellickson 1991) goes to the heart of the mechanisms of other explanations of violence and short-circuits them.

The ATCC's institutional procedures are activated when a civilian resident of the ATCC region has been accused of aiding one armed group or another, becoming "*comprobado*," or implicated, and is threatened with execution. Rather than being killed outright as he or she normally would be absent the institutional rules, the procedures call for turning the accused over to the ATCC's governing council, the *Junta Directiva* (below, I analyze the conditions where armed actors would agree to this).[18] In a region where government authority is distant, the Junta acts like a court and conducts investigations of the implicated person, using its advantage over armed groups in local information. ATCC leaders meet about the case and interview acquaintances of the accused, including family, friends, and neighbors. They further draw on local village committees that monitor compliance with agreements and inform on violators of neutrality.[19] If the person is an ATCC "*socio*" and has signed a

---

[17] ATCC#4, La India, 10/2007.
[18] This is a stylization of the ATCC procedures, which sometimes unfold differently from one case to another. The ATCC's Junta Directiva is a different structure than the village-level juntas de acción communal previously discussed.
[19] ATCC#3, La India, 10/2007.

membership contract letter, they will present this letter to the accusing group as a form of character witness.[20] They may also leverage their bilateral relationships with each of the armed groups to confirm the accusation with the rival of the accusing group. The information is then compiled and discussed with the accuser. If the implicated person is found to be a noncollaborator, by the agreement he or she is absolved of wrongdoing by the accuser.

If the implicated is found to be a collaborator, he or she has two options depending on the response of the accuser. Conditional on good behavior and "correcting," he or she can stay in the area (if he or she is found "guilty" again, the armed actor will have the "right" to mete out punishment). Alternatively he or she might be given funds from the ATCC (and sometimes even the armed actor) to leave the region and find land elsewhere. If he or she still decides to stay, the ATCC acknowledges it can no longer provide protection.[21] This procedure effectively sorts noncollaborator civilians from collaborator ones who participated in the conflict. It reduces both the potential for false accusations and the incentive for residents to participate in the conflict since it becomes more costly to do so (and gain whatever selective benefits they may) in secrecy.

There is substantial evidence that this procedure has been effective. The impression among the civilians of the ATCC (and academic analysts) is that it has saved many lives. According to one resident:

Of note is the right to life that has been achieved through dialogue. There have not been deaths but people have been threatened by armed groups. So, we asked for meetings with them and asked them to respect life. They told us that we would have to remove [the accused] for this reason or that reason … We have had to remove some people from the zone or turn them over to the competent authorities so they would pay their sentence there [or to other armed groups]. But that has been a big achievement in the region, and has been able to rescue the lives of many people. (Hernández Delgado 2004, 356)

If accurate, this characterization does much to explain the lull in violence observed in the region during 1990s. The ATCC clearly fostered an environment where pacifist civilians had fewer entanglements with armed actors, noncollaborator residents could be liberated from threats by investigations, and exposed collaborators could reform or flee.

ANALYSIS OF THREATS AND CONCILIATIONS, 1987–2007

To better understand the severity of the threats and the ATCC's ability to protect residents, I collected and compiled a new dataset on *threats* as well as deaths from the region. The main purposes of this effort are twofold: first, to

[20] ATCC#11, La India, 11/2007. Early on, membership was conceived loosely as support, participation, and adherence to pacifist norms but has been increasingly formalized over time.
[21] ATCC#4, La India, 10/2007.

assess if differences in violence outcomes depend on whether the civilians' investigations confirmed the reasons for threats, and second, to describe the information flows of the region and how civilians generate *credible* information.

Since the conciliation of threats has been an oral, day-to-day process with almost no written records available, the dataset – this oral history – was recovered based on in-depth interviews, in some cases with multiple follow-ups, with over ten "conciliators" with specific knowledge of and participation in conciliations.[22] I also spoke with a number of people who were actual victims of threats and expressed their gratitude to the ATCC for saving their lives. These interviews yielded detailed information on sixty-seven named threat episodes involving ninety-eight people between 1988 and 2007, with the majority of recorded cases occurring from 1998 onwards.[23] Based on conciliator estimates, these figures likely represent only about a third to a half of the total episodes of conciliation in the ATCC's history. Although many episodes are certainly missing, the cases that were recalled for the dataset are likely the most representative and important cases (i.e., extreme cases of either saving lives or of killings).[24]

---

[22] ATCC#1,3,4,6,10,17,18,19, 8/2008; ATCC#20, Cimitarra, 8/2008; ATCC#15, 11/2007, ATCC#3,12, Bogotá, 8/2008. Some written confirmation of approximately fifteen conciliation cases could be found in the meeting minutes of dialogues although the data collection process depended on the memory of conciliators. A number of conciliators (including women) were present at each dialogue, and the dates, results of investigations, outcomes, and other conciliation characteristics were compiled to the best of their knowledge. To improve subjects' recall, they consented to discussions with other conciliators in small groups to help jog their memories. They then helped revise the compiled lists of cases for accuracy. Unfortunately, it was more difficult to collect information on threats from the distant past – from the early 1990s – because some conciliators had either died (of natural causes), moved away from the region, or simply did not remember cases clearly. During this early period, conciliation processes were also less formal, with smaller groups of conciliators or conciliations carried out only by ATCC presidents, meaning there were fewer people to recount the history.

[23] Data on the following variables was collected for each threat: year; gender and age of accused; threatening group; reason for threat (informant, material aid to enemy, coca, etc.); how the ATCC learned of the threat; how the conciliation took place and why it worked (if it did); whether investigation showed the charge of the threat to be true or false; and result for the accused. It should be noted that, according to the ATCC, regardless of whether the threat victim is found to be guilty or innocent, death threats are never considered a legitimate way of resolving disputes. This information was collected not to cast blame, but rather to give a fair accounting of why different events unfolded as they did. Seven episodes did not involve armed groups or have validated accusations and a small number of individuals were accused in multiple episodes. This does not include an additional thirty-five cases of killings associated with the coca economy in the post-2000 period that were not conciliated.

[24] One leader from the early 1990s reported investigating somewhere between 70 and 100 such cases. These implications would usually first begin with light threats to deter certain behaviors and, if those were not effective, would then escalate to death threats (although only a handful of cases went this far; ATCC#15, Bogotá, 11/2007). Other conciliators who served toward the late 1990s also recalled dealing with at least seventy such cases (ATCC#1, ATCC#4, La India, 11/2007).

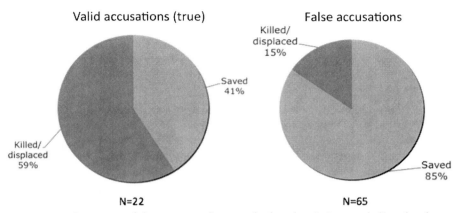

FIGURE 7.3 Outcomes of threats according to whether the victim was believed to have collaborated
Source: Interviews.

Conciliators also provided their assessments of the validity of the accusations, yielding examples of both "neutral" people being "vouched for" and saved and collaborators being identified and turned over. Indeed, the analysis of the thirty-six threat cases where the reason for the threat was determined to be "false" (in some cases ex-post), fifty-five people were saved while seven were killed and three were forced to displace. With only about 15 percent of the threat victims killed, the difference between these cases and those where the reasons for threats were confirmed ("true," i.e., participating in the conflict) is noteworthy. Of these twenty-four "true" cases involving thirty-seven people, nine people reformed and stayed, nine people were killed, and four were forced to displace (the outcomes for some of the people remain unclear). Figure 7.3 show the difference in homicide rates between these two groups, which is found to be statistically significant with a chi-squared test.[25]

Narrations of actual cases illustrate more clearly the danger the victims face and how the cases are resolved. In one example from 1995, a man who was marked for death was protected by intervention from the ATCC:

Don Diego, a middle-aged wood-cutter, was accused by the guerrillas of providing aid to and being an informant for the paramilitaries. When Don Diego got word they were going to kill him, he went to the ATCC for help. The ATCC (along with the guerrillas)

---

[25] It is conceivable, although unlikely, that judgments about whether a threat victim was falsely or validly accused were influenced by hindsight bias based on the outcome (e.g., the kind of thinking that "if they were killed or continually threatened, then they must have been guilty of the charge").

investigated his case by talking with neighbors and monitoring his actions going forward and found the accusation to be false. They determined that another wood-cutter had informed the guerrillas on him and had been spreading lies for his economic benefit – to kill Don Diego so he could take his wood and push him out of business. Upon word of this, the guerrillas relented and Don Diego remained safely in the zone. Instead, they punished his accuser.[26]

This case is emblematic of the many instances in which the ATCC leverages its local information network to protect "innocent" civilians (as residents refer to them) from the dangers of the armed conflict. While in this episode, guerrillas made a death threat based on a denunciation, underscoring their ability to project into the zone, it was also common in the 1990s for paramilitaries to bring similar threats.

In another instance, a man who was identified as aiding the paramilitaries was exposed and sentenced. He did not ultimately "correct himself" or comply with the ATCC's finding against him and suggestion that he leave the region, essentially renouncing his protection from the ATCC. He was eventually killed by a guerrilla assassin:

Señor George was implicated by the guerrillas for supporting the AUC around 1999. The FARC was going to kill him, but they notified the Directiva that he had given help and food to the paramilitaries. Testimony of George's neighbors gathered by the ATCC confirmed the FARC's belief that he provided the aid and had a revolver (an armed civilian). The ATCC also asked the AUC if they had received help from him. George was given 200,000 COP (about US$90) to leave the region but he instead spent the money. The ATCC could not force him to leave since he was a student and son of La India, but said they were not responsible for what might happen. Before long, George was killed by a guerrilla assassin.[27]

A case like this is tragic, but outcomes of this sort where an actual ATCC member insists on breaking covenant appear to be relatively rare (although more frequent among nonmember residents). Studying episodes of mediation with various outcomes illustrates how the process of vouching works and when it fails.

In a last example, an ATCC leader was falsely implicated in the early 2000s, and even though the evidence cleared him, he opted to displace from the region for a time because he feared his life remained in danger:

An (false) accusation was made against Don Franklin by paramilitaries for supposedly giving aid to the guerrillas. He was implicated because guerrillas earlier attacked a paramilitary motor canoe on the river and then fled past his house in their escape. The ATCC interviewed the man's neighbors to collect evidence of his participation and the

---

[26] ATCC#1, 4, La India, 10/2007.
[27] ATCC#4, La India, 10/2007. This did not constitute a death for the ATCC's 1990s count because he was killed in 2000, beginning the new era of violence (or effectively became a combatant).

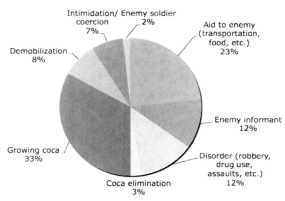

FIGURE 7.4 Reasons for threats (and killings) by armed groups
Source: Interviews.

neighbors cleared him. Although he left the zone for several months to Bogotá as a security precaution, he soon returned and resumed his daily activities.[28]

The ATCC was once again effective in saving a threatened leader. Nevertheless, this case also illustrates the complexities of removing threatened civilians from dangerous situations. Although the man in this case was able to return to his normal life, the process is not a utopia and not all, but many, cases of non-collaborators investigated by the ATCC are resolved so satisfactorily.

The dataset of threat conciliations also provides descriptive insights about how the armed conflict and concomitant threats unfolded and were dealt with. First, there were threats from many actors, and the conciliations demonstrate how the ATCC was able to adapt to dynamic conditions over time and across space. Second, hinting at the blend of armed group motives, there were diverse reasons for threats, including providing aid and information to the enemy, coca cultivation, eliminating demobilized fighters, countering delinquency, and coercing leaders (Figure 7.4). Third, the ATCC obtained advance information about threats – sometimes from residents, sometimes from armed actors, but always with the help of a dense interpersonal network – which allowed the organization to take action in a number of different ways (Figure 7.5). Fourth, the ATCC relied on a variety of appeals and investigation techniques to enhance the credibility of the information presented to the armed groups about threat victims (Figure 7.6). Fifth, the ATCC was able to intervene and save people even in various cases where armed groups were intent to kill (even with lists of targets) and did not first approach the ATCC and inform them of the

[28] ATCC#9, La India, 10/2007.

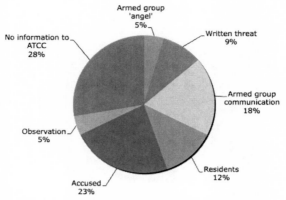

FIGURE 7.5 Information channels: how the ATCC learned of threats
Source: Interviews.

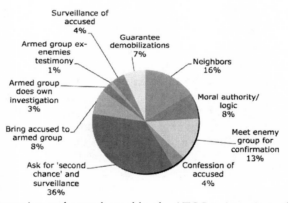

FIGURE 7.6 Information and appeals used by the ATCC to investigate threats
Source: Interviews.

threat. Lastly, in some of the cases where conciliations were not successful, the ATCC was able to rescue victims and get them to safety.

The data on threats and the presence of informants also provide insight on the geographic variation in the balance of armed group control by villages in the region. For instance, as shown in the graph in Figure 7.7 and the map in Figure 7.8, the villages with the most threats by the guerrillas were La Ceiba, Mate de Guadua, and El Pescado, on the east side of the Carare River, closer to the alleged guerrilla camps in the mountains.[29] Paramilitary threats were most

---

[29] In some cases, individuals were threatened by multiple armed groups.

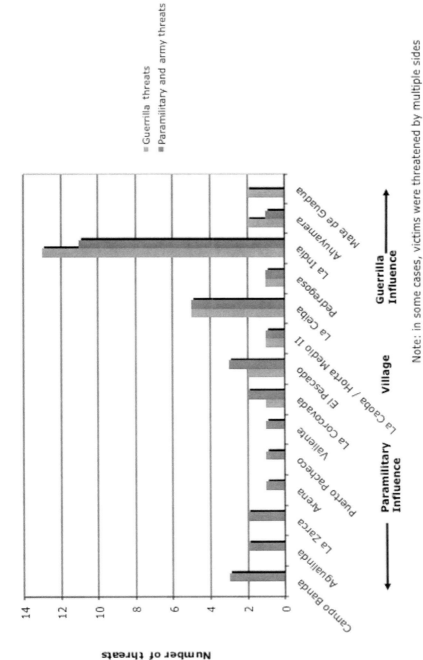

FIGURE 7.7 Distribution of threats and killings among armed groups by ATCC villages, 1991–2007

Source: Interviews.

Note: in some cases, victims were threatened by multiple sides

■ Guerrilla threats
■ Paramilitary and army threats

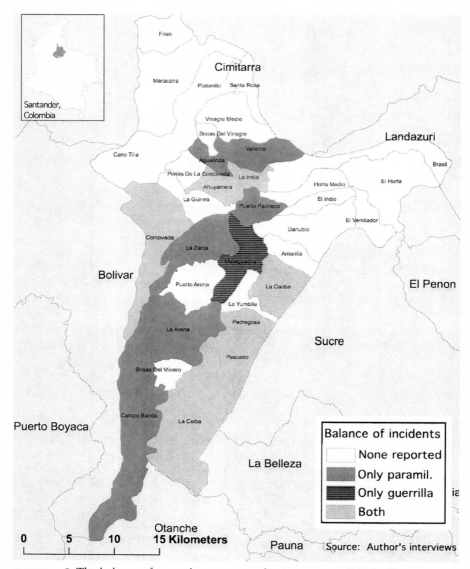

FIGURE 7.8 The balance of control among armed groups across ATCC villages,
1987–2007
Source: Interviews.

prevalent in villages such as Campo Banda and La Zarca, closer to the paramilitary bases in San Tropel and Puerto Araujo. The data again reinforce the
characterization that there existed conditions of largely dominant (though
incomplete) control by the paramilitaries where one would expect violence.

Lastly, the threat conciliation data also enable comparisons between violence in the ATCC "area of influence" and the immediate surrounding areas. This comparison suggests the ATCC experienced similar levels of armed conflict danger as its neighbors but suffered fewer actual killings. I pooled data on events from CINEP, Equipo Nizkor (based largely on press reporting and some police reports), Zamora (1983), and Vargas (1992) at the village level to classify killings by whether they were committed within the ATCC area of influence or in (rural) neighboring areas in the six municipios in which the ATCC is located. This data was then matched with the interview data I collected on (successful) threat conciliations within the ATCC region to gauge the number of killings *that might have occurred* absent the ATCC (conciliations plus the actual killings). I was able to classify data back in time over the thirty-two-year period from 1975, twelve years prior to the ATCC's founding, through 2007. These series are displayed in Figure 7.9 and mapped in Figure 7.10.

From about 1980 leading up to the ATCC's founding in 1987, the ATCC zone suffered much higher conflict homicide rates (per 100,000 residents) than neighboring villages. Because the greater repression might have made social organization even less likely, the trends argue against the ATCC forming solely because of mild conflict conditions. By contrast, in the post-1987 period after the ATCC was founded, the homicide rate in the ATCC region over time trends slightly lower than in the neighboring areas.[30] However, the dashed line, which represents the number of killings *and threats* that were resolved in the ATCC region – the counterfactual scenario – rises up to approximate the actual killings that occurred in the neighboring areas. Consistent with the ATCC becoming more effective by strengthening its conciliation institutions with a delegation of conciliators after increasing threats in the late 1990s, the number of successful conciliations is also shown to increase over time (the gap between the dashed total ATCC victims line and the solid line representing number of ATCC victims killed). These trends corroborate that the ATCC suffered far less violence than its neighbors despite experiencing similar or greater levels of danger from armed groups.[31] They also

---

[30] The interview data has some gaps in coverage due to memory lapses, especially in the early years. Press data is also missing for the year 1995 due to a gap between the two press datasets. There are slight discrepancies in the timing of events in the two datasets, again likely a memory issue for interview subjects. Despite these issues, although the graph displays the count of people killed in the ATCC area from the interview data for purposes of consistency with the threat counts, the CINEP/ Nizkor data of people killed yields a similar total number of victims over the same time period (sixteen versus twenty-two).

[31] By raw numbers of fatalities, the ATCC suffers relatively fewer killings over the time period. Note that while there is little reason to believe there were many threat victims that were saved or spared in the neighboring zones, this is not counted nor verified through these data because of the limited types of events in press coverage and challenges in covering the broad neighboring zone territory during fieldwork. This may produce an underestimate of rescues in neighboring zones. But by the same token, the ATCC's superior coverage based on its level of organization, press reporting, and interview data biases toward killings in the ATCC zone being overreported.

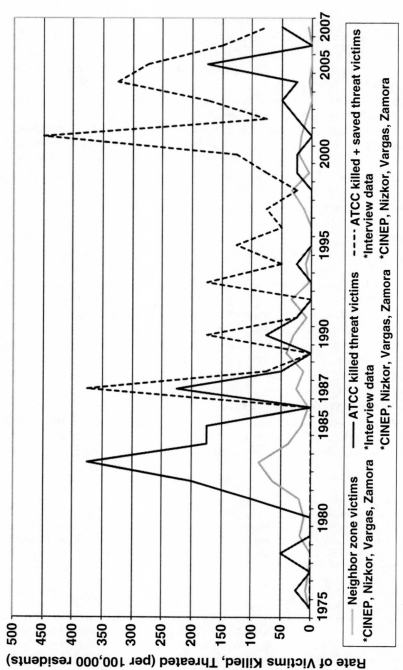

FIGURE 7.9 Threat and killing rates in the ATCC zone vs. neighboring areas
Source: Interviews and other sources.

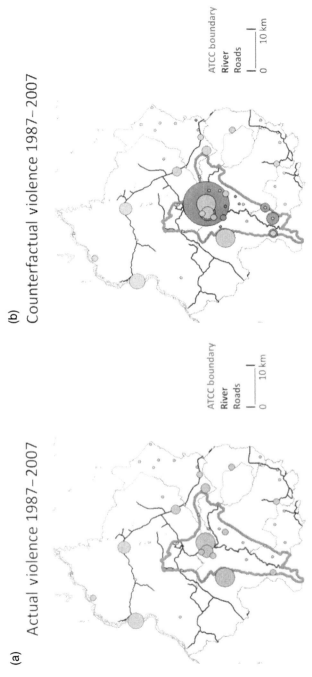

(a)

Actual violence 1987–2007

(b)

Counterfactual violence 1987–2007

ATCC boundary
River
Roads

0   10 km

FIGURE 7.10 Maps of actual and counterfactual violence in ATCC and neighboring regions, 1987–2007
Source: Interviews and other sources.

demonstrate how well-organized communities such as the ATCC are capable of suppressing violence even better than the average junta council.

CONDITIONS FOR THE MAINTENANCE OF LOCAL ORDER IN WARTIME

The ATCC functioned in a context of continued threat, danger, and denunciations, yet little to no violence occurred against its members. The success of the ATCC rests on three interlocking conditions: an institutional process to deal with denunciations, a shift in civilian preferences to abide by neutrality and not aid armed actors, and "favorable" preferences of armed actors (and favorable policies to "sweeten" the deal).

Condition 1: Institutional Investigatory Capacity. A civilian organization can mediate the flow of information and provide credible, balanced signals to armed actors about the participation of residents in the conflict.[32] As an institution, it has set procedures and is larger than any single person. This allows the process to be applied to any particular case without being *ad hoc* – it endures over time for more than a "single shot" game.

The institution need only provide information, as it can rely on "out-group policing" by the armed actors to enforce punishments when necessary (a variant of Fearon and Laitin's (1996) "in-group policing"). Similar to the Law Merchant institution that helped resolve disputes among traders in medieval Europe (Milgrom et al. 1990), the onus is on the individual in the community to stay out of trouble with the armed actors. Since the institution only provides information, it cannot restrict residents (whether few or many) from participating in the conflict and thereby running the risk of being denounced and killed if they are "outed." In other words, it stays an execution, but only until a verdict is reached. The institution alone cannot broadly eliminate violence against civilians, only against "virtuous" ones.

I found that investigations by the ATCC, or clarifications ("*aclaraciones*"), as the residents refer to them, actually unfold in a variety of ways. While it is most common for armed actors to bring suspects before the ATCC for inquiry, they do not always defer to this procedure and may be intent on eliminating targets on their lists – the ATCC does not always learn about threats or gather information strictly "by the book" as I first expected. In these circumstances, ATCC civilian informants that know of threats may leak that information to the Junta. Alternatively, some combatants in the armed groups with affinities for the civilians (referred to as "angels" or "friends of peace") may oppose a particular "limpieza," or "cleansing," and surreptitiously alert the ATCC.[33] Usually once the

---

[32] Participation can include active fighting but also acts short of this, including giving information, food, shelter, etc.

[33] ATCC#11, La India, 11/2007.

ATCC is made aware of threats it is able to intervene – even when the armed groups were originally quite determined to eliminate suspected collaborators.

Condition 2: Civilian Pacifist Preferences. To eliminate violence against civilians, the civilians must also confront the "preference problem," or the problem that some civilians prefer to participate in the war more than others (or alternatively, are less "deterrable" from collaborating with an armed group). Preferences for participating in the conflict can be influenced by various sources. As discussed in other literatures, there may be substantial selective benefits to aiding or joining an armed group (Lichbach 1994). Examples from the ATCC region include payments for aid; threats for not providing aid; payments for cultivation of coca, from which cocaine is made; or gaining an advantage against one's neighbor. These rationalist/materialist benefits may be counterbalanced by other factors that work to keep civilians out of conflicts. For one, economic development and economic opportunities can reduce the desperation that may drive poor residents to grow coca or seek other selective payments from armed groups.

Norms of nonviolence and pacifism or the philosophical and ideational belief that peace and nonviolent advocacy are morally superior to war and killing, are another way to keep civilians from getting entangled with an armed group. The pervasiveness of religion and spirituality can shape these moral antiviolence beliefs, as some ATCC residents asserted the Seventh-Day Adventist theology did in their region.[34] For instance, civilians that obey strong norms of nonviolence may be less inclined to participate in coca cultivation, even if they are economically disadvantaged. These nonviolence norms and the "culture of peace" are often the focus of peace-building strategies.

Various events and circumstances surrounding the founding of the ATCC likely contributed to building a "culture of peace" and norms for neutrality, nonviolence, and nonparticipation in the conflict. First, the ultimatum to displace led to a sorting process where less resolute residents left the region or joined their armed actor patrons (Hernández Delgado 2004, 329). Second, once the ATCC was founded, solidarity was strengthened by the persisting threat environment (García 1996, 251). Third, there was some social indoctrination and awareness raising (*"concientización"*) by the ATCC in its early years. Large meetings were held in the plazas and the recordings of meetings with armed actors would be played on loudspeakers as a form of ideational coordination. There were also educational programs in the villages to explain the purpose and functioning of the ATCC and educate residents about human rights. The community also later founded a peace radio station that would politely decline requests to play *narcocorridos* or other violence-themed

---

[34] ATCC#1, 7, La India, 10/2007. Many of the leaders of the Adventist church were also leaders in the ATCC, though the organization also featured prominent participation of other denominations, including Pentacostals, Evangelicals, and Catholics.

songs.[35] Fourth, the institutional investigation process gave further motivation to civilians who were considering aiding armed groups to straighten up or leave the organization or the region for fear of being targeted (as did the protection of upstanding residents). Fifth, a "Group of Conciliators" was established to mediate interpersonal disputes so they would not be resolved through outside actors. Sixth, the accords also won commitments from the armed actors to refrain from imposing on civilians by asking for support, making nonparticipation in the conflict more permissible.

Norms can be a powerful force for nonviolence but alone are not sufficient to protect civilians from violence since the politics of civil war show that many upstanding people can be falsely implicated as enemy supporters (Kalyvas 2006). This is confirmed by evidence on the variation in the strength and pervasiveness of ATCC norms over time. For instance, although many residents were very spiritual and pacifist before 1987, violence was rampant and many exemplary residents were killed by false accusations.[36] There was no way to "vouch" for pacifist citizens who had been implicated, so pacifist and opportunistic citizens alike were killed. While norms were strengthened after 1987, it is unlikely that the degree of faith and spiritual purity of residents alone brought about the extreme reduction in violence.

Condition 3: Armed Actor Incentives for Compliance. Civilian information systems and pacifist norms can be helpful but will not eliminate violence if armed actors have no incentives to abide by (agree to) the civilians' institutional procedures in the first place. Why should armed actors not simply kill a civilian implicated with helping their enemy? Some amount of joint interest among the armed actors to preserve or not directly target the civilian community must exist (i.e., this argument is less likely to apply to genocidal situations or "draining the sea"). However, this does not mean that an armed actor alone has no interests in committing violence against civilians (this might depend on the choices of its rivals). For instance, all armed actors may seek to coerce support of the population through violence, though they all may also prefer accuracy to avoid angry backlashes.[37]

The ATCC civilians pursued a cooperative strategy through negotiations and dialogues to get armed actors to buy into their process. They negotiated symmetrical, transparent agreements so that armed groups could be confident they were not losing civilian support to other groups (and they tape-recorded meetings for added transparency). The investigation process reduces the burden on armed actors to carefully select their victims to deter enemy collaboration

---

[35] To such requests, the disc jockey would say, "So sorry, but we can't help with that." (*"Que pena, pero no le podemos colaborar con eso"*).

[36] ATCC#3, La India, 10/2007.

[37] As one respondent suggested, "Armed actors want to feel like they're needed by the civilian population. They want to solve all civilian problems, even intrafamily disputes." ATCC#3, La India, 10/2007.

since the ATCC bears these costs. The ATCC also discarded strategies and policies that might run against armed actor preferences and upset the institutional equilibrium. For instance, since the armed groups wanted to be seen as the legitimate law of the land and were sensitive to bad publicity, the ATCC more conciliatorily opted not to publicly denounce suspected perpetrators of acts of violence by name.[38] The ATCC also chose not to prohibit the armed groups from passing through their territory since it belongs to "all Colombians" (but insisted they did not bring arms into communities), which allowed for the independent verification of the fair implementation of its institutional procedures.[39]

Civilians may also even provide some benefits to armed actors by acting as neutral arbiters and serving as a channel of communication between enemy groups. First, the ATCC helped the armed actors negotiate various prisoner-of-war exchanges.[40] Second, the ATCC has facilitated negotiations for armed actor demobilizations by guaranteeing the security of combatants as they reintegrate into civilian society. In the mid-1990s, some members of the local FARC fronts (including a commander) took advantage of the ATCC's arbitration and laid down their arms.[41] Third, ATCC peace overtures also reportedly facilitated cease-fires – a mutually beneficial "*descanso*," or rest. As one resident eloquently described the armed groups' desire to avoid unnecessarily antagonizing their enemies, "When passing a beehive, don't throw stones."[42] This jibes with accounts from World War I of troops from opposite trenches tacitly colluding to not fight (Axelrod 1984). Although not directly related to the armed actors' accession to the ATCC's investigation procedures, these benefits help "grease the deal" and can allow for bargaining leverage across issues, including civilian security.

In the ATCC's experience, armed actors have generally fought through the civilian population, being loath to engage in direct confrontations with the enemy.[43] Limiting civilian defections by limiting casualties appears to have become a second-best option to paying the costs of winning the civilians' full allegiance. The perception of fairness of this civilian arrangement turns out to be central to its stability and compliance. By implication, the process depends

---

[38] ATCC#3, 6, La India, 10/2007.

[39] This indeed was a concern of the guerrillas and later the paramilitaries. In response to the initial proposal, a guerrilla commander said, "Compañeros, these conditions that you are demanding are not fair, you would have to also impose them on the army and the paramilitaries, who are your greatest enemies" (García 1996: 196).

[40] ATCC#3, La India, 10/2007.   [41] ATCC#6, La India, 11/2007.

[42] ATCC#4, La India, 10/2007. "Si yo voy a pasar por el lado de las abejas, mejor no tirar la piedra."

[43] ATCC#15, Bogotá, 11/2007. One respondent told me, "It's not convenient for the armed groups to fight" ("*no le conviene*"). Instead they prefer the safer option of fighting a dirty war for civilian support. Another respondent said, "The entire armed actor effort of the 1990s was to regain control of the people." ATCC#3, La India, 10/2007.

on the armed actors' access to high-quality, transparent information to independently verify the workings of the ATCC. Ironically, *sapo* armed actor informants embedded within civilian society are a central source of confidence in the institution.[44]

Accounts from the combatants (from archives, interviews, and secondary reports) support this view of their preferences and strategies toward civilians. The AUC paramilitaries had relatively greater control and capability than the guerrillas, and therefore greater incentives and opportunities to commit violence. However, there is evidence that both groups could be persuaded by community processes. Consistent with the paramilitary bloc apparently committing more abuses outside the ATCC zone than within it (as illustrated by the San Tropel killings and the data in Figure 7.9), the narratives indicate that the armed groups of the region were not simply especially respectful or did not generally prefer to avoid targeting civilians.

The accounts instead suggest that the use of violence is conditional on community organization and collective action. This insight is borne out in a verbatim transcript of a meeting between the ATCC leader, the representatives of the relatively poorly organized villages of San Tropel and Santa Rosa on the border of the ATCC, and a paramilitary subcommander held in 2001 in Santa Rosa, Cimitarra (from the ATCC archive; see full dialogue in Appendix B). When Santa Rosa residents voiced concerns about being stigmatized by the guerrillas, they probed whether the paramilitaries would leave and allow them the kind of autonomy enjoyed by the ATCC. The paramilitary subcommander present tellingly responded, "The entire community would have to decide ... But if only two or three people don't want our presence, then we'll continue to be here." Freedom from armed group incursions would depend on the level of community cohesion, indicating the guarantees of the ATCC process itself were pivotal in affecting the group's calculus and diminishing violence, rather than some inherent characteristics of or changes within the armed group.

Another ex-paramilitary subcommander from the bloc provides additional confirmation.[45] He noted that violence was more frequently employed prior to 2000 because they had not yet learned how to interact with civilians. Worried about losing support and seeking less costly strategies, they became increasingly willing to delegate the maintenance of order, but mainly to well-functioning village councils.

The AUC paramilitaries would be expected to have relatively *fewer* incentives to commit violence in the zones neighboring the ATCC where their control was even more dominant. However, as noted by a village representative from neighboring San Tropel, there was both greater control and greater repression, "For us it hasn't gone very well, since we're 100 percent dominated by the Autodefensas" (2001 meeting in Santa Rosa, ATCC Archives). A similar

---

[44] ATCC#1, La India, 8/2008.   [45] Exc#7, Bogotá, 8/2009.

pattern can be seen with the guerrillas. One resident who moved to the ATCC region from another part of Sucre municipality under heavier guerrilla control said that the guerrillas would not investigate gossip there, but would simply kill "at once."[46]

Greater background on the motivations behind the paramilitaries' stances toward communities and their ambivalence is found in additional archival minutes from a meeting with a different AUC subcommander in an ATCC village from September 2003.[47] In the verbatim exchange, Comandante Montoya, true to his group's counterinsurgent, "self-defense" mission, initially proclaims his solidarity with the campesinos, "We truly believe our work should go hand in hand with the community ... to free this zone from the guerrilla. We're here because there are campesinos ... It is for this reason in some circumstances we accept your opinions, but in others we disregard them because this war is difficult." He later derides the guerrillas, professes his own group's humaneness, and also acknowledges the weight of the accords signed with the ATCC:

It's the guerrillas that attack you. In our ideological principles we respect life and come from the communities – we aren't ordered to kill campesinos. Commander Botalón talked to me about the accords and we believe we are complying with them. We accept your claim to the right of neutrality. But ... since the conflict is intensifying, the population should choose a side.

Montoya allows the right of neutrality and claims to have respected it, but also maintains the possibility of an exit from this clause. His blunt words express his first-best preference for civilian allegiance. However, he later vacillates between allowing civilians to live independently and public displays of strength through tacit threats for civilian support.

Montoya goes on to more clearly express his main concern: that of civilians' defection to the guerrillas. Acknowledging that the AUC does not depend much on the population for material support, he wants to assure the accords are being reciprocally upheld:

We don't need things [drugs, food, and arms] from you the way the guerrillas do. I recommend you don't compromise yourselves [with the guerrillas]. That's not a threat, it's a suggestion ... *The campesino compromises himself when he conceals information about where the guerrillas are and about their activities.* This is indeed a problem. Such houses [and traitors] shouldn't be allowed to do this because they'll be killed. *The campesino that dedicates himself just to his family doesn't have any problem; if he acts to the contrary, he will see* (emphasis added).

Montoya acknowledges that they try to avoid pressuring civilian involvement, but again, there is a tension in his rhetoric between "suggestions" to gain civilian support and using "threats" to deter defections. The contradictions suggest preferences that, although conflicted, are settled on the second-

---

[46] ATCC#21, La India, 10/2007.   [47] Pseudonym; edited for clarity.

best option. He would like civilians to inform on guerrillas, but his main priority is that they at least do not aid them. In the ATCC's solution to this dilemma of armed groups, the threats are mainly against enemy collaborators, while noncollaborators are left alone.

The Jekyll-and-Hyde balancing act of these paramilitaries is confirmed by Colombian scholars Gutiérrez Sanín and Barón (2005). They concur that the paramilitaries have been willing to allow civilians space for autonomy within certain constraints, "[Commander] Botalón tolerates trade unionism and collective action not controlled by the paramilitary, as long as it clearly distances itself from the guerrilla" (20). The authors observe the group's interest in maintaining order on the cheap, though also suggest it is tenuous, as the possibility of the breakdown of that order is never far away, "Botalón ... has learnt to calculate keeping in mind long-term horizons, which involves higher levels of self-control [and] replacement of pure repression by less expensive mechanisms ... Naturally, this does not prevent occasional outbursts of murderous violence" (22). With the theory developed here, these outbursts are now better accounted for.

EXPLAINING A RESURGENCE OF VIOLENCE, 2000–2007

Starting in 2000, violence returned to the ATCC region after nearly a decade with few if any civilian victims. Why did this occur? What changed? The fluctuation in this phase provides a good opportunity to test the theory of the effect of civilian institutions on new data. Although the new violence could reflect some amount of institutional breakdown of the ATCC, I find that the critical change was the degradation of norms of neutrality and nonviolence among the population due to exogenous factors.

The ATCC's residents were again put at greater risk as the guerrillas increased their presence in the region. Levels of contestation increased between the guerrillas and the then-dominant paramilitaries. With the contestation, violence increased as well. In 2001, paramilitaries began killing campesinos who resisted selling their land to *coqueros*, coca-growing campesinos involved with the AUC.[48] Guerrillas began collecting a "*vacuna*," or "vaccination" payment from civilians for protection, and when residents did not pay, they started killing too.[49] Conciliator estimates suggest about thirty-five civilians were killed in all.

In this period, the ATCC institution was actually strengthened, not weakened. For example, a formal *Tribunal* consisting of thirty elected members was established to improve the process of investigating denunciations. Information gathering was improved with the formation of village committees and delegates. An economic development report was

[48] ATCC#6, La India, 8/2008.   [49] ATCC#3, La India, 8/2008.

conducted and the ATCC also formalized its bylaws and began a membership drive to reassociate its "*socios*" (ATCC 2006; a membership contract document is displayed in Appendix B). Mediation efforts were also increasingly formalized with teams of conciliators and do not appear to have decreased in effectiveness.[50] Variation in the ATCC's institutions therefore does not appear to be the source of increased selective violence.

Instead, the change in the distribution of people in the population who were normatively committed to neutrality and noninvolvement in the armed conflict is associated with the increase in individuals killed.[51] The distribution shifted for two main exogenous reasons, both related to the fading of important norms that were formed from earlier experiences of suffering great violence and overcoming it. In the post-2000 period, there were two new populations in the ATCC region that were not committed to the norms inculcated at the ATCC's founding. First, beginning around 1999, the region saw the arrival of new migrants who had not experienced the ATCC's history, did not have the same average level of commitment to avoid the conflict, and did not have a good understanding of how the organization worked. The population in the region swelled by as many as 2,000 people, many of them coming from the department of Bolívar to plant coca. With the influx, La India was full of people. Prices rose, brothels opened, and a resident complained about the "drinking and loud music all day long."[52]

These migrants and newcomers were drawn by the region's tranquillity. Some initially joined the ATCC but did not uphold their commitments and later violated the ATCC's rules. These newcomers tended to try to have their cake and eat it too: they wanted the protection (and perhaps camaraderie) of the ATCC's "public umbrella," yet also wanted the easy gains from illicit activities. Coca divided the people, as the ATCC made an agreement with the armed actors not to get involved with the crop because "it was their thing."[53] As an ATCC leader stated in a meeting with *coqueros*, "He who plants coca is not to get involved in the organization" (September 20, 2002, in the village of Ahuyamera). Indeed, the ATCC's members report not knowing many of the victims from this time, although they suggest that many of the thirty-five murders occurred against residents of villages some distance to the southwest of La India, such as La Corcovada and La Zarca – villages with coca farms and *coqueros*. This account corresponds with data on coca cultivation across villages I calculated based on UN aerial surveys, as displayed in the map in Figure 7.11.

The immigrants were, either by nature or experience, more opportunistic than the ATCC population, or were simply less morally committed to neutrality and so were enticed by armed actors into the coca economy. Given the relatively low incomes of these *coquero* civilians, coca profits were a tempting way

[50] ATCC#12, Bogotá, 8/2008.   [51] ATCC#3, 11, La India, 8/2008.
[52] ATCC#17, La India, 7/2008.   [53] ATCC#11, La India, 8/2008.

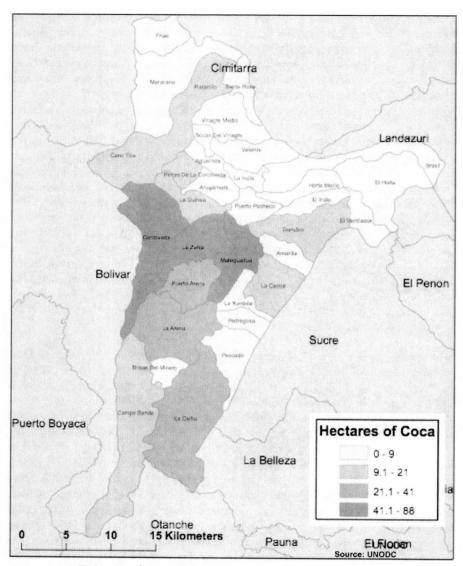

FIGURE 7.11 Estimates of coca production in ATCC villages, 2003
Source: UN Aerial Survey using 2003 data; calculations and map by author.

to increase their earnings.[54] But it also entailed risks: once a civilian begins growing coca and selling it to one of the armed actors, he or she is seen as participating in the conflict, sometimes triggering a response from the enemy armed group. In these cases, despite the ATCC's commitment to protecting the lives of all civilians, there was little the ATCC could do. At times, these incidents of violence had spillover effects, intensifying competition and conflict among armed actors, causing some pacifist residents to be seen as "guilty" merely by association. These concerns are confirmed in meeting minutes from discussions in 2002 between the ATCC and the coca growers in the region.[55] However, unlike in the cases of collaborating *coqueros*, the ATCC was still generally able to mediate successfully on the behalf of noncollaborators.[56]

In a sense, the ATCC was a victim of its own success. Anecdotal evidence suggests that the "peace" and growth the ATCC created during its nonviolent era of the 1990s created the moral hazard of attracting these new migrants to the region to share in its prosperity.[57] For instance, a current ATCC member said he moved to the sanctuary of the ATCC region from elsewhere because of the danger of gossip and slander he faced there.[58] Yet, similar to how the gentrification of a run-down neighborhood can push out longtime residents, success can sow the seeds of its own demise. As the American baseball player Yogi Berra once said, "Nobody goes there anymore, it's too crowded." This reflects a partially "endogenous" source of change in the equilibrium of violence, as the institution itself, while beneficial, can also produce instability and be "self-undermining" (Greif and Laitin 2004). Residents said the ATCC was unable to counteract this trend: as an informal organization, it does not have the governing powers to set boundaries and keep migrants out.[59] These examples demonstrate the pernicious influence that coca and the prospects of easy money can have on a local civilian institution.

Second, a growing number of youth who were born around the time of the ATCC's founding came of age around 2000. These youths were not old enough to remember the formation of the community and so were less likely to be instilled with the community's neutrality norms (recall the plight of Señor George). They were born into the ATCC system and had not agreed to

---

[54] As one *coquero* declared in a meeting with the ATCC, "I am the owner of this farm here and I also plant coca, but I am not ashamed since we are in a precarious economic situation … I'd like it if those that have coca crops and are landowners were to plant agricultural crops and buy cattle, that will help us end with coca" (Archive, 2002).

[55] As one ATCC leader stated, "The policy of the ATCC is to not get involved in questions of coca. If some campesino has some kind of problem with the state, he'll have to face the consequences. The problem is that this brings disputes between the [armed] groups over the territory and forced displacement" (Archive 2002).

[56] ATCC#4, La India, 8/2008.   [57] ATCC#15, Bogotá, 10/2007.
[58] ATCC#22, La India, 8/2008.   [59] ATCC#3, La India, 8/2008.

live in the area of their own volition (rather by that of their parents).[60] These youths "created disorder" and were often paid by armed actors to be informants (often using the money to buy small prizes, such as soft drinks or new shoes).[61] Again, once a youth is involved in the conflict, there is little the ATCC can do. If a family's adolescent is found to be continually causing trouble, the Junta tells the family to leave. The parents cannot go against the community's request without losing the ATCC's protection and facing potentially lethal retribution from an armed group.

That the ATCC could do little for these victims is not to say that members of the Association were not greatly pained by the killings. This became clear to me one night when an ATCC founder and I got to chatting, sitting in plastic chairs on his cement-strip porch and drinking sugary soft-drinks as the heat of the day finally began to fade.[62] I gently asked about the resumption of violence, a period that few had discussed with me in detail. He looked up and, gazing off into the darkness, listed the names of the victims, one after another, in cadence, but pausing between each one for emphasis, perhaps, or respect or remorse. When he finished, he was fighting back a tear. I was amazed that, even after a few years, he could recall almost every single one. Even though the conflict-related activities were "their thing" – a choice of most of the victims and separate from the ATCC – I sensed regret and sorrow that the ATCC was not able to do more.

As the ATCC and other communities have realized, maintaining their process requires continuing collective action and active management. An implication from this discussion is that, in addition to mediation procedures, community processes to maintain norms are central to staving off the return of violence in the long term. Stability requires policies to counteract the self-undermining processes triggered by their successes. Alternative development programs can directly affect violence against civilians insofar as they can prevent civilians from participating in the conflict out of opportunism or desperation. Although coca cultivation in the region has declined in recent years, the ATCC has continued working with residents to keep them from growing coca.[63] Some residents have also participated in the government's "*guardabosques*" (forest ranger) subsidy program to eradicate coca on their farms. Programs to provide opportunities for the community's youth are equally important for stopping violence.

CONCLUSIONS

This chapter profiled some of the unarmed, nonviolent strategies that are used against heavily armed combatants in civil war settings to protect human rights.

[60] ATCC#3, La India, 8/2008.   [61] ATCC#3, La India, 7/2008.
[62] ATCC#11, La India, 8/2008.   [63] ATCC#11, La India, 8/2008.

The ATCC experience as a single but important community suggests that civilians are not powerless and can effectively organize against repression to make life in lawless wartime settings a little more predictable and ordered. The ATCC civilians did not wait for intervention or focus on national-level peace negotiations or military strategies. Instead, they took matters into their own hands. I explored how and whether their efforts – the mediation, production of credible information, and behavioral norms – functioned as an explanation for reduced violence.

I developed an empirical framework and methods for measurement to study this form of "peace building" in the midst of conflict. The dataset of threat conciliations helped trace the ATCC process and even provided quantification of how the armed conflict and concomitant threats unfolded and were dealt with. Under the ATCC investigations mechanism, individuals found to have been wrongly suspected of collaborating were less likely to be killed than those found to have collaborated. The ATCC's cooperation and institutions set it apart in the eyes of armed groups from its violence-suffering neighbors. These findings suggest that existing theories of violence such as the balance of control have limitations since they do not completely explain violence: denunciations against individuals were short-circuited and the production of violence did not lie solely with armed groups. The findings have broad implications for civilian agency, community autonomy and later resilience, and peace building in civil wars.

Perhaps one sobering implication is that peace is not simply or easily "created" or "built." The absence of violence emerged through a subtle inter-action between mediation, nonviolent civilian norms, and armed actor preferences. There are also limitations on where civilian organizational processes succeed – they are again not a panacea. Along with successes, communities face challenges and failures. The ATCC suffered continued pressure from armed actors and, at times, outbursts of violence. As the ATCC and other communities have realized, stability requires continuing cooperation to counteract the self-undermining processes triggered by their successes. These may include strengthened mediation procedures, community processes to maintain norms, or even alternative development programs that limit civilians' participation in the conflict out of opportunism or desperation. The ATCC has continued working to keep residents from growing coca and provide opportunities for youth.[64]

Organizations such as the ATCC exemplify what could be, what is possible. These kinds of communities brave great risks and costs in resisting pressures from armed groups and yet are crucial inspirational models. To the extent that local peace institutions take hold across many communities, grassroots move-ments may have broader effects on belligerents' behavior at the macro level,

---

[64] ATCC#11, La India, 8/2008.

including resolving uncertainty, the reduction of violence, and supporting national peace negotiations to bring conflicts to a close. The replicability of experiences such as that of the ATCC should certainly be studied further, but there is reason to believe they can generalize to other communities.[65]

The ATCC's context of a frontier area with shifting conflict dynamics and little state presence or rule of law resembles other conflict-ridden parts of the world. Some of the ATCC's features may be distinct, but within Colombia similar investigation procedures have been implemented by certain village councils and Indigenous groups in the crossfire, including the Nasa Indians in the Cauca department. Many communities may be lying in wait to mimic these processes, though less organized or highly endangered communities may consider less institutionalized protective strategies. By unpacking the details of how local, nonviolent protection institutions work beyond the mantra of "resistance," new communities and NGOs will hopefully be better able to understand and apply these models when and where they are needed. The next chapter continues this task by comparing towns in the department of Cundinamarca.

---

[65] Similar mediation programs have been implemented in some American cities to end cycles of gang violence (e.g., see Project CeaseFire, today known as Cure Violence: www.cureviolence.org).

8

Discovering Civilian Autonomy in Cundinamarca

I'm going to tell you a story/ about why my town cried/ It happened in the early morning/ disturbing a deep quiet/ The uniformed troops/ knocking as they could/ awakened many people/ according to them guerrillas/ They broke into homes/ of whom they never should have/ asking for papers/ along with the prosecutor/ hurting feelings/ and opening many wounds . . .

We struggle to keep ourselves/ united in love/ and forget that the State/ scarred our heart/ May the experience we lived/ help us not falter/ We ask the God of all/ give us your grace and strength/ so Quipile won't cry/ and that way is reborn.[1]

           – "The Day Quipile Cried"
           Berenice Cabra Jímenez

Para adelante cuando unidos; solos jodidos.

United we move ahead; alone, we're screwed.

           – Resident of Vianí (V#1, Vianí, 3/2009)

If you head west from the Colombian capital of Bogotá, just after dropping off the central plateau you will find a number of small, isolated, mountainous coffee-growing towns. In the 1990s, FARC guerrillas came to these towns,

---

[1] Translated to the English by the author. "El Día Que Quipile Lloró": Voy a contarles la historia/ Por la que lloró mi pueblo/Ocurrió muy de mañana/Perturbando un gran silencio/Las tropas de uniformados/A golpes como pudieron/Despertaron mucha gente/Según ellos guerrilleros/Penetraron en las casas/de quienes nada debían/y pidiendo documentos/Junto con la fiscalía/Maltrataron sentimientos/y abrieron muchas heridas . . .
 Luchemos por mantenernos/Unidos en el amor/Y olvidemos que el estado/Hirió nuestro corazón/Que la experiencia vivida/Nos sirva pa` no caer/Pidamos al Dios de todos/Nos de su gracia y poder/Pa` que Quipíle no llore/Y así vuelva a renacer.

massing their forces as part of their strategy to eventually cordon off and lay siege to the capital. These towns were subjected to pressures and violence that many had not experienced since the bipartisan violence of the 1950s. No known formal civil society peace organizations emerged to respond to the conflict. Yet even in this region, could the variation in the social and organizational landscape have impacted how this new period of armed conflict would affect the civilian population?

This chapter explores additional town cases in the department of Cundinamarca that were selected with the aid of universal data and statistical models (as discussed in Chapter 6). The cases are similar or "matched" on many of their characteristics except for differences in their historical densities of junta councils. The goal of this exercise is to further test theory as well as assess the accuracy of the statistical analysis.

I compare here the neighboring rural towns between Bogotá and the Magdalena River of Quipile (key-PEE-lay), which historically had a low number of junta councils, with Vianí (vee-ah-NEE) and Bituima (bee-TWEE-mah), which together are similar in size and population to Quipile (and were historically the same county) but had many more juntas in 1985 relative to their populations.[2] I qualitatively investigate several central questions about these cases to assess their fit with theory: What was the status of junta councils on the ground and what other forms of social unity or divisions have existed? What role if any did they play in affecting the nature of the armed conflict and violence? An additional task throughout this chapter is to assess the quality of the case matches using qualitative data and confirm whether the similarities and differences encountered in the statistical analysis actually exist.

I argue by way of the Millian method of difference that the towns have many conditions in common – including conditions that might predict violence – but exhibit social differences. Despite being only several hours away from Bogotá by car today, they have been historically and similarly isolated from state presence. They are wedged between the touristic and commercial towns of Anolaima, the self-proclaimed "fruit capital" of Colombia, and Villeta, the self-proclaimed "*panela*" (sugarcane) capital of Colombia. They are also wedged between roads running northwest and southwest away from Bogotá (and therefore roughly equidistant from the city) but are isolated, and only recently accessible by paved or semipaved roads.[3] The populations are purely "campesino," or mestizo, with almost no Indigenous or Afro-Colombian residents. The towns are impoverished and have poor provision of public services. Critically, and consistent with being small neighbor municipios, these towns

---

[2] It is appropriate to consider Vianí and Bituima together because they are historically almost a single area. One resident described them as "brother" towns. B#1, Bogotá, 3/2009.

[3] These towns are not only isolated, but also forgotten. When I presented my preliminary research at a think tank in Bogotá, the Colombian audience did not even realize that these counties existed. They did not know where they were and thought they were perhaps villages.

faced similar projections of force by armed groups. The army only really came to these regions during the implementation of Plan Patriota to disperse the guerrillas and keep them from approaching the capital. For these reasons, Quipile and Bituima-Vianí are nearly ideal selections for representativeness of many Colombian towns. Further, their cultural conservativeness and relatively long institutional legacies make them tougher tests for collective action.[4]

Contiguity implies similar topographical, geographical, political, and cultural environments, but the physical separation between these towns makes contamination effects unlikely. Although the counties are situated in the mountainous terrain of majestic, verdant Andean peaks, they are divided by a small set of higher peaks. Historically, some communication passed through the corregimiento of La Sierra, but because of the peaks, the towns developed separately. Indeed, they are located in separate geographic subregions (provinces) of Cundinamarca, with Quipile known as the "ceiling" of Tequendama, while Vianí and Bituima are situated at the southern end of Central Magdalena (Figure 8.1).

Based on the differences in the junta councils data, I expected to see differences on the ground in historical levels of organization and horizontal social relations. Given civilian autonomy theory's predictions for how variation in these organizations affects violence, I therefore also expected to see differences in how civilians were able to respond to the dynamics of armed conflict, conditional on their levels of organization. However, I did not expect to find full-blown peace organizations such as "peace communities." If these organizations had existed, they surely would have already been reported in the press. Rather, I expected I might find subtler and less well-known forms of social cohesion and responses to the conflict. In correspondence with their measured values of juntas then, I expected to find levels of organization increasing from low levels in Quipile (which had few juntas), to a high degree of collective action in Vianí, and even more in Bituima.

The analysis of the social life and armed conflict in the towns in this chapter is based on firsthand field research carried out in 2009. I conducted forty interviews with a variety of people with historical knowledge of social processes and the armed conflict in these zones as well as additional interviews with ex-combatants that operated in the region.[5] When possible and as much as

---

[4] In other words, their eras of colonist cooperation are in the distant past. Bituima and Vianí were founded in 1772 and 1853, respectively, and were on the old road from the Magdalena River to Bogotá. Quipile was founded in 1900.

[5] As noted in Chapter 4, to increase the precision of historical knowledge and periodization, the body of interviews benefits from people who arrived in the towns at different times or became involved with the juntas at different times. An interesting outcome of the interviews was the revelation of the different cognitive frames the residents of the different towns would subtly express as they would respond to questions and think about social concepts through common catchphrases. These sayings that came out during conversation are telling of cross-town differences (it is equally telling what is not said). I include them in their original form in direct quotations as much as possible.

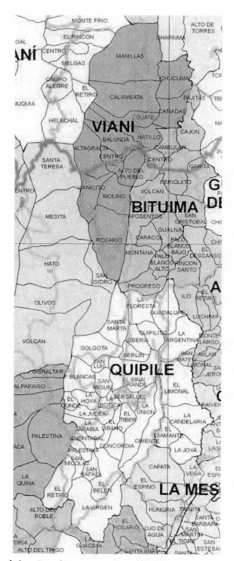

FIGURE 8.1 Villages of the Cundinamarca municipios
Source: Cundinamarca Secretaría de Planeación.

possible, I visited the villages in the countryside and spoke with villagers when they traveled to the town centers or Bogotá. Despite the absence of formal peace organizations, I was surprised at how openly many subjects were willing to discuss not only the history of the conflict and acts of violence, but also depravities in the local political system. The information from these interviews is supplemented by available secondary sources.

Despite my own initial skepticism at detecting differences on the ground, I did in fact encounter the expected variation in precursor social conditions and autonomy examples in my field research. Quipile historically had divided social relations and few if any responses to armed groups.[6] Vianí was characterized by more unified and pacific social relations, and some "weapons of the weak" tactics. Bituima, with the highest density of juntas, had both unity of social relations *and instances of collective civilian resistance to armed group hostility*. However, there were also displacements and collaboration with armed actors in many villages across the towns. I assess the effect of civilians' actions on violence in three ways: civilians' accounts, ex-combatant accounts, and additional indicators of patterns of violence. In line with theoretical predictions, the fieldwork highlights even greater differences in levels of violence across the towns than is seen in the quantitative data.

The residents of Quipile were disadvantaged in being able to cope with armed groups relative to those of Vianí and Bituima due to several factors. Quipile is relatively impoverished in experience with the voluntary provision of public goods and projects. It historically had lower levels of education (or a smaller educated class to help organize), greater (perceived) inequality of social relations, was more geographically and politically fractured, and there were few outsiders to nurture communal cooperation. In contrast, while Vianí and Bituima were not greatly organized compared to some towns in other parts of the country, they were in some ways predisposed for social organization. Not only were there stronger juntas, more unity, fewer social problems, and other local organizations and associations, but there were also fortuitous (exogenous) twists of fate ("critical junctures") that helped them build these foundations.

The story of organization does not end there. On a deeper level, I also find that conflict hurt social organizations such as juntas. So, even though there were some collective actions against violence, they were not always coordinated directly through the medium of the juntas. As I discuss at the end of the chapter, I find a possible new, intervening explanation in clientelism as another reason why juntas were weakened. Comparisons with the ATCC point to reasons why clientelism can be the death knell of local organizations in some contexts but not others.

This chapter differs in its content and purpose from the analysis of the ATCC on several grounds. First, it serves as a qualitative test of observable implications of theory and is more tightly linked with the statistical analysis. These cases are separate from those used to *generate* theory. Second, rather than directly testing new mechanisms by linking them to micro-level outcomes, the emphasis is on showing that new civilian mechanisms are at least plausible. This is because in the absence of formal human rights organizations, there is

---

[6] That Quipile historically had fewer juntas does not necessarily mean that the juntas there never played important roles, just that they were generally weaker.

less reporting of information about violence and how civilians interacted with armed groups compared to what is available for the ATCC investigations mechanism. Third, and as a result of this different purpose and these informational challenges, this chapter is structured differently than the previous one.

The sections that follow are organized by causal and historical progression up through the recent period of armed conflict. Within each section, I first explore Quipile – the "negative" case – and then contrast it with Vianí and Bituima. This chapter proceeds by first recounting experiences with La Violencia, then preexisting social capital and juntas, then the incidence of conflict, then responses to conflict and civilian interactions with armed groups, then clientelism, and lastly outcomes of (the dependent variable of) violence. I conclude with a summary of findings and methodological contributions and indicate how the insights from this chapter compare with the findings from the other chapters and may generalize more broadly.

This, then, is the story of how these communities made it through the war years ...

MANIFESTATIONS AND IMPACTS OF LA VIOLENCIA

Understanding the local manifestations of La Violencia of the 1950s is important because historical tranquility could mean any later relationship found between civilian social organization and violence could be spurious. There are also additional lessons about how peace was restored and whether historical conflict triggered local collective action and cooperation in the form of junta councils. Information on the events of this era was gathered by speaking with elderly residents of these communities who were youths when La Violencia occurred as well as asking middle-aged adults what they remembered being told by their parents.

Their stories confirm that La Violencia affected all three towns: residents spoke of fear, threats, violence, and displacement, often with partisan motivations, and of the presence of guerrilla bands, or "*chusma*."[7] Impressively, residents could often recall specific events and episodes. One town had only bipartisan conflict, while others had guerrilla bands in addition to bipartisan conflict and killings. In support of the larger claims of this book, some of the residents also recall civilian responses to deal with the violence even in these early times. Most people attributed the decline in political tensions and the ultimate end of violence to the National Front pact at the national level, but

---

[7] The term "*chusma*," translating to "rabble" or "mob" in English, was used in the vernacular as a catchall phrase for an armed band. In some parts of Colombia, where there was conflict between multiple bands, there was fighting between the Chusma and the Contra-Chusma. Interestingly, my findings do not completely concur with the categorizations of La Violencia by Guzmán et al. (1963). I found violence in all three towns, whereas Bituima is not listed in Guzmán et al.

some suggested that juntas at the local level helped repair social relations and build unity (and possibly political homogeneity as well).[8]

Residents of Quipile report that it was primarily a politically Conservative town in the 1950s and experienced Liberal–Conservative partisan conflict and killing, with Liberals tending to suffer greater persecution. According to what one woman's mother told her, there was also sporadic presence of "La Chusma,"[9] and a man remembered that the armed Chusma passed through the sector of La Palestina (on the southwest edge of the municipio).[10] These *bandoleros* (gunslingers) were Conservatives and purportedly killed many people. Some residents also mentioned the Chusma leader Sangre Negra, or "Black Blood" (though it is not clear whether his band operated much in Quipile).[11] In La Sierra, on Quipile's northern border with Bituima, Conservative bandits would take Liberals down from the buses and kill them (La Virgen, at the southern boundary, was a Liberal bastion and suffered less).[12] Illustrating how widespread the violence was, a man said that his Conservative father, who had been living in the predominantly Liberal neighbor town of Anolaima, had to come to Quipile to escape the violence against Conservatives there.[13] At one point, the residents united to form a local guard to keep the *bandoleros* out.[14]

Vianí was a historically Liberal town and residents recall some levels of conflict and partisan tension through 1965. One person attested that many leaders in the town were killed in the 1950s.[15] Another cited the occurrence of threats, rape, and the burning of farms. One woman from a Liberal family recalled a specific episode when Conservatives came to burn her in-laws' farm.[16] By contrast, a different woman's family received threatening letters because her father was Conservative.[17] She remembers hearing of the Chusma, or "*Chulavitas*," and recalls that her father had to hide because Liberals were going to kill him. Another man said that while there was violence in the 1950s, the old city councilmen tended to get along.[18] Residents also mentioned the bandit Sangre Negra and said that, while he did not directly attack Vianí, his band was still operating in neighboring areas to the northwest (toward Villeta and Chaguaní) in the early 1960s.[19] Similar to Quipile, Vianí also saw organization for self-defense during this time with help from residents who were former soldiers.[20] The priest of the era also reportedly tried to defuse threats before they were acted upon.[21] Some

---

[8] E.g. B#2, Bituima, 3/2009.   [9] Q#1, Quipile, 3/2009.   [10] Q#2, Quipile, 3/2009.

[11] Q#3, Quipile, 3/2009. Sangre Negra was finally shot dead by the army in Tolima department in 1964 (Time Magazine 1964).

[12] Q#4, Quipile, 3/2009.   [13] Q#5, Quipile, 3/2009.   [14] Q#3, Quipile, 3/2009.

[15] V#3, Vianí, 3/2009.   [16] V#2, Bogotá, 3/2009.   [17] V#3, Vianí, 3/2009.

[18] V#4, Vianí, 3/2009.   [19] V#5, Bogotá, 3/2009.   [20] V#4, Vianí, 3/2009.

[21] V#4, Vianí, 3/2009. The priest, who arrived in the early 1960s (see later in chapter), used Sunday Mass to discuss social problems and shame thieves, and would promote dialogue to resolve conflicts between neighbors. The man was also sufficiently brazen that he would at times

believed the arrival of the juntas around 1962 did help unite people by at least highlighting community-wide interests through the completion of public goods projects, though the juntas originally only tended to manage community funds.[22]

In contrast to neighboring Vianí, and like Quipile, the population of Bituima was characterized as largely Conservative going into the 1950s.[23] According to some residents, their grandparents said small groups of *bandoleros* would attack political enemies.[24] Some Liberal families were run out of town or killed. A single large and powerful Liberal family persecuted many Conservative families during this time. A man I met in Quipile said his family was run out of Bituima and fled to Quipile for refuge.[25]

The record is clear that these towns of Cundinamarca experienced violence during the 1950s. But did this harm collective action everywhere? Why or why not? If all towns suffered from violence and this violence can increase social homogenization or organizational responses, including the development of juntas, why did Quipile have less widespread and sustained junta presence than Vianí and Bituima? This history suggests that the social differences I find between the towns in the next section are not solely due to being historically peaceful (or for that matter solely suffering, since all towns are similar in experiencing past violence).

THE JUNTAS DE ACCIÓN COMUNAL AND PREEXISTING SOCIAL CAPITAL

How do the municipios vary in terms of the breadth and depth of junta councils, other social organizations, and horizontal social relations (social capital) from the 1960s through the beginning of armed group presence and guerrilla incursions of the early 1990s? Answering this question helps verify whether the cross-municipio juntas variable from the statistical analysis is a faithful descriptor of different municipios' social lives – understanding whether, according to people's memories, the juntas were created, existed, and were active when the data say they were. It also provides a picture of what real juntas actually do.

What emerges from the interview responses are coarse but identifiable differences in the social landscape and images of social relations. I first review the challenging social landscape of Quipile and then recount the greater levels of organization, activity, and "convivencia," or coexistence, found in Vianí and Bituima. In the next section, I proceed to examine whether the variation in conditions mapped here predisposed these latter towns to be able to respond to the conflict. For ease of comparison, the synthesis of indicators from this qualitative analysis is displayed in Table 8.1.

---

purportedly approach suspects of crimes and grab them by the collar to rebuke them, practically scaring them into reforming.
[22] V#1, Vianí, 3/2009.   [23] B#1, Bogotá, 3/2009.   [24] B#2, Bituima, 3/2009.
[25] Q#6, Quipile, 3/2009.

TABLE 8.1 *Qualitative indicators of social cohesion and organization*

	Juntas and participation	Machete fights	Cattle/ coffee theft and responses	Other organizations	Equality
Quipile	Some juntas, but low participation and activity	Frequent	Thefts of cattle, tools, coffee	Failed efforts to form cooperatives (only some success recently)	"Three climates" and related social separation
Vianí	Juntas everywhere and examples of successful cooperation (within and among juntas)	Uncommon	Some cattle theft; response of local watch committees	Crop warehouse, etc.	Equal plots carved from *latifundios*; village elders conciliate
Bituima	Juntas everywhere and examples of successful cooperation	Uncommon	Some cattle theft; Response of local watch committees	A local NGO; some villages with many stores (places to socialize)	Church divided land equally; village elders conciliate

Quipile

Quipile certainly has some examples of social capital and junta activity, but the more common tendency has been difficult and distant social relations and a predominantly weak and narrow penetration of junta councils in the municipio. In exploring the modern origins of cooperation to provide public goods in Quipile, residents did recall an auspicious episode from the late 1950s. At that time, Quipile benefitted from a proactive pastor who helped organize the town to pave roads.[26] With his help, they contracted for the use of two bulldozers (once of which they aptly named the "Conqueror") from the departmental government.

For a variety of projects, both in the past and more recent, however, the townspeople themselves did not have to contribute effort or labor. A resident recalled that in the 1950s and perhaps into the 1960s, prison "chain gang" laborers were brought in from outside the municipio to build roads.[27] The residents were not brought together to maintain associative traditions for the common good. This challenge of energizing voluntary contributions for public goods carried through to later years. According to a former resident with a long-running history of involvement in a junta, it was a struggle, for example, to build an aqueduct system for the town.[28] He requisitioned funds to buy pipe and tried to get people to participate and contribute work, but little collaboration was forthcoming.[29] Indeed, other residents lamented that Quipile has never planned to develop and take advantage of its abundant water resources.[30] Similarly, the aforementioned roads constructed during the mid-twentieth century were allowed to fall into disrepair as residents and mayors could not cooperate to repave some sections that connect Quipile to neighbor municipios until a few years ago.[31]

The distribution and activities of juntas in Quipile are consistent with the town's general trend of collective action problems as residents recall historically few and ineffective juntas. This jibes with the municipio's statistics on juntas: the 1985 dataset shows that there were only eight juntas in the entire

---

[26] Q#7, Quipile, 3/2009.   [27] Q#2, Quipile, 3/2009.   [28] Q#5, Quipile, 3/2009.

[29] Q#2, Quipile, 3/2009. This man felt "he accomplished in one year as a leader what many presidents couldn't do in twenty," but finished so exhausted and embittered by the experience that he washed his hands of communal action. Others noted that a later effort to build a small hotel complex with a pool to bring tourist revenues to the town was a similar boondoggle. The pool was built but the complex was left incomplete and now sits in disuse.

[30] Ironically, during one of my field visits the aqueduct to the town center broke due to a few days of heavy, sustained *rain* that washed out the pipe connections up the mountain, leaving the town without water for three days. I was informed this was a frequent occurrence but that not much is done about it.

[31] Q#8, Quipile, 3/2009. For instance, a junta leader from the early 1990s reported she tried to repair a bulldozer and repaired roads to a few villages, but there was insufficient commitment and the people "got tired of working." Q#1, Quipile, 3/2009.

municipio (which encompassed thirty-two villages, four urban centers, and a population upwards of 8,000 people). One man recalled that, when he arrived in Quipile in 1980, the urban centers of the county seat, La Sierra, La Botica, Santa Marta, and La Virgen did have juntas, but many villages did not have juntas.[32] Residents described a push to form some juntas in the 1960s and 1970s, but the councils did not become ubiquitous. Even when they were founded in some places they suffered from low levels of participation and meeting attendance, were not sustained and were therefore short-lived.[33] Furthermore, it is telling what people did *not* mention in interviews – residents recalled few if any major projects implemented by the juntas. Even today, there is no designated communal junta meeting room in the municipio (or "*salon comunal*").

The variation of junta activity within municipios is of course more complex. Although the Quipile juntas have generally been weak, there have been some geographical pockets of organization. For instance, several people concurred that La Sierra (close to Bituima) has had more solidarity and been better organized.[34] A visit to La Virgen to the south also revealed greater cooperation and junta activity. A current priest observed some of the better-organized villages in the municipio were Guadalupe Bajo and La Unión but that only about three of the eleven villages in his ecclesiastical district had active juntas.[35] A villager felt that some villages such as Los Guayabos were united and successfully worked in groups, but that others such as Sinaí were not very united.[36] Another person believed distant villages like La Joya did not have juntas at all.[37] Multiple people further observed that there was historically little contact *between* the juntas in the municipio and that the juntas were themselves not very united.[38]

When and where the juntas have functioned in Quipile, they would, among other things, communicate urban planning needs to the mayor.[39] Juntas could also requisition resources for projects from the Committee of Coffee Growers (*Comité de Cafeteros*; although coffee production declined in the 1980s).[40] One

---

[32] A different person disagreed and thought that juntas were in fact widespread in the municipio by the 1980s, but inconsistencies with this statement during the interview provide reasons to doubt this assertion.

[33] Q#11, Quipile, 3/2009. Another long-time resident believed many juntas did not "legalize" (registering with the government to get recognition for resources – a necessity for organizational survival) because there was not enough "push," or participation. Q#3, Quipile, 3/2009. According to someone else, some disorganized juntas only legalized about fifteen years ago. Q#9, Quipile, 3/2009. A third person conjectured that many villages perhaps did not legalize juntas out of "laziness" ("*pereza*") because it may have required making a trip to Bogotá to register. Q#10, Quipile, 3/2009.

[34] Q#8, Bogotá, 3/2009. "They're fighters, really moving ahead, awesome" ("son luchadores ... muy echada pa' adelante, bacana").

[35] Q#12, Quipile, 3/2009.   [36] Q#13, Quipile, 3/2009.   [37] Q#10, Quipile, 3/2009.

[38] Q#1, 2, Quipile, 3/2009.   [39] Q#10, Quipile, 3/2009.   [40] Q#9, Quipile, 3/2009.

resident noted that up until about 1985, junta meetings were "important," but others voiced more skepticism. One person said many people would not go to junta meetings and another believed the juntas were basically only a way to get resources or for candidates to get elected to the next office.[41] The juntas encountered problems with "anti-progressive" mayors who would skim money from some projects.[42] Juntas were strong in some areas, but were later manipulated and weakened by clientelist politics.[43] These problems with juntas are indicative of other organizational problems in the villages of Quipile. For example, even though the farmers live on thin margins they have not been able to cooperate to more cheaply transport crops to market.[44]

Widely cited explanations for the patchy functioning of juntas include the problems of lack of leadership, passivity, complacency, and dependence on local authorities to drive collective action. A man observed that juntas "only survive if they have good leaders, but there was not a strong enough culture [in Quipile] for junta leaders to keep being produced [everywhere]."[45] The "culture" issue was seconded by another woman, who used the adjective "individualist."[46] Another man, in noting the "lack of commitment" ("*falta de compromiso*"), similarly pointed out that not all villages have good leaders.[47] The former mayoral liaison to the juntas observed from his work with the councils that "the residents were not united and that the people needed a guide." Another former leader of the juntas of the municipio in the early 1990s noted a big problem was that the juntas never received national government support.[48] This statement is telling about both the juntas' ineffectiveness as well as the weary, passive attitude of people involved in the councils – waiting for outside help instead of undertaking new ventures on their own.[49] In this vein, a resident from one village said they felt they were the most forgotten village (using the diminutive, "*somos olvidaditos*"), again reinforcing

---

[41] Q#7, 13, Quipile, 3/2009.   [42] Q#5, Quipile, 3/2009.   [43] Q#3, Quipile, 3/2009.
[44] Q#7, Quipile, 3/2009. Some aqueduct associations and crop cooperatives have succeeded (though only most recently) and persist today, but several past efforts to form cooperatives for plantains and sugar failed. Q#2, Quipile, 3/2009. The Comité de Cafeteros used to be more active in the past.
[45] Q#5, Quipile, 3/2009.   [46] Q#8, Quipile, 3/2009.
[47] Q#9, Quipile, 3/2009, Q#13, Quipile, 3/2009.   [48] Q#7, Quipile, 3/2009.
[49] Q#12, Quipile, 3/2009. The impression of a current priest is that, equally in the countryside as in the town, the people are "a little difficult to get organized" ("*durita para organizarla*") and that they are lazy about coming to meetings or workshops ("*perezosa para formarse*"). They are more "individualist" and tend to "keep to themselves" ("*cada uno por su lado*"; perhaps in part from fear from conflict). He has also observed low attendance at his village masses, saying that the people believe in God but do not congregate, "They don't integrate/gel" ("*no se integra*"). This suggests that even outsiders who have come to Quipile recently have been surprised at the lack of organization in the municipio. Most organization today (in the cabecera) appears to be pushed by people from outside. Even today, differences between Quipile and the other municipios are notable to the casual observer: life in Vianí is, at least on the surface, more vibrant than in Quipile, with people associating out in the street.

The main street of Quipile, Cundinamarca, Colombia, 2009. Photograph by Oliver Kaplan.

their reliance on outside groups and a certain "learned" helplessness and lack of initiative.[50] As one person aptly summarized, there is "ignorance" in Quipile and it does not have an associative, "do-it-yourself" colonist culture.[51]

Whatever junta activity did exist through the 1980s, the juntas of today are much weaker. These already feeble organizations collapsed further due in part to effects of the armed conflict, such as fear and pressure from armed groups. One person stated that, from about 1994 on, the juntas "only became a vehicle to fill out paperwork."[52] When a village junta leader came to Quipile around 1999, he was surprised to find that communal action practically did not exist, that the juntas were "ungrounded" ("*desarraigada*"), and that each village existed as a "loose wheel" ("*rueda suelta*"), disunited.[53] Juntas have really only been strengthened since about 2005, as part of the nationwide juntas

---

[50] Q#13, Quipile, 3/2009.   [51] Q#2, Quipile, 3/2009.   [52] Q#10, Quipile, 3/2009.

[53] Q#14, Quipile, 3/2009. From that time up until a year ago there was no full assembly of juntas in the municipio. He perceived that the junta movement in Quipile "had a lack of will or precedent for working together" and that "people never proposed many ideas to move ahead – a lack of leaders." Once again, Quipile depended upon outsiders to push organizational processes forward.

An Acción Comunal trash bin in Quipile, Cundinamarca, Colombia, 2009. Rather than symbolizing successful cooperation, the bins came to be lampooned as representing the listlessness of the cabecera's junta council. Photograph by Oliver Kaplan.

"renewal" movement. They now exist in almost all villages, but in some places only in name (and the impression of many is they would fail without mayoral support). For example, around 2008, 300 people signed up to participate in the junta in Quipile's *cabecera*, or county seat, but only 50 showed up to the first meeting and there was not enough interest for continued attendance.[54] Perhaps most emblematic of the problems with juntas in Quipile, about the only thing the junta of the county seat was recently able to accomplish, and almost as a final afterthought before ending its term, was to put up "acción comunal" garbage bins around the town (what's worse, they have been graffitied, residents do not use them much, and some people actually removed them from in front of their houses because of the smell!).[55]

In Quipile and the other municipios I also asked about important social trends and indicators of social harmony, order, and how conflicts are resolved. First, I asked about the prevalence of machete fights, or "*macheteras*," in hopes of understanding the severity of social divisions and cleavages that armed actors might later exploit. In many parts of rural Colombia, as well as many parts of Latin America and the developing world, farmers carry small garden swords called machetes. The machete is a useful tool for cutting plants and brush and clearing trails and, in some cases, is the campesino's only means of self-defense. As a sociological phenomenon in Colombia, the machete is also the implement of choice for committing violence or brawling.[56]

Residents of Quipile were fairly unanimous in describing *macheteras* as a frequent occurrence from the 1970s up until the early 1990s.[57] During this period, with more difficult access to villages, many people would come to town for Sunday markets, where people would drink large quantities of alcohol and machete fights would occur over such banalities as love or loans. As one person reported, there were many machete fights "everywhere" (and what is worse, the town had no ambulance!).[58] Sometimes, four or five people would fight for up to thirty minutes. The police often did not get involved in these incidents, either arriving (conveniently) late or letting the brawlers just fight it out (though the police might later fine the fighters). A resident of a village specifically remembered that certain villages like La Candelaria were especially prone to machete fights and other incidents with drunks.[59] He recalled many fights – practically every week – in Boquerón de Hilo and Botica. Another reported they were moderately common in La Virgen.[60]

Cattle theft, an indicator of the level of disorder and local solutions for justice, is another prevalent social problem in Latin America and other parts

---

[54] Q#11, Quipile, 3/2009.   [55] Q#2, 11, Quipile, 3/2009.

[56] A resident of Vianí shared a revealing saying about parties, "If there's not a *machetera* it's not really a fiesta!" V#3, Vianí, 3/2009. Machetes have also been used for macabre ends. In Rwanda, machetes were the main implement used in the killings of that country's genocide.

[57] Another sign of belligerence there is the frequent cockfights, or *galleras*.

[58] Q#9, Quipile, 3/2009.   [59] Q#13, Quipile, 3/2009.   [60] Q#8, Quipile, 3/2009.

of the developing world where state presence and policing is scarce (livestock is a key asset of rural residents for preserving wealth).[61] The extent of theft of cattle and other kinds of robberies as well as collective responses to these incidents can be another useful standard for cross-town comparisons. Though Quipile is not a predominantly cattle-ranching municipio, some residents reported the town historically suffered many incidences of abigeato (cattle theft) as well as robberies of *trapiches* (cane presses), farm tools, and even coffee and *panela* (sugar cane) crops.[62] Nobody I spoke with ever recalled any local committees or organized efforts to deal with this issue.[63]

Viani

The municipio of Viani has exhibited subtle but meaningful differences from Quipile in social cooperation and junta councils. With a high number of juntas and juntas per capita – fifteen of sixteen villages had juntas in 1985 – the expectation is to find stronger signs of cooperation in Viani. The qualitative evidence shows that Viani had several advantages for collective action and junta persistence, which resulted in greater junta activity, additional social organizations, and harmonious social relations. Residents recalled that Viani was a UNESCO "model town" in the 1950s and an elderly woman remembers there was much social life. There was also a group of educated *literati* – intellectuals, lawyers, dentists, business people – in Viani in the 1960s.[64] Compared to Quipile, various indicators confirm Viani's historically better civil relations and procedures for social control.

Even with better social conditions, somewhat random events were critical for catalyzing social cooperation and organization. Most prominently, people spoke of the arrival of a Catholic priest in 1962, after La Violencia, who helped transform social life in the municipio.[65] In this year, the story goes, the roof of the town church collapsed, and the priest formed the first junta around the goal of bringing the residents together to raise a new roof and repair the church. The roof collapse and this priest appear to have (exogenously) helped set Viani on an organizational path. Witnessing this early success, the priest was spurred on to continue forming juntas. According to an old coffee grower I spoke with, the priest went from village to village organizing juntas.[66]

When I was able to seek out this now-elderly priest, retired and living in Bogotá, he recalled that, at least while he was there in the 1960s, the people of

---

[61] See Gitlitz and Rojas (1983) about the origins of the Rondas Campesinas in Peru. In Latin America there are several words that refer specifically to the theft of livestock and cattle-rustling, including not only "*robo de ganado*" but also "*abigeato*" and "*cuatrero*," perhaps reflecting its importance.

[62] Q#2, 8, Quipile, 3/2009.

[63] Although at times a junta *fiscal* (officer) might report problems to police inspectors.

[64] V#3, Viani, 3/2009.   [65] V#3, 5, Viani, 3/2009.   [66] V#6, Viani, 3/2009.

The church in Vianí, Cundinamarca, whose roof collapsed in 1961 (2009). A priest helped organize the community to rebuild it, kick-starting the junta councils in the municipio and the neighboring town of Bituima. Photograph by Oliver Kaplan.

Vianí were very collaborative (*"muy colaboradora"*) and that there were frequent junta meetings.[67] Vianí also received (technical) support for the juntas in the form of a government junta promoter because he was requested by the priest as well as a U.S. Peace Corps volunteer (around 1967–1968), both of whom helped coordinate and develop the juntas. The same coffee grower believes that if this priest had not come to the municipio, the juntas would not have formed as they did (i.e., they would have been more dependent on the government and less unified). He said the priest's legacy was that the "people never let the juntas die."[68]

The priest's work was likely made easier by organizationally favorable preconditions in the municipio. A series of land reforms in rural areas had the effect of creating a class of small farmers and fostered social cohesion.

[67] V#8, Bogotá, 3/2009. It was also his impression that Vianí had more junta activity than the next town he was assigned to by the Diocese (Viotá).

[68] As I find later, this had not turned out to be completely true, at least not for all parts of Vianí, but that in general the juntas have historically been strong.

The passage of two national laws in the 1930s, the agrarian reform Law 200 of 1936 and the 1936 Labor Law, impacted certain large property holders in Vianí and required that latifundios be split apart. As a resident told me, some of these "*latifundistas*" feared that rough and violent types of people might come from outside the area to claim pieces of land.[69] To prevent this from happening, a latifundio owner in what is today the village of Manillas decided to slowly sell off pieces of his property to his own sharecroppers, who he at least knew – who were trusted and loyal and with whom he had good relations. As the laborers worked off the price of the plots, he gave them deeds. As generations passed, land kept being divided among the descendants of these original sharecroppers, who live there harmoniously to this day.

The preexisting cosmopolitan population, the fortuitous efforts of the priest, and the legacy of amicable land reform in Vianí helped produce a history of early, strong, widespread, and lasting juntas. Residents recalled the existence of juntas from the 1960s and 1970s in most parts of the municipio.[70] Even in the large, isolated village of Manillas, a resident told how a group got the *personería jurídica* (legal charter) on August 11, 1970, and that the junta remained active (up until the armed conflict and guerrillas came).[71] Similarly, the old coffee grower recalls that residents also obtained the charter for his village's (Vianicito) junta early on, around 1970 (which required going to Bogotá to legalize).[72] He also recalled there was "always much" ("*siempre, mucho*") contact among junta leaders in the municipio.[73]

There is also proof of participation in juntas and various successful projects and activities. The coffee grower recalls many public works led by the junta in Vianicito and that the juntas in the municipio would hold fairs ("bazaars") to raise funds for projects.[74] A resident pointed to the example of the roads in the municipio, which were built through communal action, and noted that today all villages are accessible by roads.[75] Even more recently, in the early 1990s, a large volunteer work group of about forty-five community members united to build aqueducts with help from the Comité de Cafeteros, the juntas, and the mayor.[76] Also in this same period, all (seventeen) junta leaders from Vianí met to discuss education and school infrastructure in the municipio.

Despite the juntas' propitious beginnings, the juntas in Vianí today, like those in Quipile, are weak and poorly organized, existing in some cases in

---

[69] V#2, Bogotá, 3/2009.   [70] V#4, Vianí, 3/2009.   [71] V#2, 9, Bogotá, 3/2009.

[72] V#6, Vianí, 3/2009. Organizations are important, he said, because being able to demonstrate you can commit to contribute labor for projects makes it easier to get money and resources (from the departmental government or private organizations like the Comité de Cafeteros). As he commented, "Without the charter, people [in government/outside the community] wouldn't pay attention to you."

[73] He observed it was an advantage to have a junta in each village, as otherwise it can be difficult to reach agreements among various villages for joint projects.

[74] V#6, Vianí, 3/2009.   [75] V#4, Vianí, 3/2009.   [76] V#3, Vianí, 3/2009.

name only. One man said that village leaders were powerful up through the 1970s and 1980s but have since lost power.[77] A priest observed that when he arrived in 2003, the juntas were weak, and have really only been revived since 2007.[78] Even with this decline, a person involved with the juntas believed some good junta leaders remain. One of the strongest juntas at present is in Manillas, where residents were able to organize to build their own village chapel.[79] Today, the main activities are town cleanups, since there have been few funds for projects after the congressional grants known as *"auxilios parlamentarios"* were eliminated in 1993.[80] Problems are also attributed to historical paternalism, broken promises by mayors, exclusion of female leaders, and varying support among department governors for local juntas.[81]

Consistent with the strength of the juntas in Vianí, there are various other examples of unity and cooperation from the municipio. A person cited the village of Calambata as historically being very cohesive and said that, through their solidarity, they formed a collective sales center (*"centro de acopio"*) to avoid having to pay high quotas to intermediaries when selling crops (something residents of Quipile failed to collectively achieve).[82] In Manillas, a high-elevation coffee-producing village, the Comité de Cafeteros supported many public works. The villages of Hatillo and Cuchimira were also viewed as well-organized villages.[83] These specific examples coincide with the residents' general views of the town's social climate. As one man described it, "In Vianí, when someone needs something or is suffering, nobody closes their doors. They pitch in to help." Another man reiterated the early priest's sentiments about the people being "very collaborative."[84]

By the same token, the unity in Vianí has meant there is little crime and few social divisions or quarrels (especially in the 1970s and 1980s).[85] There are few property line disagreements and various people testified that the residents are not "bellicose" or "prone to fighting" (*"la gente no es peleadora"*). Various residents said that while in the past there were perhaps a few feuds between families or villages and some *macheteras*, they were not very common. For instance, many people would come to town for the county festival, but there would not be many fights. One longtime resident said they could hardly remember any machete fights, except perhaps a few between migrant coffee pickers. In Manillas, a resident recalled that there were "some" but not many in the 1970s and 1980s (and also attributed the "convivencia" in part to the population being 90 percent Liberal).[86] As a city councilman explained, "The people of the countryside are wholesome" (at least in Vianí).[87]

---

[77] V#6, Vianí, 3/2009. A different resident who started with the junta in 1996 said in 2002 there was no junta participation. V#12, Vianí, 3/2009.
[78] V#5, Vianí, 3/2009.   [79] V#10, Vianí, 3/2009.   [80] V#11, Vianí, 3/2009.
[81] V#12, Vianí, 3/2009.   [82] V#2, Bogotá, 3/2009.   [83] V#1, Vianí, 3/2009.
[84] V#11, Vianí, 3/2009.   [85] V#6, 9, 11, Bogotá, 3/2009.   [86] V#9, Vianí, 3/2009.
[87] "Gente de campo es gente 'sana.'" This was noted by about half the interviewees.

Vianí has some traditions of conciliation for when conflicts did arise. An old man from Manillas recalled how he and two other men were informal mediators for neighbors' conflicts because they were respected and viewed as impartial (instead of the alternative of going to the distant police inspector).[88] They would deal with problems like disputes over property boundaries or cows trampling fences and eating crops (where, for example, they would be called upon to impartially value the damage) by hearing the positions of the interested parties and then proposing a solution. After reaching an agreement, the deal would generally be solidified by the ever-important ritual of drinking beer together.[89] During the 1970s and 1980s, there were also reports of the church helping to mediate conflicts.[90] Several people also noted that junta presidents became important authorities in the countryside for conflict resolution. One person recalled how a junta dealt with the "commons" problem of water overuse by taxing the resource so residents of the village would share and conserve it.[91] A more recent junta leader said she was called on to resolve a variety of domestic and neighborly conflicts, as well as deal with some cases of rape.[92]

Even with the general unity and traditions of conciliation in Vianí, there were still some instances of insecurity in the form of cattle theft (*abigeato*), with varying reports as to its prevalence. In certain villages, prior to the arrival of the guerrillas, friends joined up to maintain order, policing certain families suspected of robbing and fighting off thieves from other towns.[93] One man recalled "quiet" strategies to maintain order from the 1970s and 1980s in the village of Hatillo, "I tried to unite neighbors for security against (cattle) theft and also against rape and muggings (*atraco*). We had secret, quiet discussions to organize collective vigilance. Neighbors would get together at night with arms, with revolvers to prevent theft – like a civil defense (*defensa civil*)."[94] The purpose of these committees was more to frighten and deter would-be miscreants, though a few perpetrators were actually purportedly killed. As the man explained, "When there's no army present, one must take justice into his own hands." These committees were said to have lasted about five years and, even though neither they nor the problem of cattle theft were long-lasting, the experience did instill trust among neighbors (the guerrillas also suppressed cattle theft when they entered the municipio).[95] The result was that residents saw it was

---

[88] V#9, Bogotá, 3/2009.   [89] This type of mediation was suspended when the guerrillas arrived.
[90] V#1, Vianí, 3/2009.   [91] V#6, Vianí, 3/2009.   [92] V#12, Vianí, 3/2009.
[93] V#2, Vianí, 3/2009. Even before La Violencia, justice was often meted out at the local level due to the long distances it was necessary to travel to reach official institutions. For instance, latifundios would have their own small holding cells for accused criminals where they would have to serve a period of incarceration. There was also a local "commissary" who would task criminals with communal labor.
[94] V#1, Vianí, 3/2009.
[95] Their arms were useless against armed groups and the committees ended around 1990, when the guerrillas arrived in Vianí.

better to resolve conflicts within the town and rely on lines of authority embedded between and within families.[96]

The existence of similar associations in Manillas to deal with a relatively small number of incidences of cattle theft was also described by multiple interviewees.[97] The neighbors would form "commissions" (posses) to investigate an allegation. They would call on the suspect(s) to turn themselves in and, if they did not come willingly, the commission of four to eight people, armed with revolvers or machetes, would go to capture (but not hurt) them. Once captured, the suspects would then be turned over to the local authorities. In sum, the social history of Vianí contains ample episodes of initiative to deal with local problems rather than waiting for help from the outside.

Bituima

Bituima has historically had an even wider coverage of juntas than Vianí and demonstrates similarly high levels of social cooperation. According to the 1985 data, Bituima had juntas early on and in *all* its villages and a high number of juntas per capita. In Bituima, as in Vianí, there were some early and key exogenous precursors to the formation of juntas that disrupted latifundio land-holding patterns and helped set parts of the municipio on a path toward local cooperation and organization. And, as in Vianí, the church also had a role to play. According to one story, Concepción Romero de Bustos, a woman who was a large landowner with property in the present-day villages of Caracol, Aposentos, Volcán, and Montañas, died a widow and without a will or heirs (inheritors). The land was received by the Catholic Church, which proceeded to divide it into equal plots of small farms, or "minifundios." These small plots helped engender a proximity and density of interaction among rural residents, as well as shared preferences, which were helpful antecedents for effective rural organizations and cooperation.[98]

Bituima experienced the same kind of historical agrarian reform process that occurred in parts of Vianí. As a result of the passage of agrarian reform laws, some large latifundio properties were broken up. Owners sold plots to the existing sharecropper renting families (*arrendatarios*) who had been there all their lives. Since many of these families had peacefully coexisted and gotten

---

[96] As the man elaborated on the issue, "When outside forces come and commit atrocities and abuses, we don't know who is ordering whom or why, so it's hard to fix the problem. In contrast, within communities, there are lines of authority and families can limit abuses of power. Families have the moral power to deal with individual thieves/ʻabusers'/delinquents. Four or five families might unite and talk with the people or parents of youths who were stealing and would tell them, for instance, to control their kids, or ʻthere will be consequences,' as in threats to kill (informal, but it worked). They might also ask for a ʻcontraprestación'/collateral/counterweight."

[97] V#2, 9, Bogotá, 3/2009.

[98] B#1, Bogotá, 3/2009. Quipile is also primarily composed of minifundios, but this did not appear to engender similarly close social relations.

along well, this fomented good social relations. The division of land also produced well-defined property boundaries (*linderos*), which helped to reduce conflict (even though residents did not always hold official deeds). Although there is a general tendency of association in the municipio, consistent with these accounts of land reform, the villages of Aposentos and Gualivá are perceived to be the most educated and equal areas today.[99] The same Quipile woman who characterized her town as "individualist" goes frequently to Bituima and distinguished the people there as being "[socially] aware."[100]

The organizational form of juntas was quickly adopted and became widespread in Bituima when it was first established in the 1960s. One middle-aged man recalled that, when he was a child (about fifty years ago), juntas existed in every village.[101] The residents also recalled the enthusiastic priest from Vianí. Juntas were "always there" and helped with local planning and a variety of public works projects, including building schools and a police post. The juntas also generally received the collaboration of mayors. A former mayor reported working well with the juntas and, even during the 1990s, mayors contracted with juntas for projects.[102] There is also evidence of unity and coordination among the juntas, as representatives from the juntas would meet in the town center. However, today, as in the other municipios, junta participation suffers from greater apathy.

Bituima has also had other social organizations. From 1990 to 1993, the community started its own nongovernmental organization (NGO) called "Todos por Bituima" (All for Bituima).[103] They received money from outside sources to build their own self-sufficient and sustainable granaries and seed banks. It was one resident's perception that the organization succeeded in improving communal work and cooperation, but that it also faced challenges because people were self-interested (the NGO reportedly dissolved once the armed groups arrived). Certain villages were also highly cohesive because of their large number of stores, which serve as important gathering places (those without stores were less integrated and communicative).[104]

Bituima, like any community, experienced some social divisions. But like Vianí, the recollections of residents point to a history of unity rather than social disorder. In one episode from the 1970s, campesinos who wanted to build a high school confronted the obstructionist ("anti-progress") and politically powerful cattle boss elites (*gamonales*).[105] While the 1980s saw some partisan conflicts and tensions because of ever-present poverty, they did not generally escalate, and grave conflicts between neighbors were rare. The record of machete fights tends to support this view. Although residents reported that some *macheteras* occurred and increased in the 1970s and 1980s, they were not

[99] B#1, Bogotá, 3/2009.   [100] Q#8, Bogotá, 3/2009.   [101] B#2, Bituima, 3/2009.
[102] B#3, Bituima, 8/2009.   [103] B#1, Bogotá, 8/2009.   [104] B#3, Bituima, 8/2009.
[105] B#4, Bituima, 3/2009.

all that common (a partially dissenting voice said, "Yes, macheteras were common, but less so now").[106] In a joint interview with someone from Quipile and someone from Bituima, both agreed that Quipile historically tended to have more machete fights.[107]

Like in the other towns, there was also some cattle theft (*abigeato*) in Bituima, but it was not as severe a problem. As one interviewee reported, residents unified to deal with this threat and would advise neighbors when they saw strangers pass by.[108] Her father, a coffee-grower whose harvest was stolen several times at night, led his neighbors in the collective responses of organizing a night watch and later pooling resources to eventually build a police post. During the 1990s, there were some reported increases in the amount of cattle theft and highway holdups, but cell phones have helped with security today by facilitating communication.

Bituima, like Vianí, has a prior tradition of local conflict resolution. Before the creation of a police inspection, Bituima had conciliation centers ("*centros de conciliación*") in some villages. According to one woman, up until the 1960s, village "elders" would mediate conflict in the countryside using their moral authority to bring disputants and enemies together. They would use "registries of trust" ("*escrituras de confianza*") that documented statements of witnesses to the dispute to reach agreements (similar to the ATCC's conciliations). The juntas were also mentioned as important arenas in this process. Junta leaders fell into this class of "elders" and were viewed as impartial conciliators that could promote dialogue. This tradition has dropped off more recently with the greater role of the police inspector, but junta leaders say some of these leadership aspects are conserved today.

In sum, the legacies of social cohesion in the various municipios demarcate one town from another. Quipile has had some hints of collective projects and unity, but was practically destined for difficulties. By contrast, both Vianí and Bituima exhibited greater organization and unity among residents. The juntas were traditionally more widespread across political subunits and more effective, despite signs of their waning in the 1990s.[109] This qualitative analysis uncovers that these differences were in part due to idiosyncratic, exogenous factors, which were not easily measured or identified in statistical cross-sectional analysis. The different origins of the juntas across municipios mean that some legalized earlier, lasted longer, and left greater imprints on their communities' social relations. The resulting differences in junta activity correlate with other forms of social cooperation and organization that are obvious even today.

[106] B#1, 2, Bituima, 3/2009.   [107] Q#8, Quipile, 3/2009. B#1, Bogotá, 3/2009.
[108] B#1, Bituima, 3/2009.
[109] Falling coffee prices also contributed to the economic and social decline of these coffee-growing municipios.

THE NATURE AND SEVERITY OF ARMED CONFLICT

This section explores the dynamics of the armed conflict over time, including a look at the severity of contestation between the armed groups and their interests, motivations, and strategies toward civilians. While assessments in the statistical model based on counts of attacks, reported events, and measures of state presence are helpful, they are less than ideal to understand the texture of day-to-day life. The qualitative assessment here seeks to better verify whether the towns were indeed in the same type of zone of control as the statistical matching procedures suggest they were – a key determinant of violence according to the balance of control theory. As in the statistical analysis, the task is to measure control apart from violence.

The characterizations here draw from four main sources: press reports, civilian and ex-combatant interviews, and work by Peña (1997), which contains around 100 additional interviews with active guerrillas from the early days of the fronts in the region during the mid-1990s. I find that these towns had similar experiences and were subject to pressure from the same armed group units, implying similar rules and modes of operation. However, while I expected zones of dominant though incomplete control based on the data on attacks, I encountered less state and paramilitary presence than expected and more guerrilla dominance. The armed groups overlapped less in space and time than I expected. According to my hypothesized scope conditions, guerrilla dominance is actually not ideal for expecting civilian resistance to armed groups, possibly creating a tougher test *ex ante* for civilian autonomy theory. Nevertheless, I find there was still sufficient fear of the out-groups by the civilians and guerrillas alike to create some incentives for autonomy.

The FARC's 22nd and 42nd Fronts

With historically little state presence, the FARC guerrillas began incursions into the towns of western Cundinamarca in the early 1990s. The counties began to feel pressure from the FARC's 22nd (Simón Bolívar) and (later) 42nd fronts (Bogotá-Villeta) as they came from outside and slowly built up presence, beginning with only a few cadres and resources.[110] Their reach continued to grow until the entire western Cundinamarca region became a conflict zone. The guerrillas used the western mountainous flank of Quipile and Vianí as a key north-south corridor (Peña 1997).

At first, the fronts claimed to want to "fight for the freedom of the people" and indoctrinate the masses. Their main enemies were the "paramilitaries and their patrons." Early commanders Negro Alfonso and El Ciego had years of experience and were seen as "clear in the military aspects," "disciplined,"

---

[110] After government forces attacked the FARC's "Casa Verde" headquarters in Meta in 1983, the FARC dispersed and shifted to Cundinamarca.

"effective," and bringing "a higher level of culture" to the front. Discipline and behavior degraded over time, however, as new commanders such as Negro Antonio were more abusive, extortionist, and rapacious.[111] In general, even though they targeted the rich, their application of violence was more widespread.

The fronts financed themselves through a variety of sources. In the 22nd Front's beginnings, the FARC secretariat transferred resources from narco-trafficking to help the front grow to forty men. They later came to finance themselves through roadblocks, kidnapping and taxing wealthy residents based on studies of economic productivity, and robbing banks (Peña 1997). They were so successful that they came to be considered one of the FARC's more well-off fronts and were frequently able to transfer large sums of money to the FARC's central Secretariat for redistribution to other fronts.[112]

Conflict Dynamics by Towns

In Quipile, the guerrillas had their strongest presence from 1994 through 2002. At first, the guerrillas tried to make friends with people, arriving with a vision of helping the campesinos. But like a "courtship," things turned bad and Quipile was ultimately hit hard by the conflict.[113] Under guerrilla dominance, there were ominous signs on the roadsides with messages such as "Do Not Proceed. FARC-EP." Beginning in 1999, they imposed a 6 p.m. curfew and if people went outside they would be tied to a pole. Even Colombian beer was banned, driving people to make *chicha* (moonshine, usually from corn). There were always police, but never enough, and few army patrols. The county seat was "taken" or attacked by the guerrillas four times.[114] They would attack the police and rob the bank (and when unable to open the safe, they would take the whole thing with them). In 2003, eight police officers were killed by the FARC in an area above the town.

The guerrillas inserted themselves into residents' daily lives and made demands of them. They made themselves indispensable so people would go to them to solve their problems. Gossip ("chisme"), invented stories, and denunciations among neighbors were commonplace ("because there's nothing else going on, no production, so everyone's in everyone else's business").[115] The civilians had to help the guerrillas (and some times the army) by providing

[111] Exc#1, Bogotá, 8/2009.
[112] "In 1995, according to statistics, Simón Bolívar was the front that collected the most money from roadblocks" (Peña 1997). It was estimated that the front spent 2 billion pesos per year and sent 30 million pesos monthly to the central Secretariat.
[113] Q#9, Quipile, 3/2009.
[114] Q#2, Quipile, 3/2009. The "*cabecera municipal*," or the municipio center around which rural villages are oriented.
[115] Q#2, Quipile, 3/2009.

food.[116] The guerrillas also demanded protection taxes (*vacunas*) and would ask people to bring them goods like prepaid cellular SIM cards. Several residents reported some forced recruitment of youth (the "sardines"), enticed by motorbikes, cell phones, money, or liquor – "the good life."

"Pico y plomo," or "Obey or a bullet (lead)," was a frequent ultimatum and one reason why, according to residents, fear was rampant.[117] People variously described the dynamic as "between two fires" (*"entre dos fuegos"*),[118] "between a rock and a hard place" (*"La espada y la pared,"* or literally, "the sword and the wall"),[119] and "small town, but huge fire" (*"pueblo pequeño y fuego grande"*).[120] People talked little with each other and followed the "law of silence."

When mayors asked for security help from the central government, officials responded that there were not enough troops to send.[121] The army was finally sent in by President Uribe in 2003, bringing security (by the time I arrived, people told me the town was very "Uribista"). There were supposedly two notable combat episodes between the army and guerrillas in the countryside where thirty-six insurgents were killed. The guerrillas and paramilitaries coincided in the municipio for about six months until the guerrillas withdrew at the end of 2003.[122]

The FARC also came to Vianí with relatively good intentions. According to one resident, they said, "We're coming to help the small landowners (minifundistas)" and were not going to ask for much from the campesinos economically.[123] They would hold ideological meetings at houses about Communism and other political topics. However, the guerrillas would soon become repressive. They had a strong presence for only about three years, but for that period it was "total subjugation" (*"sometimiento total"*).[124] Guerrillas had bases in the northwest mountainous villages of Manillas and Alto Pueblo because there was never state presence there and Vianí was a strategic corridor. There were similar curfews, where people could not go to the villages after 6 p.m. because of security risks. Holding meetings and driving cars were not allowed and stores would close early. As in Quipile, the residents were prohibited from drinking Colombian beer or Coca-Cola, and could only drink Venezuelan beer (Polar).

Residents also reported the "Pico y Plomo" policy, under which villagers felt threatened and were forced to collaborate with the guerrillas out of fear.[125]

---

[116] For instance, when they would call farmworkers in for lunch with a bell, the guerrillas would show up first to eat.

[117] Q#9, Quipile, 3/2009. This phrase is a macabre play on the Colombian program of "Pico y placa," or "Rush-hour (peak time) and (license) plates," which refers to a traffic-control program that restricts the use of cars on different days in urban areas with license plates ending in certain numbers. It also references *"plata o plomo"* (silver or lead), a phrase drug cartels would use to coerce deals through either bribes or bullets.

[118] Q#6, Quipile, 3/2009.   [119] Q#2, Quipile, 3/2009.   [120] Q#9, Quipile, 3/2009.

[121] Q#11, Quipile, 3/2009.   [122] V#3, Quipile, 3/2009.   [123] V#14, Vianí, 3/2009.

[124] V#9, Vianí, 3/2009.   [125] V#2, Vianí, 3/2009.

They had to give guerrillas lunch, were forced to be messengers, had to pay coffee "taxes," and faced extortion. In the villages, people had to serve both the guerrillas and army (as "employees"). Pressure was especially strong in the villages of Manillas, Cuchira, Cañadas, and Calambata. Forced collaboration was prevalent higher up the mountain, close to the FARC bases.[126]

As in Quipile, police and mayors were under severe threat and many had to leave. The guerrillas bombed the Bancafé bank in 2001 in a robbery attempt in the town center (again demonstrating that they were good at bombing banks, but not as good at opening safes; "So stubborn," one resident decried).[127] There was also a separate attack on the town that the army fought off. The greater tendency, though, was of state abandonment (no state presence, "*nada, nada*"). There were only six police officers in the town and, despite some shellings, only sporadic army presence. Only rarely would some patrols come from Villeta to the north. The army returned only at the end of 2002 and brought the peasant soldiers program (*Soldados Campesinos*).

The community saw the paramilitaries as a solution to their guerrilla problems at first, but it did not work out so well. The paramilitaries came around 2004–2005 and extorted their own taxes (*vacunas*), were abusive, and killed former guerrilla collaborators, saying, "This is our town."[128] There were even some reports of paramilitaries dressed as police.[129]

In Bituima, the guerrillas also arrived with some good "communicators" who amiably talked to people about ideology, brought gifts, gave food to the poor, and resolved social problems.[130] And, like in the other towns, there were signs of the guerrillas' dominance. They would be in town on Sunday drinking beer, and even the buses coming to or from the region had to pay *vacuna* taxes. They recruited youths and would give 10-year-old boys bikes and cell phones to patrol the road between Bituima and La Sierra (in Quipile) as informers. Residents were similarly fearful of speaking.

There was little military presence and few if any army informants. The army would patrol only occasionally and would not stay. Although the Pan-American Highway was developed in the late 1990s, residents did not feel it brought much more security or increased state presence.[131] According to one woman, it mainly meant more displacement as it became easier for people to go to Bogotá to look for work and return to visit family. Paramilitaries also came around 2003, before the army secured the area. They were drawn in part by the prospect of running an oil racket (a pipeline runs through Albán, the municipio to the east; Verdadabierta.com 2009). The paramilitaries were less visible, but bodies started to appear as they killed people with guerrilla ties.

---

[126] V#6, Vianí, 3/2009. The ELN also arrived to appropriate oil when reserves were discovered up the mountain (but they left when it was determined the oil was not extractable).
[127] V#11, Vianí, 3/2009.   [128] V#4, Vianí, 3/2009.   [129] V#1, Vianí, 3/2009.
[130] B#5, Bituima, 3/2009.   [131] B#1, Bituima, 3/2009.

In sum, these towns faced many difficult years of repression and conflict. Some differences are seen in the towns' conflict dynamics, but they are not marked ones. The guerrillas may have been more repressive in Quipile, while Vianí and Bituima were under a slightly looser grip, but there were largely similar armed groups and pressures throughout the region. There were attacks on towns and forced collaboration, though only a few episodes of combat. Even with the guerrillas' control, some residents still feared getting caught later by the army or paramilitary forces, which eventually did arrive. State counterinsurgency efforts finally dislodged the guerrillas in 2003 and the security situation gradually improved. The key question now is how did the civilians survive the many difficult conflict years?

JUNTAS DURING THE CONFLICT AND MECHANISMS FOR AUTONOMY

The histories of the municipios have shown differences in their social relations. Did the varying social landscapes (preexisting to the conflict) position these communities for varying experiences and assertiveness when the armed conflict arrived? Did Vianí or Bituima have fewer social divisions that armed actors could exploit than Quipile? Were they better prepared to organize to deal with armed actors and the violence and fear they imposed? How and why did armed actors' behavior change or produce variation in violence? Because of the probabilistic nature of civilian autonomy theory, resistance organizations and events were not expected to occur *everywhere* in the better-organized municipios.[132] Rather, I expected that levels of organization would make it more likely that some instances of "resistance" would occur in at least some areas. Vianí and, incrementally more, Bituima were expected to witness more and deeper collective actions than Quipile. This is indeed what I found.

I first consider the relationship between juntas and armed groups and then explore what antiviolence actions occurred. I find that, although the juntas may have created strong social bonds, they were weakened prior to and during the conflict for reasons both related and unrelated to the conflict. As a result, they usually did not become the explicit vehicles of choice for organization or resistance to violence and therefore did not directly impact how the conflict would unfold. However, as per expectations, in the more organized municipios, civilians did take individual and collective actions aimed at autonomy of decision-making and freedom from violence that could have plausibly affected the behavior of armed groups. Vianí saw some actions and Bituima in turn saw progressively stronger and more cooperative actions. Quipile had few responses, though not for lack of good intentions. While

---

[132] Again, if the protest actions were very big or extremely effective, they would likely already have been discovered and reported in the press.

drawing explicit connections between greater civilian activity and levels of violence is challenging, I find support for several observable implications from civilian autonomy theory.

The Juntas' Day-to-Day Role during the Conflict

The juntas have a vibrant past in Vianí and Bituima, but by the time the conflict reached the western side of Cundinamarca in the early 1990s, their profiles had already been reduced. The juntas were deactivated due to external reasons prior to the conflict or became dormant out of fear in many but not all parts of these municipios. This meant that the FARC could bend the juntas to its will with little if any resistance sprouting directly from the juntas, though there were some notable exceptions.

As one might expect from their weak historical legacy, the juntas in Quipile did not serve as a strong basis for civilian unity to confront the problems brought by the armed conflict. The juntas did not meet during the conflict years ("people didn't like to meet") but some residents reported that the FARC guerrillas manipulated the juntas in strongholds such as La Botica and had meetings with the population in places such as Costa Rica and La Argentina.[133] As one man explained, most people in these meetings did not truly support the guerrillas, but would say "*Sí sí sí,*" and agree with their propaganda to avoid consequences. The guerrillas pressured successive mayors to fix roads near their strongholds and forced campesinos to complete public works projects. They would make people clear trails and roads with ultimatums like, "Either you do it, *or you do it.*"[134] There was coerced collaboration for the provision of information (with *sapo* informants) because, even though Quipileños did not want to take sides in the conflict, as the same man quoted above put it, "One heads to the tree that gives shade – one goes to whichever side gives protection" (i.e., is stronger; "*Al arbol que sombra de*").

In Vianí the juntas were mostly inert, though there were some signs of juntas attempting to act strategically. According to the Personero, "The juntas always avoided taking sides and were impartial."[135] But the juntas' place as authorities in the villages had receded ("The armed groups – guerrillas – did not view the juntas as strong"). While there were no collective responses through the juntas, there are multiple characterizations of relationships between the guerrillas and the juntas. One person said the guerrillas did not co-opt the juntas but another said the guerrillas called some meetings with the juntas and frightened people.[136] When the FARC came to the village of Manillas, the junta fell quiet and did not function, only following the guerrillas' orders.[137] Even with the suppression of the juntas, there is some evidence of juntas strategically

---

[133] Q#14, Quipile, 3/2009.   [134] Q#9, Quipile, 3/2009.   [135] V#13, Vianí, 3/2009.
[136] V#1,14, Vianí, 3/2009.   [137] V#17, Bogotá, 3/2009.

managing information about the security situation (in one instance in the early 2000s, a junta cautioned a priest about where he traveled and gave him security advice based on their local knowledge).[138]

In Bituima in the 1990s, the juntas were also coerced by the FARC and they became quiet (*"callados"*) out of fear (*"zozobra"*).[139] As in Vianí, in 2002 the FARC forced residents of Bituima to attend a village meeting and to repair roads, and imposed fines if people did not participate. The guerrillas also influenced voting, candidate selection, and political decisions. Yet, in some parts of the municipio – the same areas where the church aided land reforms – a subtle social unity persisted. A woman spoke about how her village maintained solidarity even during this period of war.[140] The neighbors had lived there and gotten along for many years and had a tacit policy to solve their own intracommunal problems (there was, by contrast, relatively more gossip in the town center).

The scant evidence for the expansion of the role of juntas to deal with armed conflict would appear to be a strike against civilian autonomy theory. However, as shown later, the ties that brought the juntas about and the strengthened ties that they left appear to have facilitated civilian responses.

Uncovering Collective Actions for Civilian Autonomy

Surprisingly, even though the juntas themselves did not show broad differences in behavior or enhanced organizational capacity, the differences in social cohesion (either created or reflected by the juntas) corresponded with the extent of collective action against violence. These cases support the statistical measure of juntas reflecting preexisting or persisting social capital as a basis for cooperation. Residents in areas with more collective actions explicitly cited cooperation and communication as catalysts for their efforts, and vice versa. I explore the collective actions that occurred and the kinds of social cohesion that made them possible.

Quipile did not see any forms of organization or collective responses to violence. But this was not for lack of trying or because people had not thought about it. Rather, it was due to a lack of coordination, organization, and historically fractured social relations. As one resident told me, he and some others in the town center considered taking action and studied experiences of other communities in the early 2000s to stand up to guerrilla pressures, but nothing came of it. "Here in Quipile," he said, "we quietly looked at neutral models of other municipios such as Samaniego (Nariño) and the Nasa Indians (Cauca), and other places where people came out with white flags to protest combat and violence."[141] Because of disunity, the analysis was never translated into reality in the form of a civilian organization to overcome armed group

---

[138] V#5, Vianí, 3/2009.   [139] B#2, Bituima, 3/2009.   [140] B#1, Bituima, 3/2009.
[141] Q#2, Quipile, 3/2009.

pressure and fear. It came down to residents not having sufficient confidence in their neighbors to be assured a glimmer of safety and success. There was poor communication and little common knowledge of each other's preferences (for similar arguments, see Petersen 2001 and Chwe 2001).[142]

During one of the guerrilla attacks on the town center in the early 2000s, a priest encountered similar troubles. He tried to persuade the guerrillas to treat the townspeople as neutral, but found little public backing. As a couple of residents recalled, "Here, in one of the *'tomas'* (takings of the town), the priest came out of the church waving a white flag, and nothing happened – no one came to his side and the guerrillas laughed at him and ignored him."[143] The town's judge also tried to no avail to organize people against violence, and eventually had to displace.[144] Interestingly, the man quoted in the previous paragraph believed that if the juntas had been stronger, they could have better organized to deal with the armed conflict. He thinks the guerrillas saw civil society as weak and divided (by religion, politically, and socially), and could therefore easily influence the town through force and fear. The same was true for the moderately organized area of La Virgen to the south, where the guerrillas were seen as a problem, but there were never discussions of resistance because people did not feel they were capable of organizing against the guerrillas. They had to "*comer callados*," or eat silently (not talk out of fear, and instead sit there and "take it").[145]

With Vianí's heritage of prior social unity and local anti-cattle theft committees, some form of civil society resistance to violence might have been expected. Yet, the residents I spoke with did not recall formal resistance acts. There is some evidence of individual acts to avoid taking sides in the conflict. There were also some attempts to "humanize" paramilitary behavior, but not much collective action.[146]

Individuals in Vianí reported trying to avoid taking part in the conflict. As one man said, "Most people did not take one side or the other, and just focused on (agricultural) production and working their farms."[147] A family that had been accustomed to providing assistance to whoever passed by decided on the advice of a priest that, for their own protection, it was better to tell the army they could no longer provide food or aid (which the army accepted).[148]

---

[142] Q#2, 5, Quipile, 3/2009. A possible impediment was that some people perceived that the mayor was involved with one side in the conflict – the guerrillas – and they therefore realized they would not be able to attract widespread support. One man noted that some people tried to be individually neutral and stopped talking to police.

[143] Sandoval (2004) lists municipios with these kinds of collective actions that were supported and succeeded.

[144] Q#8, Bogotá, 3/2009.   [145] Q#15, Quipile, 8/2009.

[146] However, ex-combatants recalled several such collective actions in the Vianí-Bituima region.

[147] V#6, Vianí, 3/2009.

[148] V#3, Vianí, 3/2009. She never had problems with the guerrillas and would have given food to them too because "that's just what one did in the countryside."

Bullet holes in the door of Quipile's church from a FARC attack in the early 2000s.
Photograph by Oliver Kaplan.

In another account, a former village leader told the guerrillas how they were treating the people was wrong – stealing from the poor when they were supposed to be protecting them and threatening suspected army collaborators.[149] When the guerrillas came to his father's house one day and forced him to provision them with food, he refused and told the guerrillas not to ask civilians for such things on the grounds of hypocrisy and poverty.[150]

The civilians in Vianí did not collectively resist violence, and there were no responses through the juntas. Even in the seemingly well-organized village of Manillas, due to fear civilians never tried to organize. The guerrillas, rather

[149] V#1, Vianí, 3/2009. The guerrillas threatened this man and he had to leave (although later he and his family were able to resolve the issue with the guerrillas so he could return and live without problems).

[150] He said, "If we're poor campesinos and you're supposedly fighting for us, why are you extorting from us?" To this the guerrillas replied, "We're trying to reduce corruption, provide order; we're saviors of the motherland (*salvadores de la patria*)." He replied, "If that's true, what good are you doing?" This argument did not succeed in changing guerrilla behavior and he became a "persona non grata," a "stone in their shoe," and had to leave under threat. He brazenly told them, "If you're going to shoot me, do it in the plaza so all can see."

than the people, intervened to solve problems there. But there were some quiet civilian efforts to humanize the war. Some leaders in the municipio did try to dialogue with armed actors.[151] The same outspoken leader would explain to the army that the campesinos were mostly "innocent," and that people only aided the guerrillas because they were forced to. He asked the army to "leave us alone so nobody [neither the army nor the FARC] screws with us." He had also considered starting a family-based armed group to fight off the guerrillas (a "*defensa*"), but without a foundation of local organization (or armaments) he was discouraged. Short of this, the large families in Hatillo united to reach agreements about the problem of gossip (*chisme*) reaching armed groups. In the later years of the conflict, some local leaders reportedly spoke with army officials and the paramilitaries to communicate concerns about the killing of civilians. According to the perception of the village leader, this worked to some degree and the paramilitaries decreased their presence.[152]

In Bituima, even without many signs of enduring social organizations, there were both individual and collective protection efforts. These actions arose in the subregions with the highest degrees of historical organization and cohesion.[153] As one resident who traveled to many villages for his work noted, many people feared that the army or paramilitaries would arrive later and seek revenge, so it was better to stay independent.[154] In one act of individual resistance, a woman refused guerrilla compensation for damages to avoid appearing to be a collaborator. The guerrillas came to her village and took her family's motorbike and its permits to evade scrutiny from the public forces.[155] Not long afterwards, a truck came to the house with a new motorbike as repayment. Instead of accepting the offer, the woman said, "I don't want it and I don't want you sleeping in my barn. If the army finds out that you gave me this moto, I'm in trouble."

As expected, the collective actions in Bituima were more broadly based and more forceful than in the other towns. In one key episode in 2002, a non-collaborating and particularly united village that was tired of being afraid and endangered by pressure to collaborate with the FARC stood up against the guerrillas' dominance and demands.[156] Although there were contrasting

---

[151] V#1, Vianí, 3/2009.

[152] Some of these discussions occurred through official channels such as the mayor. Today, there are more formal "consejos de seguridad" or meetings between the juntas and the police to discuss security, but fear remains.

[153] B#6, Bituima, 8/2009.

[154] The man said that other villages had to help the guerrillas because they were desperately poor, but once they did and received benefits from the guerrillas, they were in too deep and had to keep assisting.

[155] B#7, Bituima, 8/2009.

[156] I was able to speak with several people who were present at the meeting (B#5,7 Bituima, 8/2009) as well as several other people who were not but heard about the episode through friends and relatives (B#1, Bogotá, 3/2009; B#6, Bituima, 8/2009, B#8, Bogotá, 8/2009). Residents

accounts of how events unfolded, the protest began when the guerrillas called the residents of the village to a meeting at the *polideportivo* (multisport court). The guerrillas demanded that they provision them with food and water, saying, "He who doesn't collaborate with us will be killed." In response, a woman who had been forced by the guerrillas to lend them her phone stood up and said, "I'm not giving anything to you because my sons were put in danger and almost killed by the army and could come under threat from the paramilitaries for transporting goods for you. You don't have any business here. You're not from this land. This has been our land all our lives."

At this point, the guerrilla commander threatened to kill these insubordinates right then and there. It is not entirely clear what happened next, though it triggered a reaction from the community. By one account, all the villagers present at the meeting apparently stood up in solidarity and said, "If you're going to kill her, you'll have to kill us all." One man, perhaps aided by some *aguardiente*-fueled[157] liquid courage, said, "Look, Commander, you are not God; you are not the owner of life who decides who lives or who will die. You don't even know if you'll outlive us [with the army gunning for you]."[158] The people were fearful but the close relationships of the villagers meant the man had the tacit support of his neighbors. In the face of this, the commander and other guerrillas backed off and left the meeting.

The retelling of such a hidden narrative is powerful, stunning, and consistent with what might be expected if civilian organization and legacies of cohesion are important. All of this occurred before the villagers knew the army or paramilitaries would come in force. The villagers attested to changes after their response to the guerrillas. Psychologically and organizationally, the act was crucial because the people saw that they were capable of facing and dealing with a threatening situation together. The residents "lost their fear" and, as one person said, "We felt that we could defend ourselves." Through unity, they

believed cooperation was in fact likely in this village for a number of reasons. First, its houses were close together and all shared strong friendships and would, for example, exchange food. Second, small groups of neighbors discussed the conflict (producing common knowledge and informal coordination instead of succumbing to the law of silence). Third, another man singled this village out as being more standoffish (*reacio*) and with the good "values" (good sense) to stay independent. Another said residents were more educated, aware, and unified ("*echada pa' adelante*"), with many stores and the ability to cooperate to run bazaars. In contrast, one neighboring village had "too many fights," while another village was too large for coordination. However, some also recalled that a second nearby and cohesive village resisted in a similar fashion.

[157] *Aguardiente* is a sugarcane-based alcohol produced in Colombia.

[158] An alternative account told that this man was the only one to speak up, because others were too fearful, but that he did so with tacit support of his tight-knit community. Even though this was a brave man, one woman thought he would have kept quiet in a weaker village. The process of collective memory and how people interpreted this event is perhaps equally significant as how it actually may have occurred. His words were a signal to his neighbors about what was possible and confirmed the feelings they all had.

A *polideportivo*, or "multi-sport court," in Quipile, 2009. FARC guerrillas would use these spaces to convene meetings with villagers. In Bituima, some villages voiced resistance at such a meeting. Photograph by Oliver Kaplan.

broke the "law of silence" that pervades civil wars and increased their communication.[159] One man said the residents became even more uncooperative with the guerrillas after this episode.[160]

This story is certainly inspirational, but for a couple of reasons, the concrete, measurable, lasting effects of this social mobilization on guerrilla behavior are less obvious. First, about two weeks later, the guerrilla commander from the meeting was killed. A man in another village, who the guerrillas threatened and ordered to pay a tax, was summoned to meet with them but had informed the DAS (the since-dissolved Colombian intelligence bureau) and the army arrived and killed the commander.[161] Shortly thereafter, there were reports that the paramilitaries had arrived and filled the power vacuum. Second, it is difficult to imagine the counterfactual of what degree of violence would have otherwise visited the community.

[159] B#1, Bituima, 8/2009.   [160] B#6, Bituima, 8/2009.   [161] B#5, Bituima, 8/2009.

Civilian Actions According to the Armed Groups

The civilian accounts of resistance to the guerrillas are confirmed by the guerrillas themselves. Interviews with former members of the FARC fronts from the region corroborate that civilian resistance generally occurred where it was predicted to and even make references to roles for the junta councils (or at least what the combatants believed to be juntas). Most of these ex-combatants were active members from around 1996 through 2004. Key insights come from a former member of the FARC who was originally from the region and operated there, and had a deep knowledge of Quipile, Vianí, and Bituima.[162] As an *escolta*, or escort guard, he would accompany mid-level commanders to meetings with communities (and was also privy to some commanders' discussions). Additional supporting statements are drawn from other ex-combatants that spent less time in the case-study municipios or spent time in neighbor towns (meaning their observations were not always geographically precise), though dissenting or more muted opinions about civilian activity are also encountered.

The escort guard recounts that his front saw more resistance in Vianí and Bituima than in Quipile starting around 1998 or 1999 as they attempted to consolidate power. He could recall instances of at least four villages relatively close to the town seats (cabeceras) in Vianí and Bituima that resisted guerrilla influence.[163] The episodes of resistance proceeded in a fairly similar manner to the civilians' descriptions of them. When entering a village, the guerrillas would hold meetings with residents, which he would commonly attend alongside his commander. The cadre would introduce themselves and announce their aims of resolving neighborly disputes and conducting social cleansing by saying, "We're from Front 42 of the FARC, and we're here to take charge of this village. Tell us who are the thieves and people taking advantage of the community."

The resisting villages united peacefully and collectively against the guerrillas and would not let them enter. The guerrillas would usually give notice when planning meetings with communities so that residents would attend. The guard believed that junta (or community) leaders, armed with this foreknowledge of the guerrillas' arrival, were able to meet with and organize their communities in anticipation of a pending confrontation. At one meeting, the civilians responded to the guerrillas' demands by advocating together for what sounds a lot like *autonomy*, saying, "We don't want you guerrillas here. Kill us all if you must. We don't want the army either. We want to manage our affairs amicably." Even with the strong guerrilla influence in the region, this statement

---

[162] Exc#2, Quipile, 8/2009. He operated in the area from around 1998–2000 and so was present at a different time than the civilians' report of resistance reported earlier. Thereafter, he had less experience in the region.

[163] He did not recall specific village names.

underlines civilians' fear of collaborating and becoming stigmatized, and their collective solutions.

Some forms of resistance in Quipile were reported as well, but they were of a different nature. Around 2000–2002, a handful of some of the guer- rillas' strongest collaborating villages reportedly turned against them. The residents were upset about abuses and tired of the guerrillas' demands, which included, for instance, the requirement to work two days for the guerrillas for every two days they worked for themselves. This was "not sustainable." However, the pleas were not as broadly based as in the other towns and the guerrilla response was supposedly an even stronger hand to crush opposition there.

The guard believed the differences in resistance between the Vianí–Bituima communities and the Quipile communities stemmed more from civilians' *social differences* than differing levels of pressure the guerrillas could bring to bear or military control. Both prior to and during the years of conflict, the residents of Vianí and Bituima were more unified and people had more contact with each other. In these villages it was *not* "keep to yourself" – the same description given by Quipile's priest – and the juntas worked.[164] He used the word "*nada*," or "nothing," to describe how the juntas in Quipile were almost nonexistent and did very little to unite villages.[165] In contrast to the residents in Vianí and Bituima, many Quipile civilians simply collaborated with the guerrillas out of fear.

Armed Group Responses to Civilian Autonomy

What was the impact of these movements? Interviews provide a look inside the guerrilla group and show that guerrilla leaders were surprised by the resistance put up by the civilians. They expected to be able to easily take the villages of Vianí and Bituima, the way they took the villages of Quipile. As the guard said, "The guerrillas wanted to take all of Vianí and Bituima but couldn't." The guerrillas could not order civilians like they wanted to. This caused a debate within the front about what to do with civilians (corroborated by other soldiers based on pushback from villages in Viotá).[166] They supposedly sent more cadres to obligate people to collaborate, but in contrast to his statements on responses to resistance in Quipile, they did not want to force residents too hard to collaborate because it was "bad."

Because of the civilian resistance, the guerrillas were reported to have more frequently desisted from killing. How and why might these collective actions have changed their behavior? Combatants provided a complex mix of

---

[164] "*Cada uno por su lado*," or literally, "each to his own side." He held this view of Quipile even before he was recruited by the guerrillas.
[165] Only now are Quipile's juntas being renewed, with a junta functioning today near Botica.
[166] Exc#3, Bogotá, 8/2009.

explanations and reasoning.[167] Taken together, they spotlight the group's balancing of their need for civilian support with costs of attacking and using heavily violent tactics – a balance that can shift based on civilians' actions. According to the strategic logic provided by the ex-combatants' collage of statements, the use of violence to cement control by coercion and fear loses some of its effectiveness when an organized community puts up resistance. The group goes from facing a decision of whether to kill individual resisters or community leaders to the possibility of targeting many more residents to quash resistance (since eliminating leaders in an organized village may not guarantee submission).

Many of the ex-combatants referred to the centrality of the backing and support of the entire community and being more prone to selective violence against lone individuals or small groups who resisted. To explain, a former FARC mid-level commander and infiltrator used the poetic saying, "*Una sola golondrina no hace verano*," or, "One swallow does not make a summer" (unbeknownst to me, an adage from Aristotle and Shakespeare).[168] This is to say that a single individual – a single swallow – will not signify or bring much change but a group, a flock of swallows, carries more weight. The juntas were seen as key institutions in this regard, "providing vigilance of communities and keeping local order." Hearkening back to the previous "alone we're screwed" comment by the Vianí resident, he said, "While the juntas aren't united, they won't achieve anything." Across the region, he noted some junta leaders left or were killed, but leaders of resisting communities were mainly safe because of civilian support.

Not only do civilians' chances at sustaining their communities improve if they remain united, but they are also more taken into account by armed groups. The intent of civilian cohesion then is to tilt the groups away from using fear to break a community and toward respecting existing social structures.[169] In these acts of collective resistance, civilians throw down the gauntlet to armed groups, gauging that they will not take the leap toward mass violence. In doing so, they can activate four main concerns that affect armed group calculus.

First, the guerrillas did not want to kill everyone and "end an entire village."[170] Ex-combatants cited some moral considerations, with distinctions between few killings (perhaps for some conceived greater good) versus massive

---

[167] Evidence about these reasons are provided by ex-guerrillas that operated in the case-study towns, as well as other members of the same fronts who operated in nearby towns but had knowledge of the fronts' decision-making.

[168] Exc#4, Bogotá, 8/2009.

[169] As the mid-commander said, "When entering a community, there are two possible strategies a commander can choose. He can break it and use fear, or work with it. If there's a strong structure, a commander will ask how they can work with it?"

[170] Exc#4, Bogotá, 8/2009.

killings (perhaps evoking cognitive dissonance of being for the people and yet committing atrocities).[171]

Second, resistance by organized communities may activate sensitivities about the guerrillas' reputation for using violence. The guerrillas did not want the reputation of being killers, and the distinct level of violence required to deal with an organized community would be more greatly publicized than smaller acts.[172] Organized communities may themselves also be more effective at publicizing atrocities and amplifying reputation costs (or perhaps appealing to government authorities). If the guerrillas kill, people could say the guerrillas are not the "freedom fighters" they claim to be but really are terrorists. Keeping up appearances is worth something and they wanted to avoid falling into a trap of rhetorical inconsistencies.[173] Front commanders were even reported to have debated how violence might worsen the group's image.[174] While these groups of course participated in the disreputable practice of kidnapping and the narco-economy, these revenue-generating activities may be easier to justify as the means to a revolutionary end than killing.

The ex-combatants referred to concerns about their reputations with three potential audiences. First, excessive violence could create political problems for the guerrilla group in the eyes of the broader population.[175] They worried about greater difficulties in securing the support of other villages (if those communities saw the guerrilla's true behavior, they would be more reluctant to help them). Second, sensitivity to their international image can also enter into the equation. If they are killing everywhere it may become a political liability for leaders from other countries to support them.[176] Third, they feared it might eventually bring the army to the zone. By definition, the army of a weak state with rough terrain like Colombia has difficulty projecting its power to many parts of the national territory at once. But that does not mean the army cannot be mobilized to address trouble spots when necessary or politically demanded.

---

[171] The mid-commander continued, "If one sees a strong social structure, it can change the way a group *thinks*. To kill one or two [resisting] people is one thing, but to kill a whole [resisting] community is too far" (emphasis added).

[172] This may be because mass violence may become a focal point – people in the community and neighboring areas talk about it more, the media pick up the story, etc. Killing organized resisters would be even worse given that the civilians approached them nonviolently and for dialogue.

[173] While they might also value a reputation for toughness and ruthlessness in the face of resistance, having to resort to large-scale violence could also be interpreted as an act of desperation.

[174] Exc#2, Quipile, 8/2009.

[175] As a guerrilla in Peña (1997) explained, for this reason, at least in the front's early days, they supposedly preferred roadblocks to demanding protection taxes (*vacunas*), "Today we don't demand vacunas because it scares and nauseates the masses." But roadblocks also have political costs, "The retentions are politically, economically, and psychologically costly for the movement, as much for the victims as for the soldiers that carry it out . . . It provokes a hostile attitude in the community toward the movement."

[176] The FARC was documented to have relied upon support from the Venezuelan government under Hugo Chávez (BBC 2011).

In sum, exemplifying a degree of risk aversion, the guerrillas believed they were more likely to blow their cover by targeting a village that is united against them.

A third factor is the relatively high cost of using mass violence to obtain the marginal benefit of the allegiance of new villages. Although the guerrillas generally wanted to gain the support of more and more communities (they "needed villages for power"), they already had a base and some power when, in their expansion, they ran up against resisting villages. The guerrillas did not attack the resisting populations in part because it was "not worth it" – it was not worth the risk.[177]

Fourth and lastly, the FARC fronts would debate abuses in their internal assemblies in response to civilian protests, at times exhibiting splits over what course of action to take. A plausible interpretation is that civilian pushback activated particular concerns that may have empowered more dovish commanders over their hard-line or abusive counterparts within the group.[178] Exemplifying these tensions, one commander might declare, "I won't work with this other commander because he is undisciplined."[179] Some commanders eventually faced sanctions by the group for their "errors," and abusive practices were tempered. These changes would probably have been less likely without civilian pushback.

AN INTERVENING EXPLANATION: CLIENTELISM

If Vianí and Bituima had historically high levels of juntas, why did the juntas themselves not (survive to) have a clear role in the armed conflict in these municipios? Field research indicates the opportunity for the junta councils to act was short-circuited by political clientelism and later by the conflict itself. Political clientelism is defined as the manipulation of local constituents and organizations through (short-term) political favors or payoffs to gain their support (see Martz 1997 on Colombia; Magaloni et al. forthcoming). This type of political arrangement can affect whether people look (horizontally) to their communities and neighbors to solve problems or (vertically) to mayors and local politicians – whether they wait for solutions from outside the village or neighborhood. In this study, the damaging effect of clientelism on community networks and organization would bias against observing any collective actions for protection from armed groups.

---

[177] Exc#5, Bogotá, 8/2009.

[178] Commanders might be dovish because of their personal values, background, or education; their closeness to the population; or simply because they are rational calculators who tend to believe that moderating the use of violence is a superior strategy for gaining control or extracting more resources from the population. In Kaplan (2013b), I explore this dynamic further and develop a theory of "nudging armed groups," in which civilian collective actions are able to exploit intra-armed group fissures to reform their behavior better than international humanitarian actors and the laws of war.

[179] Exc#6, Bogotá, 8/2009.

Clientelism creates resource dependencies on local politicians and their funds and can sap the intrinsic drive of individuals and local organizations to take actions by their own initiative. It becomes a system, an equilibrium, when no politician can compete for political power without these relationships. The perniciousness of clientelism for responding to the armed conflict in Colombia was cited in a United Nations study (UNDP 2003). In my analysis, in all three towns and even in areas that had strong, functioning juntas, residents complained that the juntas were weakened by two main factors related to clientelism: (1) instituting the direct election of mayors and (2) the dependence of juntas on external financial support and the subsequent elimination of that support.

In 1988, Colombia underwent a nationwide institutional change when municipal mayors ceased to be appointed by department governors and became popularly elected. Before the popular election of mayors, the juntas were the main forum where local *democratic* politics and decision-making were channeled for tasks such as public planning and the resolution of conflicts. Once mayors began running for election, they used funds and favors to co-opt support through the local juntas. This had the effect of juntas and junta leaders frequently acquiescing to local politicians for short-term benefits (vote buying). It increased the expectation that public goods provision was primarily the concern of the mayor and his administration, and not the juntas.[180] Juntas that were already weak lost even more relevance in citizens' daily lives.

Second, from 1965 up through 1993, the national government made some development funds available to the local juntas through grants known as "*auxilios parlamentarios*," or congressional assistance. This was aid programmed into the national budget for local juntas by representatives or senators for their constituents (see Borrero 1989, Leal Buitrago 1990). These funds were often matched with labor or funds from the local junta and functioned as a stimulus for activities and public works. In some cases, the main purpose of forming a junta was to take advantage of these funds (though once a junta is formed even for this reason, it may take on additional tasks of local governance).

It was a blow to the juntas when these funds were eliminated in 1993. People partly participated in junta activities as a means of getting funds and carrying out projects. The disappearance of national government funding also compounded the problem of vote buying by local politicians and the newly electable mayors, as the juntas became more autonomous but at the same time more desperate. Together, these changes were devastating for many though not all local juntas in the country. Indeed, up to the early 1990s, the junta movement had been signaling the benefits of increasing political autonomy (Borrero 1989). This was apparently sidelined.

---

[180] AC#1, Bogotá, 2/2009.

The effect of clientelism on juntas is problematic for social responses to armed conflict for several reasons. First, if local organizations are in it for "the buck" – the short-term gain – and come to rely on local politicians, their actions lose legitimacy among members of the community or village. If people do not feel that their contributions are necessary to the process or feel excluded and that their interests are not being represented in the use of funds, there is little point to contributing to local "democratic" processes, and participation and social bonds between community members can atrophy. Crosscutting social contacts and exchanges of information can also be damaged if juntas or other organizations lose importance. Under these circumstances, communities can be challenged to coordinate responses to intrusions by outside forces because they have few "standard operating procedures" and little common knowledge.

Second, mayors in a local clientelist political system may only be responsive to a narrow group of political supporters and less broadly accountable to community members. Mayors may then more easily cut deals with and sell out to armed groups to save their own political skins – deals that do not benefit the community or town as a whole but may instead privilege certain sectors or interests, such as landowners.[181] They may either fall in line with armed groups or be forced to pay off such groups to receive permission to govern or run for office. These deals may undercut community efforts to avoid violence and may block other social sectors from acting.

Third, clientelism may be further problematic if it blocks effective economic development. If clientelism derails the provision of economic opportunities, more people may come to participate in the conflict due to poverty. In this way, clientelism can both tip the balance of individuals' choices toward joining armed groups and become an impediment to a community's effort to act collectively to resist armed group recruitment.

Consistent with trends in many parts of Colombia, reports from interviews show the stranglehold of clientelism was present in all three of the case municipios of western Cundinamarca. In Quipile, juntas were reportedly late to form because residents traditionally looked to mayors to solve problems and there existed a long-standing clique, or oligarchy, of leaders. Residents pointed to the direct election of mayors as leading to more clientelism.[182] The local and national governments made juntas depend on them, since the juntas were used in political campaigns. Some juntas were even formed by local political bosses (*gamonales*) for personal ends.[183] Some mayors look to exclude junta leaders who are their political enemies from the policy process by, for example, inviting them to meetings, but only at the last minute so they cannot attend.[184] Although a few of Quipile's recent mayors were clean, many left office amid corruption scandals. In sum, clientelism is "endemic."[185]

---

[181] E.g., critiques by Quipile#8, Quipile, 8/2009.   [182] Quipile#4, Quipile, 8/2009.
[183] Quipile#10, Quipile, 3/2009.   [184] Quipile#8, Quipile, 8/2009.
[185] Q#15, Quipile, 8/2009.

In Vianí, residents spoke of how it has been common for mayors and councilmen to "buy" votes by, for instance, sending gifts to villages before elections.[186] This has moved voters to vote for "favors," not necessarily for good managers. A former councilman believed that when mayors became elected instead of appointed, it aggravated local political conflicts.[187] One person also suggested that the existence of a few powerful families has fostered a closed and monopolized political system.[188]

In Bituima, despite equal social relations and evidence of organization in some villages, the influence of gamonales in local politics persisted. One person directly attributed the weakness of juntas to the paternalist clientelism that began with the 1988 election of mayors, saying that they had functioned up until about that time.[189] Before, there was more participation in and commitment to the juntas as they were substitutes for unpopular appointed mayors. People were also more self-sufficient in taking on public works projects, but today they look to mayors to organize such projects. One person alleged some mayors have even kept petty cash in their desk drawers to buy people favors and buy votes.[190] Another person aptly characterized Bituima as "a town that never wanted to progress," which could be taken to mean that even with local grassroots initiatives, the town has remained *politically* backwards.

This analysis points to a new theory to explain how local civilian organizations interact with and affect armed conflict. Clientelism can pull the rug out from under some local organizations, leaving them to crumble in the face of conflict, while others are able to persist. This could explain why strong social organizations and peace communities arise in some areas of Colombia, but are not found countrywide.

Even with the burden of clientelism, the armed groups faced multiple considerations about how to deal with the actions of different civilian communities, with moments of restraint despite their atrocities. The next section assesses whether civilian social processes map to patterns of violence.

LEVELS OF VIOLENCE (VS. REPORTED VIOLENCE)

What types of violence occurred over time across the different municipios, and for what reasons? Like other conflict zones of Colombia, these towns suffered their share of killings and oppression. Field observation and interviews show there is significant measurement error in levels of violence based on press and police reports arising, for instance, out of civilians' fear of reporting victimization to authorities. Comparatively, the qualitative reports indicate greater overall levels of violence as well as greater disparities across the towns that are consistent with what would be expected based on differences in social

---

[186] V#1, Vianí, 3/2009.   [187] V#11, Vianí, 3/2009.   [188] V#12, Vianí, 3/2009.
[189] B#11, Bituima, 3/2009.   [190] B#1, Bituima, 3/2009.

organization. This triangulation with multiple sources of information adds further confidence to the theory and the statistical model.

The Colombian government data and CINEP's press reporting suggest that most of the violence was committed by the guerrillas, although there are some reports of acts by the armed forces and, later, by right-wing paramilitary groups. The levels of violence in these municipios as measured by the police's homicide rate data are well-predicted (close to the regression line): Quipile has a relatively higher average rate compared with Vianí and Bituima (though the counts of violent events in both data sources are inordinately low). Illustrating a common challenge in conflict zones, these sources only appear to capture the more publicized events.

Fieldwork revealed many reporting issues. First, in some of the towns, the police were entirely absent, or people were too afraid to risk reporting events to them. Furthermore, press reporting was sporadic and there were few or no formal human rights or peace organizations monitoring the situations in these towns. Even among the civilians themselves, there was apparently little sharing of information. Some tales of events that occurred in the countryside have only recently come to light, while many others remain hidden and untold.

I sought to increase confidence in measurement by considering several qualitative and observational sources of information. These are summarized in Table 8.2 and graphed in Figure 8.2. First, I sought to obtain counts of the number of crosses along country roads in these towns. In instances where people were too afraid to report cases to the authorities or hold a proper burial in a cemetery, people were buried where they lay, their graves marked with crosses that often simply read "NN," or "no name." Second, I interviewed the *personeros*, or human rights ombudsmen, of each town to get estimates of the number of claims by victims – widows and orphaned children – who began to come forward to collect government reparation monetary benefits.[191] Third, I obtained an additional estimate by speaking when I could with submunicipal "police inspectors" who were in charge of exhuming and registering the dead.[192] In general, less violence occurred in the more densely populated county seats compared with the outlying villages and corregimientos.

According to the theory of the balance of armed group control, Quipile should have expected less violence than the other towns because, if anything, it was the most strongly controlled by guerrillas. Even with the matching on armed group actions from Chapter 6, Quipile experienced slightly greater and

---

[191] Q#3, Quipile, 3/2009; V#13, Vianí, 3/2009; B#9, Bituima, 8/2009. Decree 1290 of 2008 allowed victims seeking reparation "by the administrative path" an additional two years from April 2008 to make their claims. www.fiscalia.gov.co/justiciapaz/Documentos/Decreto_1290_Abril_22_2008.pdf. It is possible that these data could exhibit an opposite bias – of over-reporting – if people have the incentives and ability to make false reports.

[192] These are unarmed, nonuniformed local residents who do office work for the police and receive reports and complaints from the population.

TABLE 8.2 *Qualitative indicators of violence*

	Quipile	Vianí	Bituima
Population (1993)	10,033	4,107	2,932
Average police homicide rate (1990–2005)	42.8	42.1	44.4
Total CINEP homicides (1990–2005)	5 (5 events)	5 (1 event)	0
"No name" crosses along roads	Many	Some (3 est.)	Some (2 est.)
Personero estimates			
Number of victim claims	200	30	25
Average annual rate	1,993 (125)	730 (45.7)	852 (53.3)
(1990–2005)			
(based on CNRR benefit claims)			
Police inspector			
Number of killings	150–400	N/A	N/A
Average annual rate	100–200		

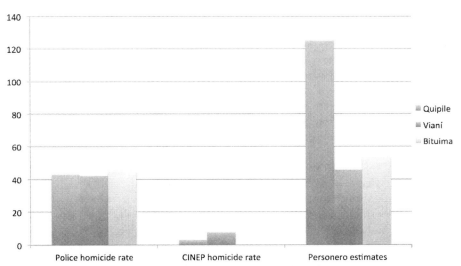

FIGURE 8.2 Estimates of violence from quantitative and qualitative sources.

longer guerrilla domination. But Quipile also suffered more violence than the other towns, or the violence at least made a greater impression on the residents with whom I spoke.

The years from 1993 to 2001 marked a period of high violence in Quipile that took several forms. First, violence was used for day-to-day social control and social cleansing. There were no robberies because guerrillas maintained order and killed thieves. As one man said, when the guerrillas came, people denounced each other for their own ends, sometimes resulting in killings. The guerrillas told fathers who were drinking too much and not caring for their children to shape up or they would be killed (though "probably many wives were glad").[193] Second, there are some examples of guerrillas more intentionally targeting suspected enemy collaborators. The guerrillas threatened some nuns who were seen walking with the police. In a letter to the priest, they said, "We'll make them whores of the countryside."[194] There were cases of guerrillas "carrying out justice" against individuals for refusing to collaborate, which they would justify by saying, "We killed this *puta* or *perro* (whore or bastard) for being a *sapo* (literally frog, meaning an informant)." In contrast, civilians were not greatly targeted during attacks on the town centers. The guerrillas would sometimes notify the population and give them time to leave or hide and mostly targeted the police or the banks (even the police closed themselves into the police station). Still, three civilians were killed in cross fire.[195]

Quipile also suffered from the stigmatization of being guerrilla collaborators. In 2003, the army and DAS (intelligence bureau) conducted a major roundup of suspected collaborators that were fingered by a single former guerrilla.[196] As alluded to in the song at the beginning of the chapter, they came with tanks and trucks early in the morning. They brought people – young, old, male, female – into the plaza, still in their pajamas, and took them to prison in Bogotá to be interrogated. In news reports they were referred to as (suspected) guerrillas. Most were let free after a few days or weeks, but some were held for up to six months. Afterwards, there was a lot of uncertainty and fear that the army lists might fall into the hands of the paramilitaries.

When the paramilitaries came they reportedly killed some of the people who the army had rounded up and then released. Around five civilians were killed in 2004 "by who knows who," and some of the bodies were dumped on the highway.[197] "The paramilitaries had good intelligence. They surrounded Quipile and La Sierra at night with hit lists." In 2008, threats began anew in the form of phone calls. About a month prior to my first visit to the town in 2009, a man who was named in an anonymous pamphlet was killed, perhaps because he was a "delinquent," had previously helped the guerrillas, or had a daughter who joined their ranks. Another man recalls at least three or four killings of suspected enemy collaborators that could also be called social cleansing.

According to additional numerical estimates from the town Personero obtained during fieldwork, there were about 200 women in the villages that were widowed as a result of the conflict.[198] He explained that victims were fearful of denouncing acts and were only coming forward now for state reparation money. He also reported three or four events he referred to as massacres, one of which involved nine victims (he was "stunned" when he

---

[193] Q#2, Quipile, 3/2009.   [194] Q#5, Quipile, 3/2009.   [195] Q#9, Quipile, 3/2009.
[196] Q#2,3, Quipile, 3/2009.   [197] Q#9, Quipile, 3/2009.   [198] Q#3, Quipile, 3/2009.

took the job and found out about all of this). A police inspector from one of Quipile's corregimientos comprising about one-quarter of the villages in the municipio said they had to recover approximately 150 bodies during the conflict years, and this was not even the most violent region of the municipio.[199] Some townspeople mentioned the figure of at least 300 deaths in the villages attributed to illegal groups and a recent anonymous pamphlet alluded to a similar figure.[200] If these estimates are correct, it would translate into an average annual homicide rate of 100–200 per 100,000 residents for the period 1990–2005, or about two to four times the rates reported by the police.

In Vianí, the FARC sought to rule by fear as well. According to a priest, the FARC would bring families to meet and say, "We have a list of people and we are not afraid to kill them."[201] As early as 1994, the guerrillas threatened a "talkative" priest and he had to leave.[202] The guerrillas would kill army collaborators and people had to lie about whether the army (or in the army's case, the guerrillas) passed by. Acts of violence certainly did occur and some interviewees said many people were killed as "accomplices." There were also reports of torture, disappearances, massacres, and high-violence pockets in the villages of Alto Rosadas and Cañadas. One respondent said he was kidnapped by the guerrillas but then let go.[203] But, according to the reparation forms filed with the Personero by victims and their family members as of 2009, there were approximately thirty victims from the conflict years – fewer than in Quipile.

According to the Personero and other residents, paramilitary forces from Puerto Boyacá to the north arrived around 2004 and were present for about two years. They reportedly killed an estimated five victims, especially pressuring Cañadas, where people were stigmatized as being former guerrillas or guerrilla supporters ("*tildados*").[204] Still, all told, people spoke of less violence in Vianí relative to Quipile during the conflict years.

In Bituima, there were also reports of violence, but it was less widespread. The Personero estimated that about twenty-five people had come forward to claim victim benefits, mostly for acts that occurred between 1998 and 2003 at the hands of guerrillas (characterized as a fairly "comprehensive" reporting of crimes). The Personero also reported there were not many crosses along roads. The paramilitaries were around for two years, from 2003 to 2005, and mainly committed violence against suspected guerrilla collaborators in the town center and some villages, killing around five people. They targeted a store owner and killed a teacher who had supposedly taught students about the guerrillas and weapons.[205] Residents of one of the resisting villages said they experienced only

---

[199] Q#16, Quipile, 8/2009. The police inspector reported these deaths to the *fiscalía* (prosecutor) but not necessarily to the police because it was too dangerous given fear of reprisals from the FARC, so most of these counts are likely not reflected in the police's statistics. The count does not include victims who were simply "disappeared."

[200] Q#9, Quipile, 3/2009.　　[201] V#1, Vianí, 3/2009.　　[202] V#10, Vianí, 3/2009.

[203] V#1, Vianí, 3/2009.　　[204] V#10, Vianí, 3/2009.　　[205] B#1, Bogotá, 3/2009.

one killing of a former guerrilla collaborator at the hands of the paramilitaries.[206]

In sum, while depictions of violence can sometimes be vague, Quipile seems to have suffered more than the other towns. This is supported by several sources of information as well as across several motivations for and types of violence.

CONCLUSIONS

This chapter's controlled comparison was designed to identify cross-town differences in civilian cooperation and collective actions and their later effects on armed group behavior. It is true that similar autonomy actions may have indeed occurred in many towns across Colombia. But with many possible confounding factors in comparisons of other sets of cases, their marginal effects would be difficult to disentangle. The structured process tracing here uses interviews to help understand the stories and motives behind different decisions. The result is a rendering of the social history of three towns over sixty years. When the conflict did reach these towns in the 1990s, it was not arriving in a barren social landscape, but rather one characterized by varied associations and corrugated legacies of social capital.

The statistical matching of cases proved to be accurate and helped highlight several significant features of the social landscape during the conflict years. There were differences in "culture," including patterns of social interaction and cooperation (*"convivencia"*/coexistence), and the junta organizations that set the towns apart. In Bituima and Vianí, the junta organizations and cooperation were more prevalent and more consistently recalled. While guerrilla dominance induced acquiescence or collaboration in a number of villages across the towns, experiences with organization proved to be a key ingredient for dealing with threats. Lack of organization inhibited community advocacy in Quipile whereas the presence of organizations enabled it in Bituima. The histories further alleviate concerns about spuriousness stemming from social organizations only thriving in peaceful conditions. The record shows the towns had *similar* social and conflict-related historical starting points: all suffered similar degrees of intercommunal and political strife during La Violencia. In sum, the evidence supports social capital as an explanation for civilians' responses to the conflict.

The relationship between social organization and conflict is also more complicated, however, as many of the juntas were weakened by armed group pressure. Guerrilla presence created an environment of fear, coercion, violence, and silence. It is not that fear and danger were absent in the resisting villages of Bituima- quite the contrary. Residents did fear the guerrillas as well as the

[206] B#6, Bituima, 8/2009.

return of the "out-group" – the army or paramilitaries – and therefore were reluctant to support the guerrillas, or in some cases, the patrolling army. Yet at the same time, preexisting social cooperation also empowered civilians as agents to retain their *autonomy*. Growing dangers created cause for action and the residents were able to overcome their fear through a history of solidarity and experiences with cooperation. The outcome was a greater "humanization" of the war and less violence suffered.

The histories show several civilian mechanisms and strategies for autonomy and protection, even though these areas were at times characterized by single group dominance. First, given that the guerrillas strove to assert authority and performed social "cleansing," civilians' simple unity and fewer local conflicts meant there were fewer inroads for armed groups to use violence. Second, civilians used some explicit organizational strategies toward the armed groups. In Bituima, some villages collectively opposed the guerrillas in the hope of increasing costs to using violence. This induced some reduction in guerrilla abuses of the population. Third, the collective actions and shared preferences for autonomy from the guerrillas meant fewer civilian alliances with them. Though the link is less clear, this in turn meant less violence and pressure later by the army and paramilitaries. Reports from the guerrillas themselves help explain why their decision-making was "sensitive" to communities that held out in unison. Even for ruthless and opportunistic armed groups, legitimacy can serve as an important lever of influence. Violence in these cases, then, is accounted for by pressure from the armed groups as well as variation in social characteristics across communities.

In comparison with the ATCC, the strategies encountered in Cundinamarca did not approach the same degrees of formality and complexity. Though impressive in their own right, they were less premeditated, less enduring, and less self-conscious. For example, the civilians' harmony and conflict resolution were less overtly managed and communities did not develop an explicit vouching system like the ATCC's. Because the Cundinamarca towns' social lives and actions are hidden narratives, with fewer formal records and less social memory, they are difficult to detect and carefully measure. Causal links between civilian social-capital mechanisms and violence are therefore not as clear as in the ATCC case.

Because of poor flows of press coverage or the subtle nature of the actions identified in these towns, these episodes were largely *unknown* histories, even though they were occurring just three hours from the capital. If these cases had been much more organized, they would already have been "discovered." They would be broadly known and lumped with the forty-plus formal organizations the media has covered. The distinctions between towns in this chapter's analysis therefore suggest that subtle and likely effective forms of civilian organization and resistance can occur widely. For instance, in the ATCC case there were paramilitaries and guerrillas who were amenable to civilian organization. Here, an additional FARC front operated similarly. Beyond these local findings, the chapter holds several more general implications for inference and the value of these research methods.

The Advantages of a Guided Search for Civilian Autonomy

Was encountering the instructive differences in civilian autonomy across these towns of Cundinamarca pure luck? Perhaps, but social science tools and models were instrumental in making an educated guess about where to look. These methodological advances are as important as the substantive findings, since data can have weaknesses, model specifications can be sensitive, and theories were made to be refined. Combining methods and triangulating multiple sources hold several advantages for understanding behavior in conflict settings.

First, combining statistical case selection with qualitative case studies facilitates making broader inferences beyond solely productive within-pair case comparisons. Matching neighbor cases within the same region helps rule out wider, nonzone specific explanations that might be difficult to measure and control for with statistics. For instance, levels of equality, variants of armed groups, or proximity to the frontier could be omitted (or poorly measured) variables that could produce spurious relationships between juntas and violence. Because these factors vary little within the localized region of western Cundinamarca, they are unlikely to account for the variation among these comparison-set towns.

Second, the qualitative explorations revealed some exogenous "twists of fate" that helped explain variation in the formation of juntas within this region that were not easily detectable with large-n methods. These unexpected events (or "qualitative instrumental variables," as they might be called) explain organizational development in Vianí and Bituima and offer hope that interventions in social-capital-challenged localities can change the "paths" they are on. Juntas (or social organizations) could be considered "treatments" that policymakers can apply to promote resilience. While organizations like the juntas may indicate preexisting cohesion and more easily thrive where cohesion exists, they can also be created in adverse circumstances and go on to have benevolent effects.

Third, beyond testing theories and mechanisms, the qualitative analysis is helpful for generating theory. Residents pointed to the explanation of clientelism to account for weakened social structures and why the junta councils did not more strongly embrace explicit mechanisms for human rights protection. This could be because they mainly existed to manage funds from the government to build (clientelist) projects. Although ATCC residents also cited the influence of clientelism, their juntas fulfilled other social functions, such as providing order and raising funds, and therefore generally remained stronger. This was likely out of necessity from being situated in an isolated, neglected colonist zone. For the same reason, they were also likely less integrated into politicians' clientelist networks. Juntas may therefore be more likely to thrive where states are weak and their survival does not primarily depend on municipal politicians.

Combating clientelism was also a motivation for the Congress to enact the national-level funding cuts in 1993. However, perversely, these cuts weakened the junta councils just prior to the surge in the armed conflict. The funding had made the juntas stronger and more active by giving them purpose and allowing them to carry out community development projects. Yet these funds were cut because they were also used for political favors.

Comparing how these cuts unfolded across my case regions underscores how they led to the greater political autonomy of juntas, but also, in many cases, to their dissolution.[207] Because the conflict arrived early in the ATCC region – before the funding cuts could weaken the junta councils – those communities were advantaged in organizing for autonomy. In contrast, by the time the wave of conflict came to the Cundinamarca municipios, national-level (external) policy changes had already weakened local organizations and they struggled to mount autonomy strategies to deal with armed groups. Of course, civilian autonomy movements may also be less common in the early phases of conflicts for ideational reasons, as communities often need time to develop repertoires of strategies. Still, my mixed-methods approach reveals that seeking autonomy is even harder, though not impossible, when clientelism is also present and threatens organizational capacity.

[207] AC#1,2 Bogotá, 3/2009.

9

Civilian Autonomy around the World

"The people are very unified so the Taliban failed. We are dead set against the army, too."
                                                    – Elder, Buner, Pakistan, 2008 (Parlez and Shah 2008b)

"Early on in this war, I met with the main religious leaders in the community: the bishop and the mother superior of the main convent. We decided that even if the mountains around us were exploding with fighting, we would not go to war.... We decided adamantly that Maloula would not be destroyed.... The situation here will not deteriorate; it's the opposite. People support each other."
                                                    – Sunni imam, Maloula, Syria, 2012 (Di Giovanni 2012)

Civilian efforts for autonomy reach far beyond Colombia. In this chapter, I explore four additional out-of-sample cases of civilian autonomy from around the globe. Although these additional cases from Colombia, the Philippines, Afghanistan, and Syria were not systematically selected for comparison, they exhibit geographical diversity, involve conflicts of diverse types and origins, and have ample documentation of civilian strategies and armed actor responses. They highlight unique aspects of civilian autonomy, including showcasing the diversity and prevalence of strategies and how they function in sectarian conflicts, Muslim-majority countries, and with the presence of international forces. They are also "tough" cases for autonomy given the intensities of the conflicts. Their displays of civilian autonomy contrast strikingly with conventional interpretations that emphasize the victimization of civilians in these conflicts.

The inclusion of these additional cases and countries shows that the main argument of this book is not culturally bounded. In fact, it shows that local civilian organization frequently supersedes cultural differences as an explanation for violence. Put differently, cohesion and organization explain differences in outcomes of violence within particular cultural groups. The cases also further showcase the diversity of innovation by civilians in war as well as the limits of their efforts when circumstances turn dire.

I first assess the civilian autonomy theory I developed in Colombia based on additional firsthand field research in Colombia on "tough," out-of-sample community cases in the highly contested demilitarized zone of the Macarena region. I then also explore the protective autonomy strategies that communities have pursued in both Muslim and Christian areas of the Philippines. Using interviews with community advocates and archival research, I conduct a quantitative analysis of the strategies implemented by communities that declared themselves "Zones of Peace." In the religious-extremist conflicts in Afghanistan and Pakistan, I document examples of community actions to avoid the NATO/government–Taliban crossfire using secondary sources and news reports. Lastly, I analyze secondary sources on communities caught between government and rebel forces in Syria and show that civilian autonomy has been attempted and proven helpful even in that extremely brutal conflict.

These cases provide helpful insights about autonomy but are not controlled studies since the influence of additional predictors of violence, such as the balance of control among armed actors, are not easily measured. Without adequate data on the complicated selection issues and precisely measured outcomes (as is available in Colombia), these cases are only a first exploration of protection and resilience in these countries. Still, these cases show that civilians have effectively organized for autonomy in diverse and challenging locations across different continents.

CIVILIAN AUTONOMY IN FARCLANDIA

In addition to the Colombia case studies from Cundinamarca and Santander, I also conducted fieldwork in the former Colombian demilitarized zone, or *Zona de Despeje* (or *distensión*) and, even there, I found examples of autonomy. Often informally referred to as "FARClandia," this region in the department of Meta, about 100 miles southeast of the capital of Bogotá, is an out-of-sample and extremely tough case for civilian autonomy. The *despeje* territory of five municipios, covering an area about the size of Switzerland, was ceded to the FARC by President Andrés Pastrana in 1998 for the Caguán round of peace negotiations.[1] The top-down negotiated cease-fire held for a short time, but it ended up being violated in many areas of the country by the guerrillas before the peace talks eventually collapsed in 2002. For this reason, and because the region became the pilot for the government's "territorial consolidation" program in the mid-2000s, FARClandia is perhaps the best-known conflict zone in Colombia. However, because the negotiations were the focus of attention – to

[1] The region includes the municipios of La Uribe, Mesetas, La Macarena, and Vista Hermosa in the department of Meta and San Vicente del Caguán in the department of Caquetá.

the neglect of conditions in the zone – FARClandia is also one of the conflict zones that is most poorly understood.

The *despeje* is a tough case for civilian autonomy because of the FARC's entrenched territorial control, as well as being the setting of peace talks while also suffering periods of shifts in control and intense conflict. The long, narrow mountain range known as the "Lying Indian" (*el Indio Acostado*) that shoots up out of the eastern plains runs through the heart of the *despeje* municipalities of Meta. This mountain range was a strategic base for the FARC, linking its coca production activities in the plains with close access to the capital and Cundinamarca.[2] Upon assuming control of this territory, FARC rule was dominant as evidenced by the guerrillas' regulation of most aspects of daily life (Campbell 2000). Nevertheless, declassified U.S. State Department cables, which provide rare insights into the conflict conditions that civilians faced within the *despeje* territory, noted that "most area inhabitants are not FARC supporters, and feel abandoned by the [Government]" (Kamman 1999, National Security Archive).

The level of confrontation between armed actors declined for a time from 1998 to 2000 because of the peace process, although there were still reports of various rights violations committed by the guerrillas and the paramilitaries (Amnesty International 2002, Vicepresidencia 2003, 2003b). Then, beginning in 2000, conflict intensified. According to a U.S. Embassy cable, while the FARC had twelve fronts in or surrounding the *despeje*, paramilitaries were reported to have expanded their presence and had three fronts in the area (Patterson 2000, 2002). As in other areas of Colombia, armed actors fought each other through the civilian population, using intimidation to exert their influence and control both during the extended period of talks and afterwards when FARC control began to erode (Vicepresidencia 2003, 2003b).

The FARC implemented forced civic action days (Kamman 1999), and there were forced displacements, kidnappings, extortion, targeted killings, and resignations by mayors (Patterson 2000). The paramilitaries, for their part, entered the zone and threatened residents not to cooperate with the FARC (Kamman 1999).[3] Short of full combat, paramilitary action was also focused on the population, as they "appear[ed] to be looking for targeted opportunities against the FARC, but [were] apparently not planning any large-scale operations" (Patterson 2002). These events led one U.S. Embassy analyst to pessimistically conclude, "The right to free political expression has effectively been limited through fear and intimidation" (Kamman 1999). Yet even in this dangerous environment some of the vibrant village junta councils helped insulate communities from violence and adapt to changing conflict conditions.

---

[2] Alias *Mono Jojoy*, the FARC's second-in-command and field marshal, was killed during airstrikes against these bases in 2010.

[3] The author of this U.S. Embassy cable ominously warned he "would not be surprised to see paramilitary massacres of civilians suspected of pro-FARC sympathies in coming weeks."

The Macarena mountain range, also known as the "Lying Indian," rising up out of the eastern plains in Meta department, within what was the demilitarized zone (*Zona de Despeje*), or FARClandia, 2011.
Photograph by Oliver Kaplan.

I visited several municipalities in the Macarena region in January 2011 and conducted interviews with a variety of residents, including several junta council leaders (and had previously interviewed ex-combatants in 2009 who had operated in Meta).[4] In this frontier region, the colonist residents had spent years building their small communities and strengthening social relations, and they had a strong tradition of junta councils (see also Molano 1987). All the juntas had legal charters (*personerías*), stayed informed about events in the zone, and were recognized by residents as the authority in the villages. The juntas also had traditions of reconciliation in the form of conciliation committees (*comités de conciliadores*), which consisted of five people who would impartially resolve conflicts in the community (adjudicating compensation when cattle would trample a neighbor's crops, etc.). As with the junta *comités* in other parts of the country, in the absence of state institutions and in conditions of armed conflict, the Macarena *comités* adapted to mediate social

---

[4] M#1,2, Meta, 1/2011. Specific municipios are not reported for anonymity reasons.

disputes even though this was beyond their official purview of monitoring junta governance and procedural issues.

Even during the most intense years of armed conflict surrounding the *despeje*, the juntas kept functioning. Villages maintained their community conflict resolution processes and, *where conciliation committees were strong*, it was preferable to resolve issues in the community rather than take them to the guerrillas. The strength of a junta would depend on the quality of its leader – whether he or she was a strong and vocal advocate for the community – and whether the junta was recently formed or had longer experience with community decision-making. In the context of the conflict, armed groups would say "you're either with us or against us," and residents looked to the juntas for protection and to dialogue with armed groups on the community's behalf. The juntas advocated for communities and were "salvation" that allowed people who preferred neutrality to say, "My side is the [community] junta."[5] Armed groups respected strong juntas and would not get involved in their community meetings, although the guerrillas would at times send representatives. By contrast, some juntas were historically weaker or more "timid" and had greater difficulty negotiating with tough commanders.

The strategy and philosophy of junta leaders was to "walk the line, neither here nor there" and not take sides in the larger armed conflict. Junta leaders participated in dialogues with armed groups and negotiated with them to avoid threats of displacement so residents could stay in their homes. During the *despeje*, if people "behaved well," they "wouldn't have any problems." One of the leaders described his relationship with the FARC guerrillas as follows, "If they greet me, I greet them. If they speak to me, I speak to them as the leader of the community, but have no other interaction."

The guerrilla commander was like the "mayor" during the *despeje* years, and while residents had to do what the guerrillas said, the guerrillas also listened to them. Notably, some guerrilla commanders were more tolerant and more willing than others to accept junta autonomy and allow communities to run their own affairs. For instance, two commanders from the FARC's 27th Front had better "political skills" and were "more aware" of the population whereas other, more militant commanders (who were more concerned with military strategy) were less concerned about the population. The juntas' independence from the armed actors was on display when the paramilitaries and guerrillas wanted the juntas to protest against government coca eradication programs and the juntas instead negotiated on their own for crop substitution programs.

---

[5] Consistent with these accounts, WOLA (2011) reports that in the early 1990s, even prior to the *despeje*, civic leaders used similar dialogues to form "peace pacts" for autonomy with guerrilla and paramilitary commanders. This tradition continued through the *despeje* period as the junta leaders later negotiated to allow the juntas and the town council to continue to function.

After the peace talks collapsed and the demilitarized zone came to an end, the military and then paramilitaries came to the region. It was "tough" (*"berraco"*) when there were multiple armed groups, and the entry of the paramilitaries was "terrible" for the population. Residents were stigmatized as guerrillas, and the guerrillas also came to see the people as paramilitaries. They were "screwed" (*"jodido"*) and it was "hard, not easy" (*"duro, no suave"*). But one man observed that the juntas were especially active in protect-ing people during this shift in control and sought to find remedies so that the "population was not pressured by multiple armed groups." As a leader, he wanted the population to be left aside from the conflict and remain "very neutral." Although there are no reports of open protests against armed actors, there is evidence of community management and negotiation with combatants.

A FARC ex-combatant that operated in Meta confirmed the general activism of some juntas there.[6] The FARC wanted the juntas to solve local problems (e. g., domestic and property boundary disputes) and would hold "orientations" and provide a document to communities with rules and norms to live by. If there were murders committed among the population, the guerrillas would join community meetings to impose order and authority. In general, however, the guerrillas reportedly respected junta decisions. For example, if civilians told guerrillas not to stay at their farms, they would respect the decision and leave. Some juntas even insisted on managing their own affairs, as did two villages in Meta that did not want army or guerrilla visits and instead preferred to maintain peace on their own.[7] As in Cundinamarca and La India, when the FARC arrived at one of the villages at night, the entire community came out to protest, with community leaders politely saying, "So sorry about this, but we want peace" (*"Me da pena con ustedes, pero queremos paz"*).

There is unfortunately little reporting and few histories on community rela-tions from the *despeje* region, making it difficult to more broadly corroborate these accounts. One of the few additional investigations of this region is Vásquez's (2013) interviews of residents of the neighboring municipality of San Vicente del Caguán in the department of Caquetá, which indicates less civilian autonomy in the interactions between the FARC and communities. The FARC exerted more control over the population in San Vicente, largely co-opt-ing the juntas, and the coca economy expanded its reach. Although community organizations were strong and "each village had a junta,"[8] communities had relatively little independence and there were not reports of resisting FARC influence. In some cases, the FARC stimulated the creation of junta councils to organize communities and then serve as interlocutors with state institutions (Cubides et al. 1989). As one man said, "The development here is a result of the guerrillas."[9] Speaking to the extent of FARC control, a woman recalled that,

---

[6] Exc#8, Bogotá, 8/2009.   [7] Precise locations were not recalled in the interview.
[8] Vásquez interview #6; translated from the Spanish.   [9] Vásquez interview #3.

"When those people [FARC] ruled here, it was they who governed. One didn't see robberies or deaths because they maintained order. Almost everyone depended on them because they generated employment. One simply did the work one had to do."[10] However, there is a contrasting account from a U.S. Embassy cable of an additional instance of activism against the FARC, where a local priest criticized the FARC's management of the zone and publicly asked them, "Who authorized you to govern San Vicente? ... Who authorized you to occupy every corner of the town, ... control economic activities, recruit minors?" (Kamman 1999). This portrayal suggests that even if civilian autonomy was not found in every part of the *despeje*, limited forms of autonomy were possible in at least some areas.

In sum, the history from the *despeje*, albeit incomplete, reveals a diversity of experiences. Although civilians lived under siege in Meta during and after the years of the *despeje* and the Caguán peace talks, communities were still able to come together to mitigate the harmful consequences of instability in surprising ways. This counternarrative begs a rethinking of conventional historiography of the region.

CIVILIAN AUTONOMY AND THE PEACE ZONES IN THE PHILIPPINES

Similar to the formally organized peace communities in Colombia, approximately 100 communities in the Philippines organized themselves as nonviolent "Zones of Peace" (ZOPs). Beginning with the founding of the Zone of Peace, Freedom, and Neutrality (ZOPFAN) in Naga City in 1988, these communities have sought to keep out and avoid entanglements with contending government, rebel, and paramilitary forces. These diverse Philippine ZOPs hold insights for civilian autonomy because many have made public declarations of their collective strategies. This systematic information makes it easier to see the distribution of civilian protection strategies used relative to the more scattered and subtle actions by the Colombian peace communities. In this section, I analyze how ZOP communities have dealt with the pressures of armed conflict and identify the possible effects these actions had to protect civilians. The analysis is based on secondary sources and interviews I conducted during fieldwork in Manila and Davao in May 2012.

The Philippines has experienced decades of conflict since the early 1970s. Government forces (Armed Forces of the Philippines, or AFP) and paramilitary units such as the Citizen Armed Force Geographical Units (CAFGU) have battled insurgent groups such as the New People's Army (NPA), the armed wing of the Communist People's Party (CPP), the Moro National Liberation Front (MNLF), and the Moro Islamic Liberation Front (MILF; the CPP was

[10] Vásquez interview #2.

founded in 1968 and the MNLF in 1969).[11] The communists' goal has been to topple the state while the Muslim insurgencies have pursued separatism with the goal of creating their own state on the southern island of Mindanao. The Muslim areas gained a degree of political autonomy through the negotiated establishment of the Autonomous Region in Muslim Mindanao (ARMM) in 1989 (McKenna 1998). Conflict intensified in the late 1980s through the mid-1990s after peace talks broke down in 1987 and President Corazon Aquino launched a "total war" policy against the NPA. Fighting spiked again in Mindanao in the early 2000s, with a series of stalled peace talks, aborted cease-fires, and aggressive government counterinsurgency campaigns against the MILF under President Joseph Estrada's "all-out war" policy. To date, the armed conflicts in the Philippines have claimed over 160,000 lives (Project Ploughshares 2013, Reuters 2014) and nearly four million people have been displaced since 2000 (IDMC 2014).

The Philippine state governs a territory of more than 7,000 islands and faces geographic and bureaucratic challenges in extending its reach to rural communities. Because of this, as one NGO staff member said, "The security situation is complex – there are not just armed actors, but also contending families, clans, bandits, paramilitaries, and corruption."[12] The Philippines' social landscape is diverse, with cultures superimposed on top of each other through waves of colonization by Muslims, the Spanish, and the United States (as well as the preexisting Indigenous Peoples). This landscape produced tense social relations in some areas and fed the armed conflicts – it did not predispose the Philippines to be an incubator of civil society peace movements. One pernicious type of social conflict that is especially prevalent on Mindanao is *rido*, or clan conflicts, as widely documented by Torres (2007). In such feuds, extended families – entire clans – carry out retributive acts against enemies, leading to cycles of violence that can last for decades. As a staff member of the Manila-based NGO Community Organizers Multiversity, which works with ZOPs, noted, peer and social pressure and the concept of *"maratabat,"* or hurt pride, provide incentives for even peaceful people to join in *ridos*.[13] Politicians and armed groups have preyed upon *rido* conflicts to incite further violence. This escalation of *rido* violence was a main reason for founding some ZOPs, such as those of Maladeg and Carmen (Catholic Relief Services 2003).

Santos (2005) identifies two main waves of ZOPs: one in the early 1990s and another in the early 2000s. Some peace zones were still being formed as late as 2010 (Cabreza 2010). According to qualitative research by Philippine (Lee 2000, Santos 2005) and international scholars (Hancock and Mitchell 2007), although the ZOPs can go by many names – sanctuaries of peace, spaces for

---

[11] The Islamist militant group Abu Sayyaf Group (ASG), which has been linked to Al Qaeda, has operated on the small, isolated southern islands of Sulu, Jolo, Basilan, and Tawi-Tawi and is generally more removed from the ZOP regions.

[12] Ma#1, Manila, 5/2012.   [13] Ma#2, Manila, 5/2012.

peace – they often form in response to a violent triggering event, suggesting that at least some ZOPs did not solely arise in historically peaceful areas. They also share strong organizational foundations, since they are launched from close community ties and often with the support of local social entrepreneurs such as Catholic priests, Muslim imams, or NGO workers and activists that help coordinate collective actions under threat of violence.[14] For instance, CO Multiversity reports that in Maguindanao in 2003, a ZOP was formed by community leaders through an agreement in which residents committed to avoid getting involved in disputes and conflict-related activities.[15] Some ZOPs are of a single ethnic or religious group (Muslim, Christian, Indigenous Peoples) while others are constituted by several groups to promote intersectarian harmony. Indeed, the use of declarations themselves (as a kind of written organizational constitution) was spread by networks of NGOs and religious organizations, becoming a norm and practice to be emulated (i.e., institutional isomorphism described by Meyer and Rowan 1977).

For a more systematic understanding of ZOPs, I coded existing qualitative community, rebel group, and military documents collected by Santos (2005). I produced a mapping of the twenty most prominent Philippine ZOPs at the level of the *barangay* (village) displayed in Figure 9.1 (a finer level of geographical detail than exists in Colombia).[16] ZOPs are found in diverse areas of the country, including in Luzon, north of Manila, as well as clusters on the southern island of Mindanao and other scattered locations. Some encompass entire municipalities while others consist of just one or several barangays.

What do ZOPs do? Based on the declarations, I compiled a detailed inventory of nonviolent protection strategies that includes their degrees of specificity, complexity, and contentiousness.[17] These diverse types of tactics can be aggregated into four general categories of clauses that correspond to the autonomy mechanisms outlined in Chapter 2: actions to strengthen community institutional arrangements, regulation of social vice (community norms), actions to protect civilians, and more contentious rules of conduct for combatants. Institutional policies include declaring the size of ZOPs, policies on migration to ZOPs, policies to manage fear and build trust, and incentives or penalties to promote cooperation. Strategies to manage social vices that could lead to

---

[14] D#1, Davao, 5/2012.

[15] Ma#2, Manila, 5/2012. Also, "Peace Covenant establishing the Zone of Peace at Sitio Cagawaran, Barangay Tugaig, Barira, Maguindanao," June 8, 2003, in Santos (2005).

[16] Some of the constituent barangays of these peace zones originally formed independently and later agglomerated into larger zones.

[17] These declared institutional practices are different from particular instances of protective actions, protests, and conflict events, which may occur within the declared ZOPs. These events would likely be seen if and when institutional procedures alone fail to deter violence. According to an NGO worker, declarations are generally a good indicator of ZOP activity, but some communities that had not declared ZOPs behaved like ZOPs, while the declarations of some ZOPs were empty statements, with little implementation. D#2, Davao, 5/2012.

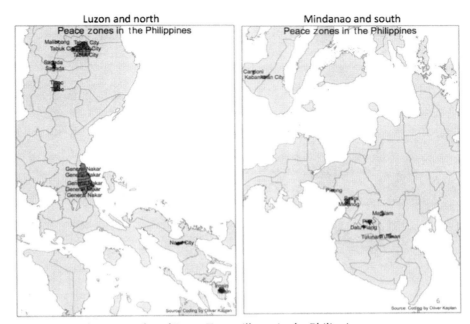

FIGURE 9.1 The geography of Peace Zone villages in the Philippines

outbreaks of disputes and violence include bans on gambling, alcohol, drugs, and firearms. Actions to protect civilians include resolving local disputes, anti-recruitment strategies (especially for youth), procedures to protect community leaders or threatened individuals, and norms of not passing information to armed groups. Rules of conduct for combatants include barring armed groups from territory, barring their use of public facilities, appeals against the harassment of civilians, cease-fires, and providing safety for wounded soldiers.

Figure 9.2 aggregates the number of different strategies declared by the twenty ZOPs (and their constituent barangays) to provide information on the prevalence and distributions of particular strategies. The analysis indicates that the majority of the ZOPs mention *multiple* armed actors as targets in their statements – a clear indicator of a preference for autonomy. However, there is also variation across the ZOPs in the specificity and sophistication of their strategies. Around three-quarters declared at least a basic package of general and definitional claims, including declarations about the contours of the ZOP, appeals against harassment of civilians, bans on firearms, and calls for ceasefires. More detailed polices (more sophisticated declarations) are found in about one-half of ZOPs, such as the Baras and Sagada zones, including dispute resolution procedures; anti-recruitment and migration policies; bans on additional vices; explicit policies to deal with trust, fear, and cooperation; and restrictions on armed actors. Indeed, ten of the declarations contentiously call for barring armed groups from community territories.

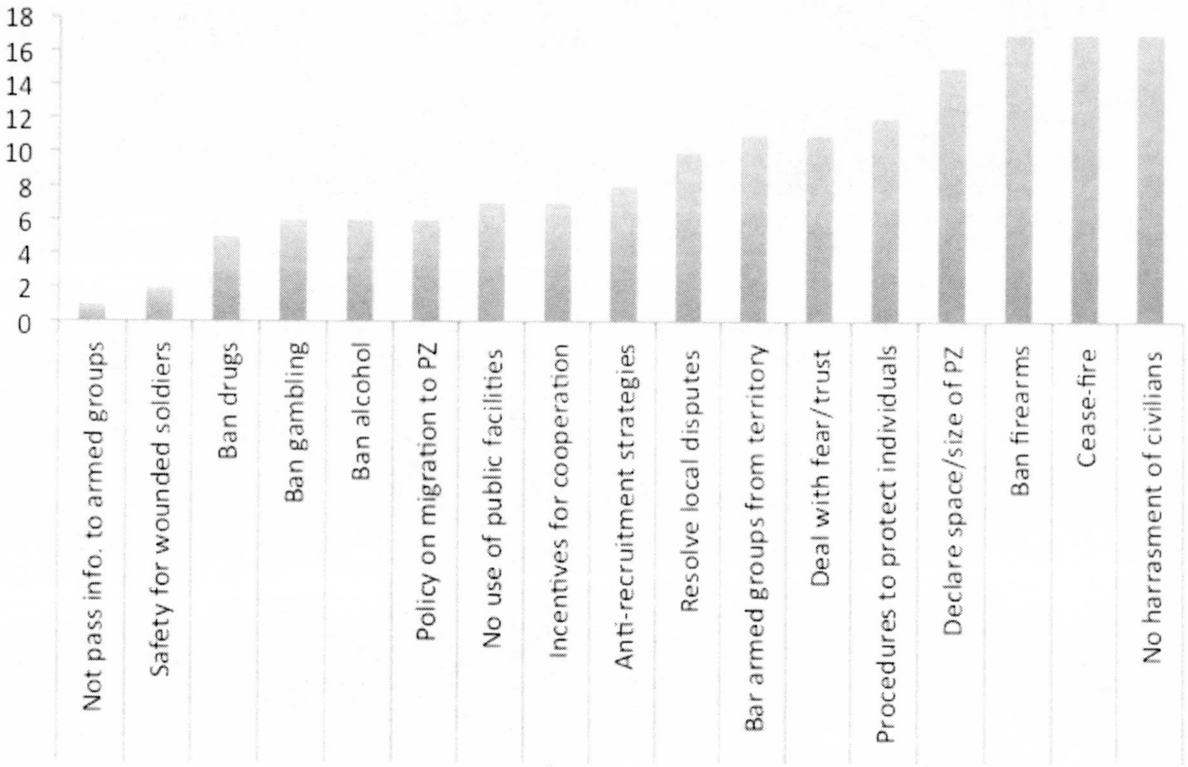

FIGURE 9.2 Frequencies of Peace Zone strategies in the Philippines.
Source: Author's tabulations, based on Santos (2005).

Similar to the peace communities in Colombia and civilian autonomy actions in other countries, social regulation (e.g., barring weapons) and norms of nonviolence to limit participation in the conflict figure prominently in ZOP declarations. Several reference the concept of *bayanihan*, or communal work and reciprocity (Catholic Relief Services 2003), evoking the *convite* or *minga* communal work groups found in Colombia. A Philippine scholar who has accompanied several peace zones emphasized the importance of moral persuasion to promote peace.[18] Such persuasion is leveraged in at least two ways.

First, within communities, women and mothers frequently compel good behavior, as the Philippines is "very matriarchal," and dialogue and education efforts are used to promote and sustain norms of nonviolence and social control. For example, an early ZOP declaration calls for "Discussion groups that will explain the situation, dissuade people from actions such as joining paramilitary civilian defense groups [CAFGU], cooperating in intelligence operations of armed groups, [or] joining fundamentalist groups."[19]

Second, in relations with rebel and government forces, communities have invoked rhetorical traps similar to those in Bituima, Cundinamarca, or the Colombian Indigenous communities. It is characteristic of ZOPs to attempt to influence armed actors by making such claims as, "You [armed actors] say you're our protectors but why do we suffer when you're here? You fight for our liberation, but we get hurt."[20] As indicated in a ZOP planning document, there is also moralistic naming and shaming for transgressions by armed actors, "Sanctions will be imposed by the armed parties on members of their own forces that violate their agreements with a Peace Zone ... Moreover, the full force of the people's judgment and condemnation will publicly be cast on parties."[21]

There is less information available on the implementation of ZOP declarations or observed collective actions to prevent violence. However, there are some positive examples, including from the Sindaw Ko Kalilintad (Light of Peace) cluster of Peace Zones. These zones were formed in Mindanao beginning in 2002 to deal with fighting between MILF and government forces in areas where some members of the population were MILF sympathizers. Local peace zone leaders and CO Multiversity built upon the existing structure of community organizations, including women's and youth groups, farmer cooperatives, and barangay councils, and trained a group of elders in mediation to resolve *ridos*. At one point, the community also warned the AFP and MILF about

---

[18] Ma#3, Manila, 5/2012.

[19] "Implementing Guidelines of our PCPR Agenda for Peace (Some characteristics of our Zones of Peace)" by the Promotion of Church Peoples' Rights, September 18, 1989, in Santos (2005).

[20] Ma#2, Manila, 5/2012.

[21] "Working Paper for the Establishment of a Policy on Peace Zones: A Proposal to the Parties to the Armed Conflict (n.d.)" by the Peace Zone Technical Committee, Multi-sectoral Peace Advocates, in Santos (2005).

Courtesy of Hearts of Peace (HOPE) · Naga City

A flyer promoting the ban on firearms in the Naga City Zone of Peace in the Philippines. Solimon Santos personal archive. Photograph by Oliver Kaplan.

fighting near the community, saying, "Don't do your shooting here because it will affect our water pipes."[22] The combatants apparently acquiesced to the community's demands.

What have been the perspectives of armed actors toward the ZOPs? Statements by government forces and insurgent groups indicate that they have at times been willing to abide by the nonviolent demands of the ZOPs and armed actors have been signatories to various ZOP declarations. However, the armed actors exhibit ambivalence toward ZOPs similar to that of the armed actors in Colombia toward the peace communities. ZOPs have initially been viewed as threatening, and armed actors have been wary of yielding perceived battlefield advantages to the enemy. Both government and rebel forces have therefore attempted strategies of co-optation. Guarantees of reciprocity and fairness, which have been aided by the ZOP's commitment to autonomy, have been helpful for stabilizing the agreements and inducing the armed actors to respect the population's wishes. This has led to diverse and evolving perspectives on the ZOPs, including toward the notion that peace should be community-based and toward greater restraint by the military.

For example, different parts of the Philippine government have been skeptical of peace zones at different moments, with the military starting out as especially skeptical for fear of ceding military advantages to insurgents. In reference to Naga City, one of the most prominent ZOPs, a military commander believed that "the outlawed Communists will enjoy the golden opportunity to propagate their prescribed doctrine,"[23] while another commander worried that it would place the National Democratic Front (NDF; an umbrella organization for the NPA, the Communist Party of the Philippines, and other revolutionary organizations) on "equal footing" and provide them with a sanctuary.[24] The military has also expressed concerns about the absence of reciprocity and ceding terrain, as one commander noted that "all of the demands and responsibilities are being made only on the side of the Military, while *no similar demand* is being made on the rebels ... the situation is unjust and ... in favor of the rebels and against the Military."[25] In this vein, General Rodolfo Obaniana starkly proclaimed, "I do not believe in peace zone[s]" (Mallari Jr. 2007).

---

[22] Ma#2, Manila, 5/2012.

[23] "Comments, Reaction and Position of the Camarines Sur Constabulary/Integrated National Police Command to the Proposal of the Hearts of Peace (HOPE) to Make Naga City a Permanent Zone of Peace, Freedom and Neutrality (ZOPFAN)" by Lt. Col. Rufo R. Pulido (n. d. but March 1989), in Santos (2005).

[24] Col. Marino L. Filart, PC Regional Commander, letter to Naga City Mayor Jesse M. Robredo, February 28, 1989, in Santos (2005).

[25] "Comments, Reaction and Position of the Camarines Sur Constabulary/Integrated National Police Command to the Proposal of the Hearts of Peace (HOPE) to Make Naga City a Permanent Zone of Peace, Freedom and Neutrality (ZOPFAN)" by Lt. Col. Rufo R. Pulido (n. d. but March 1989), in Santos (2005).

In interviews, military officers reported mixed results of ZOPs. One mid-level officer thought the Sagada ZOP does not work and is likely "an NPA sanctuary, a front, a ploy" and believed that, at the height of insurgency, social cohesion and formal governance can break down while insurgent shadow governments gain influence.[26] However, the same officer also noted that strong barangay captains, ulamas (Muslim religious leaders), and tribal chiefs can help deal with the NPA and that the NPA is not able to dismantle all informal civil society institutions. Another military officer observed that there is variation in barangay captains and participation in barangay governance from one locale to another.[27] More exuberantly, in a Philippine military trade publication, General Ariel Bernardo notes how different AFP institutions can "produce a force multiplier effect to the whole process of establishing a PZ" and called the peace-oriented approach "preferable [to] continued military confrontation" (Bernardo 2010).

More political parts of government that have broader views of the conflicts (and peace efforts) have generally held more favorable views toward the ZOPs and have adopted more conciliatory stances with the passage of time. Under President Estrada in the mid-1990s, some peace zones were designated as Special Development Areas (SDA) and received additional development support from the government.[28] As a government peace commission noted, "The development of 'Peace Zones,' while starting out as an attempt to manage conflict, has become a process of empowerment."[29] Similarly, the government's peace advisor (OPAPP) later stated that, "Zones of Peace should not be viewed as ... hindering ... a negotiated settlement" and recommended "self-imposed restraint on the part of the Armed Forces of the Philippines from conducting military/combat operations in the areas covered by the Peace Zone declaration."[30] Philippine congressional legislation has called for ensuring the "integrity and autonomy" of ZOPs.[31] In interviews, an official from OPAPP noted that "a day without the breakout of hostilities is another day of peace [so] if more and more communities declare peace zones, so much the better."[32] Some of the peace zones have also been favored by the government for their roles in

[26] Ma#4, Manila, 5/2012.
[27] Ma#5, Manila, 5/2012. For these officers, limiting comments to barangays and informal autonomy actions was perhaps a more politically acceptable way of addressing this subject.
[28] Yet, in interviews, an official from OPAPP noted the limitations of the state-imposed SDAs by saying "You cannot legislate peace zones." Ma#6, Manila, 5/2012.
[29] 1993 Report of the National Unification Commission, section on "Respect for and Recognition of Community Declarations of Peace Zones," in Santos (2005).
[30] "Memorandum for Her Excellency Gloria Macapagal-Arroyo from Secretary Eduardo R. Ermita, Subject: 'OPAPP Position on the Current Debate re Advisability of the Peace Zones of the Country,'" May 7, 2003, in Santos (2005).
[31] House Bill No. 1867, Thirteenth Congress, "An Act Declaring a National Policy on Peace Zones," July 28, 2004, in Santos (2005).
[32] Ma#6, Manila, 5/2012.

ensuring the durable reintegration and protection of insurgent ex-combatants (similar to the role of the ATCC in Colombia).

Rebel groups have also exhibited ambivalence, alternating between opposing and supporting the ZOPs. The NPA registered initial opposition in reference to the Sagada ZOP, stating, "We cannot agree outright to an indefinite 'total troop pullout' by NPA units from Sagada or any other locality, nor to a permanent local truce. To do so is to abandon the local people."[33] Skepticism toward ZOPs is also seen on the part of the MILF as made clear in a press release, which asked, "What can this so-called 'peace sanctuary' offer? Nothing."[34] Yet, in another letter by the NDF (NPA), the emphasis on reciprocity comes out, "If it is true that the AFP Officers and Civilian Officials respect the declared 'Peace Zone,' the NDF will also ... respect the people's declaration."[35]

The views of rebel groups toward ZOPs also evolved over time, as evidenced by public statements in support of the ZOPs. The NPA has outright supported principles of protection enshrined in peace zone declarations.[36] Similarly, MILF Chairman Salamat Hashim stated, "The assurance we can give is that we will keep our armed presence away from these Sanctuaries of Peace."[37] The Ginapaladtaka Space for Peace was described by a MILF leader as "a noble contribution alongside the peace process."[38] A former mayor confirmed that the ZOP efforts have contributed to respect for rights in at least some occasions, "We earned the promise from the leaders [of the AFP and the NPA] that they would respect our rules ... There were violations [of the peace zone that had never gone public]. But ... We assert the agreement so [the AFP and the NPA] were compelled to punish their own people" (Cabreza 2010).

---

[33] "Once More on the Question of Peace: On the Proposal for the Demilitarization of Sagada." Joint Statement of the CPDF Provisional Council and the NPA Chadli Molintas Command, January 30, 1989, in Santos (2005).

[34] MILF Central Committee Press Release, "Gov't resorting to dirty tactics," June 15, 2003, in Santos (2005).

[35] "Letter of National Democratic Front Far South Region Media Liaison Officer Raul Tan to Whom It May Concern [translated from Cebuano]," September 13, 1991, in Santos (2005).

[36] One statement proclaims, "We support points 5, 10, and 11 of the proposal: First, that the civilian population not be harassed, intimidated, or subjected to other criminal acts by the contending forces. Second, that customs and traditional practices be respected and observed. And third, that suspects not be tortured or killed, and be investigated with the participation of the people." "Once More on the Question of Peace: On the Proposal for the Demilitarization of Sagada." Joint Statement of the CPDF Provisional Council and the NPA Chadli Molintas Command, January 30, 1989, in Santos (2005).

[37] Message from Ustadz Ameerul Salamat Hashim, Chairman, MILF (By Mohamad Nur, Chief of Staff, Office of the MILF Chairman, Camp Abu Bakar As Siddique), responding to request to "give approval and safety assurance" of a peace zone, May 31, 2005, in Santos (2005).

[38] Remarks delivered by Von Al Haq, MILF CCCH member, during the Declaration of the GINAPALADTAKA Space for Peace and Children as Zones of Peace, at Takepan, Pikit, North Cotabato, November 29, 2004, in Santos (2005).

This review of Philippine ZOPs points to their richness, diversity, and intermediate forms of success, suggesting that Philippine civilians have crafted one of the strongest autonomy movements around the world. While some "lose their steam or cease to exist"[39] and some have suffered periods of combat (Alipala 2008), there is evidence of successful implementation, since many persisted long enough to convene to discuss lessons learned in 2003 (Catholic Relief Services 2003). Another NGO staff member observed, "[ZOPs] may not be the safest areas, but are safe compared to many other communities."[40] Further analysis that accounts for conflict conditions is required to determine the extent of implementation of declared policies and whether and how ZOPs have affected violence.

At least one indicator of success is that some of the ZOPs have persisted and continue to work toward peace at the local level and new ones continued to form (Cabreza 2010, Fernandez 2011). In one instance from 2014, villagers from the Sagada Peace Zone mobilized to evict any rebels that might be present in their region and verify their departure to convince the military that there was no threat to the area and therefore no reason for them to remain either (Quitasol 2014). The movement for civilian autonomy from conflict in the Philippines could also be far broader than what is accounted for here, as many communities may have employed autonomy strategies without formally declaring ZOPs. At the time of this writing, as peace talks continue between the government and the MILF, one can point to the hopeful reality that some ZOPs have endured long enough to survive the most trying period of conflict.

CIVILIAN AUTONOMY IN AFGHANISTAN AND PAKISTAN

The Afghan and Pakistani conflicts share several similarities with the Colombian context, including diverse community strategies for protection and cases of civilian autonomy. First, like Colombia, these countries have rural peripheries with historically weak state presence, leaving many communities to confront pressures from multiple armed actors, be they Taliban, NATO/ISAF, or Afghan National Army (ANA) forces,[41] or other paramilitary groups and bandits. Second, due to tribal and cultural differences, there are different histories of social organization, cohesion, and resistance across local communities. Lastly, the Taliban insurgency appears to fit some of the theoretical conditions for having sensitivity to civilian actions: like the armed groups in Colombia, they appear to have hybrid characteristics. They have an ideological-religious aspect, are concerned with legitimacy (e.g., see Mullen 2009 on Taliban institutions), and have published rules on how to conduct warfare and interact with

[39] Ma#2, Manila, 5/2012.   [40] Ma#7, Manila, 5/2012.
[41] International Security Assistance Force.

civilians (Rubin 2010b). However, they are also known drug traffickers, indicating different strains and motivations within the group.

Afghanistan has wide subnational variation in the strength of local institutions, tribal structures, and social cohesion. There are differing traditions of maintaining local order from one zone to another and among ethnic groups (e. g., the Pashtun Wali codes of conduct; Malkasian 2013). These organizations and traditions are enablers of self-rule in relation to the government as well as the Taliban – being wary about dangerous entanglements, stigmatization as enemy collaborators, or abuses of authority. The civilians also hold preferences for autonomy, stemming either from tribal traditions or from more immediate concerns for protection. For example, at a *shura* (tribal meeting) in the Zhari District of Kandahar Province, a vocal elder told U.S. military officers, "I'm not going to let the enemy or you in my village. I'm going to take care of security myself" (Brulliard 2010).

These preferences, combined with social cohesion and organizational capacity, have produced a variety of autonomy actions. In the context of the conflict, Hazaras in Jaghori District of Ghazni Province peacefully resisted the initial incursion of the primarily Pashtun Taliban into the district (around 1997, pre-9/11) by dialoguing with them to maintain their autonomy and minimize violence (Suleman and Williams 2003). In Helmand Province, villagers in some districts organized to take up arms against foreign troops (U.S. and NATO) to protect their homes and voice their anger after losing relatives in air strikes (Gall 2009). In the eastern province of Nangarhar, a village rose up against the Taliban, apparently as a response to Taliban violence and abuses as well as to an entreaty of development resources from the Afghan government (Gopal and Rosenberg 2009). Shortly thereafter, the rest of the tribal brethren of the 400,000-member Pashtun Shinwari tribe followed suit (Filkins 2010).[42] The ability of these communities to organize for protection has been attributed to their relatively close social relations.

Tribal elders and local politicians in some local towns, including the Musa Qala district of Helmand Province, also organized to peacefully resist the Taliban by negotiating local cease-fires. In Musa Qala in 2006, residents nonviolently pressed for neutrality and also sought to limit the presence of NATO forces (Gall and Wafa 2006). According to Semple's analysis (2009, 81), the fifteen-member district tribal jirga (council) signed a written agreement

---

[42] As Filkins reports, although this action was against the Taliban, it also exhibits autonomy motives, "Tribal loyalties are strong and the tension between the Shinwaris and the Taliban long-standing. The Shinwari elders did not merely declare their opposition to the Taliban. Although they declared their allegiance to the Afghan government, they directed at it a nearly equal measure of fury, condemning 'all the corruption and illegal activities that threaten the Afghan people.' ... 'We are doing this for ourselves, and ourselves only,' said one of the elders. 'We have absolutely no faith in the Afghan government to do anything for us. We don't trust them at all.'"

with the provincial governor stating that only the police were to be allowed within 5 kilometers of the district center.[43] As with the Colombian cases, acceptance of the civilians' initiative would depend on their organizational capacity, as the governor of Helmand recounted, "They made a council of elders and came to us saying, 'We want to make the Taliban leave Musa Qala.' At first we did not accept their request, and we waited to see how strong the elders were." NATO/ISAF forces withdrew for a time and the tribal elders "mobilized all tribes and subtribes in the area to apply social pressure to the Taliban" to call off their attacks (85). The fighting decreased for five months as the Taliban respected the ban on entering the bazaar and "the jirga succeeded in turning them back the first time that a commander tried to enter with arms" (82). According to a UN assessment, it was the "non-ideological local Taliban" who most respected the jirga (85).

Unfortunately, in 2007, the accord frayed, as the jirga did not have the necessary resources to deliver tangible benefits to the community and was unable to maintain support and legitimacy (recalling the clientelist challenges seen in Colombia). Although some rumors suggested the bargain came to be dominated by the Taliban, "There was no evidence of the Taliban exploiting it strategically," and it was instead destabilized by an ISAF airstrike against a Taliban leader close to the protected zone, which triggered a Taliban incursion (88). The Musa Qala movement had promising origins and proved to be well organized. However, with strong strategic interests among the armed actors to control the territory and shifting conflict dynamics, it was not quite able to credibly signal its neutrality or capacity to manage local security on an enduring basis. With the agreement discarded, insecurity persisted as the territory continued to be contested militarily (Goldstein and Shah 2015).

Pakistan, in the same theater of conflict, has similar examples. In some instances, civilians armed to form local-based *Lashkar* militias to resist Taliban violence, especially in the "lawless" FATA tribal region (Perlez and Shah 2008; Wilkinson and Marwat 2008; Taj 2011). The town of Buner (near FATA) adopted a hybrid approach using both armed and nonviolent collective actions (Parlez and Shah 2008b). According to news reports, the residents of this town preferred to manage their own security affairs to avoid getting caught in the crossfire, "The villagers in Buner say they would prefer to handle the Taliban on their own, rather than have the heavy hand of the army come and do it for them." Residents first armed to punish Taliban aggressors and then formed a "peace committee" composed of elders and politicians and passed a resolution declaring Buner a zone free of both the army and the Taliban. The resistance and efforts at self-governance in Buner succeeded for a time, as seen

---

[43] According to the analysis of one community elder, "The Taliban stopped fighting because we convinced them that fighting would not be to our benefit." Another resident said, "The Taliban are not allowed to enter the bazaar with their weapons. If they resist with guns, the tribal elders will disarm them" (Gall and Wafa 2006).

in the elder's statement at the beginning of the chapter. However, they were undercut the following year after the government agreed to allow the Taliban to impose Sharia (Islamic) law in the neighboring Swat Valley and the Taliban gained the upper hand (Perlez 2009).

In the nearby Dir District, civilians also rejected the Taliban in response to violent transgressions (Tavernise and Ashraf 2009). When Taliban suicide bombers attacked a mosque, killing thirty civilians, it was the "last straw," and the residents of the town armed to fight them off. Lastly, the elders of Landi Kotal and Jamrud Tehsil decided to form a peace committee to negotiate with the Taliban instead of creating an armed lashkar (the option promoted by the government) in hopes of avoiding aggravating local conflicts or inviting retaliation by arming (Shinwari 2008). Overall, some of these civilian efforts appear beneficial, including at least temporary increases in security, although other communities have faced repression in retaliation for collective actions.

Several government policies in these countries are also at least partly predicated on the importance of social organizations and civilian autonomy. While civilians may not strongly support the government or international forces (though this is of course the counterinsurgents' first preference), the Afghan government has hoped that some programs will enable communities to at least amicably manage their own affairs and development and not defect to the Taliban. Examples include the National Solidarity Program's establishment of village development councils and other initiatives to strengthen local communities (Gall 2010).[44] An episode from Nawa District reflects this approach. A key factor distinguishing the success of the case of Nawa in ejecting Taliban insurgents versus neighboring and more intransigent Marja was the strength of local chiefs and their resistance to the Taliban (Chandrasekaran 2010).[45] In another instance, paralleling the successful efforts of the Nasa Indians' Indigenous Guard to free FARC kidnap victims in Colombia, members of a local development council in Ghazni Province mobilized to win the release of government development workers that were captured by an armed group

---

[44] Beginning in 2003, the World Bank and the Afghan government built community decision-making capacity and promoted local-based development through this program. It has reached over 23,000 communities in most of the country's districts but its relevance for counterinsurgency and stability outcomes has not yet been evaluated.

[45] As Chandrasekaran explains, "A patch of desert in Helmand province that was transformed into farmland by canals designed by American engineers in the 1950s, Marja was populated from scratch by the country's late king with settlers from a variety of tribes. The rank and file moved to Marja, but the chiefs didn't. This decades-old experiment in Afghan social engineering has now complicated efforts to find the same sorts of tribal leaders who influence the population in other Afghan communities. They simply don't exist in Marja. . . . Why, then, did the Taliban fold in Nawa? Residents interviewed in the bazaar earlier this year said it was in part because the insurgency enjoyed little support in the community. Locals chafed at the Taliban's taxation, and they grew tired of the near-constant firefights between the insurgents and a team of British police trainers holed up in the district center. Tribal leaders made it clear they wanted the bad guys out, in part so they could reassert themselves as the chief power brokers in the area."

(NPR 2013). These vignettes show tribal cohesion has a role in rejecting extremists and has implications for more tactful counterinsurgency.

Civilian organization and autonomy are also cornerstones of policies to deal with detainees that are captured on the battlefield or arrested in raids. With the establishment of the "community-release program," ISAF and U.S. military policy migrated toward supporting ATCC-style investigation processes (Rubin 2010a, Bumiller 2010).[46] The U.S. military's Joint Task Force 435 began to work with communities and local institutions to deal with suspected insurgents because they had difficulty obtaining the necessary local information to adjudicate their status or prosecute them. Further, holding prisoners involves costs, since detentions that are perceived as illegitimate (e.g., due to false accusations) and even legitimate detentions can anger the population.[47] Under this program, the detainees sign pledges to stay away from the insurgency, and tribal elders then also agree to "vouch" for them with a signed contract to ensure that they do not return to war.[48] This process implicitly relies on well-organized communities in *areas of conflict* to guarantee suspects will not become insurgents. The program raises the autonomy-related questions of whether fractured communities would be less able to absorb and vouch for detainees and whether the Taliban could adopt a similar process to limit killings on their part of suspected government collaborators?

Lastly, the U.S. military has trained several villages to fight and defend themselves (Tyson 2008 and Rubin and Oppel 2010). Armed villages appear to receive public goods and be allowed autonomy as long as they do not aid the Taliban (the government does not necessarily request strong forms

---

[46] "Now, in Afghanistan, detainees who are deemed not to be a threat are handed over to local elders on the understanding that it is the community's responsibility to ensure that they stay on the right side of the law" (Rubin 2010a). A similar program has been used to deal with detainees in Iraq.

[47] Indeed, Kalyvas's local grudges figure prominently in these cases, "In interviews, former detainees and their families said the Americans were routinely misled by informants who either had personal grudges against them or were paid by others to give information to the Americans that would put the person in jail. In addition, many Afghans have experienced the detentions as humiliating, and found almost unbearable the depths of poverty borne by their families during their internment." As an elder said in one case, "'The information you had about these men was wrong in the first place. We are confident they were not involved with insurgents. If they were, we wouldn't be here to sign for them'" (Rubin 2010a).

[48] In one episode of releasing a detainee back to his community, "A United States Marine commander who was acting as the prosecutor, told the prisoner: 'This letter right here is a sworn pledge from all of your elders that they're vouching for you and that you will never support the Taliban or fight for the Taliban ever again.' ... But what is preventing him from rejoining the Taliban? The Marines say the village elders who vouched for him will help keep him in check, as will a parole-like program. The Marines will meet with him regularly and pump him for information about his friends" (Bumiller 2010). Democratic governments involved in counterinsurgency campaigns (as opposed to illegal paramilitaries or guerrillas) will not typically use threats and killing as coercive tools, but will instead arrest suspects, sometimes with slow judicial processes.

of allegiance). Likewise, the United States considered replicating an "Anbar" tribal strategy for the Pakistani tribal areas (Schmidt et al. 2007; interest may have declined after the Pakistani government commenced a counter-insurgency campaign in early 2009). Afghanistan and Pakistan have seen more arming by local communities than has Colombia. Even so, these countries are also home to many traditions and examples of nonviolent advocacy and dispute resolution.

CIVILIAN AUTONOMY IN SYRIA

The Syrian civil war began in March 2011, when the regime of Bashar al-Assad violently cracked down on antigovernment protestors and an armed rebel movement mobilized in response. The civil conflict in Syria is one of the most brutal in recent memory. It has seen the use of cluster munitions, chemical weapons, barrel bombs, mass starvation, and beheadings and mutilations on the part of the regime as well as the use of extra-lethal violence by rebel forces. In a country with a population of 23 million, estimates indicate more than 150,000 civilians have been killed, over 6.5 million have been forcibly displaced within the country, and an additional 2.5 million are refugees in neighboring countries (UNHCR 2014). The violence was so dire that the UN stopped officially counting civilian deaths in January 2014.

Since the earliest days of the Syrian civil war, international actors have been at a loss about how to stop the violence against civilians and decisively bring the conflict to an end. Numerous proposals were either implemented only half-heartedly or were deemed impractical. Failed international proposals to stop the violence included the establishment of no-fly zones, safe zones and humanitarian corridors, military interventions, observers, peacekeepers, cease-fires (e.g., for the holiday of Ramadan), providing adequate support and armaments to the ("moderate") rebels, and invoking the Responsibility to Protect doctrine. Western decision-makers were paralyzed by war fatigue, casualty aversion, fear of resistance from geopolitical rivals such as Russia and Iran, and potential spillover of the conflict to neighboring countries. The reluctance to mount a humanitarian intervention was underscored by U.S. President Barack Obama's "red line" comment, which threatened consequences for the Syrian government's use of chemical weapons but did not result in action. Limited intervention was only threatened to secure Syria's stockpile of chemical weapons after the Syrian regime used Sarin gas against civilians and killed an estimated 1,500 in Hama in November 2013. By contrast, intervention was not seriously contemplated in response to the tens of thousands of civilians that had been killed by conventional weapons up to that point.

The focus on belligerents in these proposals meant that the actions of the civilian population were largely neglected. The combination of violence and paralysis of international policymakers left civilians to their own devices. As I detail in this section, Syrians on the ground were not solely waiting for help from the outside. According to disparate and less-known subnarratives, many Syrians found their own ways to get by and survive the violence. Indeed, while many individuals have taken part in the conflict in some form or been affected by it – Syrian civilians have certainly suffered a heavy toll – there are also examples of creativity and collective actions for autonomy from the conflict. As in Colombia and other countries, resilient Syrians were able to hold out, stay in their homes, and avoid aligning with a particular side in the conflict.

Despite limitations of access and press reporting, I identify three types of civilian autonomy movements in Syria rooted in preexisting social cooperation and organization: 1) intersectarian harmony; 2) ethnic minority enclaves; and 3) other general protests and actions against violence. When these disparate examples are collected and compared, it becomes evident that citizen collective action for autonomy in Syria endured long into the conflict in diverse forms. Some of these nonviolent mobilizations for autonomy blended with the broader freedom and democracy protest movement that called for the removal of the Assad regime (and that some rebel fronts also supported).[49] Other autonomy efforts had less close links with the broader pro-democracy movement. The accounts of the civilian autonomy efforts indicate varying degrees of success at avoiding violence, with greater challenges and suffering all around as the conflict dragged on and intensified.

Civilians in Syria faced dangers from a mix of combatants: the Syrian military, the Shabiha pro-regime Alawite militias, the Free Syrian Army (FSA) and then, as the conflict evolved, jihadist and extremist Islamist rebel groups such as the Al Qaeda-affiliated Jabhat al-Nusra (Al-Nusra Front) and the Islamic State of Iraq and Syria (ISIS). These different belligerents worked to build networks of cadres and supporters within different communities and fought to a stalemate (Fahim 2012, Barnard and Saad 2013a) in which civilians were widely targeted and extra-lethal violence was reportedly used by the regime (Baker 2014) and some rebel fronts (Barnard 2012a, 2012b, Chivers 2013a; especially against captured regime soldiers). Given these conflict conditions, many Syrians remained ambivalent about which side to support long into the conflict, with one man saying, "This armed revolution, I refuse it as much as I refuse the regime" (Barnard and Saad 2013a). Instead, most civilians have been concerned with survival, worried about the regime as well as extremist (Islamist) or undisciplined rebels (Solomon 2012). According to one woman, "People feel it's 'with us or against us.' I personally am with no one, I am against the whole thing. It's killing our children" (Solomon 2012). This analysis shows that throughout the conflict – early on and even in later periods, though to a lesser extent – some people acted upon these sentiments, with some individuals and communities holding out and trying to avoid participating in

---

[49] For instance, local organizations such as the Local Coordination Committees (LCCs) sought to establish civilian governance in both contested areas and areas "liberated" by insurgents.

the conflict. However, as the conflict continued to intensify, the economy collapsed, supplies were cut off, and resources were depleted, many (though not all) autonomy-seeking civilian populations were strained and buckled.

Oases of Intersectarian Harmony

Prior to the onset of conflict, Syria was known as a haven of sectarian harmony and religious freedom, and religious identity was not generally viewed as an important social cleavage (McDonnell 2014). While the conflict did much to tear at Syria's social fabric (Stors 2013), some communities have been referred to as "oases of tolerance" and remained de facto safe zones – just not the (military-backed) ones that most international policymakers and commentators imagined and hoped to establish. I review how two such religiously tolerant communities actively worked to prevent being dragged into intersectarian conflicts.

One of these oases is the town of Maloula (or Maaloula), about 30 miles north of the capital of Damascus (England 2008). Maloula, where the ancient language of Aramaic is still spoken, had a mix of Christian and Sunni Muslim residents as well as important ancient Christian religious sites, such as the Convent of St. Takla. Maloula was initially caught between the contending forces of the Syrian government and the FSA, and later also the Islamist Jabhat al-Nusra front. Even with these pressures, unity was seen among the population in the reluctance of residents to classify themselves by religion, instead simply saying, "I am from Maloula" (Di Giovanni 2012). As illustrated in the quote by the Muslim imam from Maloula at the beginning of the chapter, there was a commitment among religious leaders to keep the community from devolving into intersectarian violence and engaging in the larger armed conflict that was being fought around them.

The cohesion and good relations between sects was, at least for a time, translated into an ability to manage the pressures of the armed conflict and avoid attacks by armed actors. In referring to the intensification of the conflict in the middle of 2013, one resident reported that, "For months the rebels have been around Maloula but there has been a sort of an understanding with the residents that they would not enter ... they do not seem to have touched churches or homes" (BBC 2013). In September of 2013, the rebels moved against the town but, as described by a rebel-affiliated activist, they quickly withdrew, citing the key role of influential community elders, "When the rebels moved in, the elders of the town were afraid of [government] airstrikes and shelling. They wanted us to go, so we left" (Sly 2013). Rebels stated that the motivation of the withdrawal was to protect the community, "To ensure no blood is spilt and that the properties of the people of Maalula are kept safe, the Free Syrian Army announces that the town of Maalula will be kept out of the struggle between the FSA and the regime army" (AFP 2013). According to one of the town's nuns, residents maintained freedom of movement between rebel and government territory (Barnard and Saad 2013b). Consistent with the demands of reciprocal treatment among armed actors seen in other conflicts, the rebel withdrawal was conditional on government forces and militias not entering the town (AFP 2013).

Eventually, more intense fighting did come to Maloula in the second half of 2013, as the more extreme al-Nusra front came to the area and the Syrian government mounted a counteroffensive. Although the contestation eventually ended in heavy damage to the town and mass displacement, al-Nusra and the FSA did not want to be seen as targeting Christians, since this could have made the United States more reluctant to intervene militarily on the side of the rebels (although the Mother Superior of the local convent was held by the rebels for several months, she confirmed she was not mistreated; Sly 2013, Barnard and Saad 2014). Similar to concerns of the FARC rebels in Colombia, FSA rebels worried about the potential consequences for their reputation of being associated with targeting cohesive nonviolent communities. Nevertheless, the incursion by al-Nusra led to retaliatory shelling by government forces, leaving Maloula a ghost town. With the incursion by al-Nusra (and social cohesion also apparently finally breaking down), a Christian resident reported having been betrayed by the Muslim residents (Bowen 2013, Fisk 2013).

Similar sentiments for autonomy and maintaining local order among diverse sects are found in the neighboring town of Yabrud (Yabroud). As a Christian resident said, "The regime wants us to fear Muslims, but I don't fear my brothers" (Tice 2012). Another man from this community extended this sentiment to the armed actors in the conflict, saying, "I don't care if you are a loyalist or a dissident, respect yourself by respecting me" (Tice 2012). In Yabrud, there was a civilian council to negotiate with the different armed actors so that neither side would fight over the town (Barnard 2014). There were also conflict management procedures to deal with disputes and cool tempers. One resident cited restraint in response to a Shabiha militia incursion, "They [the Shabiha] broke into many houses, my father's house, stealing and breaking things. We did not react strongly. We did not want to bring the war here (Tice 2012)."

Other news reports confirmed the ability of Yabrud to endure even several years into the conflict, into 2014, noting that when "Islamist insurgents tried to make inroads, they were largely rebuffed or ignored" (Barnard and Saad 2014, Barnard 2014).[50] A rebel noted respect for the neutrality of the Christian residents of the town, saying, "We don't have any problem with Christians, they are living among us for thousands of years. Before, with and after Assad" (Barnard and Saad 2013b). According to one resident, governance by the town's local council was also working to limit government incursions and

---

[50] According to one report, "Mediation, rebels say, helped keep Yabroud relatively untouched by fighting until recently. Yabroud has essentially governed itself, with some local Christians remaining, even as the war turned sectarian elsewhere" (Barnard and Saad 2014).

manage violence, "I personally consider Yabrood to be an area free of government control. . . . We have not suffered a lot compared to other cities in Syria" (Saeed 2012). The security situation remained stable until the end of 2013 when, as with Maloula, rebels finally entered Yabrud. Government forces then moved on the town in 2014 and eventually gained control, provoking mass displacements of the population (Barnard 2014).

These cases of intersectarian oases held out for nearly three years by pursuing neutrality and promoting intersectarian norms so that disputes would not provide openings for belligerents, even becoming receptors for displaced Syrians from other parts of the country (Barnard 2014). They are noteworthy since it is not obvious that such harmony can be maintained in the context of a war that pits family against family, where the regime explicitly used the strategies of dividing the sects and polarizing the opposition by framing them as terrorists and extremists, and where even children in some communities voiced desires for retribution against members of other sects (Kirkpatrick 2012, Karam 2012). However, with the intense and enduring conflict, a politicized environment, and cut supply lines, the cases also show the limitations of autonomy under extended periods of siege.

Autonomy Among Ethnic and Religious Minorities

Similar to some of the minority populations in Colombia and other countries, many of the ethnic and religious minority groups in Syria did not historically have strong interests in national-level political conflicts. In addition to the instances of intersectarian bridging found in some diverse communities, more ethnically and religiously homogenous communities also organized around their identity-based social ties to stay out of the conflict and avoid the effects of the war. Non-Sunni ethnic and religious minorities made up about 33 percent of Syria's prewar population, with about 10 percent of the population belonging to the ruling Alawite sect, a Shia offshoot. The non-Sunni (and non-Alawite) populations, especially Christians, historically aligned with the government and, fearing an Islamist takeover, were anxious about how the rebels might treat them were they to come to power. But they were also repulsed by the regime's brutal tactics and did not want to weaken the pro-democracy movement or antagonize the rebels by overtly siding with the regime.[51]

The behavior of Syrian Christian groups, including the Armenians and Assyrians (Syriacs), exhibits clear motivations and actions for autonomy. Armenian residents of Aleppo armed for self-defense while their religious leaders publicly called for the group's neutrality. On September 14, 2012, the

---

[51] Although many of the Alawite minority form the Assad regime's base of political support, there were also some splits as some Alawites favored a transition to democracy (DePetris 2013, Oweis 2013). Some but not all members of the other minority groups have preferred and pursued neutrality and autonomy.

leaders of the three Armenian churches in Aleppo issued a joint statement underscoring the neutral positioning of the community:

What adds to our anguish are the unsuccessful attempts of presenting the Syrian Armenians as taking part in the armed battles of the current Syrian crisis or trying to actually drag them into such a conflict … We reiterate today, that the peaceful co-existence that the Syrian Armenians have cultivated throughout the decades continues … and it will definitely stay against all kinds of violence and armed collisions … We are not worried. We fear the situation for the whole country, for all the people in Syria. But we are not taking sides in this crisis. (Armstrong and Williams 2012)

The religious leaders of the Assyrian Christians also made similar calls for neutrality and respect of their populations (Jawad Al-Tamimi 2012, Cheikhomar and Austin 2013). These Christian groups were able to remain intact for a short period of time, but many Armenians eventually ended up leaving the country for greater safety in Armenia (Malek 2012), while many Assyrians fled to Turkey.

The Palestinians living in Syria were welcomed to the country in the 1950s as refugees and, like the Christians, became wary of opposing the Assad regime because their rights had historically been protected by the Syrian government. Yet the Palestinians also did not want to be seen as opposing the revolution and become subject to rebel attacks. As expressed by one man from the Yarmouk district (originally a refugee camp) on the outskirts of Damascus, there was a strong preference for neutrality, "The Assad regime wants us to express our support for his regime, and the opposition wants us to demonstrate against the Assad regime" (Sands 2011, Nordland and Mawad 2012). During the first few years of the conflict, Yarmouk was left largely undamaged. As the conflict progressed, however, some rebel fighters took refuge within the district, provoking government retaliation. After an initial displacement due to fighting, community leaders were able to negotiate local cease-fires to allow them return and again asserted neutrality (AFP 2012). The autonomy actions yielded some small gains but were ultimately to little avail, as insurgents continued to infiltrate the neighborhood, prompting the government to respond with airstrikes (Barnard 2012c) and a siege that caused starvation among the residents. When Islamic State militants entered the fray in Yarmouk in late 2014, a mass displacement of the remaining population ensued.

The Kurdish minority of about 2.5 million people also took actions for autonomy from the conflict between the Assad regime and largely non-Kurdish Sunni rebels. They have sought to create an enclave from the conflict in the northern part of the country, a move that also hews toward seeking greater political autonomy (Solomon 2014). As a Kurdish man from the town of Ras al-Ain, on the border with Turkey, said, "I don't want the rebels in my town. Why would I want Assad's planes to come and bomb us? I don't want Assad, nor do I want the rebels" (Burch 2012). Kurdish populations aimed to avoid taking sides in the conflict, but some Kurds have also armed and formed militias to protect their towns and, in some cases, have fought on both sides of the conflict (Chivers 2013b). Similar to the other minority populations, the reclusive Druze population took a neutral stance, largely refusing military service and refraining from joining the rebels (Sands 2012, Naylor 2015). The Sunni tribes in eastern regions have also been hesitant about taking sides (Khalek 2012).

With community organizations, preexisting social cohesion, leaders, and no strong preferences for either side of the conflict, minority groups in Syria positioned themselves early on to stay out of the conflict. The initial efforts consisting of negotiation and public statements held promise for many groups. Unfortunately, their security deteriorated in the long run as more Islamist rebels gained strength and the regime resorted to stronger tactics.

Additional Autonomy Examples

Syria also has additional instances of civilian autonomy not directly related to intersectarian unity or minority enclaves. In various regions there were non-violent protests for community autonomy and against the conflict (distinct from protests against the regime or larger political goals). In the face of FSA transgressions against civilians, protestors have called out, "The people want the reform of the Free Syrian Army. We love you. Correct your path" (Barnard 2012b). Nonviolent pro-democracy activists mounted similar protests in the town of Saraqeb in Idlib Province against rebel excesses (NOW 2013) and in Mayadeen to demand that Jabhat al-Nusra fighters leave town (Khalek 2013). Later protests in Idlib against al-Nusra's abuses and rigid interpretations of Islam successfully forced the group to withdraw from the town of Maarat al-Numan and won the release of kidnap victims (members of the FSA; Naylor 2016).

Activists also engaged in public protests against abuses of both Islamic State militants and government forces. In Aleppo and the village of Kafranbel, citizens used witty signs and slogans to draw attention to their conditions and shame the armed actors (Mackety 2014). Similar protests were mounted against ISIS in Mosul, Iraq, to halt the destruction of cultural sites, including the city's famous Minaret (Arango 2014). There is even evidence of civilians "nudging" armed groups to reform (Kaplan 2013b) in Mosul by exploiting fissures between ISIS's domestic and foreign fighters. When an old man cursed a foreign fighter for denouncing his beard as being too short, local ISIS fighters stood up for the man and turned on the foreigner, beating and detaining him (Bradley 2016).

There have also been hunger strikes and negotiation efforts for "local autonomy" to break starvation sieges by government forces and ensure food deliveries to embattled communities (Hassan 2014). Small-scale cease-fires were brokered in several Damascus suburbs, and pressure by residents from the towns of Moadamiya and Barza got rebels to agree to a cease-fire so food could enter (although there were also some reports of rebel reneging). The Assad regime accepted some of these cease-fires and they even became a prong of U.S. and Russian diplomatic strategies (Barnard 2014).

Finally, there are several examples of other autonomy strategies oriented toward community governance. The activist-run pirate TV station AleppoTodayTV provided early warning of battles to residents so they could avoid getting caught in the crossfire (Amos 2012). In rural areas, given the unpredictable nature of the fighting and targeting of communities, some populations took to hiding in caves for shelter (Chivers 2013c), similar to the Communities of Populations in Resistance in Guatemala (Falla 1994). Lastly, in areas that fell under rebel control and even contested areas, security remains a problem and civilians have frequently taken it upon themselves to organize junta-like Local Coordination Committees (LCCs) to make community decisions and perform government functions such as policing and managing disputes (Kirkpatrick 2013, Amos 2012b). Activists in Raqqa and outside of Syria formed the group "Raqqa Is Being Slaughtered Silently" to monitor the conflict's civilian toll and report on and protest Islamic State abuses (Abdulrahim 2014, Sly 2013).

Civilians in Syria have suffered greatly from the effects of the conflict, yet their actions also highlight many examples of resilience. They have pursued a variety of autonomy strategies, including neutral positioning, negotiation, norms and managing disputes, early warning, and protests and shaming. While the examples discussed are not controlled comparisons, they show the potential for civilians to act on their own behalf even in extremely challenging conditions, including the rapid onset of conflict and Syrians' limited experience with civil society organization and self-governance, having historically lived under strict authoritarianism. The record indicates that few civilian efforts for autonomy in Syria have ultimately succeeded or endured, so the examples also point to the limitations of civilians when facing ideologically violent groups and government forces pursuing brutal tactics and "final solutions" over an extended period of conflict. Yet, these communities may have held out longer than they would have with less organization and no community strategies. If the war had ended sooner, perhaps they could have endured long enough to remain intact.

International policymakers have fixated on various diplomatic and intervention scenarios but, with the failure of the doctrine of "Responsibility to Protect" (R2P), they were left with a blind spot and did not consider the role that local institutions could play to keep people safe. Given the rapid onset and intensity of the conflict and insufficient external support, it was a challenge for the disparate local autonomy efforts to connect with each other to stitch together a broader movement to end the war. These diverse autonomy efforts therefore also raise the question of whether outcomes would have been different if these models had been identified, supported, and extended by western governments, international organizations, or local actors earlier in the conflict. In sum, although Syria may seem worlds away from Colombia, the Colombian campesinos hold lessons for Syria and Syria, conversely, is also instructive for other conflicts around the globe.

CONCLUSIONS

The cases reviewed in this chapter are tough cases where reports of widespread violence might lead one to discount the odds of encountering civilian agency and autonomy. Yet evidence from these conflicts supports aspects of the civilian autonomy theory. The presence and capabilities of social organizations varied across the landscapes but were still found in war-torn regions. These organizational bases served as helpful platforms for implementing community autonomy strategies, from community management and promotion of pacifist norms to more contentious protests and shaming. There were even cases of the sophisticated investigations mechanism that was innovated and perfected by the ATCC in Santander. Finally, the collective strategies influenced armed actors and helped avoid violence in at least some circumstances and for some amounts of time. Although these cases are some of the most well-known conflicts and have figured centrally in debates of global security and received broad press coverage as they occurred, there was little awareness of local civilian autonomy activities due to biases in reporting and our collective focus of attention. This chapter therefore serves as a needed corrective to our myopia.

Still, these cases point to many outstanding questions to be studied for a more rigorous analysis. An implication for inference from these cases is that effective civilian protective strategies are likely to be found in other countries and conflict situations that resemble the moderate (and even harsh) conditions found in some places and periods in Colombia (but are embattled as conflict intensifies).[52] Some conflicts may resemble these conditions more than others depending on armed actors' preferences and modes of operating. Some countries may also have greater preexisting bases for collective action across their social landscapes to facilitate civilian strategies than others. It will become easier to assess the causes and effects of civilian strategies and organizations through controlled comparisons as more data becomes available at the local level in these settings.

---

[52] A discussion after a presentation of this research in 2009 with a former U.S. military officer who served in Iraq revealed that, even there, community organization parlayed protective benefits. In the Sadr City district of Baghdad, elder sheiks of organized communities were better able to tell Al Qaeda (AQI) militants to leave them alone and keep them out relative to unorganized communities.

10

Conclusions and Policy Implications

To you that want violence, this ended in shit; for the right to life, peace, and work.

Ustedes que quieren violencia y esto acabó carajo; por el derecho a la vida a la paz y el trabajo.

— ATCC leader's diary (1990s)

This book brings a new perspective to civilian agency and civilian responses to the dangers and uncertainty of armed conflict. I focus on the civilians' collective action problem – opposite that of armed group recruitment – of how to keep from participating in the conflict and avoid the tyranny of the relatively fewer combatants and militant extremists. It is a puzzle that some communities apparently solved this collective action problem and were able to protect themselves while others did not. This book addresses this puzzle by taking civilian institutions seriously as an explanation for violence. In doing so, it both contrasts with and complements state-based, structural explanations of civil wars and refines our understanding of the production of violence.

The bottom-up approach shows that collective action for peace, and not just for violence, is possible even in settings of armed conflict. This is more than wishful thinking. Social organizations and cohesion function as an important buffer between communities and armed actors, enabling strategies to limit the fighting to only the combatants and the aggrieved. The nonviolent strategies that communities use to avoid getting caught in the crossfire are diverse and work because they are adapted to different threats of violence. However, these strategies can be difficult to observe because civilian autonomy is often a hidden behavior in rural, isolated areas. It does not always get reported as "news" – it is the dog that did not bark. This is in part because autonomy is not easy to define or identify when it occurs. The theory of civilian autonomy I developed therefore first involved the conceptual ground clearing of supplying a definition of autonomy in civil wars.

The theory then posits that armed groups' motivations and abilities to use violence vary based on the ability of civilians to impose costs on them and avoid entanglements with them, as captured by levels of civilian organization. The challenge thus became analyzing whether armed groups would have used more violence if not for civilian organizations.

Some *formal* autonomy organizations, such as the ATCC, are capable of innovating remarkably sophisticated and effective civilian autonomy strategies to help deal with violence. These include "weapons of the not-so-weak" that directly engage armed actors. Even under changing conflict conditions and amid denunciations of suspected armed group collaborators, the ATCC's investigation institution often proved effective for limiting violence against civilians who opted to not participate in the conflict. Even some juntas, such as those in Belén de los Andaquíes, can carry out these kinds of procedures. As the ATCC is fond of pointing out and as the ATCC leader's diary at the beginning of the chapter attests, they have outlived many of the members of the armed groups of their region. The ATCC case demonstrates that social networks and information flows can be traced empirically and that identities can be sorted out in the "fog of war" of counterinsurgency.

Some *informal* social organizations across rural Colombia even proved capable of reaching for civilian autonomy as well. The junta councils and the social cohesion among ethnic minority populations were found to most effectively limit violence because they are likely less political and more community-oriented than other organizations, namely cooperatives and land reform councils. The role of the junta councils in the case towns of Bituima, Quipile, and Vianí in Cundinamarca confirmed that protection through social cohesion is a broader phenomenon than previously believed. With relatively many juntas, Bituima and Vianí saw more forms of civilian cooperation ("weapons of the weak") and even some forms of protest, were viewed differently by armed actors, and suffered less violence than Quipile. Civilians in these and other towns mobilized to resist war in a variety of ways. They reoriented existing institutions, networks, and shared histories, and channeled collective tragedies and experiences with violence into cooperation. These were at times catalyzed by technical and epistemic support from external actors, including government promoters, the Peace Corps, NGOs, and churches.

Civilian autonomy was documented across multiple locations and armed actors. In Colombia, it was observed in relation to the FARC guerrillas, the paramilitaries, and in some cases, the public forces. The compilation of experiences from other countries further highlights the true breadth of civilian autonomy. Across the many contexts, there is a remarkable consistency not only in autonomy strategies themselves, but also the rhetoric surrounding them. This is seen among communities as well as in the responses of armed actors, including their ambivalence toward and acceptance of civilian autonomy.

In the rest of this chapter, I review the scholarly implications and policy implications of this research. I then outline a future research agenda. I conclude with some final thoughts on the broader significance of the book.

THE NUANCES OF CIVILIAN AUTONOMY

This study does not make a blanket statement about the effects of civilian organization on violence. Rather, it has a more nuanced view. I found that the effects of civilian autonomy organizations are conditional, depending on conflict intensity (with limits at intense levels of fighting) and varying across armed groups, time periods, and types of violence. Some kinds of organizations may provide protection but other organizations may be seen as threatening and be targeted. Some organizations may respond to and deal with violence but others may also be weakened by violence. The juntas appeared more effective in managing selective violence under moderate conflict conditions while qualitative evidence showed that strategies of deeper cooperation (e.g., protest or arming) can deal with even graver threats of violence.

By contemplating circular relationships and the conditions for effective civilian agency, the theory and findings also explain several puzzles. They help clarify some of the contrasting claims among the existing works about *when* autonomy strategies will be effective. For instance, while Valentino observes few civilian actions in response to mass killings and Kalyvas attributes civilian self-rule only to armed groups' permissiveness, the civilian autonomy results point to a middle ground of conflict conditions and hybrid armed actors where civilians can contribute to their own security. Incorporating the circular relationship also clarifies why in some settings we hear of many acts of resistance and in others only acquiescence, and why social leaders are targeted in some cases and, elsewhere, leaders and organizations endure.

The success of civilians' collective actions is conditional because, while civilians have levers of influence over armed groups, these levers are finite. Civilians' strategy choices depend on types of violent threats, which in turn may determine the overall effectiveness of protection through solving particular problems of violence. Certain strategies, such as community management (to limit armed group inroads) and coordinated protests (to leverage reputations) appear to be the most prevalent strategies. By contrast, investigations of suspected collaborators and early warning systems for combat require more capacity and are therefore found to be less common, though these have not yet been well systematized.

The canvassing of armed groups' viewpoints highlighted their preferences and how their choices are affected by civilian strategies – their "sensitivities." First, ex-combatants reported perceiving differences in the level of social organization across communities and treating organized communities differently. They viewed these communities as better managed, more trustworthy, and also more threatening in their potential to mobilize against them. Second, some armed groups can be induced to reduce their use of violence if, for instance, they can save face when they back down, or benefit from interacting with civilian organizations by reducing manpower costs for managing communities. Sometimes collective appeals to morals can nudge groups to change their default positions on using violence. These strategic interactions explain why civilians appeared most frequently able to affect selective violence and attempts at coercion. A broader implication, though, is that the behavior of armed groups is not destined for an inexorable deterioration as they, for instance, become more resource-based (Weinstein 2006). Instead, their behavior can be reformed over time in response to civilians.

Additional qualitative evidence indicates which types of armed groups are and are not amenable to civilian strategies. Two cases of armed group demobilization show that civilians have less influence as armed groups become *less political* and turn more toward pure banditry. In the latter half of the 2000s in the ATCC region, certain paramilitary units either did not demobilize or remobilized after the official paramilitary demobilization. With mainly the hard-core criminal and drug-trafficking elements left, the ATCC encountered more problems dialoguing with this group and having their investigations honored.[1] Similarly, Jehovah's Witness groups in Mozambique that had successfully held out against Renamo rebels faced greater difficulties in having their pacifism respected by bandit groups that arrived after Renamo disbanded (Wilson 1992).

Junta councils may fail to protect civilians in many places for several reasons. One is that they can be weakened by clientelist dependencies. At least some communities with formal organizations like the ATCC and some juntas can still act. But juntas may also either decay or fail to provide protection if they become too politicized. And, even when juntas achieve civilian autonomy, they may need to balance their neutrality by censoring their political aspirations. Survival and managing risk in the midst of war may therefore sometimes carry the price of forfeiting advocacy for broader political and economic rights (e.g., labor rights or land for peasants).

Civilians were not found to have much influence over severe forms of violence or broader conflict dynamics through either organizing or trying to opt out of the conflict. However, this does not mean civilians are never able to affect conflict dynamics or indiscriminate violence. For example, the ATCC and other organized communities assisted with combatant demobilizations, worked to reduce participation in the coca economy, and were able to help victims of forced displacement remain in the area so they could later return to their homes or resettle nearby (interviews; CNRR 2009, 2011). Further, the findings of some massacre-proofing effects and an interaction between the juntas and anti-Patriotic Union party violence suggest that the juntas may have limited the killing by countering political stigma against residents. To the extent that the violence constituted a politicide, the juntas could also have implications for genocide and mass atrocities prevention. Further study will help clarify whether "peace communities" can bring a broader peace.

---

[1] ATCC#3,4, La India, August 2008.

THE HISTORICAL AND STATE-BUILDING FOUNDATIONS OF CIVILIAN AUTONOMY

Civilian autonomy in Colombia's conflict did not appear out of nowhere. Colombia's peace movements were rooted in the country's historical social and political context and arose as a response to the conflict. The country's political tensions surrounding the urban–rural divide and contrasting state-building philosophies pre-positioned certain organizations like the juntas for later autonomy in the conflict (accounting for why the juntas, more than other organizations, merit attention for this topic). The same historical half-neglect of the juntas also explains why little is known about how they behave in conflict settings. This disengagement reflects the larger urban–rural disconnect of the highly unequal Colombian society. Other countries with instances of civilian autonomy exhibit similar historical cycles of social capital formation in the shadow of state neglect.

This research adds to the knowledge base on the little-studied period of Colombian history following the La Violencia period of the 1950s through the present day, during which time there were attempts to reshape the social landscape. There are many studies on La Violencia and the later expansion of guerrilla fronts, paramilitaries, and narco-trafficking. Yet, apart from some national level histories of this interim period (e.g., Zamosc 1986, Bagley 1989, and Sánchez et al. 2007), there has been little unpacking of the societal changes and interventions that were designed to prevent a return to conflict. The prior conflict was so devastating that there was a tendency to wear historical blinders during this era, to remain in denial about the possibility that the conflict would again metastasize and instead focus attention on the promise of progress that lay ahead.

At a national level, this history highlights the more than fifty years of experience Colombia has in what is known today as community-driven development (CDD), with the juntas embodying an alternative, decentralized state-building strategy. Of course, the junta councils and other programs did not keep conflict from resurging entirely. As a result, some communities organized under suspicions of their autonomy being political, a fear cast by the shadow of the early guerrillas' Independent Republics. They grappled with how to credibly commit to and signal the apolitical nature of their wartime autonomy.

This study's local-level analysis of counterfactual scenarios therefore answers the deeper question of where and why interventions succeeded or failed to dampen the later effects of conflict. In the process, it catalogues the histories of neglected and marginalized populations and the Acción Comunal social movement. The ground-level case studies reconstruct the social histories of small communities whose experiences tend to go unrecorded. These histories whisper that community social capital can be sustained over time against steep odds and contribute to local order.

METHODOLOGICAL CONTRIBUTIONS

Civilian autonomy is a question that begs for methodological rigor and a careful research design. This study's attention to case selection and data collection was indispensible for producing a transparent evaluation of civilians' strategies. The analysis involved the competitive testing of hypotheses across a broad spectrum of cases. By migrating to new and more tractable organizations (like juntas) and standard geographic units (like municipios), I was able to study cases with divergent values on key variables to construct plausible counterfactuals. This helped avert possible bias in the selection of cases.

This analysis of civilian autonomy integrates multiple methods: a quantitative overview of these cases and process-tracing case studies and fieldwork. These methods took advantage of multiple datasets and levels of analysis, including the substantial generation of new data. For instance, interviews in the ATCC zone yielded a unique within-case database of threats and ex-combatant interviews elicited their views of civilian social movements. The combination of methods helped deal with the threats to inference of measurement error and bias. Quantitative control variables (in Chapter 5) and multiple sources of more precise qualitative measurements (in Chapter 8) were suggestive though not conclusive about organized areas being *more* rather than less likely to report acts of violence to official sources. These efforts assuage concerns of reporting bias undermining the relationships encountered between social cohesion, strategies, and violence.

A key part of the research design involves case selection procedures. I used the quantitative data to select cases for fieldwork and qualitative study with statistical matching techniques. This set up a quasi-experiment on the juntas for selected towns in Cundinamarca, accounting for observed and possible unobserved variables and balancing the concerns of researcher security and mobility. The matching of cases helped control for difficult-to-measure global shocks to communities (nonregion-specific factors) to better parse the effects of juntas from other variables. This can be especially advantageous when confounding variables are correlated with a key causal variable or data is missing for parts of the sample. For instance, inequality (equality) washed out the juntas' effect in the large-n tests, likely because it also reflects social cohesion – one of the possible causal pathways through which the juntas are thought to affect violence. But inequality is not a factor that varied locally among the matched towns, suggesting that the violence-limiting effects are due to the additional capacity and strategies of the juntas and not conditions of equality. The dialogue between quantitative and qualitative methods also helped structure the data collection, producing more easily interpretable and generalizable findings. For instance, the histories of the Cundinamarca towns are not just any histories, but histories with clear expectations about similarities and differences and where they fit in the global distribution of cases. Similarly, the

306 Conclusions and Policy Implications

ex-combatant perspectives on the selected towns are not random but are also structured according to differing values of the quantitative data.

The research methods were also helpful for untangling the two-way relationship between civilian populations and armed actors. Conflict can destroy organization but also spur it on, and organization can then work to limit conflict. A look at the history of La Violencia and the following years tells that, on average, juntas are not found in historically more peaceful locations. The similarities of the quasi-experimental cases of Cundinamarca in their early patterns of conflict – having all experienced La Violencia – also helped rule out reverse causality for the effect of juntas and cohesion. The matching of cases also guided the search for exogenous causes to explain differences in the junta councils across towns, or what could be called "qualitative instruments." In Bituima and Vianí, these included random events such as the collapse of a church roof, the arrival of an enthusiastic priest, or a particular type of land reform.

The various methods and tests across the different chapters tended to reinforce each other. No single method or test provided a complete picture. Some are better at testing implications of civilian strategies while others are better at providing an overview of organizations. However, the small contributions of each approach add up to a larger portrait, or gestalt, of civilian behavior. The inconsistencies across methods also suggested new conditions, questions, and unresolved issues, reinforcing this study's explicit interaction between theory building and theory testing.

A general and enduring contribution of the research design and methods is the framework for evaluating civil society and conflict resolution programs to protect human rights. Civilians' institutional efforts to solve their problems were known prior to this study, but there was no good framework to evaluate them. Perhaps these protective solutions have not yet had a broader impact on policymaker consciousness because their mechanisms have not been well articulated or measured, making it hard to show what they do or that they work. My approach incorporates competing structural explanations for violence to establish plausible counterfactual scenarios where civilian collective action is absent. This pushes past simply studying the resilience to bounce back from harm to identify civilians' independent and proactive efforts to prevent violence. This analysis moves in this direction but still necessarily glosses over the details and richness of the experiences of many communities.

POLICY IMPLICATIONS

This study has a number of policy implications for security in weak states. If armies in such states were stronger or more legitimate, there would be little need for civilian organizations and autonomy in conflicts and, for that matter, no civil wars to begin with. Bringing about grandiose changes in such state institutions is not an easy task (e.g., if territory could be easily controlled, resources denied to insurgent groups, or international interventions decisively mounted, conflicts would already be over). By contrast, the adoption of civilian-oriented policies is relatively more incentive-compatible and the key limitations are usually not interest or resources, but knowledge and capacity. I review implications for civilians, NGOs, and governments.

Civilian Communities

For communities, this study provides a roadmap to evaluate their particular situations relative to the experiences and conditions in other towns. For civilians, collective action in wartime continues to be a risky choice. However, civilians can take steps to strengthen community bonds in advance of the arrival of conflict. Communication and interaction can build common knowledge and trust, and have been helpful for assessing the conflict environment and mitigating uncertainty. They can learn about strategies and gain knowledge about their effectiveness. The more communities become aware of their options, their conditions, and their support bases, the more able they will be to make informed choices and act. Communities should further consider adapting their strategies to address particular motivations for violence.

Other actors should pay attention to community autonomy efforts since the "micro" actions of individual communities may spread and have broader effects. As a by-product of their organizations, civilians can augment Hobbesian notions of order in "ungoverned" spaces. The junta councils, for example, provide lessons about local alternative forms of justice and conflict resolution and the long-term effects of decentralized state-building programs. Civilian actions may also affect the onset, intensity, and duration of conflicts, especially if civilian behaviors deter or impede other actors. Some civilian mechanisms may reduce the potential amount of recruits, information, material resources, or combat territory available to both rebel and state actors, and thus influence how fighting in civil wars unfolds. Civilians' collective strategies to limit participation in illicit crop cultivation and trafficking can similarly inform counternarcotics programs (e.g., Kaplan 2012). Structures like juntas also provide alternatives for youths to get involved with pro-social projects that are bigger than themselves, to promote peace instead of getting involved in war.

Though this analysis is at the local community level, if resistance to conflict by civilians can be replicated across localities, the cumulative effect of these efforts may promote negotiations among state and rebel leaders and solutions at the macro level of the conflict. Indeed, these insights are potentially widely applicable, as most civilians would like to avoid conflicts even though they may not always be able to do so. For instance, some newer rural civilian organizations in Colombia have suggested they are considering various models for organizing resistance to armed actors.

The author (right) sharing research findings with the ATCC in La India, Santander, Colombia, 2013.
Photograph by Oliver Kaplan.

External Actors

External actors such as IOs and NGOs have historically been eager to support local processes. Civilians, compared to foreign governments and their interventions or peacekeeping forces, have strong interests in conflict resolution (and little patience for top-down negotiations) but may lack adequate resources or knowledge which international actors may be eager to supply. Past outside interventions such as the Peace Corps and Acción Comunal programs have broadly reshaped the social landscape. In Colombia alone, the UN's Redes program, USAID (for example, the ADAM and CSDI programs as part of Plan Colombia funding), the European Union's Peace Laboratories, Germany's GTZ, Switzerland's Suippcol program, and World Bank analyses (2000, 2004) are all predicated on the hypothesis that social cohesion and local capacity can effectively protect civilians and promote peace. The Colombian government's efforts include the Social Action Agency's Peace and Development Program, the National Peace Prize, and alternative justice processes such as *casas de justicia* (houses of justice), among other programs. International NGOs such as Peace Brigades International, Fellowship of Reconciliation, and many Colombian NGOs accompany communities that are pressured by armed groups.

These programs hold general notions about how "social capital" promotes "peace," but they are not always explicit in specifying protection mechanisms or aware of which mechanisms are operating.[2] The careful measurements in this analysis help clarify which activities may work to reduce violence, and when. A first promising way communities can be assisted is through the provision of alternative funding sources for community projects to circumvent clientelism. Second, external actors can help transport general knowledge of "best practices" and detailed knowledge of how certain mechanisms function. For instance, the capacity, procedures, and information flows needed for the ATCC investigation system to function can be digested and explained to other communities. When tailoring programs to communities, it will be helpful to assess local armed group dynamics and preferences.

The involvement of international actors must also be considered with caution. Although international development programs can bring various benefits, they are not without controversy (e.g., Easterly 2007). INGOs can have positive human security effects, but only if they are not motivated by "rent-seeking" (Murdie 2014). A particular challenge for supporting civilian autonomy movements is that external aid projects can be perceived by nonstate armed actors as part of a counterinsurgency strategy. In these circumstances, the implementation of aid projects can stigmatize communities and make them targets, leading to more, rather than less, violence (Crost et al. 2014). Depending on the national political dynamics, democracy promotion projects may incur similar risks. International actors must also be aware of the incentives their actions create and the messages they may relay (either advertently or inadvertently) to civilians and activists through their engagement. They must be wary that encouraging civilian autonomy could create a moral hazard if it leads civilians to confront armed actors or remain in situations where they may have low odds of success. For these reasons, it may be wise to work to unite communities preventively, prior to the onset of conflict, rather than in the thick of the fight.

Counterinsurgents and Warfighters

Lastly, this research pertains to government counterinsurgency programs. Governments face the problem of how to implement public policies and provide security in regions where they have little presence. Protecting the population is the ethical choice and also central to gaining civilian support in

---

[2] The UNDP 2003 study recommended the following policies: "i) Systematization of experiences; ii) strategies of social communication; iii) training of moderators and mediators; iv) training of local leaders . . . ; and v) execution of agreements with organizations that give credit to experiences along the lines already mentioned."

counterinsurgency (Sewall et al. 2007), and armies have improved at gauging bases of support and addressing civilians' concerns to "win hearts and minds." Yet as military strategies of counterinsurgency increasingly result in stalemates, states may look for new ways to deal with local security risks without alienating civilians. The debate today among counterinsurgency specialists over the merits of decentralization to extend government reach is a repeat of Colombia's experiment that began over fifty years ago. Autonomy and its decentralization (or delegation) of power can be perceived as hostile to governments, though it does not have to be. Insights from civilian autonomy theory point to how government operations can protect civilians without abandoning their goals.

Before considering the implications that civilian autonomy theory holds for counterinsurgency, it is important to address whether there is a place for them in a book that puts nonviolent civilian agency at the forefront. This is a delicate issue, especially because the goal of civilian autonomy is to deescalate war, and distilling implications for warfighters could possibly do the opposite. I never-theless believe that, to promote respect of autonomous communities by armed actors, it is appropriate and necessary to address these implications here. This is not to say, however, that this text encourages counterinsurgency campaigns or any kind of belligerency. This project was forged out of the ashes of the Afghanistan and Iraq wars – two wars in which armed actors (including international, state, and nonstate forces) had poor understandings of the pref-erences and social dynamics of civilian communities, and civilians suffered extensive harm as a result. Unfortunately, the Colombian conflict tells a similar story, but it also offers an opportunity to study and learn about these dynamics. This discussion recognizes that counterinsurgency campaigns have been a fact of modern warfare (and also historical warfare). Even so, they can still be informed by new and more humane approaches to resolving conflicts, and civilian autonomy may represent a nonviolent alternative to insurgency and counterinsurgency.

If counterinsurgents cannot control an area, they should be wary of insuffi-cient half measures that may end up putting local institutions in greater danger. Moving intermittently in and out of zones is tempting when resources are limited, but it entraps and entangles localities without being able to protect them, which is not good for anybody. If communities are punished for this by insurgents, some portion of the blame may ultimately fall on government forces as well (see Oxfam 2009).[3] Arming communities may contribute to security in

---

[3] Similar critiques have also been raised by a consortium of NGOs, including Oxfam, about the United States' proposed Afghanistan Social Outreach Program (ASOP) to arm villagers to provide for their own protection, claiming that the effort may not be sustained and may invite retaliation against communities. The still-young experience of Canadian forces with development projects in the Afghan village of Deh-e-Bagh suggests that international forces should embrace towns that want to reject extremists, but only if their protection can be assured (Pearson 2009).

some cases, but can ultimately be risky if civilians are not sufficiently powerful or accountable or do not have adequate support, making them open targets (e.g., Khan 2009).

Counterinsurgents should consider how to work with local institutions and allow them to function and police themselves as a way to avoid heavy-handed measures that could stigmatize them or cause unintended damage and push civilians toward the enemy (Jaffe 2009).[4] This includes sensitivity with detainees and suspects. Samuel Huntingon highlighted the benefits of such an approach in his assessment of U.S. military strategy in Vietnam in 1967, observing that, "Efforts to arrive at such political accommodations [over communities] with the VC [Vietcong] are preferable to intensification of the war in the Delta" (Huntington 1967).

It becomes the responsibility of the state to provide sufficient security guarantees to win the allegiance of communities. Many accounts of civil conflict observe that most civilians are not extremists and instead largely seek to survive periods of instability and protect their livelihoods (e.g., Kriger 1992, Nordstrom 1992). If international forces are sufficiently cautious and eventually make good appeals to local communities, they have better chances of winning or discouraging them from supporting insurgents. This logic is consistent with new principles of restraint articulated by Admiral Mullen and the Powell Doctrine's decisive use of force when force is to be used (Shanker 2010; in other words, pursue counterterrorism unless counterinsurgency can be comprehensively implemented). These kinds of community-based alternatives to military strategies may allow government forces to operate with a smaller footprint or redeploy to more vulnerable areas. The ramifications for international relations are clear since the United States has given over $10 billion in foreign aid to Colombia alone over more than a decade under Plan Colombia, primarily for military equipment and training.

Planning ahead, we should think about how to strengthen communities for both current conflict settings and for future peace and stability. However, while counterinsurgency strategists have become concerned with understanding the "human terrain," in many cases, the deep analysis of communities is still sorely missing (McChrystal 2009). There is still a poor understanding of what civilians want, how their communities are organized, and how their institutions function. My ethnographies from Colombia and elsewhere suggest, however, that armed actors are capable of *learning* how to respect and interact productively and accountably with autonomous communities. Indeed, shifting the focus from military to civilian alternatives can provide payoffs, including in areas such as supporting local cease-fires, reducing illicit crop cultivation, and

---

[4] Indeed, the United States appears to have experimented with this concept in areas it cannot completely control during a pullback of forces in Afghanistan from remote villages to more populated areas. Commanders appealed to village elders and even an insurgent leader to develop a local security plan for after U.S. forces withdraw from the village of Damesh in Nurestan.

fostering development. Since communities may be targeted if they are seen as too political, development aid and capacity building should be done cautiously so as not to make local institutions appear to insurgents as part of the opposition. Local and national elites can play crucial roles to either help or hinder the development of horizontal social relations in local communities.

A RESEARCH AGENDA ON CIVILIANS IN WAR

This section maps out remaining challenges for studying civilian behavior and conflict outcomes and outlines a research agenda. While I found some support for civilian autonomy theory, the research agenda to understand the nuances of civilian behavior in different conflict settings is wide open. Because this study touches on many interrelated topics, it points to many new questions in diverse areas.

First, there is much room to improve the specification and measurement of civilians' strategies for protection and their alignments and preferences vis-à-vis armed groups. Civilian processes of strategy selection (as well as armed groups' responses) are complex and hinge on information, expectations, and social and cognitive processes. My theoretical treatment of strategy here is a simplification, and there are many facets that could be examined further.

In the realm of the measurement of strategies, several additional techniques may become feasible as more data is collected. First, additional case studies can provide measures of organizations and strategies across additional units, and careful village comparisons can contribute to an accumulation of findings. Second, survey questions could be helpful for identifying civilians' preferences and decisions, if truthful responses can be elicited. Third, data on observational measures of political preferences can help separate the influence of organization and cohesion from political leanings. Data on protests could also be used to at least test revealed preferences and visible strategies of alignment and autonomy. In sum, there is a need for deeper analysis of how additional autonomy mechanisms function and influence armed actors beyond the few analyzed herein. There may yet be strategies that remain unknown to the broader world and have not been systematized.

Second, there are many unknowns about civilians' decisions to use violent versus nonviolent strategies. Why do civilians tip from pacifism to arming or back from arming to nonviolence? When do armed efforts succeed and when do they fail? What are armed groups' views of civilians under arms? When and why do armed civilians ally with macro-actors?

Third, there are many remaining questions about the capacity of the junta councils and a need to better disentangle the mechanisms through which such organizations can affect violence. This is a complex issue because there are many concurrent pathways and limited available data. For instance, levels of funds and resources, projects, social cohesion, existing social capital, political alignments, and clientelism are all ways in which the juntas might themselves affect outcomes of interest or stand in for other factors that do. New insights about these factors should inform whether the juntas can be viewed as a "treatment" in experimental terms or whether societal patterns are path dependent and hard to shape (external stimuli appear to effectively promote community cooperation in at least some post-conflict circumstances; see Fearon et al. 2009 on Liberia). This will also inform how external organizations can best aid communities, including further probing whether bolstering juntas enhances security.

More broadly, the challenges of researching the junta councils show the need for capacity to collect and maintain data at the micro level on the social landscapes and organizations of developing countries. Data collection will be most useful if it samples the full spectrum of units of analysis – both "treated" and "untreated," organized and unorganized communities. Additionally, repeated measurement over time will help account for unit-specific, time-invariant characteristics such as social histories or preexisting capacities. Lastly, research could benefit from further clarification about possible reporting biases since the availability of information may depend on both the levels of community organization and levels of security.

Fourth, social capital and the internal dynamics of peaceful civilian organizations merit further study. How do civilians mobilize and sustain collective action and participation in violent environments? Are selective incentives or other appeals most common? How do people coordinate and communicate? How can they be supported? What are the limits of organizations? Why do breakdowns and defections occur? What are the day-to-day management tasks and strategies that *leaders* of these organizations use to both meet their goals and protect themselves in the process?

Fifth, this research represents only a first look into the reverse causal relationship of the effect of armed conflict on social organizations – when conflict weakens or stimulates social organization. This points to open questions about the sequencing of the creation of councils: Can they be formed in the midst of conflict to survive and aid in protection, or must they be established prior to conflict as a preventative measure? Do they require sustained support (e.g., by the government or external actors) under threat, or can they survive on their own?

Sixth, there is much more to learn about how armed groups view and respond to civilians. Why do some armed groups at times set up civilian councils and rely upon them but other times do not? If armed groups can easily create civilian organizations, what does this imply for the importance of preexisting civilian structures? What determines when armed groups can co-opt civilian organizations? In Colombia, there are still questions about why paramilitary groups vary in their attitudes and strategies toward the junta councils, as some were respectful while others were much more brutal. There is also more to learn about the conditions and types of groups that will be influenced by civilians. For instance, what guarantees (or consequences) will move armed groups to not target organizations? This calls for more extensive study of the different types of armed groups and their sensitivities and motives than what were found in the case studies. As seen here, one productive avenue for studying these questions is to collect information from ex-combatants.

FINAL THOUGHTS

Looking ahead, what are the prospects for Colombia and for autonomy movements in the near future? What are the prospects for civilian autonomy around the world? With the help of the initiatives of Plan Colombia, the conflict in Colombia has abated and state presence has expanded to reach many more towns, albeit at a nonnegligible human cost. Paramilitary groups have been disbanded and rebel groups have been weakened and repelled. Even as fighting continued, the government negotiated and signed a peace agreement with the FARC in 2016 and announced talks with the ELN, putting peace within reach. Like the years after La Violencia, the present conditions would seem an opportune moment to rebuild civil society and consolidate accountable state presence and security. However, while violence against civilian populations affects fewer communities, it still continues.

Emergent armed "criminal bands" (BACRIM) have spread to over 150 municipios and narco-trafficking, though slightly diminished, remains a concern (MAPP/OEA 2010; Corporación Arco Iris 2008 estimates criminal bands are present in over 250 municipios, or one-quarter of the country). These emergent groups are less organized and centralized, less political, and more criminal than other armed groups. These characteristics may make them depend relatively less on the population and harder to negotiate with. This may mean civilians have less leverage with them to gain protection than they have had with other armed groups. But it may also mean that civilians may be able to avoid transgressions by minimizing entanglements with these groups and staying out of their way. According to civilian autonomy theory, community management strategies would seem to be most useful, though other strategies may still be effective in some circumstances.

In a wider, global view, while civilian autonomy may not broadly occur in all conflicts, existing examples may reflect the tip of an iceberg. A lesson of the juntas is that there may be the potential for civilian autonomy and protection rooted in underlying social processes, perhaps not everywhere, but at least in more countries and communities than commonly believed. Indeed, new cases of civilian autonomy (at least in its primordial form) continue to be discovered, even in contexts where they are least expected (e.g., Libya, Syria, Mali, Iraq, and Ukraine).

As much as organizational strengthening is a key catalyst for civilian protection, careful analysis and understanding of examples is also necessary for awakening cooperation. This was seen in a number of my case studies, where civilians were not able to stand up for themselves due to a lack of reassurance and a meager understanding of organizing. Armed with information and ideas, communities can see what is possible, which limitations have been encountered in the past, and how to assess their own situations and capabilities. This speaks to the importance of sharing best practices, which some networks of communities are already doing, both within Colombia and internationally. To minimize harm (Anderson 1999) in acting collectively to deal with threats, communities and their supporters must carefully assess the security situation and organizational capacity, and gain the consent of residents, which all require good local information networks. This research can be informative for these tasks with its mapping of community history, protection mechanisms, contextual conditions, and armed group psychology.

I sought to answer questions about civilian autonomy, but the reality is that conflict conditions, communities, and available resources to manage conflict differ from one place to another and are ever evolving. So, more importantly, I asked difficult questions and put forward an approach for seeking answers. With interest in community-driven development, counterinsurgency, and, now, "countering violent extremism" on the rise again, the topics of civilian behavior and violence are also growing in attention and importance. As this conversation continues, we should look to civilians as a source of peace.

Appendix A

Archives Consulted

ATCC Community Archives, La India, Santander, Colombia
Ministry of Interior Archives, Bogotá, Colombia
Solimon Santos Personal Archives, Manila, the Philippines
The National Security Archive, Colombia Project, Washington, D.C. http://
    nsarchive.gwu.edu/colombia/

Appendix B

Supplementary Documentation on the ATCC

A NOTE ON VARIABLES AND "CASES"

The complex explanatory framework in Chapter 7 runs the risk of the number of independent variables exceeding the number of cases (the "n-k problem"). Under these circumstances, there is not ample variation to test and rule in (or out) different factors. I argue that the ATCC's investigation institution inter-acts with civilian "pacifist" norms to limit violence against civilians. This arrangement is further primarily supported when a third condition is present – that armed actor preferences are not excessively hostile to the institution's existence.[1] When variables representing alternative hypotheses such as Military Balance of Control and Armed Actor Resources are considered, even more cases are required for testing.

As a solution, I tap three kinds of variation within the ATCC meta-case. First, I look at temporal variation in the dependent variable of violence against civilians over time. In the ATCC case, the changes in violence can be roughly classified into the three different time periods. Second, I examine cross-sectional variation in violence between the ATCC region and communities in neighboring regions (lumped together). These cases are relevant "controls" since they likely share similar characteristics, including armed group fronts, geography, and perhaps demography.[2] Third, I consider counterfactual worlds as

---

[1] This presumes the counterfactual argument that if armed actors were more hostile than they actually were toward civilians, the institutional arrangement would have been unstable. This claim can be assessed by asking civilians and ex-combatants why the armed group agreed to and benefited by the civilian arrangement.

[2] I do not delve into counterfactuals for neighboring cases since they are not interesting or analyzable – one can only assume that if they had a civilian process, civilians would have been more protected (although the "thought experiment" of these counterfactuals makes one wonder why civilian institutions did not arise there). This would however add an additional three "cases."

additional cases (Fearon 1996). In theory, counterfactual cases can be derived
for each variable-time-period (e.g., what would have happened in case c
during year y if independent variable x had been present, or not present?).
The Table B.1 presents the various relevant factual and counterfactual cases.[3]
I identify variation across eleven real and counterfactual sub-cases within the
ATCC meta-case, which should help add confidence to civilian autonomy
theory with more cases than the seven independent variables (counterfactuals
are highlighted).

QUALITATIVE DISCUSSION OF ADDITIONAL EXPLANATIONS FOR TRENDS IN VIOLENCE

This section assesses how various extant explanations account for the observed
trends in violence over time. Specifically, it seeks to account for the surprising
era of the absence of violence during the 1990s. Beyond shifts in territorial
control, these explanations are: general (national) trends in violence and peace
overtures, changing rebel organization and discipline, and increased international support (see Table 7.1). I assess these hypotheses with various "cases"
within the ATCC meta-case.

General Trends in Violence and Negotiations? One explanation for a reduction in violence in the Carare region during the 1990s could be that either the
country or the wider Magdalena Medio region saw general trends toward less
violence against civilians in the conflict. This could be due to some kinds of
macro-level changes in rebel strategies, government counterinsurgency strategy,
or the initiation of macro-level peace negotiations or ceasefires unrelated to the
local decisions made by the ATCC or their armed actor counterparts. However,
none of these explanations fully account for the sustained reduction of violence.

Although violence decreased nation- and region-wide at some points in the
1990s, it fluctuated during this period. National homicide rate data (Figure 3.1)
show that violence against civilians was generally stable throughout the 1990s
until it began to surge even higher in 1998. Kline (2003) reaches a similar
conclusion. This trend likely corresponds with the regrouping of the paramilitary forces into the AUC and ACCU umbrella organizations in late 1990s.

Recorded trends in violence from the Magdalena Medio region and the
department of Santander also do not correspond with the ATCC's history.
Statistics from the Colombian government show that the Magdalena Medio
region and the department of Santander were no less violent and civilian
deaths were steady (or even increasing) throughout the 1990s. This is further
confirmed by CINEP data, which uses an alternate source for counts of

[3] I consider cases as "relevant" according to whether the variation is interesting. Cases with values on
the military control variable that predict a low-threat environment are not "interesting" because it
becomes impossible to distinguish any independent effect of the civilian process since the values of
both variables make the same prediction of low violence – a case of "equifinality."

TABLE B.1 *Real and counterfactual subcases*

Period/Case	ATCC (institution, norms)	Control variable value*	Outcome prediction	Observed outcome[4]	Reality or counterfactual
1975–1991/ ATCC	Absent	Contested/ dominant	Violence	Violence	Reality
1975–1991/ Neighbors	Absent	Contested/ dominant	Violence	Violence	Reality
1975–1991/ ATCC	Present[5]	Contested/ dominant	Low violence		Counterfactual
1991–2000/ ATCC	Present	Contested/ dominant	Low violence	Low violence	Reality
1991–2000/ Neighbors	Absent	Complete/ dominant	Violence	Violence	Reality
1991–2000/ ATCC	Present (weak norms)	Contested/ dominant	Violence against opportunists		Counterfactual
1991–2000/ ATCC	Absent	Contested/ dominant	Violence		Counterfactual
2000–2007/ ATCC	Present (degrading norms)	Contested/ dominant	Violence against opportunists	Rising violence	Reality
2000–2007/ Neighbors	Absent	Contested/ dominant	Violence	Violence	Reality
2000–2007/ ATCC	Present (strong norms)	Contested/ dominant	Low violence		Counterfactual
2000–2007/ ATCC	Absent	Contested/ dominant	Violence		Counterfactual

Present = norms and institutions present
Present (weak norms) = institutions present but weak pacifist norms among residents
Absent = institutions and norms absent
* Military balance is estimated by period, even though there are more fined-grained variations of balance within periods. Predictions of violence in each period are presented as helpful simplifications.

violence (OPI 2005; Holmes et al. 2007). AUC paramilitary violence was notably ruthless in the neighborhoods of the regional capital of the oil town

---

[4] Variation in the dependent variable of violence can further be disaggregated according to variation in the "pacifist norms" of the ATCC process. Although not all potential counterfactual cases are discussed, this variable accounts for differences in violence against pacifist-norm-abiding (ATCC member) civilians versus violence against nonnorm-abiding civilians in the region. The investigation institution theoretically only provides a protective benefit to civilians who abide by pacifist norms of noninvolvement in the armed conflict (not participating in the coca economy, for example). In cases where norms are weak, the institution will protect civilians that do not participate in conflict activities but not those that do, leading to low to moderate levels of violence.

[5] This could be further disaggregated into whether or not norms are present in addition to the investigatory institution, but I desist since it is not an "interesting" comparison.

of Barrancabermeja. According to García, in the first half of 1989, there were seven massacres within 100 kilometers of La India (264), while the ATCC area remained a relative oasis of peace. An interview subject also told of a massacre of six people found in a mass grave in the nearby town of Puerto Pinzón, in the department of Boyacá to the south, around 1996 (the case was under investigation by the Attorney General's office). Other ATCC residents who migrated from neighboring regions also testify that violence continued in their towns of origins, and some residents had family members who were victims.

Peace negotiations are fairly ubiquitous in recent Colombian history, but they do not seem to have been effective at tempering the conflict (García Durán 2005, 2006).[6] Although the government negotiated with the FARC and established the demilitarized zone in the Macarena region, this did not occur until 1998 and does not explain reductions in violence that occurred prior to that date. Overall, decisions at higher levels of politics do not seem to explain what occurred locally in the ATCC.

Resources of rebels. Weinstein (2006) suggests that rebel organization can explain abusive behavior against civilians. The resources available to rebel groups are seen as a main determinant of organizational structure. Since resource-rich groups attract economically motivated recruits and do not depend as much on civilians for support, they are more likely to have more abusive soldiers and be more lax in disciplining bad behavior (allowing soldiers "pillage" rewards). This theory would predict civilian violence to decrease when either illegal armed groups lose resources or become better organized.

In the case of the Carare region near Cimitarra, the level of resources available to illegal armed groups did not decline during the 1990s, and, if anything, actually increased. The Magdalena Medio region, including its southern edge, is known as the most oil-rich part of the country. Oil rackets and siphoning from oil pipelines by rebel and paramilitary groups was fairly common, according to interview accounts. Further, although Colombia is not known to have many diamond deposits, it does have emeralds, and emeralds and the emerald are trade prevalent in Magdalena Medio and the Carare region (Hernández Delgado 2004). As some of the campesinos have said, emeralds could be spotted with the naked eye in the riverbeds.[7] There are several reports of rebel and paramilitary groups emerging as protection rackets for

---

[6] As García Durán characterizes the period from 1993 to 1999, "After the failure of the peace process with the largest guerrilla groups in Caracas and Tlaxcala [in Gaviria's term], the armed forces ... declared 'total war' on all guerrilla groups. Ironically, this produced only mediocre results and left the guerrillas militarily stronger than ever. ... Although the Samper government (1994–1998) ... did try to construct a new model for negotiation with the guerrilla groups, all of its efforts were torpedoed by the weight of the political crisis produced by the investigation of the Attorney General's Office regarding the receipt of funds from drug trafficking in the election campaign which brought Ernesto Samper to the Presidency." Kline (2003) also notes that negotiations occurred throughout the 1990s, but to no avail.

[7] ATCC#24, La India, 10/2007.

esmeralderos, or emerald prospectors, as well as for local wealthy *ganadero* cattle ranchers (UNDP 2003). However, in the analysis of an interview respondent who was knowledgeable about the emerald trade in the region, while armed groups certainly took advantage of emerald rents when they could, it was not the principal source of their financing (and in fact, the FARC's 23rd Front may have been relatively resource-poor). Instead, a greater part of the guerrilla groups' operations was supported by *resource transfers* from other nearby FARC fronts in the department of Bolívar to the north, who were involved in gold mining in the Serranía de San Lucas mountain range, or by kidnapping.

In addition to oil and emeralds, the coca crop from which cocaine is made provided another source of income for armed groups. Many of the paramilitary groups have their origins in protecting drug traffickers (groups that emerged in Cimitarra were a union of drug traffickers and *esmeralderos*; Observatorio del Programa Presidencial de Derechos Humanos y DIH 2001: 6). Although there are reports of coca cultivation from the early 1990s in the region, coca production did not flourish until the end of the decade (interviews; Echandía 1999). However, even if little coca were produced in Santander in the 1990s, the FARC central committee collected coca profits and distributed the funds to its regional fronts.[8]

Surrounded by coca fields, emeralds, and oil, resources were certainly available to the armed groups and evidence suggests that, as time progressed, the rebel groups in Colombia only became more economically motivated, rather than less (e.g., a "war system"; Richani 2002). Since the theorized connection between resources and organization implies that violence should increase over time as groups' resource bases increase, resources per se do not convincingly explain the low levels of violence and abuse towards civilians during the late 1980s and 1990s (but are perhaps consistent with the abuse of civilians observed in the 1980s). The theory is further undermined when considering that, according to Weinstein, once groups tend toward opportunism and abuse, they are set on a path-dependent process and their behaviors become difficult to reverse. Despite stable or increasing resources, the organization of illegal armed groups in the area generally improved over time.

The local FARC fronts reformed by supposedly purging rogue commanders who committed abuses. This was not done out of pure good-heartedness, but rather in response to demands made in initial meetings with the ATCC. The FARC realized it was losing the support of civilians, and in response to the ATCC's entreaty, the FARC commander apologized for the past behavior and said he would hold abusive commanders accountable. Braulio Herrera, a leader in the political party associated with the FARC, the Union Patriótica, came to the region as part of the dialogue with civilians to regain support. He ordered that

---

[8] ATCC#3, La India, 8/2008.

abusive commanders be eliminated, and it was later reported that perhaps as many as seventy-eight men were "executed" or "thrown in the river," never to be seen again (interview; García 1996, 207, 269; Restrepo 2005, 2006). This process may have played a role in the FARC's improved treatment of civilians. Yet, it is not clear that this purge would have taken place without the initiation of dialogue by and pressure from the civilian leaders.

The increasingly dominant paramilitary groups in the region appear to have also improved their organization during this period, though not until the end of the decade.[9] In 1997, the various independent paramilitary groups merged to form the AUC (Autodefensas Unidas de Colombia) umbrella organization. Reports suggest that as a result of this merge, they became more effective and coordinated. But, interviews and statistics indicate that the paramilitaries were responsible for a larger portion of the threats than the guerrillas during this period. Paramilitary organizational consolidation did not coincide with the earlier decrease in violence seen by the ATCC.

Patterns of violence against ATCC civilians do not appear to be solely a function of armed actor resources and organizational structures. First, reforms did not coincide with changing resource endowments or reductions in violence. Second, although abuses, torture, and impertinent threats did occur in the region, much of the violence and denunciations were also characterized as purposive and coercive, and not a result of poor troop discipline. Third, some of the organizational reforms resulted from civilian pressures.

International Support? National and international actors seeking to support the ATCC could have raised the reputational costs to armed actors of transgressing against the ATCC by raising the organization's profile. However, this is not a likely explanation for the armed actors' apparent benign treatment of the ATCC since it only gradually gained international attention.

The ATCC did garner some early attention in the country shortly after the time of its founding, including by winning the Alternative Peace Prize in 1991, which generated some international press (e.g., Yarbro 1990). But as one of the first movements of its kind, it did not receive the kind of public profile and attention that other similar civilian communities receive today (especially given the early state of the internet for communication at that time). There is little evidence that either international governmental organizations (IGOs, such as the UN) or nongovernmental organizations (NGOs) were involved in the organization's founding (it arose indigenously) or with any kind of human rights monitoring programs or "accompaniment," such as those of Peace Brigades International and Fellowship of Reconciliation (e.g., Mahony and Eguren 1997).[10] The ATCC has only had part-time Peace Brigades

---

[9] Commander Botalón's rise in 1994 may have improved paramilitary control and discipline.

[10] Nor is there much evidence of any kind of "boomerang effect," where NGOs lobbied foreign governments to put pressure on the Colombian government to protect the ATCC (Keck and Sikkink 1998).

15 de febrero de 2002

Señores

ASOCIACION DE TRABAJADORES CAMPESINOS DEL CARARE

ASUNTO INVITACIÓN

Por medio del presente me dirijo respetuosamente a ustedes, para invitarlos a una reunión que se efectuara el día 1° de marzo del año en curso, a las 10 de la mañana en el corregimiento de Santa Rosa del municipio de Cimitarra (Santander)

En esta reunión se trataran temas de suma importancia y que en un futuro nos pueden llegar a beneficiar en el buen desarrollo de nuestra región.

A esta reunión asistirán personas delegadas del estado mayor de las ACMM de Puerto Boyacá y otras personalidades que en un futuro próximo pueden llegar ha colaborar con el desarrollo de obras que beneficien nuestra comunidad

Con esta invitación queremos hacer participe a toda la comunidad, por este motivo solicitamos a ustedes invitar a toda la comunidad ha asistir a dicha reunión.

Atentamente.

ESTADO MAYOR
ACMM PUERTO BOYACA

COMANDANTE MAICOL
LIDER SANTA ROSA

FIGURE B.1 Communication from the paramilitaries to the ATCC.

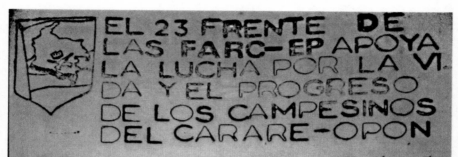

FIGURE B.2 Communication from the FARC to the ATCC.

accompaniment since 2000. The Colombian government's "peace ambassador" lent only tepid support to the process (García 1996).[11] In addition, much of the positive press garnered by the ATCC came *after* its long period without violence. The ATCC also tempered its public stance toward the armed groups in a way that limited international attention to abuses. It has had a policy of not implicating specific armed groups in their public

---

[11] Rafael Pardo, the Presidential Peace Advisor, said, "The national government is not interested in regional peace accords ... because ... they cause the guerrillas and violence to displace from one region to another ... but he also offered 'all the institutional support possible'" (García 1996, 283).

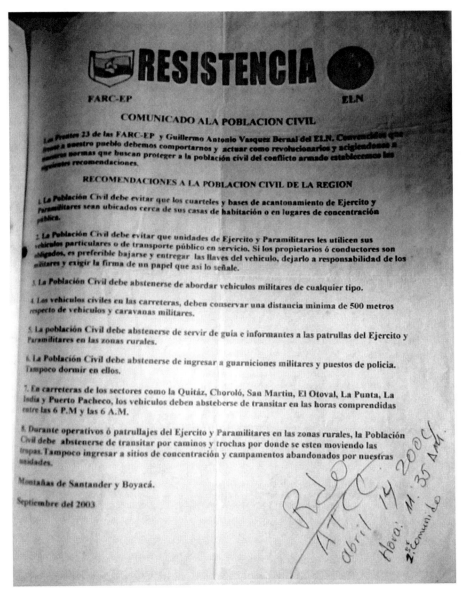

FIGURE B.3 Warning from the FARC to the ATCC.

denunciations of threats or human rights violations, only referring to the culprits as "the enemies of peace."

In sum, most accounts would have otherwise predicted that, during the 1990s, violence against civilians would have prevailed just as it had in the preceding fifteen years.

AUTORIZACIÓN

Los abajo firmantes e identificados como aparece al pie de las mismas, mayores de edad e integrantes de la micro región de la india, área de influencia de la ATCC, autorizamos a ███████ ███████, para que organice una comisión que canalice la posibilidad para que el/ los grupo/os de FARC que se encuentra/an en nuestra área nos permita/an lograr un dialogo con ellos.

Para mayor constancia se anexan las firmas.

Dada en la india a los ███ días del mes ███ de 2004.

FIGURE B.4 ATCC authorization to seek dialogues with the FARC.
"We the signers below, adult members of the region of La India, area of influence of the ATCC, authorize _____ to organize a commission to look into the possibility that the FARC groups found in our area will allow us to dialogue with them."
La India, 2004.

Verbatim transcript of meeting between the ATCC leader, the junta leaders of San Tropel and Santa Rosa (on border of the ATCC), and a Paramilitary Subcommander, 2001, in Santa Rosa, Cimitarra (from the ATCC archive).

ATCC LEADER: The association is always willing to help people of a good heart [but] . . . there was some misinformation because they [some paramilitaries] said that the leaders of the ATCC had come to supposedly create an ATCC here in Santa Rosa and regarding this there was a disagreement in the high command and that the commander stated he would not permit that they create an ATCC in Santa Rosa.

PARAMILITARY SUBCOMMANDER: If tomorrow we come to spread terror, the community will quickly be the one to react (form opinions) and organize itself and say that, "We don't want your presence." I've spoken with some members of this community and they have told why the ATCC before didn't take Santa Rosa into account and why the ATCC does so now, so I want you to explain this to me.

SANTA ROSA JUNTA LEADER: We can't blame the ATCC leaders for this. . . . Unfortunately here in Santa Rosa we've been a totally un-united community and while we are not united and organized we won't get anywhere.

ATCC LEADER: Every armed group is jealous with the people. This region is delicate because here there does not exist the total domination of any of the armed groups and there exist split territories; but there is a dividing line and it's the association . . .

SANTA ROSA JUNTA LEADER: Our problem is, if we're going to have the Autodefensa here, then we're going to continue with the comment that Santa Rosa is land of the paras; so we should look for another horizon, because tomorrow they'll have us marked (tildados) as paramilitaries and before long the guerrillas will come and they'll take-out some innocent people. So, I want to keep looking for a way to keep living at the margin of whichever group. By that I don't mean that I'm against the paras or the guerrillas.

ATCC LEADER: If this war were directed at the guilty, there wouldn't be problems and we wouldn't have to worry. . . . If it were really a directed war, more innocent people would not die.

PARAMILITARY SUBCOMMANDER: If all the community said that they didn't want our presence here we would respect the decision.

SAN TROPEL JUNTA LEADER: We've had a lot of contact with the ATCC and the paramilitaries. I want to tell (the community) that there are many times that we are afraid to express ourselves before the commander for the fear of what they'll say after the meeting. I want to tell you that they have changed their philosophy a little and have ended their assault a little against the community . . . For us it hasn't gone very well, since we're 100% dominated by the Autodefensas, whereas the situation is different here (in Santa Rosa).

SANTA ROSA WOMAN: Will you (paras) still be here regardless of whether the community wants you here?

PARAMILITARY SUBCOMMANDER: Yes, we're going to be here whether they want us or not.

SANTA ROSA WOMAN: And if the community organizes itself and says no?

PARAMILITARY SUBCOMMANDER: Regarding this it would have to be that the entire community decides it.

SANTA ROSA WOMAN: So it's the community that decides it.

PARAMILITARY SUBCOMMANDER: But if there are only two or three people that don't want our presence, then we'll continue to be here.

ASOCIACION DE TRABAJADORES CAMPESINOS DEL CARARE

Per. Jur. 190 1987 Gobernación de Santander.

(TRANSLATED FROM THE SPANISH)

ASSOCIATION OF FARMWORKERS OF CARARE
ATCC
ACT OF INDIVIDUAL COMMITMENT OF THE AFFILIATE

INTRODUCTION: *Through the present certificate, I voluntarily commit myself, purposefully and without any pressure that might coerce my will, to be part of the thought and work toward the defense of the lives, work and welfare of my companions to which the ATCC endeavors through its process of peace toward the prospect of safe coexistence in the area of influence of the ATCC.*

I COMMIT MYSELF TO:

1. Act within the stipulated statutes of commitments and obligations that give me the right to be associated with the ATCC and to be able to access the economic, political, cultural, and social benefits that it offers its associates.

2. I commit myself to be receptive, to accept training, and inductions that allow me to learn about things related to the process of the ATCC, its organization and its peace proposal.

3. I make myself responsible for the obligations that I have as an affiliate of the ATCC for its support and economic, political, and social strengthening, according to the established statutes and other agreements that are approved by the general assembly and the delegates.

4. Upon signing this certificate I accede to the procedure and decision that the ATCC makes regarding my association to the organization, and I authorize it to investigate and verify the information supplied. In the case I am not accepted as an associate I accept the decision and I expect to be able to count on another possibility to be evaluated should I request it.

5. Upon signing this certificate I declare and give proof of not being linked to any violence-generating action or illicit activity that could jeopardize the organizational goals and construction of peace led by the ATCC.
   Note:
   ❖ To become an affiliate, in the case of having been linked to illicit cultivation, it is necessary to have at minimum one year of disassociation from the illicit action.
   ❖ In case of having been linked to an illegal armed group, it is necessary to have at minimum 5 years of dissociation from the armed organization.
   ❖ In any circumstance, the ATCC reserves the right to deny admission

6. Upon signing this certificate I recognize the ATCC as the rural organization that personifies the goal of peace and life that we seek to live better.

7. I commit myself to not go to armed groups to mediate my personal, neighborly, community or political conflicts. To solve my conflicts I will first resort to the ATCC and in case the ATCC is not able to provide a solution, I will go before the competent judicial authorities by referral through an act made by the ATCC. In addition, I will not resort to illicit actions to improve my living conditions.

8. I commit myself to maintain the good names of the ATCC and its members, to clarify any comment that arises about them before it becomes a destructive rumor for the organization and risks lives and the image of the process.

FIGURE B.5A ATCC Membership Document circa 2007.

9. Upon signing this act I assume the responsibility of being aware of the actions and instructions given by the board of directors and the assembly of delegates relating to the political, social and economic process of the ATCC.

10. Upon signing this certificate I commit to fulfill my economic, cultural, political, and social obligations as an affiliate in the presence of the community, the delegates, the executives and the process of the ATCC. When When I fail these obligations I lose the rights given to me as an affiliate by the statutes, the community and the law.

    Note: The economic obligations of the affiliate will be understood as:
    - Contribution of affiliation.
    - Maintenance contribution to the ATCC

11. Upon signing this act I am conscious of my responsibility for and role in the management of my own welfare and progress.

12. Upon signing this act I assume the commitment to actively participate in each action the ATCC convenes in the defense of life and other non-negotiable rights that guarantee human existence.

13. As an affiliate of the ATCC I along with my fellow members commit to setting an example through my way of life, to demonstrate my unwavering commitment to peace and non-violence.

14. I commit to complying with my utmost ability to the principles and the statutes of the ATCC.

As an affiliate that who meets his obligations toward the ATCC, I have the right:
- ❖ To voice within the organizational process of the ATCC but not to vote to elect or be elected to the board or assembly of delegates, but this restriction does not apply for the work committees or projects of the association or your community.
- ❖ That my life and goods be defended when they are threatened.
- ❖ That once I have fulfilled the requirements established by the statutes to be a member, I be accepted by the association as such.

Name of Affiliate: _____

C. C. N. _____ Expedida _____

Signature del Affiliate: _____

Fingerprint

Name of Delegate or Leader _____
C. C. N. _____ Expedida _____

Name of Junta de Acción Comunal President _____
C. C. N. _____ Expedida _____

Witnesses _____
C. C. N. _____ Expedida _____

Signed on _____ ____day of the month of _____ in the year_____

Note: this certificate is personal and non-transferable and loses its validity at the time in which the associate fails to fulfill the established commitments.

FIGURE B.5B ATCC Membership Document.

Glossary

This study uses a specialized set of Colombian vocabulary in Spanish and English, as well as acronyms related to Colombia's armed conflict and social setting.

Abigeato	Cattle theft.
ACCU	Autodefensas Campesinas de Córdoba y Urabá (United Self-Defense Forces of Córdoba and Urabá); a private army mobilized by the Castaño family to combat the FARC in northwest Colombia, which later grew into the United Self-Defense Forces of Colombia (AUC).
ACR	Agencia Colombiana para la Reintegración (Colombian Agency for Reintegration); the Colombian government entity, created in 2011 (previously the High Advisory for Reintegration), that oversees efforts to reintegrate demobilized fighters into Colombian society.
ANUC	Asociación Nacional de Usuarios Campesinos de Colombia (National Association of Peasants); community land reform councils in rural areas.
ATCC	Asociación de Trabajadores Campesinos del Carare (Peasant Workers Association of the Carare River); a civilian community organization in the department of Santander that created its own mechanisms for mediating and mitigating the effects of the armed conflict.
AUC/Autodefensas Unidas de Colombia	United Self-Defense Forces of Colombia; a paramilitary umbrella organization formed in 1997 to consolidate the country's disparate paramilitary

	groups. At its peak, the AUC had an estimated 31,000 members. The organization demobilized from 2003 to 2006.
Autonomy	Self-rule; the goal of seeking independence from armed actors as a response to conditions of civil conflict and state absence. In conflict settings, *de jure* civilian autonomy involves independence in decision-making. De facto civilian autonomy reflects freedom from threats or violence achieved through the implementation of community autonomy strategies.
BACRIM/Bandas Emergentes/Aguilas Negras	Criminal bands or neo-paramilitary groups that appeared in the post-paramilitary demobilization era.
Bazaar	Party (fiesta) or fair, usually to raise funds for community needs or projects.
Berraco	Tough, or a tough guy.
Bestia	A mule, used for transportation.
Cabecera	The county seat of a municipio (urban center).
Cabildo	The political council that governs an Indigenous community.
Campesino	A farmer or peasant; usually a mestizo of mixed Spanish and Indigenous descent.
Chévere, Bacano	Awesome, great.
Chisme	Gossip; unreliable information circulated within communities or shared with armed actors as part of false denunciations.
Chusma/contra-chusma	Bandit groups during La Violencia.
Coca	The plant from which cocaine is derived.
Cocalero Movement	A social protest movement led by coca growers in the Amazon region of Colombia, primarily the department of Putumayo, that received support from the FARC and negotiated for benefits with the Colombian government.
Comité de Cafeteros	The local committee of coffee growers in a municipality.
Consejo Comunitario	The governing political council of an Afro-Colombian community.
Convite/Minga	Community service and shared labor; the act of working toward a common goal ("minga" is used among Indigenous groups).
Convivencia	Peace; coexistence; harmony.

Corregimiento	A subsection of a municipio with a small urban center; larger than a village but smaller than the county seat.
DANE	Colombian Census Bureau.
DAS	Departamento Administrativo de Seguridad (Administrative Department of Security); Colombia's former intelligence agency, which was dissolved in 2011 following a series of scandals, including evidence of links between the agency and paramilitary groups and illicit surveillance of leftist politicians, judges, journalists, human rights defenders, and other civilians.
DIGIDEC	Dirección General de Integración y Desarrollo de la Comunidad (General Directorate of Community Development and Integration); the bureau of the Ministry of Government that managed the junta council portfolio; the office was absorbed into the Ministry of Interior in 1996.
Eje Cafetero/Coffee Axis	Colombia's main coffee-growing region, comprising the departments of Risaralda, Caldas, Quindío, and the southern part of Antioquia.
ELN	Ejército de Liberación Nacional (National Liberation Front) guerrilla group; Colombia's second-largest guerrilla group, formed in 1962.
FARC	Fuerzas Armadas Revolucionarias de Colombia (Revolutionary Armed Forces of Colombia); Colombia's largest guerrilla group, founded in 1964.
Indigenous Guard	A nonviolent community self-defense movement established in 2001 by the Nasa Indigenous community in Cauca, southwestern Colombia.
Inspector de Policía	Police inspector; an unarmed, nonuniformed civilian who does administrative work for local police and registers complaints from the population.
Junta de Acción Comunal (JAC)	A community action board of a village or neighborhood; a decision-making body whose duties include planning public goods projects.
Law of Silence	An unspoken rule whereby members of a community cease to communicate with each other for fear of reprisals from the controlling armed group, undermining the potential for community-based resistance.
Liberation Theology	A Roman Catholic ideological movement with roots in Latin America that places poverty at the center of

	Biblical interpretation, calling for social change and critiquing the structural causes of poverty.
Limpieza	"Social cleansing"; the tactics used by paramilitary groups to eliminate individuals or groups identified as criminals, drug users, social deviants, or military objectives.
Machetera	A fight with a machete (garden sword).
Magdalena Medio	A large valley in central Colombia spanning five departments and surrounding the Magdalena River, the country's primary waterway; the resource-rich region has historically been one of the most violent and contested parts of the country.
Medellín Cartel	The drug-trafficking network led by Pablo Escobar, responsible for hundreds of targeted assassinations and widespread violence during the 1970 and 1980s; it contributed to the founding of the early paramilitary group Death to Kidnapers (MAS) in the Middle Magdalena region.
Ministry of Government (Gobierno)	The national government ministry in charge of the junta council program.
Municipio	A municipality; a town or county.
National Front (Frente Nacional)	A coalition formed by the Liberal and Conservative political parties in 1958 to bring an end to La Violencia. It consisted of a power-sharing agreement to alternate the presidency between the two parties each electoral cycle and was maintained until 1974.
NN	"No nombre", or "No name"; found on umarked graves or crosses to mark the dead.
Peace zones/Zones of peace	Self-declared autonomous communities in conflict areas in the Philippines that seek to be free of the influence or presence of armed actors.
Personero	A human rights ombudsman for a municipio.
Plan Colombia	U.S. anti-drug and counterinsurgency aid package that has given approximately $10 billion in aid to Colombia's government and military institutions since it began in 2000.
Plata o Plomo/ Pico y Plomo	"Bribe or a bullet" or, variably, "Obey or a bullet"; a guerrilla policy of intimidation and fear to coerce civilians to cooperate; a play on "pico y placa," an urban traffic control initiative.
Procuraduría	Inspector General; the national government branch responsible for overseeing the conduct and operations of politicians and political institutions; it also

	investigates and prosecutes corruption by government officials.
Raso	A foot soldier in an armed group.
Sapo	An informant; literally, a frog.
Secretariat	The leadership council of the FARC, comprising seven commanders.
Socio	A member of an organization.
Soldados Campesinos	Peasant soldiers recruited and deployed as part of a strategic program to increase Colombian military presence in municipios that lacked state presence and were seen as vulnerable to armed actor control.
Tildado/Señalado	"Marked"; literally, "signaled" or "accented"; to be identified as a supporter, sympathizer, or informant of an armed group.
Toma	A guerrilla assault on or taking of a town.
Unión Patriótica	The Patriotic Union party; the leftist political party founded by members of the FARC in 1985. Over 3,000 members of the party were systematically assassinated by right-wing forces, leading to its eventual dissolution.
Vacuna	A "vaccination payment" or protection tax extorted by an armed group.
Vereda	Village; a subsection of a municipio; smaller than a corregimiento.
La Violencia	The large internecine political conflict that occurred from 1948–1958, pitting members of the Liberal and Conservative parties against each other in bloody battles, primarily in rural areas. An estimated 200,000 people were killed over the course of conflict.
Zona de despeje	The former demilitarized zone located in the department of Meta, and known colloquially as FARClandia. This territory, covering about 16,216 square miles (42,000 square kilometers) in southern Colombia, was granted to the FARC by President Andrés Pastrana in 1998, before the failed 1998–2002 Caguán peace talks.

References

Abdulrahim, Raja. 2014. "In Syria, Activists in Raqqa Try to Confront Militant Islamist Group." *Los Angeles Times*, May 5, 2014.

Abouzeid, Rania. 2012. "Who Will the Tribes Back in Syria's Civil War?" *Time.com*, October 10, 2012.

Acemoglu, Daron, Simon Johnson, and James A. Robinson. 2002. "Reversal of Fortune: Geography and Institutions in the Making of the Modern World Income Distribution." *The Quarterly Journal of Economics* 117(4): 1231–94.

ACIA (Asociación Campesina Integral del Atrato, Chocó), Consejo Comunitario Mayor, and Red de Solidaridad Social Presidencia de la República. 2002. *Medio Atrato: Territorio de Vida*. Quibdó: Red de Solidaridad Social; ACIA.

AFP. 2012. "Palestinian Refugees Reclaim Syrian Camp." *AFP*, December 21, 2012.

AFP. 2013. "Syria Rebels Announce Withdrawal from Christian Town." *AFP*, September 10, 2013.

Al-Ansary, Khalid and Ali Adeeb. 2006. "Most Tribes in Anbar Agree to Unite Against Insurgents," *The New York Times*, September 18, 2006.

Albertus, Michael and Oliver Kaplan. 2013. "Land Reform as a Counterinsurgency Policy: Evidence from Colombia." *Journal of Conflict Resolution* 57(2): 198–231.

Alipala, Julie. 2008. "Army Air Strikes Defeat Peace Zone Agreement Signed in Jolo." *Philippine Daily Inquirer*, April 30, 2008.

Almond, Gabriel A. and Sidney Verba. 1963. *The Civic Culture: Political Attitudes and Democracy in Five Nations*. Princeton, NJ: Princeton University Press.

Amnesty International. 2000. *Colombia: Return to Hope: Forcibly Displaced Communities of Urabá and Medio Atrato Region*.

Amnesty International. 2001. *Annual Report Colombia*.

Amnesty International. 2002. "Colombia: San Vicente Del Caguán after the Breakdown of the Peace Talks: A Community Abandoned." AMR23/098/2002, October 16, 2002.

Amos, Deborah. 2012a. "In Syria, Aleppo Today Is Must-See TV For Survival." *National Public Radio*, November 28, 2012.

Amos, Deborah. 2012b. "Syrian Villagers Hope Their Example Will Be A Model." *National Public Radio*, December 10, 2012.

Anderson, Mary B. 1999. *Do No Harm: How Aid Can Support Peace - or War.* Boulder: Lynne Rienner Publishers.

Anderson, Mary B. and Marshall Wallace. 2012. *Opting Out of War: Strategies to Prevent Violent Conflict.* Boulder: Lynne Rienner Publishers.

Arango, Tim. 2014. "Tears, and Anger, as Militants Destroy Iraq City's Relics." *The New York Times*, July 30, 2014.

Arjona, Ana. 2014. "Wartime Institutions a Research Agenda." *Journal of Conflict Resolution* 58(8): 1360–89.

Armstrong, Martin and Lauren Williams. 2012. "Armenian Christians Torn in Syria's Civil War." *The Daily Star (Beirut)*, October 1, 2012.

Asociación de Trabajadores Campesinos del Carare. 2006. "Estatutos." ATCC Archive, September 2006.

ASOPROA. 2006. ASOPROA: Fortalecimiento de la organización campesina para la prevención del desplazamiento y el impulso al desarrollo local.

Axelrod, Robert. 1984. *The Evolution of Cooperation.* New York: Basic Books.

Azam, Jean-Paul. 2006. "On Thugs and Heroes: Why Warlords Victimize Their Own Civilians." *Economics of Governance* 7(1): 53–73.

Bagley, Bruce. 1989. "The State and the Peasantry in Contemporary Colombia." *Latin American Issues* 6.

Bagley, Bruce and Matthew Edel. 1980. "Popular Mobilization Programs of the National Front: Cooptation and Radicalization." In *Politics of Compromise: Coalition Government in Colombia*, eds. Ronald G. Hellman and R. Albert Berry. New Brunswick, NJ: Transaction Books.

Baker, Aryn. 2014. "'Systematic Torture and Killing': A New Report Points Fingers at Syria's Assad." *Time*, January 20, 2014.

Bakke, Kristin M. 2014. "Help Wanted? The Mixed Record of Foreign Fighters in Domestic Insurgencies." *International Security* 38(4): 150–87.

Ball, Patrick. 1998. *Liberal Hypocrisy and Totalitarian Sincerity: The Social and Ideological Origins of the National Non-Government Human Rights Movements in El Salvador, Pakistan, and Ethiopia*, Ph.D. thesis, University of Michigan.

Barnard, Anne. 2012a. "Syrian Insurgents Accused of Rights Abuses." *The New York Times*, March 21, 2012.

Barnard, Anne. 2012b. "In Syria, Missteps by Rebels Erode Their Support." *The New York Times*, November 9, 2012.

Barnard, Anne. 2012c. "Syrian Airstrike Kills Palestinian Refugees." *The New York Times*, December 17, 2012.

Barnard, Anne. 2014a. "Syrian Government Forces Seize Town in a Deep Blow to Opposition." *The New York Times*, March 16, 2014.

Barnard, Anne. 2014b. "Syrian Rebels Say Cease-Fire Deals Prove Deceptive." *The New York Times*, January 16, 2014.

Barnard, Anne and Hwaida Saad. 2013a. "Undecided Syrians Could Tip Balance of Rebellion." *The New York Times*, January 5, 2013.

Barnard, Anne and Hwaida Saad. 2013b. "Assault on Christian Town in Syria Adds to Fears Over Rebels." *The New York Times*, September 11, 2013.

Barnard, Anne and Hwaida Saad. 2014. "Nuns Released by Syrians After Three-Month Ordeal." *The New York Times*, March 10, 2014.

Barnett, Donald and Karari Njama. 1966. *Mau Mau from Within: Autobiography and Analysis of Kenya's Peasant Revolt.* Letchworth: MacGibbon and Kee.

Bates, Robert H., Avner Greif, Margaret Levi, Jean-Laurent Rosenthal, and Barry Weingast. 2000. *Analytic Narratives*. Princeton: Princeton University Press.

Bavier, Joe. 2009. "Congo Villagers Take Up Arms against LRA Rebels," Reuters UK, January 16, 2009.

BBC. 2011. "Venezuela Links to Farc Detailed." *BBC*, May 10, 2011.

BBC. 2013. "Syria Rebels Withdraw from Ancient Christian Town of Maaloula." *BBC*, September 6, 2013.

Bejarano, Ana Maria and Eduardo Pizarro. 2001. "The Coming Anarchy: The Partial Collapse of the State and the Emergence of Aspiring State Makers in Colombia." Manuscript.

Bernardo, Ariel B. 2010. "Spaces for Peace: Societal Influence through Grassroots Peace Building." *Army Troopers Newsmagazine*, July–August 2010: 7–13.

Bobbio, Norberto. 1988. "Gramsci and the Concept of Civil Society." In *Civil Society and the State*, ed. John Keane. London; New York: Verso.

Borrero García, Camilo. 1989. "Acción comunal y política estatal: un matrimonio indisoluble?" *Documentos ocasionales CINEP*, No. 57, Centro de Investigación y Educación Popular (CINEP).

Bouvier, Virginia M. 2006. "Harbingers of Hope: Peace Initiatives in Colombia." *USIP Special Report* (#169).

Bouvier, Virginia M. 2009. *Colombia: Building Peace in a Time of War*. Washington, D.C.: USIP Press.

Bowen, Jeremy. 2013. "Syrians 'No Longer Trust Neighbours.'" *BBC News*, September 15, 2013.

Bradley, Matt. 2016. "Rift Grows in Islamic State Between Foreign, Local Fighters." *Wall Street Journal*, March 25, 2016.

Brulliard, Karin. 2010. "In Targeting Taliban Stronghold, U.S. Depends on Afghans' Reluctant Support." *The Washington Post*, July 16, 2010.

Bumiller, Elisabeth. 2010. "U.S. Tries Luring Taliban Foot Soldiers Back to Society." *The New York Times*, May 24, 2010.

Buonanno, Paolo, Paolo Vanin, and Daniel Montolio. 2009. "Does Social Capital Reduce Crime?" *Journal of Law and Economics* 52 (February 2009): 145–170.

Burch, Jonathon. 2012. "On Syrian Border, Mixed Feelings for Rebel Liberators." *Reuters*, November 15, 2012.

Cabreza, Vincent. 2010. "Another Peace Zone in Mt. Province?" *Philippine Daily Inquirer*, September 21, 2010.

Campbell, Duncan. 2000. "Heart of Darkness." *The Guardian*, June 19, 2000.

Cante, Freddy and Luisa Ortiz, eds. 2005. *Acción Política No-violenta, Una Opción para Colombia*. Bógota: Centro Editorial Universidad del Rosario.

Cárdenas, Juan Camilo. 2008. *Social Preferences among the People of Sanquianga in Colombia*. CEDE, Universidad de Los Andes.

Catholic Relief Services. 2003. "Reflections on Creating and Sustaining Zones of Peace: Lessons from Mindanao, Philippines." Catholic Relief Services Peace & Reconciliation Program, Davao City, Philippines.

Caviedes, Mauricio, ed. 2007. *Paz y Resistencia: Experiencias Indígenas desde la Autonomía*. Bogotá: CECOIN.

Ceballos, Miguel and Gerard Martin. 2001. *Participación y Fortalecimiento Institucional a Nivel Local en Colombia*. Bogotá: Centro Editorial Javeriano, Pontificia Universidad Javeriana; Washington, D.C.: Center for Latin American Studies.

Chandrasekaran, Rajiv. 2010. "In Afghanistan, Why Does Counterinsurgency Work in Some Places but Not Others?" *The Washington Post*, July 25, 2010.

Cheikhomar, Ammar and Henry Austin. 2013. "Caught in the Middle: Christians Suffer amid Syria's Civil War." *NBC News*, August 11, 2013.

Chenoweth, Erica and Maria J. Stephan. 2011. *Why Civil Resistance Works: The Strategic Logic of Nonviolent Conflict*. New York: Columbia University Press.

Chivers, C. J. 2013a. "Brutality of Syrian Rebels Posing Dilemma in West." *The New York Times*, September 5, 2013.

Chivers, C. J. 2013b. "Some Syrian Kurds Resist Assad, Defying Conventional Views." *The New York Times*, January 23, 2013.

Chivers, C. J. 2013c. "Syrians, Fleeing Home, Crowd in Roman Caves." *The New York Times*, March 23, 2013.

Chwe, Michael Suk-Young. 2001. *Rational Ritual: Culture, Coordination, and Common Knowledge*. Princeton, NJ: Princeton University Press.

CINEP. 2003. *Comunidades de Paz de San Francisco de Asís, Nuestra Señora del Carmen y Natividad de María: Chocó, Colombia*. Bógota: CINEP.

CINEP. 2007. "Presentación - Falsos Positivos." *Noche y Niebla* 34/35.

Cohen, Jean L. and Andrew Arato. 1994. *Civil Society and Political Theory*. Cambridge, MA: MIT Press.

Collier, Paul and Anke Hoeffler. 2004. "Greed and Grievance in Civil War." *Oxford Economic Papers* 56(4): 563–595.

Colombia Ministerio de Gobierno. 1980. *Dirección General de Integración y Desarrollo de la Comunidad 20 Años de Desarrollo de la Comunidad 1959 - 1979*. Bogotá: DIGEDEC.

Comisión Nacional de Reparación y Reconciliación (CNRR). 2007. *Disidentes, Rearmados y Emergentes: ¿Bandas Criminales o Tercera Generación Paramilitar?* Área de Desmovilización, Desarme y Reintegración. Bogotá: CNRR.

Comisión Nacional de Reparación y Reconciliación (CNRR). 2009. *Una Historia de Paz para Contar, Recontar y No Olvidar: Cartilla Sobre la Historia de la ATCC*. Equipo de Memoria Histórica. Bogotá: CNRR.

Comisión Nacional de Reparación y Reconciliación (CNRR). 2011. *El Orden Desarmado: La Resistencia de la Asociación de Trabajadores Campesinos del Carare (ATCC)*. Grupo de Memoria Histórica. Bogotá: CNRR.

Coronel-Ferrer, Miriam. 2005. "Institutional Response: Civil Society." Background paper, Human Development Network Foundation, Inc.

Corporación Nuevo Arco Iris. 2008. "Preocupante Aumento de Bandas Armadas en Colombia." Available at: www.nuevoarcoiris.org.co/sac/?q=node/231.

Crost, Benjamin, Joseph Felter and Patrick Johnston. 2014. "Aid under Fire: Development Projects and Civil Conflict." *American Economic Review*, 104(6): 1833–1856.

Cubides, F., Jaramillo, J. E. and Mora, L. 1989. *Colonización, Coca y Guerrilla*. Bogotá: Editorial Alianza.

Cubides C., Fernando. 2006. "La Participación Política del Campesinado en el Contexto de la Guerra: El Caso Colombiano." In *La Construcción de la Democracia en el Campo Latinoamericano*, ed. Hubert C Grammont. Buenos Aires: CLACSO, Consejo Latinoamericano de Ciencias Sociales.

DANE (Departamento Administrativo Nacional de Estadística). 1962. *Directorio Nacional de Explotaciones Agropecuarias (Censo Agropecuario) 1960*. Bogotá: DANE.

DANE (Departamento Administrativo Nacional de Estadística). 1971. *Censo Agrope-cuario, 1970–1971: Datos Preliminares.* Bogotá: DANE.

DANE (Departamento Administrativo Nacional de Estadística). 1978. *Directorio Nacional De Entidades Cooperativas 1975–1976.* Bogotá: Departamento Adminis-trativo Nacional de Estadística.

DANE (Departamento Administrativo Nacional de Estadística). 1985. *Divipola.* Bogotá: DANE.

DANE (Departamento Administrativo Nacional de Estadística). 1987. *Colombia Esta-dística.* Bogotá: DANE.

DANE (Departamento Administrativo Nacional de Estadística). 1997. División Político-Administrativa de Colombia / República de Colombia. Bogotá: Departamento Administrativo Nacional de Estadística, DANE.

DANE (Departamento Administrativo Nacional de Estadística). 2000. *Divipola.* Bogotá: DANE.

DANE (Departamento Administrativo Nacional de Estadística). 2007. *Divipola.* Bogotá: DANE.

DANE (Departamento Administrativo Nacional de Estadística). 2008. *GIST Data Repository* [cited 2008]. Available from https://gist.itos.uga.edu.

Daniel, James M. 1965. *Rural Violence in Colombia since 1946.* Washington, D.C.: Special Operations Research Office.

De Friedemann, Nina S. 1979. "Ma Ngombe: Guerreros y Ganaderos en Palenque." Available at: www.lablaa.org/blaavirtual/antropologia/magnom/ninao.htm.

DePetris, Daniel. 2013. "Alawite Group against Assad." *The Epoch Times*, October 28, 2012.

Di Giovanni, Janine. 2012. "Mountaintop Town Is a Diverse Haven From Syria's Horrors." *The New York Times*, November 22, 2012.

Doughty, Kristin and David Moussa Ntambara. 2005. "Resistance and Protection: Muslim Community Actions during the Rwandan Genocide." Available at: www.cda inc.com/cdawww/pdf/casestudy/steps_rwanda_case_study_Pdf.pdf.

Dudley, Steven. 2003. *Walking Ghosts: Murder and Guerilla Politics in Colombia.* Taylor & Francis, Inc.

Duncan, Gustavo. 2006. *Los Señores de la Guerra: De Paramilitares, Mafiosos y Autodefensas en Colombia.* 1st ed. Bogotá.

East View Cartographic, Inc. 2002. *VMAP Level 1 GIS Vector Data.* East View Cartographic, Inc.

Easterly, William. 2007. *The White Man's Burden: Why the West's Efforts to Aid the Rest Have Done So Much Ill and So Little Good.* First Edition. Penguin Books.

Eastman, Jorge Mario. 1982. *Seis Reformas Estructurales al Régimen Político: Resulta-dos Electorales de 1930 a 1982.* Bogotá: Ministerio de Gobierno.

Echandía Castilla, Camilo. 1999. *El Conflicto Armado y las Manifestaciones de Vio-lencia en las Regiones de Colombia.* Santa Fé de Bogotá: Presidencia de la República de Colombia, Oficina del Alto Comisionado para la Paz, Oberservatorio de Violencia; Imprenta Nacional.

Eckstein, Harry. 1975. "Case-Study and Theory in Macro-Politics." In *Handbook of Political Science*, eds. F. Greenstein and N. Polsby. Reading: Addison-Wesley.

Edel, Matthew. 1969. "The Colombian Community Action Program: Costs and Bene-fits." *Yale Economic Essays* 9(Fall 1969): 3–58.

Edel, Matthew. 1971. "Determinants of Investments by Colombian Community Action Boards." *Journal of Developing Areas* 5(2): 207–221.

El Espectador. 2015. "Colombia, El Segundo País Con Más Desplazados: Ya Son Seis Millones." December 2, 2015.

El Tiempo. 1996. "Campesinos Impiden Toma Guerrillera En Santander" (Campesinos Impede Guerrilla Attack in Santander). *El Tiempo*, April 12, 1996.

El Tiempo. 2001a. "Paz: 500 Diálogos Clandestinos" (Peace: 500 Clandestine Dialogues). *El Tiempo*, November 11, 2001.

El Tiempo. 2001b. "Paeces Impiden Ataque De Las Farc" (Paez Impede FARC Attack). *El Tiempo*, November 14, 2001.

El Tiempo. 2002a. "Lo De Nosotros Son Las Veredas" (What's Ours Are the Villages). *El Tiempo*, September 11, 2002.

El Tiempo. 2002b. "No Les Serviremos Ni a Uribe Ni a las Farc" (We Won't Serve Uribe nor the FARC). *El Tiempo*, July 29, 2002.

El Tiempo. 2002c. "FARC Acechan a Juntas Comunales." *El Tiempo*, July 25, 2002.

El Tiempo. 2004. "Comunales Preocupados Por Politización Y Amenazas." *El Tiempo*, December 7, 2004.

El Tiempo. 2005. "A Prueba, Neutralidad de Ocho Comunidades de Paz en el Urabá." *El Tiempo*, March 9, 2005.

El Tiempo. 2008a. "Por ser de izquierda, asesinaron a líder comunitario en San Vicente del Caguán." *El Tiempo*, December 15, 2008.

El Tiempo. 2008b. "Acusan a 'Botalón' por Masacre en Cimitarra (Santander)." *El Tiempo*, August 8, 2008.

El Tiempo. 2009. "Por masacre de 12 taladores en Cimitarra, aseguran a 'Botalón'" (For Massacre of 12 Woodcutters in Cimitarra, 'Botalón' Is Imprisoned). *El Tiempo*, January 7, 2009.

El Tiempo. "Justicia y Paz: 5 años" (editorial). 2010. *El Tiempo*, July 25, 2010.

Ellickson, Robert C. 1991. *Order without Law: How Neighbors Settle Disputes.* Cambridge: Harvard University Press.

Elster, Jon. 2000. "Analytic Narratives by Bates, Greif, Levi, Rosenthal, and Weingast: A Review and Response." *American Political Science Review* 94(3): 685–702.

England, Andrew. 2008. "Syria's Religious Tolerance Belies Critics." *Financial Times*, September 15, 2008.

Equipo Nizkor. 2001. "Colombia Nunca Más: Crímenes de Lesa Humanidad (Zona 14ª 1966, Tomo I)." Proyecto Nunca Más, Colombia.

Estado Mayor del Bloque Oriental FARC-EP. 2002. "Contra las Instituciones del Estado."

Fahim, Kareem. 2012. "Stalemate Deals Grief and Fury in Syria." *The New York Times*, January 23, 2012.

Falla, Ricardo. 1994. *Massacres in the Jungle: Ixcán, Guatemala, 1975–1982.* Boulder: Westview Press.

Fals Borda, Orlando. 1960. *Acción Comunal en Una Vereda Colombiana: Su Aplicación, Sus Resultados y Su Interpretación.* Bogotá: Universidad Nacional de Colombia, Departamento de Sociología.

FARC-EP. Date unknown. "Boletín informativo del Comité Temático de las FARC-EP N 11."

Fearon, James. 1994. "Domestic Political Audiences and the Escalation of International Disputes." *American Political Science Review* 88(3): 577–592.

Fearon, James D. 1995. "Rationalist Explanations for War." *International Organization* 49(3): 379–414.

Fearon, James D. 1996. "Causes and Counterfactuals in Social Science: Exploring and Analogy between Celular Automata and Historical Processes." In *Counterfactual Thought Experiments in World Politics: Logical, Methodological, and Psychological Perspectives*, eds. Philip E. Tetlock and Aaron Belkin. Princeton: Princeton University Press.

Fearon, James D. and David D. Laitin. 1996. "Explaining Interethnic Cooperation." *American Political Science Review* 90(4): 715–735.

Fearon, James D. and David D. Laitin. 2003. "Ethnicity, Insurgency, and Civil War." *American Political Science Review* 97(1): 75–90.

Fearon, James D. and David D. Laitin. 2008. "Integrating Qualitative and Quantitative Methods." In *The Oxford Handbook of Political Methodology*.

Fearon, James D., Macartan Humphreys, and Jeremy M. Weinstein. 2009. "Can Development Aid Contribute to Social Cohesion after Civil War? Evidence from a Field Experiment in Post-Conflict Liberia." *The American Economic Review* 99(2): 287–291.

Fernandez, Edwin. 2011. "Officials Want Harassed Village Declared Peace Zone." *Philippine Daily Inquirer*, February 9, 2011.

Ferro, Juan Guillermo and Graciela Uribe Ramón. 2002. *El Orden de la Guerra: Las FARC-EP entre la Organización y la Política*. Bogotá: CEJA.

Filkins, Dexter. 2010. "Afghan Tribe Vows to Fight Taliban in Return for U.S. Aid." *The New York Times*, January 28, 2010.

Fisk, Robert. 2013. "Syria Crisis: In Sacred Maaloula, Where They Speak the Language of Christ, War Leads Neighbours into Betrayal." *The Independent*, September 25, 2013.

Forero, Juan. 2005. "Colombia War Spills Into Indians' Peaceful World." *The New York Times*, May 2, 2005.

Fumerton, Mario. 2001. "Rondas Campesinas in the Peruvian Civil War: Peasant Self-Defence Organisations in Ayacucho." *Bulletin of Latin American Research* 20(4): 470–497.

Funes, Maria J. 1998. "Social Responses to Political Violence in the Basque Country: Peace Movements and Their Audience." *The Journal of Conflict Resolution* 42(4): 493–510.

Gall, Carlotta. 2009. "U.S. Faces Resentment in Afghan Region." *The New York Times*, July 3, 2009.

Gall, Carlotta. 2010. "U.S. Hopes Afghan Councils Will Undermine Taliban." *The New York Times*, June 19, 2010.

Gall, Carlotta and Abdul Wahhed Wafa. 2006. "Taliban Truce in District of Afghanistan Sets Off Debate." *The New York Times*, December 2, 2006.

Galula, David. 1965. *Counter-Insurgency Warfare Theory and Practice*. Second Printing edition. Praeger.

García, Alejandro. 1996. *Hijos de la Violencia: Campesinos de Colombia Sobreviven a "Golpes" de Paz*. Madrid: Libros de la Catarata.

García Durán, S. J., Mauricio 2005. "*To What Extent Is There a Peace Movement in Colombia? An Assessment of the Country's Peace Mobilization, 1978–2003.*" Ph.D. dissertation, University of Bradford.

García Durán, Mauricio. 2006a. *Movimiento por la paz en Colombia. 1978–2003*. Bogotá: UNDP Colombia, CINEP, COLCIENCIAS Colombia.

García Durán, S. J., Mauricio. 2006b. "De Turbay a Uribe: Sin Política de Paz pero con Conflicto Armado." In *En la Encrucijada: Colombia en el Siglo XXI*, ed. Francisco Leal Buitrago. Bogotá: Grupo Editorial Norma.

Geddes, Barbara. 2003. *Paradigms and Sand Castles: Theory Building and Research Design in Comparative Politics*. Ann Arbor: The University of Michigan Press.

George, Alexander L. 1979. "Case Studies and Theory Development: The Method of Structured, Focused Comparison." In *Diplomacy: New Approaches in History, Theory and Policy*, ed. P. G Lauren. New York: The Free Press.

Gettleman, Jeffrey. 2007. "Chaos in Darfur Rises as Arabs Fight with Arabs," *The New York Times*, September 3, 2007.

Gettleman, Jeffrey. 2009a. "Armed with Little but Resolve, and Defending a Hollowed Village," *The New York Times*, February 18, 2009.

Gettleman, Jeffrey. 2009b. "For Somalia, Chaos Breeds Religious War," *The New York Times*, May 24, 2009.

Gettleman, Jeffrey. 2009c. "Radical Islamists Slipping Easily Into Kenya," *The New York Times*, July 22, 2009.

Gettleman, Jeffrey and Eric Schmitt. 2009. "US Aided a Failed Plan to Rout Ugandan Rebels," *The New York Times*, February 6, 2009.

Gitlitz, John S. and Telmo Rojas. 1983. "Peasant Vigilante Committees in Northern Peru." *Journal of Latin American Studies* 15(01): 163–197.

GMH. 2013. *¡Basta Ya! Colombia: Memorias de Guerra y Dignidad*. Bogotá: Imprenta Nacional.

Goldstein, Joseph and Taimoor Shah. 2015. "Taliban Strike Crucial District in Afghanistan." *The New York Times*, June 19, 2015.

Gómez-Suárez, Andrei. 2007. "Perpetrator Blocs, Genocidal Mentalities and Geographies: The Destruction of the Unión Patriótica in Colombia and Its Lessons for Genocide Studies." *Journal of Genocide Research* 9(4): 637–660.

Gopal, Anand and Matthew Rosenberg. 2009. "Afghan Villagers Attack Taliban, Sever Ties with Militants." *The Wall Street Journal*, July 19, 2009.

Greene, David. 2010. "A Village Clings to Hope Amid Dagestan's Dangers." *National Public Radio*, March 18, 2010.

Guerra Curvelo, Weildler. 2004. *La Disputa Y La Palabra: La Ley En La Sociedad Wayuu*. Bogotá: Ministerio de Cultura.

Guevara, Che. 1961. *Guerilla Warfare*. (Stone, I. F., *The Authorized Translation*). Vintage Books.

Gutiérrez Sanín, Francisco. 2008. "Telling the Difference: Guerrillas and Paramiliataries in the Colombian Civil War." *Politics & Society* 36(3).

Gutiérrez Sanín, Francisco and Mauricio Barón. 2005. "Re-Stating the State: Paramilitary Territorial Control and Political Order in Colombia (1978–2004)." *Crisis States Program* Working Paper no. 66. Bogotá.

Guzmán Campos, Germán, Orlando Fals Borda, and Eduardo Umaña Luna. 1963. *La Violencia en Colombia, Estudio de un Proceso Social*. Bogotá: Ediciones Tercer Mundo.

Hafner-Burton, Emilie. 2008. "Sticks and Stones: Naming and Shaming the Human Rights Enforcement Problem." *International Organization* 62(4): 689–716.

Hafner-Burton, Emilie. 2009. *Forced to Be Good: Why Trade Agreements Boost Human Rights*. Cornell, NY: Cornell University Press.

Hancock, Landon E. and Christopher Mitchell, eds. 2007. *Zones of Peace*. Bloomfield, CT: Kumarian Press, Inc.

Hartlyn, Jonathan. 1988. *The Politics of Coalition Rule in Colombia*. Cambridge: Cambridge University Press.

Hassan, Hassan. 2014. "Hope Springs in Syria? How Local Cease-fires Have Brought Some Respite to Damascus." *Foreign Affairs Snapshot*, January 22, 2014.

Heaton, Laura and Maggie Fick. 2010. "Field Dispatch: The Arrow Boys of Southern Sudan – An Army of the Willing." Available at: www.enoughproject.org/ publica tions/arrow-boys-sudan.

Henao Delgado, Hernán and María Teresa Arcila Estrada. 1993. *Nariño, Antioquia*. Medellín: CORNARE; Universidad de Antioquia (INER).

Henderson, James D. 1985. *When Colombia Bled: A History of the Violence in Tolima*. Tuscaloosa, AL: University of Alabama Press.

Hernández Delgado, Esperanza. 2004. *Resistencia Civil Artesana de Paz: Experiencias Indígenas, Afrodescendientes y Campesinas*. Bógota: Editorial Pontificia Universidad Javeriana: SUIPPCOL.

Hirschman, Albert O. 1970. *Exit, Voice, and Loyalty: Responses to Decline in Firms, Organizations, and States*. Cambridge, MA: Harvard University Press.

Holmes, Jennifer S., Sheila Amin Gutiérrez De Piñeres, and Kevin M. Curtin. 2007. "A Subnational Study of Insurgency: FARC Violence in the 1990s." *Studies in Conflict & Terrorism* 30(3): 249–65.

Houghton, Juan and William Villa. 2005. *Los territorios Indígenas Colombianos: Teorías y Prácticas*. Bogotá: Centro de Cooperación al Indígena, CECOIN.

Human Rights Watch. 2003. *"You'll Learn Not to Cry: Child Combatants in Colombia."* Human Rights Watch Report.

Human Rights Watch. 2015. "Colombia: Top Brass Linked to Extrajudicial Executions." June 24, 2015.

Humphreys, Macartan and Jeremy Weinstein. 2006a. "Handling and Manhandling Civilians in Civil War." *American Political Science Review* 100(3): 429–447.

Humphreys, Macartan and Jeremy Weinstein. 2006b. "Handling and Manhandling Civilians: Derivation of Hypotheses." Appendix.

Humphreys, Macartan and Jeremy M. Weinstein. 2008. "Who Fights? The Determinants of Participation in Civil War." *American Journal of Political Science* 52(2): 436–55.

Huntingon, Samuel P. 1967. "Political Stability and Security in South Vietnam." Report to USAID, December 1967.

Inglehart, Ronald, Miguel Basáñez, and Alejandro Menéndez Moreno. 1998. *Human Values and Beliefs: a Cross-Cultural Sourcebook*. Ann Arbor: University of Michigan Press.

Internal Displacement Monitoring Centre (IDMC). 2010. "Colombia Current IDP Figures." Available at: www.internal-displacement.org/idmc/website/countries.nsf/ (httpEnvelopes)/A7E1B7BD7528B329C12575E500525165? OpenDocument#sources.

Internal Displacement Monitoring Centre (IDMC). 2014. "Philippines IDP Figures Analysis." February 2014. www.internal-displacement.org/south-and-south-east-asia/ philippines/figures-analysis.

Internal Displacement Monitoring Centre (IDMC). 2015. "Syria IDP Figures Analysis." December 31, 2015. www.internal-displacement.org/middle-east-and-north-africa/ syria/figures-analysis.

Ivan García, Jorge. 1994. "Asociaciones De Seguridad Rural Son Un Invento Viejo" (Rural Security Associations are an Old Invention). *El Tiempo*, December 16, 1994.

Jaffe, Greg. 2009. "U.S. Plans to Shift Forces to Populated Areas of Afghanistan." *The Washington Post*, September 22, 2009.

Jawad Al-Tamimi, Aymenn. 2012. "Syria's Assyrians, Caught in the Middle." *The Daily Star* (Beirut), December 7, 2012.

Justicia y Paz (Comisión Intereclesial de Justicia y Paz). 2003. "Colombia: Desplazadas forzadamente familias del Cacarica." September 12, 2003.

Kalyvas, Stathis. 2006. *The Logic of Violence in Civil War*. Cambridge: Cambridge University Press.

Kalyvas, Stathis and Matthew Kocher. 2009. "The Dynamics of Violence in Vietnam: An Analysis of the Hamlet Evaluation System (HES)." *Journal of Peace Research* 46(3): 335–55.

Kamman, Curtis W. 1999. "FARC Abusing Civilians in 'Despeje.'" Confidential Cable 004726. United States Embassy, Colombia; National Security Archive, May 10, 1999.

Kant, Immanuel. 1970. *Kant's Political Writings*. Hans Reiss, ed. translated by H.B. Nisbet. Oxford: Oxford University Press.

Kaplan, Oliver. 2010. *Civilian Autonomy in Civil War*. Ph.D. thesis, Department of Political Science, Stanford University.

Kaplan, Oliver. 2012. "A New Approach to the Drug War" (A novel model offers hope for communities battling narcos and militants). *National Interest*, July 26, 2012.

Kaplan, Oliver. 2013a. "Protecting Civilians in Civil War: The Institution of the ATCC in Colombia." *Journal of Peace Research* 50(3): 351–367.

Kaplan, Oliver. 2013b. "Nudging Armed Groups: How Civilians Transmit Norms of Protection." *Stability: International Journal of Security and Development* 2(3): 62.

Kaplan, Oliver. 2013c. "Shootings and Shamans: Indigenous Group Authority Structures and Civil War Violence in Colombia," working paper.

Kaplan, Oliver and Enzo Nussio. 2015. "Community Counts: The Social Reintegration of Ex-combatants in Colombia." *Conflict Management and Peace Science*. DOI: 10.1177/0738894215614506

Kaplan, Oliver and Enzo Nussio. 2016. "Explaining Recidivism of Ex-combatants in Colombia." *Journal of Conflict Resolution*. DOI: 10.1177/0022002716644326

Karam, Zeina. 2012. "War Rips Apart Families, Neighbors in Syria as Political, Sectarian Loyalties Take Over." *Associated Press*, November 30, 2012.

Keck, Margaret and Kathryn Sikkink. 1998. *Activists Beyond Borders*. Ithaca, NY and London: Cornell University Press.

Keohane, Robert O. 1984. *After Hegemony: Cooperation and Discord in the World Political Economy*. Princeton, NJ: Princeton University Press.

Kernell, Samuel. 1986. *Going Public: New Strategies of Presidential Leadership*. Washington, D.C.: CQ Press.

Khalek, Rania. 2013. "Syria's Nonviolent Resistance Is Dying to Be Heard." *Al Jazeera America*, September 9, 2013.

Khan, Riaz. 2009. "Tribal Elders Gunned Down by Taliban in Pakistan." *The Associated Press*, September 24, 2009.

King, Gary, Robert O. Keohane, and Sidney Verba. 1994. *Designing Social Inquiry: Scientific Inference in Qualitative Research*. Princeton, NJ: Princeton University Press.

Kirkpatrick, David D. 2012. "Syrian Children Speak of Revenge against Alawites." *The New York Times*, September 3, 2012.

Kirkpatrick, David D. 2013. "Syrian Civilians Take Reins in Test of Self-Government." *The New York Times*, March 1, 2013.

Kline, Harvey F. 2003. "Colombia: Lawlessness, Drug Trafficking, and Carving Up the State." In *State Failure and State Weakness in a Time of Terror*, ed. Robert I. Rotberg. Washington, D.C.: Brookings Institution Press.

Krasner, Stephen D. 1982. "Structural Causes and Regime Consequences: Regimes as Intervening Variables." *International Organization* 36(2): 15–205.

Kriger, Norma J. 1992. *Zimbabwe's Guerrilla War: Peasant Voices*. Cambridge, New York: Cambridge University Press.

Kuperman, Alan J. 2000. "Rwanda in Retrospect." *Foreign Affairs*, January/February 2000.

Kuran, Timur. 1991. "Now Out of Never: The Element of Surprise in the East European Revolution of 1989." *World Politics* 44(October): 7–48.

Lacina, Bethany. 2006. "Explaining the Severity of Civil Wars." *Journal of Conflict Resolution* 50(2): 276–289.

Ladrón de Guevara and Andrés Dávila. 1998. "El Ejército Colombiano: Un Actor Más de la Violencia." In *Las violencias: inclusión creciente*, ed. Jaime Arocha Rodríguez. Santafé de Bogotá: Centro de Estudios Sociales Fac. de Ciencias Humanas Univ. Nacional.

Laitin, David D. and Avner Greif. 2004. "A Theory of Endogenous Institutional Change." *American Political Science Review* 98(4): 633–652.

Leal Buitrago, Francisco. 1990. *Clientelismo: El Sistema Político Y Su Expresión Regional*. 1st ed. Bogotá: Instituto de Estudios Políticos y Relaciones Internacionales.

Leal Buitrago, Francisco, ed. 2006. *En la Encrucijada: Colombia en el siglo XXI*. Bogotá: Editorial Norma.

Lederach, John Paul. 1997. *Building Peace: Sustainable Reconciliation in Divided Societies*. Washington, D.C.: United States Institute of Peace Press.

Lederach, John Paul. 2003. "The Mystery of Transformative Times and Spaces: Exploring a Theology of Grassroots Peacemaking." In *Artisans of Peace: Grassroots Peacemaking Among Christian Communities*, eds. Mary Ann Cejka and Thomas Bamat. Maryknoll, NY: Orbis Books.

Lederach, John Paul. 2005. *The Moral Imagination: The Art and Soul of Building Peace*. Oxford: Oxford University Press.

Lee, Zosimo E. 2000. "Peace Zones as Special Development Areas: A Preliminary Assessment." In *Building Peace: Essays on Psychology and the Culture of Peace*, eds. A.B.I. Bernardo and C.D. Ortigas. Manila: De la Salle University Press.

LeGrand, Catherine. 1986. *Frontier Expansion and Peasant Protest in Colombia, 1850–1936*. Albuquerque, NM: University of New Mexico Press.

León, Juanita. 2004. *No somos machos, pero somos muchos*. Bogotá: Grupo Editorial Norma.

Levitsky, Steven and Gretchen Helmke. 2006. *Informal Institutions and Democracy: Lessons from Latin America*. Baltimore, MD: The Johns Hopkins University Press.

Lichbach, Mark. 1994. "What Makes Rational Peasants Revolutionary: Dilemma, Paradox, and Irony in Peasant Rebellion." *World Politics* 46: 383–418.

Lichbach, Mark. 1998. "Contending Theories of Contentious Politics and the Structure-Action Problem of Social Order." *Annual Review of Political Science* 1998(1): 401–424.

Lieberman, Evan S. 2005. "Nested Analysis as a Mixed-Method Strategy for Comparative Research." *The American Political Science Review* 99(3): 435–452.

Llano Cano, John Jairo. 2006. *El Movimiento Comunal en Colombia.*

Lohmann, Susanne. 1994. "The Dynamics of Informational Cascades: The Monday Demonstrations in Leipzig, East Germany, 1989–91." *World Politics* 47(October): 42–101.

Lorente, Luis. 1985. *Distribución De La Propiedad Rural En Colombia, 1960–1984.* Bogotá: Ministerio de Agricultura; Corporación de Estudios Ganaderos y Agrícolas.

Luttwak, Edward N. 1999. "Give War a Chance." *Foreign Affairs* 78: 36–44.

Mackety, Robert. 2014. "Syrians Protest Assad and Islamist Militants." *NYTimes.com*, The Lede Blog, January 3, 2014.

Magaloni, Beatriz, Alberto Díaz-Cayeros and Federico Estevez. Forthcoming. *Strategies of Vote-Buying: Poverty, Democracy, and Social Transfers in Mexico.*

Mahony, Liam and Luis Enrique Eguren. 1997. *Unarmed Bodyguards: International Accompaniment for the Protection of Human Rights.* West Hartford, CT: Kumarian Press.

Malek, Alia. 2012. "Syrian Armenians Seek Shelter in Armenia." *The New York Times*, December 11, 2012.

Malkasian, Carter. 2013. *War Comes to Garmser: Thirty Years of Conflict on the Afghan Frontier.* London: Oxford University Press.

Mallari Jr., Delfin. 2007. "Solcom Chief Slams 'Peace Zone.'" *Philippine Daily Inquirer*, October 4, 2007.

Mao, Zedong. 1961. *On Guerrilla Warfare.* New York: Praeger.

MAPP/OEA. 2010. "Décimo Cuarto Informe Trimestral del Secretario General al Consejo Permanente sobre la Misión de Apoyo al Proceso de Paz en Colombia." OEA/Ser.G CP/doc. 4486/10, April 26, 2010.

Martz, John D. 1997. *The Politics of Clientelism: Democracy and State in Colombia.* New Brunswick, CT and London: Transaction Publishers.

Marwell, Gerald and Pamela Oliver. 1993. *The Critical Mass in Collective Action.* Cambridge: Cambridge University Press.

Mason, David T. 1996. "Insurgency, Counterinsurgency, and the Rational Peasant." *Public Choice* 86(1–2): 63–83.

Masood, Salman. 2009. "Taliban Ambush in Pakistan Kills 8 Militiamen." *The New York Times*, September 25, 2009.

McAdam, Doug, Sidney Tarrow and Charles Tilly 2001. *Dynamics of Contention.* Cambridge: Cambridge University Press.

McCarthy, John D. and Mayer N. Zald. 1977. "Resource Mobilization and Social Movements: A Partial Theory." *The American Journal of Sociology* 82(6): 1212–1241.

McChrystal, Stanley A. 2009. "COMISAF Initial Assessment (Unclassified)." U.S. Department of Defense, September 21, 2009. www.washingtonpost.com/wp-dyn/content/article/2009/09/21/AR2009092100110.html

McDonnell, Patrick J. 2014. "In Syria's Capital, Residents Recall a Sectarian Tolerance Gone By." *Los Angeles Times*, April 19, 2014.

McKenna, T. 1998. *Muslim Rulers and Rebels: Everyday Politics and Armed Separatism in the Southern Philippines.* Berkeley, CA: University of California Press.

Meyer, John W. and Brian Rowan. 1977. "Institutionalized Organizations: Formal Structure as Myth and Ceremony." *American Journal of Sociology* 83(2): 340–363.

Milgrom, Paul R. and Weingast Barry R. 1990. "The Role of Institutions in the Revival of Trade: The Law Merchant, Private Judges, and the Champagne Fairs." *Economics and Politics* (2): 1–23.

Ministerio de Gobierno. 1993. *Censo Nacional Calificado de Juntas de Acción Comunal, 1993*. Santa Fé de Bogotá: Ministerio de Gobierno, Dirección General de Integración y Desarrollo de la Comunidad (DIGIDEC).

Molano, Alfredo. 1987. *Selva Adentro: Una Historia Orral de la Colonización del Guaviare*. Bogotá: Ancora Editores.

Molano, Alfredo and Alejandro Reyes. 1978. "Los Bombardeos en el Pato." *Controversia* 89.

Molano, Alfredo, Daniel Bland, and Lance Selfa. 1994. "The Dispossessed." In *La Historia al Final del Milenio: Ensayos de Historiografía Colombiana y Latinoamericana*. Bogotá, Colombia: Editorial Universidad Nacional, Facultad de Ciencias Humanas, Departamento de Historia.

Moreno, Guillermo Cardona. 2008. *Acción Comunal: Cincuenta Años Vista a Través de los Congresos Nacionales*. Manuscript.

Muana, Patrick K. 1997. "The Kamajoi Militia: Civil War, Internal Displacement and the Politics of Counter-Insurgency." *Africa Development* 22(3/4): 77–99.

Mullen, Michael. 2009. "Strategic Communication: Getting Back to Basics." *Joint Forces Quarterly* (55 October): 2–4.

Murdie, Amanda. 2014. *Help or Harm: The Human Security Effects of International NGOs*. Stanford, CA: Stanford University Press.

National Public Radio. 2013. "Grants to Rural Afghan Villages Pay Off." March 18, 2013.

Navarrete-Frías, Carolina and Francisco E. Thoumi. 2005. "Illegal Drugs and Human Rights of Peasants and Indigenous Communities: The Case of Colombia." Management of Social Transformations Policy Papers (15), United Nations Educational, Scientific and Cultural Organization (UNESCO).

Naylor, Hugh. 2015. "In New Sign of Assad's Troubles, Syria's Druze Turn Away from President." *The Washington Post*, July 17, 2015.

Naylor, Hugh. 2016. "Al-Qaeda Affiliate Faces Unusual Backlash from Fed-up Syrians." *The Washington Post*, April 13, 2016.

Nechama Tec. 1993. *Defiance: The Bielski Partisans*. 1st ed. New York: Oxford University Press.

Nordland, Rod and Dalal Mawad. 2012. "Palestinians in Syria Drawn into the Violence." *The New York Times*, July 30, 2012.

Nordstrom, Carolyn. 1992. "The Backyard Front." In *The Paths to Domination, Resistance, and Terror*, eds. JoAnn Martin and Carolyn Nordstrom. Berkeley: University of California Press.

Nordstrom, Carolyn. 1997. "From War to Peace – Examples from Sri Lanka and Mozambique." In *Cultural Variation in Conflict Resolution: Alternatives to Violence*, eds. Douglas P. Fry and Kaj Björkqvist. Psychology Press.

NOW News. 2013. "Syrians Protest against Islamist Group Violations in Idlib." *NOW News* (Beirut), January 25, 2013.

O'Donnell, Guillermo. 1999. "Polyarchies and the (Un)Rule of Law in Latin America: A Partial Conclusion." In *The (Un)Rule of Law and the Underprivileged in Latin America*, eds. Guillermo O'Donnell Juan E. Méndez and Paulo Sergio Pinheiro. Notre Dame, IN: University of Notre Dame Press.

Ober, Josiah. 2008. *Democracy and Knowledge*. Princeton, NJ: Princeton University Press.

Observatorio de Paz Integral. 2005. "La Población Civil y el Conflicto Armado en el Magdalena Medio, 1996–2004." Barrancabermeja.

Observatorio del Programa Presidencial de Derechos Humanos y DIH. 2001. "*Panorama Actual del Magdalena Medio*." Bogotá: Vicepresidencia de la República de Colombia.

Offstein, Norman. 2005. *National, Departmental, and Municipal Rural Agricultural Land Distribution in Colombia: Analyzing the Web of Inequality, Poverty and Violence*. CEDE Working Paper. Bogotá: Universidad de Los Andes.

Oficina del Alto Comisionado para la Paz. 2006. *Proceso de Paz con las Autodefensas*. Bogotá: Presidencia de la República de Colombia.

Olson, Mancur. 1965. *The Logic of Collective Action: Public Goods and the Theory of Groups*. Cambridge, MA: Harvard University Press.

Oquist, Paul H. 1980. *Violence, Conflict, and Politics in Colombia*. New York: Academic Press.

Ortiz Sarmiento, Carlos Miguel. 1985. *Estado y Subversión en Colombia: La Violencia en el Quindío, Años 50*. Bogotá, Colombia: CIDER Uniandes, Fondo Editorial CEREC.

Otis, John. 2010. "What's Andy Warhol Doing in Rural Colombia?" *Global Post*, March 10, 2010. Available at: www.globalpost.com/print/5529759.

Oweis, Khaled Yacoub. 2013. "Fearing Stark Future, Syrian Alawites Meet in Cairo." *Reuters*, March 23, 2013.

OXFAM and other NGOs. 2009. "Caught in the Conflict: Civilians and the International Security Strategy in Afghanistan." Available at: www.humansecuritygateway .com/documents/OXFAM_Civilians_InternationalSecurityStrategy_Afghanistan.pdf.

Páez Segura, José Antonio. 2005. *Los Espacios Humanitarios: Una Pedagogía en la Vida y Para la Vida*. Bucaramanga: Programa de Paz y Desarrollo de Magdalena Medio (PPDMM).

Palacios, Marco. 2006. *Between Legitimacy and Violence*. Durham, NC: Duke University Press.

Patterson, Anne W. 2000. "From the Outside Looking In: Meta/Caquetá Residents View the Despeje." Confidential Cable, 010660. United States Embassy, Colombia; National Security Archive, December 4, 2000.

Patterson, Anne W. 2002. "Colombia's Meta Department–FARC Engaged in Hostile Activities/Paramilitaries Not a Factor.'" Confidential Cable 001202. United States Embassy, Colombia; National Security Archive, February 7, 2002.

Pearce, Jenny. 1997. "Sustainable Peace-Building in the South: Experiences from Latin America." *Development in Practice* 7(4): 438.

Pearson, Craig. 2009. "New Afghan Strategy Tackles One Village at a Time." *CanWest News Service*. Available at: www.canada.com.

Peña, Carina. 1997. "La Guerrilla Resiste Muchas Miradas: El Crecimiento de las FARC en los Municipios Cercanos a Bogotá: Caso del Frente 22 en Cundinamarca." *Análisis Político* SEP/DIC 1997(No. 32): 83–99.

Peñaranda, Ricardo. 2006. "Resistencia Civil y Tradiciones de Resistencia en el Suroccidente Colombiano." In *Nuestra Guerra Sin Nombre: Transformaciones del Conflicto en Colombia*, eds. María Emma Wills, Francisco Gutiérrez and Gonzalo Sánchez Gómez. Bogotá: Grupo Editorial Norma, Instituto de Estudios Políticos y Relaciones Internacionales (IEPRI).

Perlez, Jane and Pir Zubair Shah. 2008a. "Pakistan Uses Tribal Militias in Taliban War." *The New York Times*, October 24, 2008.

Perlez, Jane and Pir Zubair Shah. 2008b. "As Taliban Overwhelm Police, Pakistanis Hit Back." *The New York Times*, November 2, 2008.

Perlez, Jane. 2009. "Taliban Seize Vital Pakistan Area Closer to the Capital." *The New York Times*, April 23, 2009.

Petersen, Roger. 2001. *Resistance and Rebellion: Lessons from Eastern Europe.* Cambridge: Cambridge University Press.

Pizarro León-Gómez, Eduardo, Ricardo Peñaranda and Pierre Gilhodes. 1991. *Las Farc (1949–1966), de La Autodefensa a La Combinación de Todas Las Formas de Lucha.* Bogotá: Tercer Mundo Editores.

Popkin, Samuel L. 1979. *The Rational Peasant: The Political Economy of Rural Society in Vietnam.* Berkeley, CA: University of California Press.

Presidencia de la República de Colombia. 2013. "Presidente Santos, en la entrega del documento 'De la violencia a la sociedad de los derechos.'" December 10, 2013.

Project Ploughshares. 2013. "Philippines-CPP/NPA." *Project Ploughshares.* http://plough shares.ca/pl_armedconflict/philippines-cppnpa-1969-first-combat-deaths.

Putnam, Robert D. 1993. *Making Democracy Work: Civic Traditions in Modern Italy.* Princeton, NJ: Princeton University Press.

Quitasol, Kimberlie. 2014. "Villagers Help Search for Rebel Camp in Sagada." *Philippine Daily Inquirer*, May 16, 2014.

Raghavan, Sudarsan. 2010. "In Somalia's War, a New Challenger Is Pushing Back Radical al-Shabab Militia." *The Washington Post*, May 27, 2010.

Ramírez, María Clemencia. 2001. *Entre el Estado y la Guerrilla: Identidad y Ciudadanía en el Movimiento de los Campesinos Cocaleros del Putumayo.* Bogotá, Colombia: Instituto Colombiano de Antropología e Historia, Colciencias.

Ramírez, Sara and Christopher Mitchell. 2009. "Local Peace Communities in Colombia: An Initial Comparison of Three Cases." In *Colombia: Building Peace in a Time of War*, ed. Virginia Bouvier. Washington, D.C.: USIP Press.

RECORRE. 2007. Red de Comunidades en Ruptura y Resistencia (RECORRE) www.prensarural.org/recorre, 2007 [cited 2007].

Rempe, Dennis M. 1999. "The Origin of Internal Security in Colombia: Part I — A CIA Special Team Surveys La Violencia, 1959–60." *Small Wars & Insurgencies* 10(3): 24–61.

Restrepo, Gloria Inés. 2005. "Dinámicas e Interrrelaciones en los Procesos de Resistencia Civil: Estudio de Caso Comparado de los Procesos de Resistencia Civil Organizada de la Asociación de Trabajadores Campesinos del Carare y la Comunidad de Paz de San José de Apartadó." B.A. thesis, Universidad Nacional de Colombia.

Restrepo, Gloria Inés. 2006. "Dinámicas e Interacciones en los Procesos de Resistencia Civil. Estudio de Caso Comparado entre la Comunidad de Paz de San José de Apartadó y la Asociación de Trabajadores Campesinos del Carare." *Revista Colombiana de Sociología* 27(2).

Restrepo, Jorge Alberto and Michael Spagat. 2006. "El Conflicto en Colombia: Quién Hizo Qué a Quién? Un Enfoque Cuantitativo (1988–2003)." In *Nuestra Guerra sin Nombre: Transformaciones del Conflicto en Colombia*, eds. María Emma Wills Francisco Gutiérrez and Gonzalo Sánchez Gómez. Bogotá: Grupo Editorial Norma, Instituto de Estudios Políticos y Relaciones Internacionales (IEPRI).

Rettberg, Angelika. 2006. *Buscar la paz en medio del conflicto, un propósito que no da tregua: un estudio de las iniciativas de paz en Colombia (Desde los años 90 hasta hoy).* Bogotá: Universidad de los Andes.

Reuters. 2014. "Philippines, Muslim Rebels Sign Final Peace Deal to End Conflict." *Reuters*, March 27, 2014.

Richani, Nazih. 2002. *Systems of Violence: The Political Economy of War and Peace in Colombia.* Albany, NY: SUNY Press.

Roldán, Mary. 2002. *Blood and Fire: La Violencia in Antioquia, Colombia, 1946–1953.* Durham, NC: Duke University Press.

Romero, Mauricio. 2003. *Paramilitares y Autodefensas, 1982–2003.* 1st ed. Bogotá, D. C.: Instituto de Estudios Políticos y Relaciones Internacionales, Universidad Nacional de Colombia: Editorial Planeta Colombiana.

Romero, Simon. 2008. "Two Colombias, at War and at Peace." *The New York Times*, September 7, 2009.

Romero, Simon. 2009. "An Isolated Village Finds the Energy to Keep Going." *The New York Times*, October, 16, 2009.

Rubin, Alissa J. 2010a. "As U.S. Frees Detainees, Afghans Ask Why They Were Held." *The New York Times*, March 19, 2010.

Rubin, Alissa J. 2010b. "Taliban Overhaul Image to Win Allies." *The New York Times*, January 21, 2010.

Rubin, Alissa J. and Richard A. Oppel Jr. 2010. "U.S. and Afghanistan Debate More Village Forces." *The New York Times*, July 12, 2010.

Rubio, Mauricio. 1997. "Perverse Social Capital – Some Evidence From Colombia." *Journal of Economic Issues* 31(3).

Ruhl, J. Mark. 1980. "The Military." In *Politics of Compromise: Coalition Government in Colombia*, eds. Ronald G. Hellman R. Albert Berry. New Brunswick, NJ: Transaction Books.

Saeed, Abdirahim. 2012. "Syria: An Attempt to Live a Normal Life." *BBC*, December 24, 2012.

Salazar, Boris and María del Pilar Castillo. 2001. *La Hora de Los Dinosaurios: Conflicto y Depredación en Colombia.* Bogotá: CEREC, Universidad del Valle.

Sánchez Torres, Fabio. 2007. *Las Cuentas de la Violencia: Ensayos Económicos Sobre el Conflicto y el Crimen en Colombia.* Bogotá: Grupo Editorial Norma: Universidad de los Andes, Facultad de Economía.

Sánchez, Fabio and María Del Mar Palau. 2006. "Conflict, Decentralisation, and Local Governance in Colombia, 1974–2004." *CEDE Working Paper*. Bogotá: Universidad de Los Andes.

Sánchez, Gonzalo, and Donny Meertens. 2001. *Bandits, Peasants, and Politics: The Case of "La Violencia" in Colombia.* Austin: University of Texas Press, Institute of Latin American Studies.

Sandoval, Luis. 2004. *La Paz en Movimiento.* Vol. 1 and 2. Bogotá: ISMAC.

Sands, Phil. 2011. "Syria's Palestinians Try to Stay Neutral amid Turmoil." *The National* (UAE), May 5, 2011.

Sands, Phil. 2012. "Syria's Druze community: A Silent Minority in No Rush to Take Sides." *The National* (UAE), February 22, 2012.

Sanford, Victoria. 2003. "Peacebuilding in a War Zone: The Case of Colombian Peace Communities." *International Peacekeeping* 10(2): 107–118.

Sanford, Victoria. 2004. "Contesting Displacement in Colombia: Citizenship and State Sovereignty at the Margins." In *Anthropololgy in the Margins of the State*, eds. Veena Das and Deborah Poole. Santa Fe: School of American Research.

Santos, Jr., Solimon. 2005. *Peace Zones in the Philippines: Concept, Policy and Instruments*. Quezon City: Gaston Z. Ortigas Peace Institute.

Sarmiento Anzola, Libardo. 1998. *Municipios y Regiones de Colombia: Una Mirada Desde la Sociedad Civil*. Bogotá: Fundación Social, Vicepresidencia de Planeación.

Schmidt, Eric, Mark Mazzetti, and Carlotta Gall. 2007. "U.S. Hopes to Use Pakistani Tribes against Al Qaeda." *The New York Times*, November 19, 2007.

Schock, Kurt. 2005. *Unarmed Insurrections: People Power Movements In Nondemocracies*. Minneapolis, MN: University of Minnesota Press.

Scott, James C. 1985. *Weapons of the Weak: Everyday Forms of Peasant Resistance*. New Haven, CT: Yale University Press.

Scott, James C. 1992. *Domination and the Arts of Resistance: Hidden Transcripts*. New Haven, CT: Yale University Press.

Seawright, Jason and John Gerring. 2008. "Case Selection Techniques in Case Study Research: A Menu of Qualitative and Quantitative Options." *Political Research Quarterly* 61(2): 294–308.

Semelin, Jacques. 1993. *Unarmed against Hitler: Civilian Resistance in Europe, 1939–1943*. Westport, CT: Praeger.

Semple, Michael. 2009. *Reconciliation in Afghanistan*. Washington, D.C.: US Institute of Peace Press.

Sepúlveda Roldán, David. 2004. *Saiza: Esplendor y ocaso, un pueblo fantasma del Nudo de Paramillo*. Tierralta (Córdoba): Corpocodesa, ACNUR, Opción Legal.

Sewall, Sarah et al. 2007. *The U.S. Army/Marine Corps Counterinsurgency Field Manual*. University of Chicago Press Ed. University of Chicago Press.

Shanker, Thom. 2010. "Joint Chiefs Chairman Readjusts Principles on Use of Force." *The New York Times*, March 3, 2010.

Sharp, Gene. 1973. *The Politics of Nonviolent Action*. Boston: P. Sargent Publisher.

Sharp, Gene and Joshua Paulson. 2005. *Waging Nonviolent Struggle: 20th Century Practice and 21st Century Potential*. Manchester, NH: Extending Horizons Books.

Shinwari, Ibrahim. 2008. "Elders Refuse to Form Lashkar in Landi Kotal." Available at: www.dawn.com/2008/10/07/local6.htm.

Simmons, Beth A. 2009. *Mobilizing for Human Rights: International Law in Domstic Politics*. 1st ed. Cambridge University Press.

Sivard, Ruth L. 1993. *World Military and Social Expenditures 1993*. Washington, D.C.: World Priorities.

Sly, Liz. 2013. "Syrian War Makes Sudden Appearance at Convent in Historic Christian Town." *The Washington Post*, September 9, 2013.

Snapp, Trevor. 2010. "Sudan's 'Arrow Boys' Challenge Militants." *National Public Radio*, August 2, 2010.

Solomon, Erika. 2012. "In War-Torn Syria, Secrets and Double Lives." *Reuters*, November 14, 2012.

Solomon, Erika. 2014. "Special Report: Amid Syria's Violence, Kurds Carve out Autonomy." *Reuters*, January 22, 2014.

de Sousa Santos, Boaventura and Mauricio García Villegas. 2004. *Emancipación Social y Violencia en Colombia*. 1st ed. Bogotá: Grupo Editorial Norma.

Starn, Orin. 1999. *Nightwatch: The Politics of Protest in the Andes.* Durham, NC: Duke University Press.

Stoll, David. 1993. *Between Two Armies in the Ixil Towns of Guatemala.* New York: Columbia University Press.

Stors, Michel. 2013. "'Their Agendas Have Ruined Us': Religious Tolerance the Latest Casualty of Syrian Conflict." *National Post*, February 20, 2013.

Sudarsky R., John. 2007. *La Evolución del Capital Social en Colombia, 1997 - 2005.* Bogotá: Fundación Antonio Restrepo Barco.

Suleman, Mohammad and Sue Williams. 2003. "Strategies and Structures in Preventing Conflict and Resisting Pressure: A Study of Jaghori District, Afghanistan, under Taliban control." *Steps Toward Conflict Prevention Project (STEPS)* working paper, Collaborative for Development Action (CDA), March 2003.

Taj, Farhat. 2011. *Taliban and Anti-Taliban.* Newcastle upon Tyne: Cambridge Scholars Publishing.

Tarrow, Sidney. 1994. *Power in Movement: Social Movements, Collective Action and Politics.* New York: Cambridge University Press.

Tarrow, Sidney. 2007. "Inside Insurgencies: Politics and Violence in an Age of Civil War." *Perspectives on Politics* 5(3): 587–600.

Tavanti, Marco. 2003. *Las Abejas: Pacifist Resistance and Syncretic Identities in a Globalizing Chiapas.* New York: Routledge.

Tavernise, Sabrina and Irfan Ashraf. 2009. "Attacked, Pakistani Villagers Take on Taliban." *The New York Times*, June 10, 2009.

Taylor, Michael. 1988. "Rationality and Revolutionary Collective Action." In *Rationality and Revolution*, ed. Michael Taylor. New York: Cambridge University Press.

Thoumi, Francisco E. 1997. *Drogas Ilícitas en Colombia: Su Impacto Económico, Político y Social.* Santa Fé de Bogotá: Planeta Colombia Editorial, S.A.

Tice, Austin. 2012. "In Syria, an Oasis from the War." *The Washington Post*, July 15, 2012.

Tilly, Charles. 1992. *Coercion, Capital and European States: AD 990–1992.* Cambridge, MA: Wiley-Blackwell.

Time Magazine. 1964. "Colombia: Death of Black Blood." *Time*, May 8, 1964.

Tobler, W. R. 1970. "A Computer Movie Simulating Urban Growth in the Detroit Region." *Economic Geography* 46: 234–240.

Todd, Molly. 2010. *Beyond Displacement: Campesinos, Refugees, and Collective Action in the Salvadoran Civil War.* Madison, WI: University of Wisconsin Press.

Torres Restrepo, Camilo. 1963. "La Violencia y los Cambios Socio-Culturales en las Areas Rurales Colombianas." *Asociación Colombiana de Sociologia: Memoria del Primer Congreso Nacional de Sociologia*: 95–152.

Torres Sánchez, Jaime and Fabio Barrera Téllez. 1982. *Colombia Represión, 1970–1981.* 2 vols. Bogotá: CINEP.

Torres III, Wilfredo Magno, ed. 2007. *Rido: Clan Feuding and Conflict Management in Mindanao.* Makati City: The Asia Foundation.

Triana y Antorveza, Humberto. 1966. *La Acción Comunal en Colombia: Resultados de una Evaluación en 107 Municipios.* Bogotá: Ministerio de Gobierno, Direccion General de Integracion y Desarrollo de la Comunidad.

Tulio Rodríguez, Marco. 1982. *Los Municipios Olvidados.* Bogotá: El Tiempo.

Tyson, Ann Scott. 2008. "New Joint Effort Aims to Empower Afghan Tribes to Guard Themselves." *The Washington Post*, March 31, 2008.

Tzu, Sun. 2005. *The Art of War*. Boston, MA; London: Shambhala.

U.S. Department of State. 2000. "1999 Country Reports on Human Rights." *Bureau of Democracy, Human Rights and Labor*, February 25, 2000. Available at: www.state.gov/www/global/human_rights/1999_hrp_report/colombia.html.

United Nations. 1998–2006. *Cultivos Ilícitos de Coca: Estadísticas Municipales*. SIMCI, United Nations.

United Nations Development Program (UNDP). 2003. *El Conflicto, Callejón con Salida: Informe Nacional de Desarrollo Humano para Colombia – 2003*. United Nations Development Program, ed. Hernando Gómez Buendía.

United Nations High Commissioner for Refugees (UNHCR). 2010. "UNHCR Global Report 2010."

United Nations High Commissioner for Refugees (UNHCR). 2014. "Syria Tops World List for Forcibly Displaced after Three Years of Conflict." March 14, 2014.

USAID. 2009. "Religion, Conflict and Peacebuilding Toolkit." Available at: www.usaid.gov/our_work/cross-cutting_programs/conflict/publications/docs/Religion_Conflict_and_Peacebuilding_Toolkit.pdf

Valentino, Benjamin. 2004. *Final Solutions: Mass Killing and Genocide in the Twentieth Century*. Ithaca, NY: Cornell University Press.

Vargas Velásquez, Alejo. 1992. *Magdalena Medio Santandereano*. Bogotá, D.C., Colombia: CINEP.

Varshney, Ashutosh. 2002. *Ethnic Conflict and Civic Life: Hindus and Muslims in India*. 2nd ed. New Haven, CT: Yale University Press.

Vásquez Delgado, Teófilo. 2013. *Territorios, conflicto armado y política en el Caguán: 1900–2010*. Universidad de los Andes, Master's thesis, Department of Geography, January 22, 2013.

Verdadabierta.com. 2009. "El Pájaro' señala a capitán de la Policía de nexos con 'paras' y 'narcos.'" August 25, 2009.

Vicepresidencia de la República de Colombia. 2001. "Iniciativas Comunitarias de Paz en Colombia: Semillas que Abren el Camino de la Paz. Fondo de Impresiones para la Paz." *Observatory on Human Rights in Colombia Monthly Newsletter* May 2001(15).

Vicepresidencia de la República de Colombia. 2003a. "Los Derechos Humanos en el Departamento de Meta." Programa Presidencial de Derechos Humanos.

Vicepresidencia de la República de Colombia. 2003b. "Panorama Actual de los Municipios que Conformaron la Zona de Distensión." Programa Presidencial de Derechos Humanos, December 2003.

Villarraga Sarmiento, Álvaro. 2003. *Vida, Dignidad y Territorio: Comunidades de Paz y Zonas Humanitarias en el Urabá y Atrato*. 1st ed. Bogotá D.C.: Fundación Cultura Democrática; Ministerio del Interior; Programa de las Naciones Unidas para el Desarrollo; Programa por la Paz, Compañía de Jesús; Fondo de las Naciones Unidas para la Infancia; Instituto de Estudios para el Desarrollo de la Paz.

Washington Office on Latin America (WOLA). 2011. "In La Macarena, Colombia, a Program on 'Autopilot.'" June 10, 2011, video interview. www.wola.org/commentary/in_la_macarena_a_program_on_autopilot.

Weinstein, Jeremy. 2006. *Inside Rebellion: The Politics of Insurgent Violence*. Cambridge: Cambridge University Press.

Wilkinson, Isambard and Lakki Marwat. 2008. "Pakistan Chieftain Hunts Down Taliban." *Telegraph* (UK), September 22, 2008.

Wills, María Emma, Francisco Gutiérrez and Gonzalo Sánchez Gómez, eds. 2006. *Nuestra Guerra Sin Nombre: Transformaciones del Conflicto en Colombia*. Bogotá: Grupo Editorial Norma, Instituto de Estudios Políticos y Relaciones Internacionales (IEPRI).
Wilson, K. B. 1992. "Cults of Violence and Counter-Violence in Mozambique." *Journal of Southern African Studies* 18(3): 527–582.
Wirpsa, Leslie, David Rothschild and Catalina Garzón. 2009. "The Power of the Bastón: Indigenous Resistance and Peace Building in Colombia." In *Colombia: Building Peace in a Time of War*, ed. Virginia Bouvier. Washington, D.C.: USIP Press.
Wood, Elisabeth. 2003. *Insurgent Collective Action and Civil War in El Salvador*. New York: Cambridge University Press.
World Bank. 2000. *Violence in Colombia: Building Sustainable Peace and Social Capital*. World Bank Publications.
World Bank. 2004. *Voices of the Poor in Colombia: Strengthening Livelihoods, Families, and Communities*, eds. Jairo A. Arboleda and Patti L. Petesch. Washington D.C.: World Bank.
Yarbro, Stan. 1990. "Village in Colombia Battles Violence, Wins Peace Prize." *Christian Science Monitor*, December 4, 1990.
Zamora, Gloria Lucy. 1983. *Los Moradores de la Represión: en el Magdalena Medio*. Bogotá: Centro de Investigaciones y Educación Popular.
Zamosc, Léon. 1982. *Los usuarios campesinos y las luchas por la tierra en los años 70*. Bogotá: CINEP.
Zamosc, Léon. 1986. *The Agrarian Question and the Peasant Movement in Colombia: Struggles of the National Peasant Association, 1967–1981*. Cambridge: Cambridge University Press.
Zamosc, Leon. 2001. "Peasant Struggles of the 1970s in Colombia." In *Power and Popular Protest: Latin American Social Movements*, 2nd ed., eds. Susan Eckstein Merino and Manuel Antonio Garretón. Berkeley: University of California Press.

Index

ACIA, 74
ACR, 103
Afghan National Army (ANA), 286
Afghanistan, 26–27, 59
  armed self-defense, 290
  autonomy actions, 287
  civilian resistance, 287–288
  community-release program, 290
  conflict, 271, 286–287
  government, 287, 289
  organizational capacity, 288
  social cohesion, 287
  territorial control, 288
  tribal jirga, 285
  tribal structures, 287
  U.S. war, 310
AFP, 276, 281, 284–285, 296
Afro-Colombian
  autonomy, 74
  collective territories, 74
  conflict resolution, 74
  consejos comunitarios, 74, 130, 157
  organizations, 13, 25, 112
  population, 74, 130
agricultural cooperatives, 13, 39, 107, 110,
  131, 281
al-Assad, Pres. Bashar, 291
Alawite, 292, 295
Aleppo, 295
al-Nusra Front, 292–294, 297
Al-Qaeda, 292, 299
Amazon region, 138
Amazonas (department), 138

Anbar Province, 28
Anolaima, 170–171, 180, 220, 225
Antioquia, 53, 74, 82, 104, 123, 138
ANUC, 13, 131
  activism, 132
  effects, 71
  measurement, 132
  militancy, 132
  stigma, 132
Arauca, 138
Armed Forces of the Philippines. *See* AFP
armed groups
  attitudes toward violence, 36, 40, 55, 57, 60,
    116–117, 256
  behavior, 8, 10, 18, 23, 26, 34, 60, 127, 255,
    266, 303
    abusive, 54
    norms, 54–55
    violent behavior, 18, 57, 184, 256
  characteristics, 55–60
  choice set, 26, 35
  civilian collaboration, 48
  civilian response, 16
  coercion, 9, 11, 19–20, 35, 43, 49, 60, 71,
    134, 208
  competition, 34
  control, 4, 18, 23
    territorial, 55–56, 114, 189
    urban, 15
  costs, 11, 57
    military costs, 51
    of using violence, 11, 47, 59, 120, 258
    reputation, 257

CPSIA information can be obtained
at www.ICGtesting.com
Printed in the USA
LVOW12*1929260118
564149LV00005B/112/P